FIXING FAMILIES

FIXING FAMILIES

Parents, Power, and the Child Welfare System

Jennifer A. Reich

ROUTLEDGE
NEW YORK AND LONDON

Published in 2005 by
Routledge
Taylor & Francis Group
270 Madison Avenue
New York, NY 10016

Published in Great Britain by
Routledge
Taylor & Francis Group
2 Park Square
Milton Park, Abingdon
Oxon OX14 4RN

International Standard Book Number-10: 0-415-94726-X (Hardcover) 0-415-94727-8 (Softcover)
International Standard Book Number-13: 978-0-415-94726-8 (Hardcover) 978-0-415-94727-5 (Softcover)

Library of Congress Cataloging-in-Publication Data

Reich, Jennifer A.
    Fixing families : parents, power, and the child welfare system / Jennifer A. Reich.
        p. cm. -- (Perspectives on gender)
    Includes bibliographical references and index.
    ISBN 0-415-94726-X (hardcover : alk. paper) -- ISBN 0-415-94727-8 (pbk. : alk. paper)
    1. Child welfare--United States. 2. Family social work--United States. 3. Problem families--Services for--United States. I. Title. II. Series: Perspectives on gender (New York, N.Y.)

HV741.R438 2005
362.7'0973--dc22   2004030689

Taylor & Francis Group
is the Academic Division of T&F Informa plc.

Visit the Taylor & Francis Web site at
http://www.taylorandfrancis.com

and the Routledge Web site at
http://www.routledge-ny.com

Dedication

To my bookend babies, Harrison and Lilia

CONTENTS

ACKNOWLEDGMENTS

Unlike many of the families I study, I have been blessed with a large support system that has made writing this book possible. My mentors and friends at the University of California, Davis helped me immeasurably to develop my ideas and exercised unwavering support for this project from its infancy. Of particular note, Carole Joffe has been a mentor, supporter, and friend to me over the last 10 years; her love for research— and belief in its power to transform social worlds—is infectious, as is her respect for the importance of balancing personal and professional life. Ryken Grattet provided advice, encouragement, friendship, focus, and inspiration to push my analysis further. Bill McCarthy discussed my fieldwork experiences and conveyed the importance of not just good sociology, but of good writing. Daniela Kraiem shared her legal expertise and served as my sounding board and editor, reading many painful early drafts. With her humor and brilliance, Anna Muraco contributed to this work from inception to completion.

Along the way, the work has changed and grown, in large part due to those who generously shared their ideas, read my work, and discussed with me the larger questions with which I was grappling. I am indebted to Amanda Noble, who introduced me to the world of drug policy and child welfare, Dave Meyers, who checked my facts and reassured me that what I had to say was worth saying, and Andrew London, who generously reviewed the entire manuscript more times than could reasonably be expected of anyone. This book was improved by the comments of Meika Loe, Madonna Harrington Meyer, Anne Nurse, and the anonymous reviewers from Routledge and Cambridge University Press. Melanie Egorin, Michael Alan Sacks, Melinda Milligan, John Dale, Yali Bair, Marika Brussel, Rosemary Powers, Ellen Scott, Jen Dunn, Laura Schmidt, and Laura Carpenter provided encouragement, commiseration, and occasionally, library resources. Past and present members of the UC Berkeley School of Social Welfare, including Karie Frasch, Devon Brooks, Alan Brookhart, and Dan Webster provided explanations of social services data and policy background. Lori Bowermaster helped with transcription.

At the UC Office of the President, Steve Handel, Margaret Heisel, Dennis Galligani, Bob Tacconi, Simon Flores, Theo Hobbs, Ronald Roth, and Alicia Wilkins offered flexibility and camaraderie. I was able to further develop this project while a fellow at the University of California, San Francisco (UCSF) Institute for Health Policy Studies (IHPS). There, Claire Brindis and Dan Dohan provided encouragement and pragmatism in equal measures, as well as detailed comments on drafts. Hal Luft, Josh Dunsby, Stuart Henderson, Christopher Jewell, Joanna Weinberg, Margaret Daniel, and members of the IHPS writing seminar provided feedback on chapters and insistence on relevance to "the real world." At the University of Denver, Cathy Potter, Nancy Wadsworth, Caryn Aviv, Pete Adler, David Shneer, Susan Sterett, Sam Grossman, Amber Mallory, John Reader, Seth Masket, and Vivian Masket provided some combination of feedback, encouragement, food, and much-needed pep talks, as did many Mitcheners in many places. Dorene Miller, Arianna Nowakowski, and Ernestine Florence (at UCSF) kept me organized and well-equipped to work. Deserving special accolades, Paul Colomy, Nancy Reichman, and Jennifer Karas not only read portions of the manuscript, but in the final stages consulted on the smallest decisions necessary to finish it. While purging old files recently, I discovered evidence that as far back as high school research papers, I was already concerned with issues of reproduction and families. Beth Schneider, Denise Bielby, and Dick Flacks at UC Santa Barbara nurtured that interest, trained me to think sociologically, and provided the foundation on which this research is built.

I am most grateful to Myra Marx Ferree for taking me under her wing and adding this book to her series. Her editorial work has greatly improved the final product. Michael Bickerstaff, Amanda Rice, and the production staff at Routledge have been wonderful to work with. Ilene Kalish and Kim Guinta helped me enormously in the early stages of converting this from dissertation to book.

The UC Davis Consortium for Women and Research, the UC Davis Humanities Institute, the UC Davis Department of Sociology, and the Agency for Healthcare Research and Quality provided financial support for portions of this project. Beyond material support for the research itself, this book would have been impossible to complete without the help of many people, including Valeria Santos, Zerfie Alamu, and the exceptional staffs of the Model School in Berkeley and the Fisher Early

Learning Center in Denver, who made sure my own family was cared for while I studied other families.

I owe a great deal to the many players in the Child Protective Services (CPS) system. The members of the CPS committees taught me about the system. The dedicated social workers shared their days and nights with me. The attorneys offered me their insights and experience. The presiding judge and referees of the juvenile court granted me entrance to their courtrooms and allowed me to watch them work. The parents in CPS trusted me with their histories, experiences, and most confidential proceedings. Without them, there would be no book. Although the aforementioned CPS system players may not agree with everything I have written, I hope they feel their trust in me was well placed.

In writing of families, I became even more grateful for my own. My sister Stephanie Reich has been my cheerleader, colleague, friend, and source of strength. My father John Reich, an immigrant to the United States from Hungary, has helped me since the earliest days to consider the meanings of family life in police states. As is often the case with immigrants who love their adopted country with a respect many of us who are native born fail to articulate, he encouraged me to critique our culture while demanding that I acknowledge the luxury of being free to do so. From my grandmother Violet Reich, who would freely recount stories of struggles to plan families during the Holocaust as readily as she would pass on a recipe from the Old World, I learned the centrality of family life and the ways it is always situated in sociopolitical contexts. My mother Nancy Gottlieb provided me with insight into the complicated ways women strive to define themselves while caring for others; I cannot remember a moment when she told me the importance of reproductive autonomy to women's lives, just as I can't recall a time when she wasn't communicating that same message. My brother Markus Reich increased my understanding of social worlds beyond my own. Jo and Doug Scudamore and Mark Christman have always expressed their greatest confidence in me, for which I am grateful.

I have left for last those who are always first in my life. Thank you, Harrison and Lilia, for reminding me what a blessing healthy, happy children are, and for granting me insight into the emotions of parenting. In sharing my life with you, I have gained a new understanding of what is at stake. And to David Scudamore, who has supported me in every way possible—from discussing cases, explaining medical diagnoses, reading chapters, and adding a level of pragmatism to my work, to countering my episodic whines of exhaustion with encouragement and chocolate chip cookies—I am grateful for your support, insight, patience, and love.

1
INTRODUCTION

In northern California, in the early part of 1996, a three-year-old boy lost consciousness in his home after his mother "disciplined" him by beating him and throwing him on the floor. The older of his two sisters—ages six and eleven—noticed that he wasn't breathing and called emergency services. The story of this boy, whom I will call Adam,[1] became the lead story in the area, with television and newspaper coverage providing frequent updates not only on his medical condition, but on the conditions that led to this tragic moment. After several days in a coma in the hospital, Adam died.

Like other battered children whose violent deaths expose the inadequacies of the social services designed to protect them, Adam's death became a flashpoint for public policy in the county in which he lived at the time and the two neighboring counties in which his family had also recently lived. Newspaper articles revealed that child welfare agencies in at least two of these counties had, on multiple occasions in the prior two years, investigated allegations that Adam and his sisters were in danger, and finding the allegations credible, had opened cases on them. Their mother—a single woman known to be a methamphetamine user—completed parenting classes, evidenced by the certificate of completion that hung on a wall near where Adam's unconscious body was found, and other county-provided services. By virtue of having an open case, the family would have received monthly visits from a social worker who was inspecting their home, checking on the welfare of the children, and working with Adam's mother to identify lingering needs she may have had that might prevent her from adequately caring for her three children. Having satisfied the requirements of her case plans, social workers (at least one from each county) decided that she no longer presented a danger to her children and the agencies closed their cases. Adam died six months after the last case was closed.

Adam's death and the failures that led to it became the focus of public outrage. At least fifty-seven articles, editorials, and letters of which he was the focus appeared in the largest regional newspaper that year, with more than one hundred items referencing him between 1997 and 2002. It seemed difficult at the time to live nearby and not find oneself engaged, whether at the grocery store or at social events, in a discussion of Adam's fate. The week after his death, I met a sociologist friend for lunch. Although the sunny patio at the café in the quaint downtown area seemed worlds away from Adam's family's dilapidated publicly subsidized apartment, he had lived less than ten miles away, a proximity that kept Adam's story omnipresent. As someone whose own research explores issues of drug use and child welfare intervention, my friend was acutely aware of the case. As we sat down to catch up, she almost immediately mentioned the coverage Adam and his family had received and the mammoth public response to it. Having observed other cases like this, she sighed, "It is always a blonde boy under the age of three."

Adam's death rocked the community and transformed my own life. A few months after his death, the board of supervisors for one of the counties that had monitored his family but failed to identify the serious risk he faced formed a series of oversight committees to both identify how such a failure had occurred and the necessary changes to county policy and practice. Armed with a catchy acronym that included terms like "integration" and "team," a half-dozen subcommittees were formed, each comprised of agency administrators, practitioners, and community members including religious leaders, educators, and members of community-based organizations. These committees were charged with finding ways to revise child welfare practice so that similar tragedies might be prevented. I was asked to serve on one of these committees as the sociologist.

At that particular moment, this county was not the only body committed to addressing perceived failures in the child welfare system. The federal government had just reconfigured welfare, transforming the entitlement program of Aid to Families with Dependent Children (AFDC) into a time-limited program replete with potential sanctions and work requirements called Temporary Aid to Needy Families

(TANF). Following on the perceived success of welfare reform, Congress began tinkering with the child welfare system. Since 1980, federal law has specified that whenever possible, families should be provided services to prevent the removal of children from their homes, and when that fails or is not possible, services should be provided that can enable children to safely return to their natal families. This law, and the sentiment embodied in it—that children should return to their parents whenever possible—are often blamed for cases like Adam's. Often in response to such tragedies, public sentiment reflects a belief that parents like Adam's are given too many chances, a fact which is never recognized until it's too late.[2]

The worst images of this perception are represented by one of two scenarios: in one, a child "languishes" in foster care for several years while his or her parents make half-hearted attempts to comply with service plans; the child is left without a permanent home or stable caregivers, and without a realistic expectation of ever returning to his or her parents. In the other, a parent completes required services and children are returned, only to again be neglected, abused, or, like Adam, killed. In 1997, with these situations in mind, Congress passed the Adoption and Safe Families Act (ASFA), a law that defined situations in which parents should not be provided an opportunity to regain custody, shortened the window of time in which parents who are eligible for services can regain custody of their children, and articulated a greater preference for adoption when feasible.[3] ASFA, like the local reforms I was observing, aimed to provide children with safe homes where they could remain permanently, even as it created additional hurdles for biological parents to overcome in order to maintain their parental rights. With these new federal priorities as a backdrop, the county retooled its own procedures.

Shortly after the county committees began meeting, senior administrators from the county child welfare agency, referred to throughout this book as child protective services—or CPS—unveiled the agency's new policy.[4] These reforms included a zero tolerance policy for illicit drug use, body checks of all children less than five years of age during investigations, and a commitment to more thorough home inspections. The CPS administrators claimed these policies would better identify children who face harm so they could be adequately protected. The county felt certain these changes would make a difference, and the public seemed to believe it too. Approximately one week after the reforms were announced, another toddler, Sarah, was murdered in her home. In a low-income neighborhood in the same county, Sarah's mother's boyfriend—reportedly in an effort to discipline her—held her under water in an ice-cold bath. Two-year-old Sarah lost consciousness and died a few days later in the same hospital as Adam. Like Adam's family, Sarah's had been monitored by CPS. After her single mother—who also had a long history of methamphetamine use—completed services, the case had been closed.

The public outrage that followed the news of Sarah's death was palpable. The ire revolved around two points: Sarah's death revealed that her mother's boyfriend had been molesting Sarah's siblings, and that the CPS social workers who had been monitoring their family and conducting home visits had failed to identify the serious, on-going abuse Sarah and her four siblings endured—or worse, had wrongly believed that Sarah's mother was rehabilitated and would now keep her children safe. Town hall meetings were held, the director of the agency resigned, and the media again demanded accountability. What community members most wanted, it seemed, was assurance that no other children would die on CPS's watch. Through it all, I continued to attend the monthly committee meetings.

I came to this committee with substantive training in welfare policy and an awareness that policy reformations rarely benefit biological parents. Historically, state welfare policies have failed to recognize the ways race and class intersect to limit individuals' ability to affect change in their own lives. State policies have often judged poor families and families from racial and ethnic minority groups against a white middle-class definition of adequate parenting. Central to this legacy is the reality that most families who rely on public assistance are female-headed. Thus state policies have enforced dominant definitions of gender and what it means to be appropriately maternal. I had expected agency members to voice many of the assumptions embedded in the history of U.S. welfare racism.[5]

At these meetings, I found community members, administrators, and front-line service providers who were all guided by a desire to help struggling families. Contrary to my expectations, they did not represent a monolithic state body whose aim was to dissolve poor families and families of color. Rather, they were beleaguered bureaucrats who found themselves able to do little more than provide proverbial Band-Aids to gaping wounds. Although I appreciated their sincerity, I was also aware that, in the conference room where we drank weak coffee, discussed CPS goals and practices, and tried to imagine a better system, I was also observing efforts to increase state surveillance of families. Despite class- and race-blind rhetoric, these surveilled families were almost always poor and disproportionately African American.

The CPS system is comprised of a series of interlocking agencies and service providers. In the CPS system, social workers, attorneys, therapists, parenting and anger management course instructors, drug treatment counselors, other service providers, and judges evaluate parental behavior and determine whether it is in the children's best interest to live with their parents or to live somewhere else. Social workers investigate allegations of abuse or neglect and determine whether children should remain in their homes or be placed in state custody for their own safety. They coordinate services for families whose children have been removed by the agency and who are attempting to regain custody of them. In addition, they find places for children who will not return to their parents to live long term. The other state actors are charged with either providing services to improve parents or evaluating whether they are rehabilitated. This is a complex bureaucratic system where case outcomes are often heartbreaking. The longer I observed efforts to reform CPS, the more I came to believe that the seemingly compatible, but often contradictory goals of protecting children from their families and helping families remain together are permanently in tension, a fact better understood by those who are responsible for the workings of the system.

In observing policymakers trying to improve practice without being able to resolve this core tension, I began to wonder how child welfare workers conduct their work and how state policy, despite the good intentions of its practitioners, serves in the end to reinforce dominant definitions of family life. After all, their work is to ferret out "dangerous" families from "safe" ones, to then transform the former into the latter, and to identify correctly when they have done so successfully. At stake are the very meanings of state intervention into family life. Public intervention is never equally applied, with poor families, female-headed families, and families of color receiving the bulk of state attention. CPS is a system that seeks to rehabilitate or resocialize parents so they can address those aspects of their familial life that appear to place children at risk and then adequately care for their children. These attempts to "fix" families require parents to attend meetings, demonstrate their desire to improve their lives, and comply with state definitions of adequate parenting. Embedded in these expectations are meanings of family life that reflect beliefs about gender, race, and class. It is in these ways that the therapeutic state serves to reinforce dominant definitions of family life without addressing the underlying structures of inequality that contribute to parents' perceived failures.

In Adam's case, the state failed to determine whether or not his family was a safe place for him, a public failure that was followed by demands for accountability. The public calls following Adam's death facilitated the release of information. One publicized study conducted by the county death review team found that of the 101 children who were identified as having died because of abuse or neglect in the preceding six years (the role of maltreatment in another 120 child deaths was undetermined), more than half had been in contact with CPS. One-third of the children who were killed were being supervised by the county agency when they died, but in most cases remained with their parents. The study also identified young children, children of color, and poor children to be at greatest risk, with half of the children killed being between the ages of one and four years, sixty percent coming from families that had received AFDC, and African American children disproportionately more likely to die of all causes, including abuse. This report was a Rorschach test of sorts, allowing its readers to assign a variety of meanings to it, depending on their own views. Not surprisingly, these results were interpreted by many as further evidence of agency failure. They inspired me to wonder what happens in the interactions between child welfare officials and the families that seem to be struggling, and sometimes failing. Understanding these interactions could allow for greater understanding of how state actors enact their contradictory goals and how expectations of race, class, and gender in family life are communicated.

This book aims to provide greater understanding of these interactions by detailing the inner workings of cases in the child welfare system in one northern California county. Specifically, I examine the interactions between parents and system insiders to better understand why the system operates as it does. Actors in the CPS system interpret parental behaviors in order to identify imminent danger that children face. Investigators decipher cues from parents' answers, attitudes, demeanor, and environment to create their assessments (narratives) of risk. In creating case plans and outcomes, social workers, attorneys, service providers, and judges look for signs that parents want to be or have been rehabilitated and can now be appropriate parents. Although parents have little authority or recourse in this system, they are nonetheless active participants in how these assessments, evaluations, and representations are shaped. Though they often disagree with the outcomes, parents' actions influence the depictions of them and their families.

Parents and state actors negotiate power at several critical moments of interaction: when a social worker investigates allegations of abuse and neglect; when a parent participates in reunification services, court proceedings, or meetings with social workers to regain custody of his or her children; and at the moment when the court ultimately decides whether a parent will regain custody and/or retain legal rights over his or her children. By examining these "moments," I demonstrate how parents and state actors struggle to shape case meanings and propose solutions. These critical moments of interaction provide a unique opportunity to examine how power is negotiated between individuals and the state over meanings of the family. I gained access to these moments by accompanying social workers as they investigated allegations of maltreatment or monitored cases of children who had been placed in state custody, observing court proceedings of CPS cases in the juvenile court, interviewing parents and attorneys, and reviewing court documents and reports. (The methodological appendix provides more detail about data collection.) In discussing these data, I move between my observations and the accounts provided by parents, social workers, and attorneys to understand case meanings, processes, and outcomes. These narratives may not capture "the truth" and may instead simply provide pieces of larger mosaics of what has transpired. Yet as parents and state actors present stories of themselves, their allies, and their opponents, they are revealing what they think is important—and valued—in this large welfare bureaucracy.

In this book I strive to paint a portrait of the CPS system, tinted with the intentions and perspectives of the many players who, though often making competing claims to advocate for different outcomes, are usually acting with the best of intentions. Simultaneously, I reveal how, in the end, and despite good intentions, the system participants reproduce the same fractures along lines of gender, race, and class that have always plagued state welfare systems, and in doing so, reify larger social inequalities. This book is about child protection as a *system* and not about the specifics of protecting children. Much of existing social research on this system tries to address the long-standing public controversy that circumscribes questions of whether CPS acts appropriately when it removes children from or returns them to their parents.[6] In the course of my research, I found these questions largely unanswerable, and even circular. We know agencies make the wrong decisions because trage-dies—like those of Adam and Sarah—occur. In response, some would argue that the only correct policy would be one of removing all children who are allegedly maltreated. Simultaneously, others hold that children should only be removed in the most egregious cases of abuse, since they are often safer with their flawed natal families than in the deeply troubled foster care system. These poles reveal that conceptions of ideal agency practice more often reflect concerns over who should be raising children and what constitutes appropriate parenting than they clarify how the bureaucracies that regulate them should be retooled.

Hence I avoid discussing whether CPS should or should not remove children and whether children should be placed in state custody more or less often and instead focus my analysis on questions of how the system grapples with these issues and how these efforts are often crippled by larger public and fiscal policies.

INTERVENING IN FAILING FAMILIES

What the CPS system grapples with is nothing less than the cultural and legal meanings of family. The family occupies a near mythical role in our national culture, and this role has changed and evolved over time.[7] Beginning most notably in the United States in the late 1800s, the family increasingly came to be seen as a haven from the outside world, including the seemingly harsh conditions of industry. Both its presumed universality as a site of nurture and its locus as the source of unique tradition complicate our conceptions of what families are and should be and contribute to the difficulty of child protection practice. The diversity between families and the uniqueness of each family must be appreciated. Yet these differences, which include variations in child-rearing, blur efforts to define adequate parenting. Adequate care has no universal meaning, as definitions vary with cultural and historical views about children and what constitutes their appropriate upbringing. In fact, several studies suggest that even in the same time period, state agencies and community members define child maltreatment differently, with variations also existing from community to community. In lieu of a formal definition of maltreatment, the state uses a flexible one that allows for professional judgment and interpretations of cultural standards. This practice recognizes the widespread belief that good parenting is self-evident: like pornography (another definitional challenge for public policy), you know it when you see it. Nonetheless, the child-centered model of American middle-class ideology dominates. In defining good parenthood, essayist Calvin Trillin suggests, "Your children are either the center of your life or they're not." Yet such notions—even those that children should be central to adult lives—are culturally and historically relative.[8]

Families have their own histories, cultures, and treasured rituals. As a historically private institution that was imagined to provide refuge from the outside world, families are believed to be free to nurture their unique traditions without external intervention. (In popular representations, ethnic diversity might be reduced to nonthreatening characteristics such as unique cooking styles, fashion sense, or holiday rituals.) Yet, even with these differences, The Family—as an institution—is expected to maintain social cohesion by reproducing the social norms, expectations and institutions that socialize its members. As Christopher Lasch notes,

> If the reproduction of culture were simply a matter of formal instruction and discipline, it could be left to the schools. But it also requires that culture be embedded in personality. Socialization makes the individual want to do what he has to do; the family is the agency to which society entrusts this complex and delicate task.[9]

Parents, as the leaders of families, are expected to meet these obligations, even as it requires personal sacrifice to do so.[10] Ideally, families can remain private, so long as the most vulnerable members are "adequately" cared for. However, parents who fail—or are perceived as failing—to care for their family members create a dilemma for society. In such cases, the state—obligated to protect individual citizens, especially those who cannot protect themselves—must intervene. As illustrated by the outcry on behalf of Adam and Sarah, children are seen as being most vulnerable and most in need of protection.

In the last one hundred years, children have gone from being an economic resource to possessing symbolic pricelessness, undergoing what sociologist Viviana Zelizer calls a process of "sacralization."[11] While eighteenth century rural America viewed children as a source of labor and as security for aging parents, children born after the 1920s—as a repository of love and care—were seen as a source of emotional value. This transformation marked a move from children's value stemming from their usefulness in work and as wage earners to intrinsic value as a source of emotional fulfillment. With children's increasing value came concern about children's emotional, moral, and intellectual development, and recognition that parents could be potentially harmful to children. Progressive Era concern with child health and development led to the creation or expansion of several social institutions—public schools, juvenile courts, public health interventions—each of which placed many of the responsibilities of child development outside of the home and out of parental control. These public institutions communicated new social standards for parenting and family life, and provided the mechanisms by which families could be evaluated. In doing so, the state assumed a new role: protecting children from the privacy of the family, which required state surveillance of families and their members.

Concerns about family life generally, and parental shortcomings specifically, guide public policy. Parents fail—or are perceived as failing—for a variety of reasons and in myriad ways. Some families fail to educate children, care for their health, or prepare them to be productive members of society. Through their abuse or neglect, some parents emotionally, psychologically, and physically damage their children. Some parents lack the skills necessary to help their children develop to their full potential and frequently employ poor strategies for discipline, impose inconsistent rules, or withhold affection or praise, all of which are understood to be markers of bad parenting. Others experience drug dependence or significant mental health problems, sometimes associated with the abuse or neglect they themselves experienced. Others may be simply too poor to meet their children's material needs.

Gender further defines failed parenting, with a special form of contempt reserved for mothers, particularly those who are unmarried. Because cultural expectations for mothers are higher, including the expectation that children are central to women's lives and vice versa, women receive the bulk of state scrutiny. However, fathers are not irrelevant and are measured against specific cultural definitions of adequate fathering, which remain tied to meanings of masculinity. To address perceived parental failures—whatever their causes or constructions—the state has defined a right for itself to overrule the sanctity of the family when parents violate social norms. And although discussions of "families" and "parents" who fail are gender neutral, the fact that women provide the vast majority of care to children and other family members marks mothers as the focus of public scrutiny. As such, I largely focus my discussion in this chapter of the role of the state in family life on the experiences of mothers, with recognition that poor fathers endure state evaluation, though the criteria are somewhat different. In subsequent chapters I more fully explore the gendered experiences and expectations of both men and women in CPS.

INTERSECTIONS OF THE STATE AND FAMILY

One of the most striking features of the child welfare system is that its power to dismantle families exists along side its efforts to preserve them. This paradox exposes the ways that the family is both the subject of public policy and of sentimental and material privacy. At the heart of this issue are meanings of gender in family life and what the role of the state is in defining them. Feminist explorations of the public-private duality of the family largely center on whether there should be more or less government intervention in family life. Some have argued that the best way to ensure women's economic self-determination and escape from reliance on the patriarchal family is to integrate private life as completely as possible into the public sphere. For example, domestic violence advocates commonly mobilize for a more responsive legal system, public funding for shelters, prosecutions that are not reliant on victims filing charges, and broader legislation and funding to support women's ability to leave their abusers and the bounds of the family. Publicly funded child care, access to safe and affordable abortion, and affirmative action programs in education and employment are other examples of efforts to expand the public domain.[12] Each of these proposals suggests the solution to women's inequality lies in dismantling the private patriarchal family and moving toward a broader definition of individual rights and the expansion of the state's capacity to protect them. From this perspective, the state is benevolent, protective, and trustworthy.

At the same time, other branches of feminism (by no means mutually exclusive) have argued for increased rights of privacy from state control and intervention.[13] These opposing visions of the appropriate role of the state can be accounted for by looking at the different ways social class mediates the experience of the state. Battles for reproductive rights, for example, illustrate the differences in experiences of women of different classes. While middle class women advocate for expanded state coverage for contraceptive services, poor women have been forced to resist state-sponsored campaigns of forced or coerced sterilization.[14] Welfare theorists have also articulated the need for privacy from the gaze of the state, noting that while public assistance programs provide a source of (limited) economic freedom for women, poor women have experienced the state as oppressive and invasive. Recipients of public assistance have been subjected to "unreasonable searches, harassing surveillance, eavesdropping and interrogation concerning their sexual activities" by state welfare agencies.[15] Welfare rights activist Johnnie Tillmon described the intrusion of the state, noting, "You trade 'a' man for 'the' man…'The' man runs everything…'The' man, the welfare system, controls your money. He tells you what to buy, and what not to buy. Where to buy it, and how much things cost."[16] Embodied in this description is a view of the state as patriarchal, coercive, and threatening. Middle class women, who escape reliance on public resources because they have access to private resources, are afforded greater privacy; they escape public scrutiny and are allowed greater independence. As such, they are unlikely to experience the state in the ways described by poor women.

This class division is significant for understanding how parents generally, and mothers specifically, experience state intervention. For middle-class women, who tend to be granted a wider sphere of privacy by the state, increased public funding for healthcare, child care, immunization campaigns, and parks and recreation programs bear little threat to their families, and thus are seen as solely positive. After all, they can always opt for their privacy through the purchase of private services and schools whenever they dislike the scrutiny of the public state. Family theorist David Cheal observes, "Family members define their projects with reference to personal desires, rather than public goals, and they are free to implement them to the limits of their resources."[17] Indeed, private resources provide the ability to selectively participate in only those aspects of public life—and those public resources—that are consistent with one's own desires. Alternatively, receipt of public assistance, utilization of Head Start or subsidized child care, enrollment in publicly funded healthcare, or even participation in school programs facilitates the state's ability to evaluate poor women's families and to intervene where and when it sees fit. Poor women who are dependent on state support cannot opt out of publicly funded services because they cannot afford private ones. Therefore, poor people's lives may be subject to greater public scrutiny than their middle- and upper-class counterparts.

Public resources exist for families who lack economic independence (and the privacy it provides). However, these resources may only be used as prescribed. For example, the rules dictating voucher redemption for some state-sponsored nutritional supplement programs—like the Women, Infants and Children program—regulate exactly which products and brands can be bought and in what quantities: cheese can only be bought in one pound blocks, hot and cold cereals can't be combined on the same coupon, and milk must be purchased two gallons at a time, regardless of a recipient's ability to carry or use them.[18] Although the regulations may seem cumbersome and even infantilizing, a recipient who dislikes those prescriptions can presumably refuse the benefits or services, but only by accepting hunger.

A similarly limited choice exists for women wanting to use public resources to escape domestic violence. Public intervention in domestic violence situations between adults is predicated on a belief that not all individuals within a family have equal access to power and resources. Advocates for women attempting to escape domestic violence have successfully argued for a public response that facilitates women's choices to leave a battering relationship. Because of police intervention, housing, legal aid, and transitional services, women may choose to leave a situation that threatens their safety. They could not exercise this choice without such resources. At the same time, using such services places them under the scrutiny of domestic violence counselors, therapists, social workers, police, and prosecutors, and potentially could cost them custody of their children, who can be placed in CPS care because their parents were "engaging in domestic violence" (even when they only "engage" by being beaten).[19] Here the choice to avoid public supervision can result in death.

Children lack legal rights and economic autonomy. Their vulnerable status encourages the view that abused or neglected children are prisoners trapped behind the shrouded walls of the private family in need of rescue. (Cases like Adam's and Sarah's show how claims are often material, rather than symbolic.) At the core of this understanding is that families are often dangerous places for children. As such, parents cannot always be trusted to make decisions that are in the best interests of their children. With this understanding, CPS, the state agency responsible for saving children from their parents, truncates parents' freedom to make decisions for their family; while parents are presumed able to "choose" whether to participate in other state programs on behalf of their entire family, that choice disappears once in the CPS system. Once in the CPS system, the family unit dissolves into a collection of individuals, presumed to have competing interests, who are connected by history, biology, and legal ties. To allow these individuals to remain a family, the state requires the family members to share the goal of caring for the children, even as this goal and the means to accomplish it must be taught.

THE THERAPEUTIC STATE

With the stated goal of protecting children's well-being—both in the physical sense of their survival, as well as in a broader sense of their emotional, cognitive, and social development—a core question remains: In the face of parental failure, should children be taken away and given to others to raise, or can these families be resocialized to adequately raise children?

Except in cases of horrific physical abuse or torture, current state policy presumes that parents, often victims of their own abusive, impoverished, or dysfunctional childhoods, can be rehabilitated. As mentioned, federal law dictates that "reasonable efforts shall be made to preserve and reunify families (i) prior to the placement of a child in foster care, to prevent or eliminate the need for removal of the child from the child's home; and (ii) to make it possible for a child to safely return to the child's home."[20] Within these legislative goals is a belief that the state and its actors can act in a parental capacity by resocializing and supervising parents. Parents who abuse or neglect their children benefit from the state's assumption that attempts should first be made to salvage families before dismantling them. Without this ideological and legal focus, many more children could be adopted by strangers, without the natal families having much chance to improve their lives and regain custody. This legal goal—to reform deviant parents—requires the state to provide services to families so that they may overcome their problems. At this juncture, social workers are service providers and the parents become clients.

Political scientist Andrew Polsky describes the state's therapeutic approach: "It begins with the premise that some people are unable to adjust to the demands of everyday life or function according to the rules by which most of us operate. If they are to acquire the value structure that makes for self-sufficiency, healthy relationships, and positive self-esteem, they need expert help."[21] In providing services, social workers, clinicians, attorneys, and judges deploy a medicalized vocabulary, infused with psychological terms, to address and assess familial change. Parties will cite the "need for treatment," "failure to recover," "level of bondedness," "compliance," or "therapeutic relationship" when discussing their clients' needs and failures. Rather than viewing these families as morally or irreparably damaged, the therapeutic ethos works, as sociologist Peter Conrad describes it, "by using medical means to minimize, eliminate, or normalize deviant behavior."[22]

The widespread acceptance of the therapeutic model may stem from or reflect its wider social use. After all, any number of adults, with or without children, take advantage of counseling to cope with their anxieties, gain self-insight, or improve their relationships.[23] Participation in psychotherapy has become so common that the therapy session is now an unproblematic fixture in cultural representations. Pointing to the prolific market of self-help and recovery programs that show the centrality of the therapeutic ethos, Wendy Kaminer writes, "Personal development passes for politics, and what might once have been called whining is now exalted as a process of asserting selfhood; self-absorption is regarded as a form of self-expression, as if creative acts involved no interactions with the world."[24] Broadly, self-improvement is rewarded.

Of course, voluntary participation in therapeutic processes is quite different from coerced participation in services by economically marginal populations. Polsky has described this difference:

Though the problems that bring middle-class clients to seek treatment may be serious, it is not seen as necessary to instill in them mainstream values to which they already subscribe. It should be added that they choose when to begin and end treatment. By contrast, public therapeutic intervention aimed at marginal citizens proceeds from the assumption that they cannot govern their own lives. The state seeks to "normalize" them... Lower-class clients do not seem to require merely a bit of support, like their middle-class counterparts, but instead wholesale personal and family reconstruction.[25]

Class differences—and access to resources—change the experience and goals of therapeutic intervention. While middle-class individuals may choose therapeutic treatment as a means to self-improvement, the poor are perceived as needing treatment as a means of resocializing—or normalizing—them. This "normalization" process is central to understanding state intervention in the family.

Social theorist Michel Foucault wrote that the normalizing gaze is "a surveillance that makes it possible to qualify, to classify and to punish. It establishes over individuals a visibility through which one differentiates them and judges them."[26] In the CPS system, state actors attempt to normalize parents by establishing—or making visible—clear goals for rehabilitation and specific criteria for evaluating progress and attainment. It is not simply as representatives of the state, but rather, as "therapeutic experts" that these actors examine CPS parents. Through the process—at varying moments of interaction—these professionals expect parents to acknowledge that their home life is inadequate and communicate a desire to change. Social workers expect parents to defer to their authority and their accompanying definition of the situation, and in doing so, to communicate the requisite acceptance of their need for therapeutic help.[27] While receiving services, parents again must defer to state definitions of rehabilitation and of what the parents should become. Embedded in these expectations are ideals of family life that reflect specific visions of race, class, and gender. To return to the above discussion of the state in family life, the state defines appropriate reproduction, parenting, and even victimization, and defines them differently for mothers and fathers. The therapeutic state, as it strives to normalize parents, does so with an idealized outcome that reflects its own definitions and priorities.

As I show throughout this book, parents must show—or perform—their acceptance of and cooperation with these efforts to normalize them in order to succeed. Some parents demonstrate this easily, as they actually do aspire to the better selves promised by the therapeutic process. Others may perform deference, even as they remain skeptical. Some resist state prescriptions entirely. In fact, parents selectively cooperate or resist state power and therapeutic practitioners' efforts to define their current and future lives, sometimes in ways that they know will undermine their own goals of regaining custody of their children. At each stage of the CPS process, parents are active agents who act in self-determined ways, even as they are bound by structural limitations.

OVERVIEW OF THE SYSTEM

We work for the government. We're here to help.
                    —Bumper sticker on a social worker's office door

Families in the county I studied come to the attention of CPS most often because someone calls the agency and reports suspected maltreatment. CPS offices have a hotline to which concerned individuals and legally mandated reporters can report suspected child abuse or neglect. An intake social worker screens reports and assigns each case a priority level. The most serious cases must be investigated within two hours and the least serious cases, within ten days (the more common classification); cases can be assigned an intermediate priority level and time frame for investigation depending on the assessed level of risk the child may face. An intake worker can also classify a report as unfounded and not refer it for further investigation. Cases deemed valid for investigation are referred to social workers in the emergency response unit.

After investigating a case, emergency response workers have three options. If there is no evidence to support the allegation in the report, the allegation is classified as unsubstantiated and the case is closed. If the worker finds evidence to support the allegation or finds other cause for concern, but does not believe the children are in imminent danger, the worker can open a case and enroll the parents in voluntary services, while leaving the children at home. In this case, the family maintenance unit of CPS will provide services to the parent or parents for approximately six months, after which the family's life will, hopefully, be judged improved and the case will be closed. If the parents are not seen as having improved their lives, if the risk to the children is greater than originally assessed, or if the parents are noncompliant with services, the case will again be evaluated and if deemed necessary, the children can be removed from their home and placed in protective custody.

Should the emergency response social worker find the allegations in the report to be true and believe that the children are in imminent danger, the worker can open a case and immediately place them in protective custody, "known as PC-ing." The children are then removed from the home and placed in the county-run children's receiving home or in foster care. The majority of this book deals with cases in which the state has removed children from their parents' homes, and examines what parents must do to regain custody.

Juvenile Justice

> —*The title of the television show parents' attorneys fantasize*
> *they will someday write*

Once a social worker removes children from the home, she or he must file a petition with the county juvenile court. The petition, which lists the allegations against the parents, states that the children must be placed "in the care and custody of the juvenile court" for their own safety. Within seventy-two hours of the children's removal, a detention hearing is held. Here, a juvenile court judge reviews the petition and evaluates whether the social worker was reasonable in removing the children. Though it rarely occurs, social workers fear having their petitions dismissed at this initial hearing, as it challenges their credibility and calls their ability to reasonably assess risk into question. Should the petition be upheld, the case is set for a hearing that establishes whether or not the allegations are true (called the jurisdictional hearing) and where the children should be placed (known as the dispositional hearing). These hearings, held within thirty days of the detention hearing, determine whether, based on the low legal standard of a preponderance of the evidence, the allegation is true. These two proceedings, almost always occurring concurrently during the same court appearance, typically take only ten to fifteen minutes combined, and are perceived by parents to be one hearing.

Parents have the right to challenge the allegations in a formal trial, at which time they can call witnesses, testify on their own behalf, and present evidence. However, most parents waive their right to a trial and allow the court to decide their culpability based on the information provided in the case records. Should the court find the allegation(s) to be true, the parents are legally recognized as responsible for the harm that befell their children. In order to regain custody, the parents are expected to address the issues underlying the allegations. In such cases, parents are typically offered a series of services that are coordinated and supervised by a CPS social worker from the family reunification unit. These social workers also evaluate parental compliance with court-ordered services and recommend to the court whether the children should visit their parents more frequently and eventually return home, or should be permanently placed elsewhere. Cases are reexamined in court every three to six months, with social workers filing progress reports between hearings, until the case reaches the legislatively determined time limit of six to eighteen months. At that point, the county must articulate a permanent plan for the children. These civil court proceedings are kept confidential from any related criminal proceeding against the parent so the parent may accept responsibility for their prior acts or misdeeds and make full use of the therapeutic process without fear of self-incrimination.[28]

A lawyer represents each party who appears in court. The county employs attorneys to represent the CPS agency's interests, which are largely based on social worker assessment and recommendation. A nonprofit law firm called Counsel for Dependent Children represents the children as a guardian ad litem (I also refer to them generically as children's attorneys throughout the book).[29] These attorneys advocate for what they believe to be in a child's best interest, particularly as it relates to case outcome, and ensure government adherence to legal mandates for supervision and case timeliness. All parents who communicate their intentions to regain custody of their children by attending the initial hearings are represented by an attorney. For parents who cannot afford to pay an attorney, as is the case for the vast majority of parents who enter the system, the court assigns an attorney who is contracted by the county to provide indigent legal services to parents.[30] I refer to these attorneys generically as county advocates for parents, or simply parents' attorneys. In cases where parents can afford private counsel, these same attorneys are often hired to represent these privately paying clients. On rare occasions, a parent will hire an outside attorney. If there is both a mother and father in a case—who often have competing interests or present different levels of risk to the children—they are given (or hire) separate attorneys.

With parents almost exclusively represented by one firm, the children by another, and the county by its own small staff of attorneys, a small cast of legal characters work together in almost every case. Typically, specific attorneys from the firms representing the children, the parents, and the county are assigned to a specific courtroom where virtually all of their cases appear in front of the same judge and where they handle the majority of their cases. Like the public defender who "attends to the courtroom as his regular work place and conveys in his demeanor his place as a member of its core personnel," the attorneys in the juvenile court system work in an environment that is almost identical to the normal crimes model described by sociologist David Sudnow.[31] Because the attorneys work together, they too have developed what Sudnow describes as "a set of unstated recipes" for resolving cases.[32] The ongoing nature of these proceedings—which reappear every three to six months—and of the discussions of case progress also facilitates familiarity between attorneys. The result of these dynamics is that the interactions between attorneys in this system tend to be more formulaic and less adversarial than in other court proceedings.[33] For example, attorneys might discuss their intentions for their cases before entering the courtroom, may strike deals about case specifics, and may find ways to expedite hearings by aligning paperwork ahead of time.

THE COUNTY

This book analyzes the child welfare system in one unnamed northern California county. The experiences of the parents and agents in this county's CPS system are in many ways similar to those of parents and agents in other places, though there are some points of differentiation. Federal law dictates child protection policy, but its practice is also informed by state law and then administered at the county or local level. As a result, there is great variation in practice between states and from county to county within a particular state. For example, all parents attempting to regain custody of their children in the study county receive attorneys; this practice varies, with some locales only providing attorneys when cases are set for trial. Also, not all counties provide separate attorneys for children as this county does; some rely on the county counsel's office to represent the children. This practice is becoming less common as counties recognize the conflict of interest inherent in trying to both represent government fiscal interests and children's psychological, material, and emotional interests.

California has a higher proportion of children in foster care than does the average state: one in four children in foster care nationwide lives in California, though only thirteen percent of the total U.S. population under eighteen years of age lives in California.[34] The county I studied has both urban and rural areas, with a population of more than one million inhabitants and is one of the top ten most populous areas in the state. As mentioned, when I began my research, the county was reeling from negative publicity and public accusations following Adam's death. As is often the case following high-profile CPS failures, agencies—like this one—adopt a more aggressive investigation strategy that results in the removal of more children.[35]

About 21 percent of the county's children live in poverty, while about 45 percent are low income (living at or below 185 percent of the federal poverty level, defined in part by qualification for free or reduced-price lunches). This places the county among the one-third of the state with the highest rates of child poverty.[36] Of the children in this

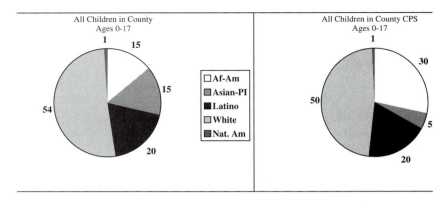

Fig. 1. Pie chart of the racial composition of county children as a whole versus children in county CPS.[50]

county, about 54 percent are white, with white children making up about 50 percent of children in the CPS system. African American children are the most overrepresented in CPS, making up almost 30 percent of the county child welfare population, but only 15 percent of the county's children. Fifteen percent of the county's children are Asian or Pacific Islanders, but they make up only 5 percent of the CPS population. Twenty percent of the county's children are Latino, comprising the same percentage of the CPS population. Native Americans are proportionately represented, comprising one percent of the county's children and one percent of the CPS system's children (see Figure 1). It is worth noting that the race of the children in CPS—for whom administrative data are collected—does not necessarily match the race of the parents in the CPS system. Underscoring this point, more than half of the white women in this study gave birth to children whose fathers were men of color, and as a result, were most likely recorded as children of color in administrative data. In light of the complex meanings of race in the system and the significant number of multiracial families included in my study, I strive throughout the book to examine how race affects investigations and case outcomes.[37]

Although this county does not receive significantly higher numbers of reports of child maltreatment than other counties, it has one of the highest rates of foster care placement per capita in the state, and hence in the country. This means that should a parent be reported for child maltreatment in this county, he or she is more likely to have a child removed by CPS than in most other counties in California. Like many counties, this county almost always removes newborn babies who test positive for illegal drugs at birth.[38] However, this county is one of the few that sponsors a universal drug testing program for newborns; rather than using markers of suspicion that reflect racism and classism, all babies born at the large university-affiliated hospital (which serves county-funded patients, though not only those patients) are tested for cocaine, amphetamine, and opiate derivatives. This creates a situation in which many children—perhaps more than in other counties—are removed at birth and placed in foster care. These differences not with-standing, the larger issues and experiences of families in this county are similar to those of families in other counties and regions.[39]

REPRESENTING "BAD" PARENTS

In this book I try to neither valorize nor demonize the parents who enter CPS. The parents who end up in the CPS system for any length of time are almost always poor. However, they are usually not simply poor, which in many cases makes them different from the poor discussed by those who write about welfare and poverty.[40] Rather, they are individu-als who face other significant social issues: histories of victimization by their own parents or partners, drug and alcohol addiction, limited success in school and the labor force, and encounters with the criminal justice system, including incarceration. Many of them are the individu-als that advocates for social justice are loath to discuss; some resemble the anecdotes that political conservatives use to justify cutting holes in social safety nets.[41] They are not necessarily "the worthy poor," and may be the ones with whom "good citizens" avoid eye contact as they lock their cars and doors.

In studying these families, I was more often than not moved by these parents' stories of survival within, and even conquest over, their social situations. I also observed some parents whose actions were so repulsive that I found it difficult to listen to the court proceedings, but I more often felt compassion for the parents whose situations and poor choices had led them into the complex web of state supervision. I was often impressed by their love for their children, angered by how they were treated, and saddened by the lot they had been handed early in life. How-ever, I also carried a cell phone and reported my comings and goings to others when I entered the worst neighborhoods in town to interview these parents. My compassion could not protect me from opportunistic crime or even malicious harm, too often part of these parents' social environments. In addition, the fact remains that many of these parents had lost their children because of their own capacity for violence.

Some parents appeared to have had their children removed from their homes by CPS for unjustifiable reasons; their cases demonstrate the often-described CPS error where children are removed from loving homes.[42] However, most of the parents did the things of which they were accused. Accepting this is an important point of entry to this book. To be clear, I am not actually interested in guilt or innocence; those terms have no legal meaning or relevance in CPS, which is a civil, not a criminal, court system. Beyond the legalistic meanings, I am equally unconcerned with efforts to identify who are good and bad parents. Instead, I focus on the negotiations of power between parents who come under the surveillance of the state and the state's attempts to rehabilitate them. Underlying this goal is a larger one: I am most concerned with questions of how the state defines who can be a family and who cannot and how those definitions are infused by, and simultaneously promote, definitions of race, class, and gender.

Although I do not want to engage efforts to define good and bad parenting, I must also acknowledge that at times I found it difficult to discuss people who do bad things to children. I remember reading an explanation by attorney Naomi Cahn on how she initially justified her decision to represent parents in child abuse cases:

> For a long time, with perhaps my first fifty clients, I believed that they had not beaten, burned, struck, or kicked their children; that they were all good mothers who would never do such things; and that their children had been unfairly removed from them. These beliefs were important to me. I was not sure that I could continue to represent my clients unless I believed they were innocent, that they were not bad mothers. There was a part of me that could not believe that a mother would really abuse her child. When friends asked me how I could represent abusive parents, I patiently explained that my clients were innocent.[43]

This book might have been easier to write if I too had been an advocate who could have convinced myself that the parents I studied did not do the things of which they were accused. In studying child maltreatment, it is often more comfortable to avoid child abuse and solely address neglect or a parent's failure to protect a child from harm inflicted by someone else. In those cases, a structural lack of power or resources can explain a parent's failure. Although the parents in this book are overwhelmingly poor and have faced structural hardship throughout their lives, most people who are poor do not harm their children, and not all people who harm their children are poor. It is perhaps this very conflict that challenges my thinking about structure and agency.

Many who write about family violence have shied away from discussing child abuse, especially as perpetrated by mothers, for fear of losing claims against patriarchy by creating ambiguities about who is the victim.[44] While fearful of being misunderstood, I nonetheless choose to write about aggressions that women and men commit against children. These aggressions are not always physical assaults. Many parents were in court because they failed to protect their children from harm inflicted by others; for exposing their children to illegal drugs, either perinatally or through use and sale in their homes; or for neglecting their children's basic physical needs. While I tell of these failings, I also avoid fixating on them. Many adults who have traveled with a toddler, cared for a baby with colic, or uncovered an adolescent scheme have some insight into how adults can be driven to ignore or harm a child. Others may have glimpsed the ways illness, depression, or addiction can leave a person unable to care. Those experiences may offer insight into how one act on one day can change a person from a good (enough) parent into a suspected child abuser—how one act can erase a normative identity and replace it with another, more deviant one.

In some cases, the abuse or neglect in the stories I tell was not a single act; rather it was patterned, developed, and rationalized over time. Nonetheless, these parents—those who turn a blind eye while their boyfriends molest their daughters, those who lock children in bedrooms while out in search of drugs, those who binge on substances so mind-altering that they forget to feed their children for days at a time, or even those who burn children with cigarettes—are more than the sum total of these acts. They are also parents who love their children, who mostly care for their children (or care for their children most of the time), and who cherish their identities as parents (even as they are challenged by the state). In studying child welfare in the Progressive Era, historian Linda Gordon described the victims and assailants in family violence cases as "unusual heroes and heroines, to be sure, for they were almost always quite wretched, innocent and guilty alike. Nevertheless, they were people with aspirations and complex emotions as well as ill luck and, often, self-destructive impulses."[45] Similarly, French philosopher Jacques Donzelot describes the families in turn-of-the century France that he wrote about as "in sum, that fringe of the working class where misconduct is joined to fatalism."[46] These descriptions apply equally to many of the families I studied in California in the late twentieth and early twenty-first century.

Throughout the book I often—but not always—identify the race or ethnicity of the people I studied. Without a doubt, race shapes the system processes and the experiences of those within it. Indeed, race structured the patterns of interactions, but did so in ways that were more fluid than fixed. In some interactions, race was more salient than in others. Discussions of the treatment of families of color in the child welfare system often raise questions about race and whether individual and systemic racism account for the disproportionate presence of children of color in the child welfare system.[47] Although I saw instances where police officers assisting social workers acted in overtly racist ways, I did not see the same behavior from social workers or attorneys. Social workers in this county were diverse in their racial and ethnic backgrounds and sexual orientations, and many were immigrants. Therefore, as race affected the negotiation of power between parents and state agents, it did so in complex ways that reflected how race shaped each party's worldview more than it revealed racist practices. Thus I mark race to provide an opportunity to unpack how each party's experiential knowledge, shaped by race, culture, and community, contributed to the outcomes of these critical moments of interaction.

When possible, I use cases to illustrate the dynamics I discuss. When comparing cases, I try to select ones that are similar enough and separate enough to permit treating them as comparable instances of the same general phenomenon. I use ethnographic descriptions to illustrate larger patterns occurring in the proceedings or interactions, and when possible use detailed accounts of cases for the "justification or illumination" of theories that arose from the research process.[48] Although I had multiple encounters with almost all the parents I discuss, I nonetheless had a limited view into their social worlds. In some cases I was in their homes, in others I watched their cases wind through the judicial process. Some parents discussed their cases with me in great detail; for others I draw mostly on what their attorneys told me. I acknowledge that I have collected fragments of the greater whole—snapshots of families moving through time and space. Nonetheless, I strive to employ rich ethnographic descriptions, interview data, and case records to provide analysis that "does not erase personality."[49]

OVERVIEW OF THE BOOK

This book is organized around critical moments of interaction in the CPS system. Looking at each stage of the CPS process allows an opportunity to examine how parents make decisions as they go through this long legal process and how the choices they make affect case outcome. Chapter 2 provides a historical overview of the CPS system. Beginning in the Progressive Era and wending through present day, I trace the ways that public policy has shifted between a preference for placing children away from their biological parents to one that has prioritized keeping children with their natal families. The historical background provides theoretical grounding for discussions of recurring issues of child protection. Chapter 3 looks at the context of CPS social work and exposes child protection work as thankless, dangerous, and stressful. In doing so, I establish a framework for understanding how the work conditions in this female-dominated profession affect the ways in which social work is practiced, and ultimately under which dependency decisions are made. Chapter 4 focuses specifically on the investigation of child maltreatment and looks at how social workers expect deference from parents when deciding whether or not to remove children from their homes. In this chapter I examine the investigations of three mothers for child maltreatment to show how deference also intersects with class race and gender. Chapter 5 examines the experiences of parents who are attempting to regain custody of their children through their participation in reunification services. In this chapter I analyze the structural barriers that inhibit parents' ability to succeed, while also showing how parents make strategic decisions about their cases. Chapters 6 and 7 look specifically at how state expectations of reunification are gendered and serve to reinforce gender-normative meanings of parenthood. Chapter 6 focuses on mothers and examines state expectations dictating that they learn self-restraint and sacrifice for the good of their children. Chapter 7 analyzes the legal and biological definitions of fatherhood and considers how men who have not experienced social markers of success can demonstrate their competence as men and fathers. Chapter 8 outlines how judges, using claims made by attorneys and social workers, measure parental rehabilitation and how the court decides long-term case outcome. In looking at measures of successful reformation, which I term demonstrable rehabilitation, we see how narrowly prescribed definitions of success limit parents' abilities to reunify with their children. Chapter 9 concludes with a broader discussion of the CPS system and points to possible policy and practice reforms.

Each chapter points out the process by which the state enacts meanings of adequate parenting and demonstrates how parents interact with these definitions in deliberate ways. Within these critical moments of interaction between parents and the state, state actors expect deference to their authority and professional definitions of social life. By looking at how those without structural power experience state intervention into their families—and strategize their cooperation and resistance to that intervention—I explicate the process by which the therapeutic state does not just demand compliance, but seeks to fix families in ways consistent with dominant beliefs about motherhood, fatherhood, and the appropriate form of family life.

2

CHILD PROTECTION: A HISTORICAL PERSPECTIVE

Child welfare historians speak of the pendulum of social welfare that swings between a prioritization of returning children to their families and a belief in the superiority of adoption. As the pendulum swings toward birth families, reunification services are prioritized, policies aim to assist needy families, and state agencies remove children with trepidation. With the pendulum's swing back toward a belief in the superior benefits of adoption, state agencies respond more aggressively to allegations of maltreatment, erring on the side of removing children rather than waiting to see if the child is harmed more severely. In this context, biological parents receive fewer "chances" from agencies and parental rights are more swiftly terminated.

This chapter describes the development of the child welfare system in the United States from the late nineteenth century to present, highlighting the state's evolving response to changing social contexts and new challenges. The public meanings of and responses to child abuse as a social problem, like all social problems, have been constructed over time through interaction between groups or individuals that make claims of meaning.[1] One defining feature of the history of child abuse and its various proposed solutions is the changing belief in what constitutes children's best interests. This historic pendulum, swinging between an emphasis on preserving families or removing children, is a significant force in shaping policy and practice. Exploring the changing meanings of child abuse in different time periods sets a backdrop for the remainder of this work and demonstrates how many themes around the family are recurrent and can be seen in the contemporary CPS system.

THE PROGRESSIVE ERA:
NEW RESPONSES TO NEW SOCIAL PROBLEMS

Although child maltreatment existed as a condition prior to the nineteenth century, its identification as a social problem needing a response occurred in the late nineteenth and early twentieth centuries.[2] As social reformers of the Progressive Era defined child abuse as a social problem and advocated for specific solutions, they reconfigured the relationship between the private family and the public state. Historians place the rise of an organized response to child maltreatment in the second half of the nineteenth century, when the impact of the well-documented stresses of industrialization, urbanization, and immigration on family life were perceived as requiring intervention.[3] As historian Linda Gordon describes,

> ...in the late nineteenth century, child abuse appeared worse than before, and indeed it may well have been worse. Urban poverty was more stressful in many ways than rural poverty: housing was overcrowded and overpriced; homes and neighborhoods were filthy, without adequate facilities for disposing of wastes; the air and water were polluted; the food in the markets was often adulterated and rotten, and the urban poor could not grow their own; there were dangers from fires, traffic, and other urban hazards; wage earners were at the mercy of periodic unemployment and grinding hours and conditions. Immigration created neighborhoods that were not communities, left mothers more alone with children than they had been in "the old country." The anonymity of urban life promoted more theft, vandalism, and violence.[4]

Growing urban unrest created a sense of crisis among middle-class social reformers, which took two forms: fear of increasing interclass tension and suspicion of immorality in poor communities. Efforts to protect children reflected "concern among bourgeois observers that working-class children deserved special attention, for they were at once the most vulnerable of marginal populations and the medium with which the ranks of certain anti-social elements would be replenished."[5] Child advocates believed that children were at risk of being exploited by their parents, corrupted by urban streets, and becoming callous and immoral as a result of their environment. Out of these anxieties rose a philanthropic practice known as "child-saving."[6]

Advocacy on behalf of children fit neatly into the belief systems of the Progressive Era social reformers, most of whom were members of the bourgeoisie. From their perspective, individuals were responsible for their own situations, which reformers "often traced to the innate inferiority of the immigrants, who constituted the great bulk of their targets."[7] Many industrial workers were immigrants who came from countries with socialist traditions and had experience with labor movements. Social reformers reasonably feared a larger threat of organized protest as the working class began to develop a sense of class solidarity that transcended ethnic lines.[8] Simultaneously, children were believed to be innocent, malleable beings who could be shaped into appropriate citizens with proper guidance.[9] Reformers believed that children would be best saved from the presumed depravity of their poor parents by being removed from their deviant homes. Historian Walter Trattner notes that concern for children was "not merely a matter of pity or compassion. Indeed, it resulted from, above all, the fact that most citizens viewed children as the key to social control."[10]

Prior efforts to protect children from their families and communities resulted in many children going to live in almshouses and other institutions, where they were often treated poorly.[11] In contrast, organized child-saving in the Progressive Era adopted the more radical solution of placing children outside their homes and communities. The first children's organization to adopt out-of-home care that placed children in homes of other families, or "placing out," was the New York Children's Aid Society (CAS), founded by Reverend Charles Loring Brace. Brace, a twenty-two year-old recent graduate of divinity school, arrived in New York in 1848 and was horrified at the visible class divisions between the wealthy classes and families who lived in destitution, leading him to create the CAS.[12] Initially the CAS offered religious, vocational, and academic training to children and provided shelter to runaways. However, the agency quickly faced a demand for services that exceeded its capacity. In 1853, believing that children were better off away from the ills of city life, Brace and his colleagues began moving city children to live with families on farms. Brace and his colleagues placed children on trains, referred to as "orphan trains," and shipped them out, a practice that came to be known as "placing out" or "shipping out."

In the first year, 207 children were placed out. In 1854 the CAS opted to send larger groups of children "because more could be accomplished with little increase in cost or the magnitude of work."[13] Between 1854 and 1930, approximately 150,000 children were placed out by the CAS or a related agency to homes in California, Colorado, Illinois, Indiana, Iowa, Kansas, Michigan, Minnesota, Missouri, Nebraska, Ohio, Texas, and Wisconsin. Smaller numbers were sent to Florida, Louisiana, North Carolina, South Carolina, and Virginia, as well as rural parts of New York, Connecticut, Massachusetts, New Jersey, and Pennsylvania.[14]

Placing out efforts focused on children who were believed to be orphans, homeless, abandoned, or neglected. Children identified as "incorrigible, who appeared to be sickly," were mentally or physically handicapped, or were African American were not allowed to participate.[15] Brace's goals for the orphan trains were twofold: he wanted to help poor children by providing them a good rural life, and he wanted to spare the city's upper classes of the poor, "dangerous classes," who, comprised largely of Catholic immigrants, were perceived as presenting a threat to social order. Reverend Brace wrote of his efforts:

> As Christian men, we cannot look upon this great multitude of unhappy, deserted, and degraded boys and girls without feeling our responsibility to God for them. The class increases: immigration is pouring in its multitudes of poor foreigners who leave these young outcasts everywhere in our midst. These boys and girls, it should be remembered, will soon form the great lower class of our city. They will influence elections; they may shape the policy of the city; they will assuredly, if unreclaimed, poison society all around them. They will help to form the great multitude of robbers, thieves, and vagrants, who are now such a burden upon the law-respecting community.[16]

Many historians have pointed out the problems inherent in placing out.[17] The children shipped out, many of whom were Catholic immigrants, were often sent to live with Protestant farmers. This rallied public criticism by the Catholic Church. Some were taken in as a source of free or cheap labor and were not educated, fed, or clothed properly. Local agents responsible for evaluating potential foster parents may have been reticent to deny approval to their neighbors, and thus overestimated the quality of foster homes. Despite the CAS program mandates for screening foster parents and for maintaining contact with them, little is known about what became of the children placed out, as case records were poor. Although Brace's program targeted orphans and reportedly required parental consent for children with a living parent, the level of consent given is a subject of controversy. Parents who consented to placements in hopes that their children would learn a trade were surprised by the lack of information about their children's whereabouts. Few children ever saw their parents again and siblings were often permanently separated when those not placed in one town were sent to another.[18] Because placing out arrangements did not involve formal indenture contracts, there was no legal remedy to mediate conflicts between the CAS and foster families, nor between the CAS and biological parents. As such, efforts by the CAS to place children on the orphan trains threatened to set the organization in open conflict with a child's parents, a situation that Brace, who considered poor parents to be an irremediable source of corruption, loathed.[19]

Some childsaving organizations, such as the Society for the Prevention of Cruelty to Children (SPCC), did not shy away from conflicts with parents, and many "were willing, even eager, to prosecute parents as a means to refashion family norms."[20] Initially the SPCC respected the reluctance of American courts to interfere with the patriarchal authority of the family and only asked courts to become involved in cases of "flagrant neglect or exploitation."[21] However, over time the members of the SPCC asked the courts to intervene in less serious offenses, including behaviors that were quite normal in impoverished working-class communities, like begging or absence from school.[22] One manner in which Brace and the leaders of other childsaving organizations, including the multiple chapters of the SPCC, aimed to rescue children from their own families was to lobby for state legislation against juvenile vagrancy, street begging, and child exploitation by parents. To ensure legislation would be enforced, the societies' agents established good working relationships with local judges and the police. In 1881 the New York chapters of the SPCC were given the power to make arrests, while other SPCC chapters routinely called upon the police to remove children from parents. Some SPCC chapters gained the right to be named temporary guardians and thus positioned themselves so that the courts usually accepted their recommendations. This transformation of the SPCC's power demonstrates the willingness of the state to involve itself in deciding family matters, an area that previously had remained private and free from public adjudication. Polsky argues that "by responding to the prodding by SPCCs for earlier action and delegating enforcement powers to their agents, the judiciary allowed itself to be invested with a new responsibility to enforce bourgeois child-raising norms within the working-class household." Although this change represented a new and significant extension of state power, the transformed role of the state drew little notice, in part because the middle class largely viewed the courts as neutral legal organs rather than as active parts of the political state. Not dissimilar to the differential experience of the courts today, the newly "inflated judicial power would be seen only by those marginal families caught directly in its path."[23]

The SPCC's new powers served to blur its role as both a charity provider and an agent of the state. In one notable case, the New York chapter of the SPCC refused to allow the New York State Board of Charities to inspect or supervise its facilities, arguing that "the SPCC [was] a law-enforcing, rather than a charitable institution and thus not subject to visitation."[24] The New York Court of Appeals' willingness to uphold the SPCC's claim that they were in fact more like police than charity workers illustrates the complicated role in which childsavers placed themselves. In poor neighborhoods, where the SPCC and its agents were seen as police agents, SPCC workers became known as "the Cruelty;" and rather than being seen as a source of assistance, their presence was dreaded and feared.[25] Parents' negative views of child protection, as well as the agencies' complicated dual functions, continue today.

Despite the controversy over whether the orphan trains were exploitative or charitable, there are some larger points of historical significance. Brace was among the first to prioritize placing children in homes and families rather than in institutions and orphanages. As social welfare historian Walter Trattner suggests, "Unlike many of his contemporaries who advocated locking up the needy behind walls of an institution, Brace contrived a way of both securing their removal and capitalizing on the beneficial influences of home life."[26] As such, he is considered the grandfather of modern foster care. For a variety of reasons, including new laws requiring children to attend school, child labor laws, unwillingness of host communities to accept more "orphans," and early efforts to provide assistance to poor mothers so they could keep their children, placing out peaked in 1875 and slowly declined until 1930.[27] However, organized child-saving campaigns continued to flourish.

Professionalization of Childsaving

In the early twentieth century, the childsaving movement altered its strategy, progressing beyond simply saving children by removing them from their parents to reforming their families' lifestyles, even if through coercion. According to historian Linda Gordon, child protection agents in the nineteenth century saw themselves as paralegal—responsible for punishing specific offenses and protecting children from specific dangers; in the early twentieth century, they tried to supervise and direct the lives of those families they considered deviant.[28] At the end of the nineteenth century, childsavers were largely volunteers from philanthropic and social organizations who worked to defend poor and abused children. In contrast, those who assumed childsaving activities in the early twentieth century were pursuing the new profession of social work. Social workers in this era struggled to devise a unique professional body of knowledge and techniques that included formalized systems for keeping case records, client diagnoses, and treatment recommendations. They had also gained new legal powers. With these powers, the pendulum swung toward greater state involvement.

Gender is woven throughout the history of social work. In the early twentieth century, men outnumbered women, but women continued to enter the profession and eventually assumed positions of leadership. The women poised to assume positions of power within the profession were white, privileged, unmarried, and childless. As social welfare scholar Mary Ann Mason notes, these women "had benefited from the efforts of the first wave of feminism and from the growing wealth of the middle class" and were "college graduates who did not need to marry immediately in order to attain financial security."[29] Their unwavering commitment to their work—even as they themselves remained unmarried or childless—and public visibility feminized the social work profession. These women were sometimes regarded as "unduly sentimental, meddlesome, sexually abnormal, or to be women who made gender trouble of one sort or another."[30] Critics of the burgeoning profession referred to the social workers as "a mobile mob of maidens mediating matrimony," as well as "half-baked young girls running around trying to tell other people how to manage their affairs [when] what they need is a family of their own."[31] Social workers struggled to downplay their femininity so as to build a credible source of professional scientific rigor, while also playing up the notion that as women, they possessed special skills for mediating domestic conflict. In doing so, they also defined class differences between themselves and their clients, and between the volunteers who had formerly run social charities and themselves as new professional women.[32]

Women social workers also made gender central to their work by advocating for motherhood as a way of helping poor children. Women reformers championed mothering as a key component of raising good citizens. In essence, "it was as mothers that these poor women contributed to society and as mothers that their virtue was measured."[33] Social workers at the turn of the twentieth century prioritized keeping children with their mothers, so long as their mothers were not immoral; this was a determination that only they, as social workers, could make.

Building on the legal powers gained by childsavers in the late nineteenth century, which included the ability to make arrests, utilize the police to remove children, and make recommendations to the court, twentieth century social reformers continued to develop their role as an arm of the state. Abandoning historical notions of familial privacy, the state, as represented by these newly empowered agents—child welfare workers— became "the superparent, determining the conditions under which natural parents could raise their children."[34] Social workers policed family life and determined the fitness of families, introducing poor families to increased public scrutiny. Simultaneously, these same social reformers advocated keeping poor children in their homes with their natal families and clarified that poverty did not intrinsically make a family immoral.

Creating Public Welfare

The reformers' efforts to advocate for the importance of family life broadly and mothering specifically led to the creation of new federal policies. Social reformers advocated successfully for the 1909 White House Conference on the Care of Dependent Children. The landmark conference gave public recognition to the importance of child well-being and lent the budding field of social work credibility, which helped the profession blossom. The conference also had several significant outcomes. First, the conference led to the creation of the U.S. Children's Bureau, a federal agency committed to research about and advocacy for children. In spite of its limited resources, the Children's Bureau became the primary and most authoritative source of information on child welfare and family life in the United States. Its creation marked the first federal recognition of the rights of children, as well as the need to create a permanent agency to study, if not to protect them.

Second, the conference provided an articulation of the importance of family life to children. The conference keynote speaker explained that "home life is the highest and finest product of civilization," and argued that children "should not be deprived of it except for urgent compelling reasons," in which case they should be placed in other families whenever possible.[35] In many ways, these sentiments continue to guide child welfare policy, which favors adoption or family-based foster care if children cannot reside with their natal families.

Third, the conference publicly declared that poverty alone did not make a parent unfit and led to the creation of a monetary support system for poor children. Known initially in gender-neutral terms as "Funds to Parents," and eventually as the "Mother's Pension" or "Widow's Pension," this federal program was among the most significant of the era.[36] The cash grant program was built on the belief that "family life of the home is sapped in its foundations when the mothers of young children work for wages."[37] Between 1911 and 1935, all but two states enacted systems to give funds to women with dependent children who lacked wage-earning husbands, ideally because of death. The Mother's Pension was not equitably awarded, and excluded most mothers who were unmarried or abandoned, regardless of their need. In 1931, 82 percent of the women receiving aid were widows. In addition, most states excluded nonwhites. Despite its disparate treatment of women, the pension program marked the beginning of public assistance for poor families in the United States and held important symbolic value.

The Mother's Pension also defined a new role for the government and laid the groundwork for future welfare programs, including the Social Security Act of 1935. Title IV of the Social Security Act created Aid to Dependent Children (ADC) (which in 1964 evolved into the Aid to Families with Dependent Children (AFDC) program), a federal entitlement to assistance for mothers who were deprived of the financial support of the fathers of their children.[38] The Social Security Act of 1935 also made small grants available to states to help them support "preventative and protective services to vulnerable children," though most funds went to support foster care.[39] In concert, these programs communicated the symbolic importance of public support for children's well-being and a preference for children being raised in their own families. With this, political sentiment swung toward a prioritization of natal families over other homes or institutions for poor children.

The dual histories of U.S. child protection and welfare policy are entwined, with single mothers figuring prominently in each.[40] Whereas social welfare policy held that poverty did not intrinsically make a parent unfit, pensions were not intended for morally questionable parents, no matter how poor. Assessing that moral worth became the self-appointed duty of social workers. Should a mother request assistance, she was also inviting suspicion of her worthiness as a mother and on-going surveillance by a social worker who could revoke her grant. A worthy mother was one who did not work outside her home, devoted herself completely to her children, "and led a conspicuously virtuous life with no male companionship."[41] A mother's sexual behavior was of paramount concern when determining her morality. To be clear, mothers deemed immoral did not receive grants and their children were easily removed from their custody. Out-of-wedlock births demonstrated a mother's immorality and presented a great challenge to social welfare agencies. Illustrating this, more than three-fifths of the children born out of wedlock in Boston in 1914 became wards of child welfare agencies within the first year of their lives.[42]

Social welfare has been both a blessing and a curse for poor women. While it provides much needed support for poor women and their children, it has also been a means for the state to evaluate and police individual families. As social welfare scholar Laura Frame points out,

> ... while "welfare" through the Social Security Act was an important entitlement in name, it has never been truly universal. A variety of policy and implementation mechanisms have always made it a source of support offered judiciously by welfare officials. The implicit and explicit "suitable home" policies of the early mothers' pensions, ADC, and later AFDC (Aid to Families with Dependent Children) have all served as a means of behavioral regulation and caseload containment, as well as maintaining a critical link between the welfare and child protection systems.[43]

The work of childsavers led to the creation of much needed financial support for single mothers and a public prioritization of child well-being that identified mothers as a key part of that well-being. This can be seem in more contemporary examples, such as when, in 1994, Representative Newt Gingrich (R-GA) advocated for orphanages for poor children, a proposal that received little support, in large part because of the collective belief in the superiority of families—even those who struggle financially—over institutions. However, the very existence of this proposal also shows the disdain for providing poor families with material support. This same anxiety existed from the beginning of state welfare policy. As childsavers identified the key role of mothers in children's lives and the need to assist them, they also emphasized that children needed suitable homes, as they defined them, thus intertwining cash welfare and child welfare agencies. The conjoined roles of social workers as providers of help and monitors of parental behavior were to some extent contradictory. This convoluted relationship continues today.

1920s TO 1960s: "BATTERED CHILD SYNDROME" AND THE FIRST FEDERAL RESPONSE TO CHILD ABUSE

Between the 1920s and late 1950s, public awareness of child maltreatment seemed to disappear. There are several possible explanations for this. A decline in the first wave of feminism after World War I may have led to a waning interest in family violence.[44] The introduction of psychoanalysis as a method of social work also changed approaches to child maltreatment; social workers focused on those who could most benefit from new therapeutic techniques, which "generally excluded child abusers, whose problems were among the most difficult and who did not choose to seek help."[45] Through the 1930s, the effects of the Great Depression, when the need for public assistance far exceeded available aid, served to disorganize social work and to erode agency specificity. This, and U.S. involvement in World War II, led to declining attention to child abuse. During the 1950s, child abuse and neglect did not rate among the top concerns of social workers and were not of great interest to the public, since the idea of "involuntary intervention by community agents into family life on charges of child abuse was unthinkable, most abhorrent, in the climate of conservatism throughout the 1950s."[46]

Beginning in the mid-1940s, with the widening availability of x-ray technology, pediatric radiologists' reports in medical journals increasingly described skeletal injuries and multiple fractures in children, although they rarely identified causes. Following a landmark 1957 article by a radiologist claiming that a child's injuries were likely caused by "misconduct and deliberate injury," concern for the beaten child dramatically increased.[47] A series of insignificant federal reforms in 1958 adjusted funding for child welfare, and a short-term advisory council was formed to make recommendations about future directions for child welfare services. Following the council's recommendations, a new national research agenda was established. In the 1960 reauthorization of Social Security, the Children's Bureau, a federal agency committed to aiding public and private child welfare practitioners and scholars, received one million dollars to study child abuse. These funds were designated for projects that showed "promise of substantial contribution to the advancement of child welfare" and allowed the Children's Bureau to provide funding for child abuse research.[48] Through these grants, the agency built a network of researchers whose work focused specifically on child abuse, helping to compile better information about child maltreatment and creating broader public awareness of child abuse.

Perhaps most influential in the rediscovery of child abuse was a 1961 lecture at the American Academy of Pediatrics annual meeting by C. Henry Kempe, M.D., a pediatric radiologist. Kempe identified "battered child syndrome," a new medical diagnosis to address severe manifestations of nonaccidental injuries to children, many of which were uncovered on x-rays. As a pediatric radiologist diagnosing child abuse, Kempe did not face many of the challenges encountered by other pediatricians who regularly interact with parents, including confusion over whether the child or parent is their patient and fear of retribution from parents. In addition, a coalition between radiology, general pediatrics, and psychiatry formed to address this newly identified "illness" of child abuse.[49]

This new diagnosis gained significant public attention and led many states to pass laws that required doctors, teachers, and other professionals who work with children to report any suspected child abuse. By 1968, all fifty states and the District of Columbia had some version of a mandatory child abuse reporting law.[50] States have continued to broaden mandated reporting laws, with California now requiring photographic processors, firefighters, and dog catchers to report suspected child abuse.[51] Throughout the 1960s, with the Children's Bureau's new apparatus for research and information dissemination and a clear medical definition, child abuse continued to gain public attention. Public policy scholar Barbara Nelson has suggested that the rediscovery of child abuse "occurred in an era when issues of equity and social responsibility dominated public discourse," flowing from the beginnings of the civil rights movement in the late 1950s.[52] With this rebirth of awareness, greater state intervention was again seen as necessary.

1970s: RISING CASELOADS AND CALLS FOR REFORM

In 1974, Congress authorized funding for the Child Abuse Prevention and Treatment Act (CAPTA), a federal law that helped states establish services, policies, and community-based programs aimed at protecting children. (Although federal foster care reimbursements were made available to states in 1961, CAPTA represents the first broad-based effort to support child welfare agencies in providing comprehensive services.) In strategizing this legislation, Senator Walter Mondale (D-MN), CAPTA's sponsor, was aware of the importance of framing child abuse as a universal issue rather than as an extension of existing welfare policies. As Barbara Nelson explains, "to his mind the real stumbling block to passing the legislation would occur if it were considered poverty legislation, or if the problem were defined as deviance confined solely to the poor, rather than as a social blight which attacked all classes."[53] As such, CAPTA was marketed with the understanding that children of any race, gender, class, or national background were at risk.

CAPTA also emphasized physical abuse over other forms of maltreatment; in doing so, child abuse came to be seen as something separate from a parent's right to discipline a child, a right that "Congress would no doubt have supported if pressed."[54] Between the shaping of battered child syndrome and the marketing of CAPTA, child abuse could be seen as a medical disorder affecting all Americans, one that caused identifiable harm, and likely resulted from psychic illness in the perpetrator that could be treated by professionals.

In the first year of CAPTA, only three states had reporting laws that met federal standards to qualify for CAPTA funds. However, most states quickly revised their statutes, and by 1978, forty-three states qualified for federal funds.[55] CAPTA created the National Center on Child Abuse and Neglect to develop and maintain standards for states and locales to respond to maltreatment reports. New monies for child protection services, statutory requirements for reporting abuse, expectations that state agencies would intervene aggressively, and increased public attention all coalesced to create a soaring number of children being removed from their homes and placed in foster care. As child abuse was defined and funded, policy emphasized increased intervention.[56,57]

Constructing the "Best Interests"

In 1976, the first year national statistics of abuse and neglect reports were compiled, 669,000 reports of child abuse and neglect were reported nationwide. By 1980 there were more than one million reports.[58] At the same time caseloads were increasing, new concern about children's long-term well-being entered public discourse, influencing fears that children were removed unnecessarily, "only to languish, often in a series of foster homes, with little effort made either to reunite them with their birth families or to place them for adoption."[59]

In their 1973 book, *Beyond the Best Interests of the Child*, Joseph Goldstein, Anna Freud, and Albert Solnit argued for the importance of giving a child one caregiver or "psychological parent." Given the growing concern about "foster care drift," in which child move from placement to placement without any permanency, the collective works of these authors received great attention.[60] According to these theorists, a child requires a single caregiver who may be, but is not necessarily, a biological parent, and who provides for their physical and psychological needs and offers affection, comfort, and mental stimulation. A child must have this "psychological parent" to develop normally. Further, children develop a bond to their psychological parent and can be harmed by separating from that parent. The juvenile courts adopted the psychological parent model to assess the significance of the existing parental relationship and to prioritize permanent foster and adoptive homes with new psychological parents.[61]

The first judicial use of the psychological parent concept was in the 1973 case known as *In re: B.G.* In this case, a biological mother sought to regain custody of her children who had been placed in foster care following their father's death. The foster parents who were caring for the children were not allowed to participate in the court proceedings. On appeal, the California Supreme Court, citing *Beyond the Best*

Interests of the Child, ruled that foster parents, referred to as de facto parents, have an interest in case outcome and should be allowed to appear in juvenile court proceedings. As a result, foster parents who can demonstrate they have a significant relationship with the child—usually defined as having cared for the child for six months or more—can request de facto parent status that grants them the right to participate in proceedings, call witnesses, and be represented by attorneys.

The social significance of *Beyond the Best Interests of the Child* and the other works by Goldstein, Freud, and Solnit cannot be overstated; most of the existing vocabulary and central assumptions of the contemporary child welfare system are derived from them.[62] Yet Goldstein et al.'s theories have come under significant criticism within psychology and law. Some critics argue that this theory's emphasis on a single caregiver may be unrealistic and may reflect cultural bias. Specifically, this theory overlooks the reality that children bond with adults other than their primary caretakers, including siblings, non-caretaking parents, and other family members, and fails to consider the importance of multiple caregivers as the norm in other cultures.[63] In addition, attachment has been increasingly seen as a life-course phenomenon, with different attachments to different people developing at different stages of one's life. Other works claim that there is little empirical evidence to support the conclusions of bonding assessments, used to test a child's psychological attachment to a caregiver.[64] Child psychiatrist David Arrendondo and juvenile court judge Leonard Edwards argue that in the family court context, some experts are attempting "to use attachment theory to reduce the entire spectrum of human relatedness into a limited number of discrete categories." They caution that although this approach may be useful for research, "it is of limited value in the context of the juvenile and family court."[65] Despite the critiques and theoretical challenges to the psychological parent model, it continues to dictate child welfare policy and practice. Its current application is addressed in chapter 8.

Opposition to Transracial Adoption

One of the key contributions of the psychological parent theory—and the "best interests" standard that it supported—is its focus on children's long-term well-being. At the same time the best interest standard was taking hold, a growing movement of the National Association of Black Social Workers (NABSW) was under way to ban the practice of allowing black children to be legally adopted into non-black homes. In the late 1960s and peaking in 1971, an increasing number of white families adopted black children. The combination of the decreasing availability of white infants for adoption and the new awareness of racial inequality and the accompanying desire to "save" black children shaped this trend.[66] However, the rapid increase in transracial placements and concern for children's total well-being absent a relationship with the black community caused concern among many social workers. At its first annual convention in 1972, the NABSW passed a resolution opposing transracial adoption. The resolution stated that

> Black children should be placed only with black families whether in foster care or adoption. Black children belong physically, psychologically and culturally in black families in order that they receive the total sense of themselves and develop a sound projection of their future... Black children in white homes are cut off from the healthy development of themselves as black people... We have committed ourselves to go back to our communities and work to end this particular form of genocide.[67]

The NABSW's position and their extensive advocacy work dramatically reduced rates of transracial adoptions from foster care. Public and private agencies quickly adopted policies to promote same-race adoptions.[68] The 1973 adoption of these recommendations by the Child Welfare League of America (CWLA), the oldest and largest national member organization devoted to providing "a consistent, strong, and nonpartisan voice for children both in the United States and worldwide," shows the mainstream support for the NABSW campaign.[69] Illustrating its success, interracial adoptions peaked in 1971, with 2,574 black children adopted by white parents annually, dropping to 831 by 1975.[70] This change in policy was justified as being in children's best interests. Yet on the heels of the civil rights movement, it was also a way of vocally acknowledging the value of black community, culture, and biological family.

In 1979 another policy change prioritized children's continuing ties to their families and communities by mandating payment to relatives caring for foster children. In the case of *Miller v. Youakim*, the U.S. Supreme Court ruled that states had to pay relatives who were caring for foster children—an arrangement known as kinship care—the same rate as licensed foster parents, so long as the relatives could meet the requirements for foster care licensing.[71] This colorblind policy change created new opportunities for children to remain with biological relatives and in their own communities, consistent with the NABSW's position. Kinship care, which provides children an opportunity to stay in their natal communities, has been increasing in use, particularly in cases involving children of color.[72] Many states have different requirements for foster care licensing for relatives, with California being among the most lenient.[73] Although not all relatives can meet foster care licensing requirements, the shift in policy placed a premium on children's relationships with their family history and culture.

The Indian Child Welfare Act of 1978 (ICWA) is another example of federal efforts to prioritize children living with their natal communities and to recognize the unique needs of children of color. Specifically, this legislation aims to prevent the removal of American Indian children by requiring "active efforts" to prevent removal and specifying that placement and adoption should first be attempted with relatives, tribal members, or in homes or institutions approved by the tribe before considering a non-American Indian home. In response to the widespread practice of removing American Indian children from their families and tribes and placing them with non-American Indian families and in institutions, this law specifically aims to protect the best interests of American Indian children within their tribal culture. ICWA created different requirements for social services agencies' management of cases when they involve American Indian children. The law also mandates a higher legal standard for removal of children or termination of parental rights and grants decision-making authority to tribal courts rather than county or state juvenile courts for cases involving children who qualify under ICWA. Under ICWA, tribes have the right to intervene in court proceedings and may be given additional time to prepare motions and can request the case be transferred to tribal court venues. ICWA carries both material requirements that affect child welfare practices for American Indian children and symbolic importance. Indeed, ICWA was the first federal legislation to address the role of culture in the lives of children and families who enter the child welfare system.[74]

THE 1980s: REFOCUSING ON REUNIFICATION IN THE FACE OF NEW CHALLENGES

In 1980 Congress passed the Adoption Assistance and Child Welfare Act (AACWA), which until recently remained the dominant legal framework for child welfare, foster care, and adoption. This act attempted to safeguard children's connections to their natal families and communities, and to prevent long stays in foster care without the benefits of appropriate psychological parents. The federal law provided funds to states to help with the expenses associated with adoption and reunification services, not simply foster care, a policy that made reunification or permanent adoption as financially attractive as foster care.[75] The AACWA also required states to make "reasonable efforts" to reunite children with their families, specifying that "in each case, reasonable efforts will be made (A) prior to the placement of a child in foster care, to prevent or eliminate the need for removal of the child from his home and (B) to make it possible for the child to return to his home." This law also stipulated that children could only be removed from their parents when a "judicial determination" had been made that leaving the child in the home with their family would be "contrary to the welfare of such child" and that reasonable efforts to do so had been attempted. Further, this law required that states develop a case plan for each child in foster care receiving maintenance payments from the federal government. This law was the logical outcome of the political climate of the 1970s, which included the NABSW's campaign to end transracial adoption, the passage of ICWA, the concern for children's psychological bonds with parents, and the legal rights gained by biological relatives.

The concept that state-run agencies must make "reasonable efforts" to reunify families is one of the most significant pieces of the AACWA. This provision, although vaguely worded, mandated state agencies to work with natal families to make it possible for children to return home.[76] Although the provision was found to be legally unenforceable, it prompted a shift in child welfare practice as states prioritized reunification over the termination of parental rights. By 1982 there were only 262,000 foster care placements, a noticeable decrease by almost half from the 1977 level of 502,000.

The Crack Crisis in Child Welfare

Through the late 1980s and early 1990s, foster care caseloads again grew, returning to the notably high levels of the pre-AACWA era. Parental substance abuse was identified as the cause for much of this increase.[77] Although substance abuse has posed a problem for child welfare since the Progressive Era, when the childsavers aligned forces with prohibitionists around their shared concern about alcohol consumption, child protection in the 1980s largely focused on crack cocaine.[78] Crack was different socially and politically than powder cocaine, a drug that was used recreationally among whites through the 1970s. Crack—cocaine mixed with water and baking soda to create a rock that can be smoked—is packaged in small quantities for inexpensive distribution, making it more affordable and available in low-income neighborhoods. Named for the crackling sound when it is smoked, it appeared almost exclusively in poor inner-city black and Latino neighborhoods in New York, Miami, and Los Angeles. While largely contained in specific urban areas, crack use was portrayed as a disease that could spread beyond the inner city. From the initial news reports, crack was identified as an "epidemic" that was "spreading rapidly from cities to the suburbs and was destroying American society."[79] Once again motivated by the perceived moral depravity of the poor and the risk they posed, social reformers advocated for greater intervention, with children as the identified symbol needing salvation.[80]

Concern for the children of crack users manifested in gendered ways. Crack cocaine "marked the first perceived epidemic of a heavily stigmatized illegal drug in which large numbers of women participated, many of them young with small children."[81] The novelty of female drug use allowed women to be singled out in portrayals of the crisis that crack was reportedly causing. In these anecdotal accounts, mothers were portrayed as neglectful as they chose to use drugs instead of caring for their children. Crack was also reported to increase women's sexual libido, increasing the likelihood that they would prostitute themselves for drugs, and to exterminate their maternal instinct, causing them to neglect their children.[82]

Simultaneous to the rise in crack use among women was the widespread use of fetal imaging techniques. As doctors began to diagnose, treat, monitor, or conduct surgery on fetuses, "it became natural to think of the fetus as a baby, if not from conception, then from some later (if arbitrarily chosen) point in utero."[83] In her pivotal work on abortion politics, political scientist Rosalind Petchesky describes the symbolic importance of the fetus:

> Unlike poor women and children, the fetus requires little or no social care and few if any services, and it doesn't have to go to school, get a job, or find shelter. ... Thus, fetal advocacy becomes a badge of identity signifying not only 'moral,' 'Christian,' values and defense of the (traditional, patriarchal) family, but also fiscal restraint and its corollary, tough-mindedness against the poor.[84]

With the abortion controversy as a backdrop, the newborn baby whose mother had used crack during her pregnancy became an identified victim of the crack epidemic. The "crack baby," as such newborns quickly came to be known, became a potent symbol of the crack epidemic and accompanying war on drugs. Crack babies reportedly were more likely to have a smaller head circumference, be born prematurely, and be smaller in length.[85] Crack babies were described as "irritable, inconsolable, developmentally delayed, and incapable of love," reportedly suffered from "Alzheimer's-like symptoms," and were expected to be learning disabled.[86] Medical journal articles in the mid- to late 1980s, and the popular media reports that followed, described the prenatal damage caused by drug use, and in many ways served as rallying points for state action. Studies after 1990 were more rigorous and "self-consciously responded to the alarmist tone of much of the early medical literature." However, studies that identified an effect of perinatal substance use remained more likely to be published in medical journals than those that did not. As a result, later findings that the initial effects of in utero drug exposure had been overstated were not as widely disseminated as the earlier, more alarmist research had been.[87]

In the mid- to late 1980s, crack babies provided identifiable victims of maternal substance abuse that justified increased intervention.[88] The images of crack babies were used to justify increased spending on law enforcement, prisons, and neonatal intensive care units. Indeed, the focus on harm to the fetus made it increasingly difficult to draw a line between fetal abuse caused by maternal drug use during pregnancy and postnatal child abuse. Because intervention in the latter was perceived as inarguably necessary—a fact codified in federal law—the blurred line between the two facilitated greater state action in the former. Most profoundly, the crack epidemic broadly, and the crack baby phenomenon more specifically, undermined the efforts of the 1960s and 1970s to universalize meanings of child maltreatment, and instead successfully returned child maltreatment to its historical roots as a problem of racial and ethnic minorities and the poor in the inner city.

Hospitals in the mid-1980s began administering toxicology screens to pregnant and delivering women. (This was often done without explicit patient consent for the test, but rather under the general consent form that all admitted hospital patients sign.) Momentum for testing came from medical practitioners who felt something should be done to identify drug-exposed newborns, but the tests were conducted without an identified treatment goal to which the information could contribute.[89] As drug test results became available, physicians, social workers, and law enforcement agents began imagining ways the results could be used. One of the most dramatic examples of agency efforts to use positive drug test results occurred in South Carolina. There, doctors at a large county hospital, assured that the test results would be used as leverage to force women into treatment, turned over positive test results to district attorneys in two neighboring counties. Between 1989 and 1992, when the program ended, eighty-seven women were charged criminally with neglect or distribution of drugs to a minor, while at least forty-three others were coerced into treatment with threats of prosecution.[90] Nationwide, the Center for Reproductive Law and Policy estimated that by 2000, at least 200 women from more than thirty states had been arrested and criminally charged for alleged drug use or other behavior during their pregnancies.[91]

The practice of testing pregnant and delivering women for drugs is problematic for a variety of reasons. First, testing is not applied equally. Almost all the women who have been prosecuted for drug use have been black, a pattern consistent with research that shows that after controlling for poverty and other variables, black women are still more likely to be reported for prenatal substance abuse than are other women. One frequently cited study of pregnant women who were tested for drugs at several sites in Pinellas County, Florida found little difference in the rates of substance abuse among pregnant women by race or income level, but found that black women were ten times more likely to be reported to government agencies than were white women.[92]

Second, the use of positive test results ostensibly obtained for medical reasons, but actually used for criminal prosecution, has been ruled unconstitutional. Appellate courts have thrown out all but one conviction relating to perinatal substance use that alleged child endangerment or delivering illegal substances to a minor. In the South Carolina case of *Ferguson v. City of Charleston* (2001), the U.S. Supreme Court ruled that drug testing pregnant women without consent and disclosing results to law enforcement represented an unconstitutional search.[93]

Despite these issues, the use of drug testing of pregnant women has not waned; rather, concerns have continued to grow about whether perinatal drug use constitutes child abuse or suggests parental unfitness. In the initial years of drug testing, most cases were referred to child welfare agencies. In 1989, California juvenile court judges, facing a rising number of child welfare cases involving drug-exposed infants, requested that the California legislature clarify whether those cases constituted child abuse. Following a commission recommendation for a uniform statewide policy, in 1990 the California legislature passed a law (SB 2669), requiring every county to maintain a protocol for drug screening pregnant women. The law specified that a positive drug test alone did not constitute child abuse, and that hospitals needed more information of risk to newborns than just the test results to make a report to child welfare authorities. Whether the law was successful in reducing the number of referrals to child welfare agencies is a matter of controversy. It appears that in some counties in the first few years following SB 2669's passage, referrals of positive toxicology reports to child welfare agencies did decrease. However, since the law was implemented differently in different counties and no agency was empowered to monitor implementation, some counties appear to remain committed to referring most positive drug test results to child welfare agencies, with some counties opting to use them as grounds to remove children from their parents.[94]

Crack babies and positive drug tests presented a rallying cry for greater social welfare involvement in the lives of poor women of color. At the same time, some intervention was inevitable. In the mid-1980s, a new dilemma arose when numerous infants who were medically cleared to leave the hospital after birth remained there as "boarder babies" when their parents—often ill or drug-addicted—failed to claim them. In 1988 the AACWA was amended to include the Abandoned Infants Assistance Act (AIAA). This addition allowed the Department of Health and Human Services (DHHS) to make grants to public and nonprofit agencies for demonstration projects that would prevent the abandonment of infants and young children and help to identify the unique needs of these infants and children. The AIAA was designed to assist birth families in caring for these infants and children; to recruit, train, and retain foster families; to carry out residential programs; and to provide respite care for those caring for chronically ill children. The bill also funded efforts to recruit and train health and social services personnel to work with families and residential programs.[95]

Although the AIAA focused on infants and children who were drug exposed, it also prioritized care of children with acquired immune deficiency syndrome (AIDS), a significant issue in the mid- to late 1980s (underscored by the publicity surrounding Ryan White at the time).[96] In addition, while HIV- and AIDS-afflicted children, largely from poor ethnic minority communities, presented new challenges to the child protection system, the system also had to deal with children whose parents, sometimes intravenous drug users, were either ill, dead, or incarcerated. Again, the focus on drugs and AIDS served to further racialize and urbanize the social problem of child maltreatment. As these issues gained prominence, the child welfare system became the system of children of color. During the late 1980s and 1990s, the number of minority children in foster care rose, increasing from half of the caseload in 1990 to nearly two-thirds in 1995. By 1998 African American children represented almost forty-five percent of the foster care population.[97]

THE 1990s: ATTEMPTS TO ADDRESS SYSTEM FAILURES

Beginning in the late 1980s and early 1990s, public attention focused on many of the weaknesses in child protection policies, including caseloads that were both bulging and stagnant. One perceived weakness was the ban on interracial adoption. The NABSW's resolution was effective in creating a virtual ban on transracial adoption, which had remained in place for almost twenty-five years. But as black children became increasingly overrepresented in the foster care system, the preference for race-matching in adoption came to be seen as the underlying cause of children's long stays in foster care. This perception was perpetuated by anecdotal accounts of white foster care providers who were denied the right to legally adopt the children they had cared for in their homes. In many of these stories, the children had spent much of their lives in foster care, with little or no chance of being reunited with their parents, but they were prohibited from being adopted by their white caregivers. For example, the white foster mother in one 1995 case bemoaned the county's removal of her two African American foster daughters after she and her husband were refused permission to adopt them, explaining, "We raised these girls for five years, and now I can't even take them to the bathroom."[98]

Color-Blind Child Welfare Policy

In the mid-1990s, as the media hosted debates about transracial adoption, the United States witnessed the dismantling of Affirmative Action programs and the broad adoption of an ethos of color blindness. These race politics, combined with public and fiscal pressure to address the perceived failings of the foster care system, provided the foundation for the Multiethnic Placement Act of 1994 (MEPA) and its subsequent amendments in 1996. As social welfare scholar Devon Brooks and his co-authors observed, in considering MEPA, "Congress had little empirical data on the effects of same-race placement preferences and had to rely largely on anecdotal evidence…complicated by news reports of children who had been removed from long-term transracial foster placements to achieve racial matching."[99] Nonetheless, the color-blind ethos embodied in MEPA became law.

The Adoption Anti-Discrimination Act of 1995 (S 637), an earlier unsuccessful effort to amend MEPA, specifically addressed the historical position of the NABSW. As Senator John McCain (R-AZ), the bill's author and himself a transracially adoptive parent, stated,

> In the late 1960s and early 1970s, over 10,000 children were adopted by families of a different race. This was before many adoption officials decided, without any empirical evidence, that it is essential for children to be matched with families of the same race, even if they have to wait for long periods for such a family to come along. The forces of political correctness declared interracial

adoptions the equivalent of cultural genocide. This was, and continues to be, nonsense.[100]

As amended in 1996, MEPA accomplished two things. First, it prohibited the delay or denial of any child's adoption or placement in foster care due to the race, color, or national origin of the child or of the foster or adoptive parents. Second, it required states to recruit potential foster and adoptive families who reflect the ethnic and racial diversity of the children who need permanent homes.[101] Failure to comply with MEPA can result in a loss of federal funds, in injunctive relief, and in certain cases, in an award of monetary damages. DHHS enlisted the Office of Civil Rights (OCR) to enforce this law and framed noncompliance as a violation of civil rights. The bill and amendments had many allies, and groups like the NABSW were notably silent.

In the years since MEPA was implemented, little has been done to assess its effect. Olivia A. Golden, Assistant Secretary for the Administration for Children and Families (ACF), a branch of DHHS, testified before Congress that "both ACF and the Office of Civil Rights have been rigorously enforcing MEPA since its enactment." According to Golden, "In fiscal year 1999, OCR conducted over sixty-eight activities including complaint investigations, compliance reviews, training and technical assistance."[102] Outside of OCR investigations, there has been little study of the direct effects of MEPA on the foster care population.

Increasing Attention to System Failures

Problems regarding children's excessive stays in foster care, inability to be adopted, and case mismanagement came under scrutiny again shortly after the passage of MEPA. In a federal lawsuit, *Marisol A. v. Giuliani* (1996), a group of children and adults who identified themselves as friends of the children sued the Mayor of New York and the Child Welfare Administration of New York. The plaintiffs alleged the children were unreasonably deprived of their entitlement to protection under New York law and that they had not been adequately placed or protected by the state. Stories of each of the eleven children in the suit epitomized the various failures of state-run children's services. Children were returned to abusive parents, were not provided medically appropriate care or needed services while in foster care, were born to known abusers who were not investigated, were placed in inadequate foster homes where they were abused or neglected, or were wanted by a biological parent who was not given appropriate training on caring for them. In a few of the cases, children were left in foster care limbo without a permanency plan, appropriate monitoring, or with ongoing legal ties to biological parents deemed incapable of rehabilitating. The stories of the plaintiffs were both horrific and heartbreaking. The stories ranged from that of a five-year-old girl whose drug-addicted mother physically and sexually abused her, forced her to live in a closet, and "deprived her of sustenance resulting in her eating her own feces and plastic garbage bags to survive," to a teen who had spent most of his fifteen years in various foster care placements until he was placed with a minister who took him out of state and sexually abused him until he ran away to live on the streets.[103]

In *Marisol A. v. Giuliani*, the court ruled that children had a broad right to protection by the state.[104] In the *Marisol* case, the federal court ruled that "individuals in state custody do have a constitutional right to conditions of confinement which bear a reasonable relationship to the purpose of their custody" and that the state is responsible for harm that befalls children in its care. Citing a 1987 decision, the court asserted, "the goal of the child welfare system is to 'further the best interest of the children by helping to create nurturing family environments without infringing on parental rights.'" As a result, the state must provide "custodial children with adequate food, shelter, clothing, medical care, and reasonable safety."[105] *Marisol* identified a government responsibility for safe foster care, appropriate placements, and reasonable treatment for children in state custody. It also drew national attention to the failures of the child welfare system, with accompanying calls to action.

On December 14, 1996, six months after the *Marisol* decision, President Clinton instructed DHHS, under Donna Shalala's leadership, to work toward doubling the number of children adopted or placed in permanent homes from foster care by the year 2002. On February 14, 1997, Secretary Shalala issued "Adoption 2002: Safe and Permanent Homes for all Children," a statement of goals for the child welfare system. Announcing this new program, President Clinton declared,

> With this effort we're saying no child should be trapped in the limbo of foster care, no child should be uncertain about what the word 'family' or 'parents' or 'home' mean, particularly when there are open arms to welcome these children into safe and strong households where they can build good, caring lives.[106]

Adoption 2002 built on other Clinton administration efforts to promote adoption. These included a 1996 tax credit for adoptive parents, allowing up to $5000 in a nonrefundable tax credit for adoption expenses, up to $6000 in tax deductions for "special needs children," who are usually harder to place, and some tax deductions for employer-sponsored adoption assistance programs.[107] Accompanying these newly created financial incentives was a larger reconstitution of child welfare law.

Adoption Reform

Adoption 2002 established a federal goal, but not the policies to accomplish it. In 1997 the federal government passed the Adoption and Safe Families Act (ASFA). This law, declaring that "the child's health and safety shall be of paramount concern," presented the first major revision to the 1980 AACWA.[108] Returning to the heart of the 1980 legislation, this act goes to great lengths to clarify "reasonable efforts." Both the 1980 and 1997 laws require efforts to "prevent or eliminate the need for removing the child" prior to placement of the child in foster care and to "make it possible for a child to safely return home." However, ASFA clarifies that reasonable efforts "shall not be required" in certain situations. States are not required to attempt reasonable efforts at reunification if a court has determined that the parent has subjected the child to "aggravated circumstances," which may include, but is not limited to, abandonment, torture, chronic abuse, and sexual abuse. If a parent has committed murder or voluntary manslaughter of another child of the parent or if the parent has "aided or abetted, attempted, conspired, or solicited to commit such murder or such a voluntary manslaughter," reunification services are not required. If a parent has committed a felony assault that results in serious bodily injury to the child or another child of the parent, that parent is not entitled to reunification services. Finally, if a parent's legal parental rights to a sibling have been terminated involuntarily, the parent is not entitled to services for any other child.[109]

While it seems reasonable to eliminate reunification possibilities for parents who severely injure their children, torture them over time, or who have murdered a child's sibling, the above language also excludes parents who have failed to reunify with children in the past, regardless of the cause. If a parent falls into one of the aforementioned situations, a judge may order reunification services if he or she believes it is in the best interests of the child to do so. Otherwise ASFA requires that the state begin the process of terminating parental rights immediately, and in doing so, expedite eligibility for adoption.

In addition to excluding some parents from reunification, ASFA created new barriers to reunification for parents who are eligible for services. Responding to allegations that children's cases are slow to move toward a permanent plan and that states attempt reunification long after it is clear it will not succeed, ASFA also significantly tightens the timeline in which reunification must occur. According to this legislation, a child enters foster care at "the first judicial finding that a child has been subjected to abuse or neglect" or sixty days after the child has been removed from the home. From this point, parents are legally entitled to six months to reunify with a child less than four years of age and twelve months for a child who is older. The law explains that if a child has been "in foster care under the responsibility of the state for fifteen of the most recent twenty-two months, or if a court…has determined a child to be an abandoned infant," states shall begin the process to terminate parental rights. This last section clearly departs from the AACWA and the Abandoned Infant Act of 1988, which focused more explicitly on prevention, treatment, and reunification. In contrast, this law focuses most heavily on children exiting out-of-home care via reunification, adoption, or guardianship as soon as possible.[110] Once reunification efforts are under way, the county is required to place a child "in accordance with the permanency plan," a long-term plan that exists in case a parent fails to reunify with the child within the time provided. The ASFA states that "reasonable efforts to place a child for adoption or with a legal guardian may be made concurrently with reasonable efforts" to reunify. This latter provision, known as concurrent planning, requires states to not only provide reunification services, but also "concurrently identify, recruit, process, and approve a qualified person for an adoption." Although concurrent planning is not required in all cases, particularly those of older children, it is designed to streamline the adoption process.

A final significant policy change of late-1990s adoption reform was the creation of financial incentives to encourage states to increase their rates of adoption out of foster care. In addition to the tax incentives offered to adopting families and their employers, states received financial rewards as well. Bonuses of $4000 for each adopted child and $6000 for each child with special needs are awarded to states that increase their adoption rates over the prior year. In 2001, forty-two states, the District of Columbia, and Puerto Rico received bonuses. California, which increased its adoption rates by 31 percent, received the lion's share of the reward, getting $4,030,572, compared with the second place awardee—Missouri—receiving $665,819 for their 47 percent growth. California was also awarded the DHHS's Administration for Children and Families' "Adoption Excellence Award" for adoption increases.[111] By most accounts, adoption reforms have resulted in more children being adopted. In 1996 there were 27,761 adoptions of children who had involvement with a public child welfare agency nationwide. By 1999 that number soared to 46,072, making great strides toward Clinton's announced goal of 54,000 by 2002.[112]

The reforms of the 1990s must be viewed in the larger context of welfare reform. As Clinton set out to "end welfare as we know it," he created welfare policy that mandated paid employment for parents and removed parents from their children. Through strict work requirements, the state communicated a great deal about the perceived value of poor children's relationships with their parents, as on average poor children spend more than forty hours a week in child care.[113] This is a notable change from the Progressive Era policies that created welfare out of an appreciation for mothering. As social historian Theda Skocpol wrote of the present moment in American history,

> It is not possible...to deploy a political rhetoric of honoring motherhood. Around the turn of the twentieth century, perhaps, such a rhetoric could unproblematically connect many elite, professional, middle-class, and poor American women... But in the United States today, no such unproblematic connections of womanhood and motherhood, or of public and private mothering, are remotely possible.[114]

Such welfare changes, combined with child welfare changes, suggest that motherhood is increasingly perceived as fungible.[115]

UNDERSTANDING THE CHILD WELFARE PENDULUM

Prior to the creation of the Mother's Pension in the early twentieth century, belief in the benefits of placing children out was clear. ADC and AFDC returned to a belief in the importance of children receiving care from their natal families. Battered child syndrome and the federal response to child maltreatment in the 1960s shaped a view of families as dangerous places for children. With the 1970's social movements and the 1980 AACWA, state policy was to provide reasonable efforts to reunify parents and children. The crack epidemic and accompanying war on drugs racialized and urbanized perceptions of child maltreatment and again constructed parents as predators—this time with mothers harming children even before their births. Throughout the 1990s, nostalgia for a fictional era of efficient child protection came to the forefront. Charles Brace's work and the work of volunteer childsavers became romanticized. The large number of children in foster care in middle-class white homes who were from poor, urban, black communities can be imagined as synonymous with Brace's desire to transform European Catholic immigrant children into Midwestern Christian farmers. Similarly, the vision of reestablishing institutional foster care, promoted by former Speaker of the House Newt Gingrich in 1993, and many of the tenets of the legislation passed between 1994 and 1997, reflected nostalgia for placing children out. However, the dream of reinstitutionalizing children reaches beyond Brace, who despite his xenophobia or other ulterior motives, believed in the value of home life.

The intrinsic limitation of the pendulum metaphor is that it invokes a vision of policy preferences that swing laterally between two poles. In the case of child welfare, policy swings sometimes move back and forth, and often in dizzying circles. These shifts are not just changes in policy, but in ideology. With each change in public sentiment and policy, the value of biology, community, natal families, and permanent homes, as well as the appropriate role of the state in determining familial outcome is articulated. Child welfare policy attempts in different historical periods to grapple with morality, poverty, race and ethnicity, and even the very meaning of childhood. With each shift, thousands of lives are altered. There is little doubt that at the end of the twentieth and beginning of the twenty-first century, sentiment has swung away from reunification. With race-blind politics that also sometimes overlook the significance of family history, the child welfare system is attempting to move more children into new homes faster than ever before. It is in this context that I conducted my research.

3

THE HATED DO-GOODERS: SOCIAL WORK IN CONTEXT

Thao Vue and I have just walked into the front office of Thurgood Marshall Elementary School; Thao is at this urban public elementary school because he received a report from the school nurse alleging the medical neglect of a seven-year-old boy and must now investigate. The nurse called Child Protective Services (CPS) after she couldn't reach the parents of a boy who was crying in class because of an inflamed jaw, presumably caused by an abscess from neglected dental care. He was also reported to have a bilateral ear infection and pink eye. We were at his school to take him for medical treatment.

Thao is a Hmong man in his early thirties who immigrated to the United States when he was nine years old. The youngest in his family, he was the only one of his seven siblings to get a college education and as a result he subsidizes members of his family on his meager salary as a county social worker. He has a slight build and a look of chronic exhaustion from working irregular hours with late night and weekend calls, seldom working less than six days a week. Thao has worked for CPS as an investigator for about two years, making him the second most senior worker in his unit. His job requires him to investigate allegations of child abuse and neglect, evaluate whether families need services, assess the risk children are facing, and choose whether children should be left with their parents or removed from their homes to enter the overburdened foster care system.

The nurse who had called was not there and we were asked to wait for her to return. As we waited in yellow plastic chairs opposite the reception counter, I became aware that my Hmong companion and I were the only non-African Americans I had seen and that we stood out as outsiders. Opposite from us, a woman wearing crisp white pants, an immaculate white blouse with black dots, and shabby, fraying pink bathroom slippers stands at the counter completing paperwork to withdraw her daughter from school. Her eight-year-old daughter, clean and well dressed, is spinning in circles and dancing by the counter next to her mother. The mother looks over at us between pages, confirming my suspicion that Thao (and I by association) are recognizable as social workers. In an effort to escape her accusing glare, I lower my eyes from hers and instead study her fraying slippers, now directly in my line of vision. I shift uncomfortably in my plastic chair, feeling as out of place in the lobby as the pink slippers appear with the woman's otherwise pristine outfit.

Turning my attention away from the woman and her slippers, I ask Thao, sitting next to me, how he feels about working with abused children. He explains that in his two years with the agency, he has seen few cases of severe physical abuse. He recalls a boy who was unable to sit down at school after his mother's boyfriend spanked him a hundred times, causing his backside to turn blue, and a girl with crisscross scars on her buttocks and backside from being hit with a belt or hanger. Otherwise, he explains, cases are rarely so clear cut. If they were, the job of CPS would be easier.

A heavy-set middle-aged woman, phone in hand, leans over the counter and informs us that the maternal grandmother has already picked up the child and his two siblings from school. The school nurse, who is out doing home visits, is on the phone and wants to speak with Thao. Thao walks to the counter where the office person hands him the receiver. The nurse tells Thao that her visits are taking longer than she had anticipated and asks if we could meet her at a house down the street. Frustrated with this waste of time, Thao declines and we leave.

As we walk out, the woman with the slippers and her daughter walk out beside us. We walk in parallel through the parking lot to our respective cars. Gesturing to Thao and me, the mother asks the girl, "Do you recognize either of those faces?"

The little girl shrugs and says, "No."

The mother replies, "Good. Do you know who they are?"

The girl casually shakes her head no.

The mother sneers, "They're the ones who took (a name I couldn't make out) away. They're the bad guys."

Thao ignores her, but I am shocked and ask, "Oh, *we're* the bad guys?"

The woman answers, "You're not taking my baby away."

I respond that her daughter looks well taken care of and that I wouldn't worry about it if I were her. The mother turns to the daughter and says, "They're the ones who put you in the car." The girl looks over at us, horrified. She might as well have told her that we ate children. The mother taunts, "They're gonna take you away." She then laughs, "They're gonna take you away...over my dead body."

Thao remains silent until we are back inside the county-issued lavender Ford sedan. He turns to me, hesitates, and speaks for the first time since we left the office. "I've been to her house."

* * *

When controversies about CPS arise in public, when news reports are published, congressional hearings held, or lawsuits filed, they are frequently about what the CPS investigators did wrong: they left a child in a dangerous home or they removed a child from a loving home without a valid reason. CPS workers have the unenviable job of almost always being perceived as doing the wrong thing and they work in fear of making the wrong decision. Child abuse investigator Keith N. Richards writes,

> I'm entrusted with one of the most important responsibilities society can confer; as a result, I am continually called upon to defend my actions, not only in the homes of my clients but in the office of superiors, as well as in courts of law...Wherever I go I am feared and resented, because of who I work for and because of what I do. I'm the Simon Legree of social work, the Bogeyman with a clipboard. I'm a child abuse investigator, and people always think I'm going to take their kids away. In dire circumstances, I can.[1]

Child Protective Services investigators, known as emergency response workers, are the frontline of the system. Workers in the emergency response unit are charged with investigating allegations of abuse and neglect, assessing the relative danger a child is facing, and deciding whether or not that child should be left with a parent or removed. They are sent into the field to investigate legal violations: some criminal, others violations of the state Welfare and Institutions Code, a civil legal code that dictates most of the policies affecting families. CPS workers are the long arm of the state. As public agents, they cross the boundaries into private families and decide those families' fates. However, CPS workers are not police officers. They do not have the power to arrest individuals, do not carry weapons, and cannot conduct searches or seizures in the same way police officers can. Armed with forms and business cards, they police with the threat of removing someone's child.

As agents of the state with immense power—albeit deployed bureaucratically—investigating social workers walk the line between public and private, between protecting children and the autonomy of family. Reflecting on this, Thao, an emergency response worker, explained, "We do good but we do harm to a family." This chapter examines the context of investigative CPS work. Specifically, I describe the content and culture of CPS investigative work, exploring the perception of the work as dangerous, the public criticism workers face that makes the work thankless, and the professional challenges that result from the stressful nature of the work. This chapter sets the stage for the next chapter, in which I explore investigator expectations of parents and identify the role of deference and subordination in parent–social worker interactions.

SOCIAL WORK AS THANKLESS

The government's interest in the welfare of children embraces not only protecting children from physical abuse, but also protecting children's interest in the privacy and dignity of their homes and in the lawfully exercised authority of their parents.

—9th Circuit Court of Appeals in Calabretta v. Floyd *(1999)*

Social workers often choose social work as a profession because they want to help people, and tend to prioritize job satisfaction above advancement, pay, or professional status.[2] However, social workers' power to scrutinize families and remove children undermines their ability to be perceived primarily as a resource to families. As in the Progressive Era, CPS workers are often perceived "more as law enforcement agents than social service providers."[3] Social workers are perceived as being representatives of a power structure that can threaten families. One case involving Julie Lawrence, a white emergency response worker in her early thirties, illustrates this point. Julie went to investigate the well-being of a thirteen-year-old girl who was pregnant for the second time and whose mother was threatening to force her daughter out of their home. When Julie arrived to investigate the teen's safety and to possibly enroll the family in counseling services, the mother on several occasions turned to her daughter and yelled, "See. You brought the white man to our doorstep!" When Julie asked her what that meant, the mother explained that "its all of them—welfare, CPS," illustrating how Julie's presence was perceived as representing the white power structure of the patriarchal state rather than as the mediating influence Julie aspired to be.

Parents are not the only critics of social workers. Policy makers frequently ask CPS to account for its behavior as an agency. Demonstrating this, the "Hot Issues" section of the federal Children's Bureau website offered an article promising that new regulations, announced in January 2000, "will hold states accountable for services to at-risk children with a new, results-oriented approach in Federal monitoring of state child welfare programs."[4] Promises of increased evaluation, improved auditing, and more accountability are common topics when CPS comes to the attention of policy makers; calls for reform most commonly follow scandals. This is evidenced in the declarations following the 2003 discovery in Newark, New Jersey of seven-year-old Faheem William's body in the basement of a relative's house near his two restrained brothers, who were severely malnourished and dehydrated. In the articles that followed, child welfare advocates—referring to Faheem and other unnamed prior tragedies—were quoted as saying, "We need immediate reform…we need public accountability for the deaths of these children," while the New Jersey Governor's office unveiled a plan to rename the agency, appoint a new director, and put "tools in the hands of Department of Youth Family Services (DYFS) (the New Jersey name for CPS) to allow caseworkers to make better decisions."[5]

Social workers are not only hampered by a lack of popularity. They now face the possibility of being individually sued by parents who are under investigation. Limiting their immunity from liability, the U.S. 9th Circuit Court of Appeals found in *Calabretta v. Floyd* (1999) that, absent an emergency situation, the same rules of privacy apply to social workers as other state agents. In that particular case, a social worker used a police officer to gain entrance into a home when the mother refused her access. This event occurred fourteen days after the initial report of child maltreatment was made, suggesting that the social worker did not reasonably believe that the children were in imminent danger. The court challenged the social worker's defense that her goal of child protection justified her coercion of a mother to let her in. The decision explains,

Appellants also argue that the coerced entry into the home was primarily to protect the children, not investigate crime…We held, years before the coerced entry into the Calabretta home, that even in the context of an administrative search, "[n]owhere is the protective force of the fourth amendment more powerful than it is when the sanctity of the home is involved"...Therefore, we have been adamant in our demand that absent exigent circumstances a warrant will be required before a person's home is invaded by the authorities.[6]

In light of the *Calabretta* decision, both the personal liability social workers may face and the perceived lack of judicial support for their difficult job create further professional challenges for social workers.

As an agency that protects children from maltreatment, one might imagine that CPS would receive positive press or be publicly described as a noble profession, as is medicine, for example. One survey of doctors found that those contacted by the media were "satisfied with the coverage of their work," with a majority feeling "that news coverage improves the image of the profession, informs the professional community and provides an avenue for greater public understanding."[7] In contrast to the experiences of doctors, the media almost exclusively report CPS's shortcomings, a pattern that has held true since social work's inception.[8]

CPS cases, because they involve minors, are confidential, and thus journalists have almost no ability to report on the actions of CPS social workers, nor on the broader juvenile court system. Lacking permission, reporters typically gain access to cases in two ways. First, cases become public upon the death of a child, scandal in foster care, or other investigation that removes jurisdiction from family court and places it in the realm of criminal proceedings. In these cases, something has almost always gone terribly wrong. Examples proliferate: The 2003 discovery of seven-year-old Faheem Williams's dead body in the basement of a New Jersey house; the 2002 case of Rilya Wilson, a foster child in Florida whose case was so badly managed—with social workers failing to monitor her and even falsifying visit reports—that she was missing from her foster care placement for several months before child welfare agencies noticed; or the media frenzy surrounding the video footage of Madelyne Toogood striking her four-year-old daughter in an Indiana parking lot.[9] (This week's newspaper likely offers a similar array of tragic examples.) The take-home message in each case is the same: social workers failed to adequately protect children. In the media coverage of these problem cases, social workers' names are commonly included, making professional mistakes—even those that may reflect institutional weakness—a personal nightmare.

Second, journalists gain access to information about CPS cases when a parent chooses to speak to the press. Although parents are also responsible for protecting the confidentiality of their children, no sanctions are applied to parents who violate their children's privacy. In these stories, parents or their representatives usually describe how they perceive the CPS system wronged them. A useful example can be seen in media coverage of the arrest of comedian Paula Poundstone, a formerly celebrated foster parent who, as one columnist described her, "adopted kids before Rosie O'Donnell or Calista Flockhart made them seem like a celebrity accessory and took hard-luck cases without martyring herself as a Westside Mother Theresa."[10] Poundstone was arrested in July 2001 for "lewd conduct" with her oldest daughter and child endangerment of her younger children, reluctantly transforming this celebrity into a prominent client of the CPS system. None of the many columns and newspaper or magazine articles about the case discussed who specifically had removed the children, nor represented their concerns. Instead, reports voiced skepticism of her guilt and implied that those responsible for the case made a mistake. As an example, *Los Angeles Times* columnist Patt Morrison wrote, "Things that happen between a child and an adult, from a hug to a diaper check, can be misinterpreted."[11] Social service agencies cannot legally respond to, nor challenge, these statements.

The negative portrayal of CPS in the media affects the public's understanding of the agency, which in many ways shapes parents' expectations of encounters when CPS enters their lives. For example, Mateo Estes, a Latino father in his early twenties whose children were placed in protective custody after a CPS investigation determined that he likely contributed to the spiral fracture of his stepdaughter's leg, said that he knows CPS frequently makes mistakes because he read about it in "newspapers and things, stuff like that, the library." He explained social workers' failures: "These people have left kids in homes when they should have taken them. They have put them in foster homes throughout the state where kids are being killed. Sometimes they have acted or not acted enough." Interestingly, Mateo, who contends he was wrongly accused of harming his stepdaughter, accepts the common critique of CPS as failing to remove children from dangerous homes. If a parent like Mateo, who is involved in the system, believes the media veraciously portray the agency, those without contact with the system likely accept existing coverage as accurate.

Although attorneys, public relations firms, relatives, and parents can promote their version of injustice, agencies are silenced. As an editorial in the *American Journalism Review* (*AJR*) notes, "state confidentiality laws make it difficult for reporters, and ultimately the public, to find out whether child protection systems are working well." As such, no one hears of the family who successfully reunifies; agents can't discuss case specifics and parents who want to move on with their lives are loath to publicly admit to their involvement with CPS. The consequence is that there is virtually no way that a CPS success can be reported, whereas horror stories are widely available. As the *AJR* explains, "Although fatal cases get the most press attention, they represent a small fraction of the much larger universe of neglect and abuse cases."[12] For social workers, the experience of being frequently represented negatively in the popular press is exhausting and demoralizing.

There is a third avenue for the media to gain access to case information: direct observation of the system, although it is the least utilized and most difficult to secure. One notable exception is John Hubner and Jill Wolfson's book *Somebody Else's Children*. To report on the CPS system, the authors obtained a court order to observe confidential proceedings. In granting these journalists permission to observe confidential juvenile court proceedings, provided they keep the identities of clients of the system confidential, the presiding judge stated, "Confidentiality does not mean secrecy. The public has a right to know the full story of what we do here."[13] Hubner and Wolfson acknowledge in their book that they are likely the first reporters to gain such access.[14]

It is also important to note that child protection social work as a profession has few allies. Feminist organizations, which have almost single-handedly shaped the public understanding of domestic violence, would seem a probable supporter for CPS workers. Although feminist organizations and advocacy groups have brought issues of domestic violence into public view and reformed the justice system to respond to family violence, they have often been silent on child abuse or have condemned the work of CPS. As Marie Ashe and Naomi Cahn argue, "It is our belief that most feminist writers who have attended to the reality of child abuse perpetrated by mothers have minimized the extent of such abuse, have ignored its pervasiveness, or have attempted to define it away."[15] Feminists have critiqued social workers as enforcers of state surveillance of the poor and implementers of paternalistic policies "through various forms of public relief that respect neither domestic privacy nor individual rights."[16] Whereas these critiques are essential on a macro level, feminists' abstract critique or relative unwillingness to engage in discussions of child abuse on a micro level ignores many of the realities of child maltreatment, including the sad truth that women sometimes contribute to and even perpetrate their children's abuse. It also ignores the reality that

CPS intervention often takes women and children out of dangerous homes, even if not together.

Conservative groups touting "family values" are also critical of CPS, since the agency's very nature challenges parental autonomy. For example, the Pacific Justice Institute (PJI), an organization that devotes large portions of its webpage to providing parents with advice when dealing with CPS, condemns CPS, explaining that "the juvenile court system's seemingly unbridled discretion creates a wall of intimidation, a wall preventing the kind of public accountability necessary to expose the need for judicial reform." Because parents' rights issues and CPS often intersect around corporal punishment that crosses the line into physical abuse, both PJI and the Focus on the Family, a policy group for the religious right, have released statements advising parents of their right to spank and physically discipline their children.[17]

In sum, public condemnation combined with a sustained public perception of CPS as "baby snatchers" and the risk of private violence from clients add to workers' feelings of despair. In addition, the dearth of allies and of publicly identifiable success stories makes CPS work thankless at best and unbearable at worst, illustrated by the high workforce turnover.

SOCIAL WORK AS DANGEROUS

Risk? Yes, there's risk. That's why we're here. This starship is all about risk.

—Capt. James T. Kirk, Starship Enterprise
Sign on the door of the ER unit director's office

Social workers understand their work to be dangerous. The National Association of Social Workers (NASW) expects that "at least a quarter of professional social workers will confront a violent situation on the job. Half of all human services professionals, which include lay-social workers such as family maintenance workers, will experience client violence at some point during their careers."[18] The NASW Committee for the Study and Prevention of Violence Against Social Workers states that "work-related violence against social workers is a fact of life. It is pervasive and must be addressed by every school of social work, agency and individual worker."[19] There is some evidence that incidents of threats, verbal abuse, and physical assaults of social workers by clients are on the rise.[20] Estimating the rates of victimization of social workers by clients has been difficult because of a lack of standardized measurement tools and the difficulty workers have remembering specific incidents. One study found that 88 percent of social workers reported being verbally harassed at least once in their career, sixty-four percent reported receiving threats of physical harm, and twenty-nine percent experienced noninjurious physical assault (only about eight percent reported being physically injured by a client). Another study found that 23 percent of social workers had been physically assaulted by a client during their careers.[21] The only study that specifically focuses on CPS workers found that in the preceding twelve months preceding the study, approximately 10 percent of social workers were pushed, shoved, or hit by one or more agency clients, 33 percent had been threatened "with words or in a manner that led them to conclude that the person making the threat was making a death threat," 27 percent concluded they were threatened with physical injury but not death, 9 percent received threats to harm a member of the worker's family, and 6 percent received threats to damage the worker's property. One-third of CPS workers reported feeling frightened on the job at least monthly.[22]

Anecdotal evidence of serious physical assault drives social workers' perceptions of their job as perilous. In the first year I served on a county oversight committee, there was growing concern about worker safety after a public health nurse who went on a home visit to see a baby was raped by the baby's father. This particularly chilling story reminded everyone that social work is differentially dangerous for women. The murders of social workers in Michigan and New Hampshire also prompted counties and states to evaluate worker safety and heightened social worker awareness of danger. Although these stories are unusual, the presence of a wanted poster in a CPS office hallway portraying a parent who has threatened to harm or kill a social worker is not.

The dangerous nature of CPS work, as perceived by the workers, shapes the profession and practice. One study of police officers found that the dangerous nature of police work shapes "out of the multitude of demands and expectations of their role, a working police personality."[23] Similarly perceptions of danger frame the social worker's personality. The perception that danger is omnipresent is reinforced through social worker encounters with parents who are accused of assaulting children or other adults. When emergency response workers arrive at a house to investigate an allegation of child maltreatment, they introduce themselves and explain as calmly as possible that they are there to make sure the children are safe or that they need to speak to the parents. This information is rarely welcomed. On one of the first cases I observed,

Thao knocked on an apartment door, then introduced himself to the woman who answered, the mother of the child in question who reportedly lacked eyeglasses for school. The mother sternly said, "No. If you are here to take my kid, we are gonna fight," and put up her fists. She then laughed and said, "Come on in."

Not all situations are so benign. Julie investigated a case where a mother refused her entrance and was so combative that Julie gave up and left, returning the following day with law enforcement. As she relayed the story to me, she commented that I, pregnant at the time, was lucky I was not there, explaining that the mother is "the kind who would have kicked you in the stomach."[24] The volatile and threatening behavior of the mother helped to shape Julie's understanding of the case as one where there were serious mental health issues. Julie returned the following day with law enforcement, predisposed to believe that she would likely have to take the children because their mother was seemingly unstable and prone to violence.

Parents are rarely happy to see CPS. Parents express their dislike of CPS in both overt acts, such as being threatening or combative, as well as covert ones, like avoiding an interaction. Emergency response social workers enter an investigation with full knowledge that parents dread their appearance. Although I was not a social worker, I perceived this animosity and noted it in my field notes during a ride-along with Thao. Thao was called out to investigate a child's lapse in immunizations after a mother verbally abused a receptionist and was banned from the pediatrician's office. In this low-priority case, Thao needed to verify that the mother had secured a new pediatrician and state-mandated immunizations for her child. As we sat outside the dilapidated house in a neighborhood I was becoming accustomed to visiting, I wrote in my field notes, "It's amazing how aware I am of being really hated. We knocked and saw fingers in the blinds and someone looking out. The air conditioner was running; no one answered." In that case, the mother's initial refusal to allow Thao to investigate left the powerful arm of the state temporarily impotent. However, in cases like this one, and Julie's above, social workers return with law enforcement officers for whom parents are willing to open the door, allowing social workers to complete their investigation. Technically parents can exercise their legal right to deny police and social workers entrance.[25] However, this form of resistance does not serve parents well; social workers are predisposed to believe that a case is worse than they might have believed had a seemingly cooperative parent let them in the home and pacified their concerns. This is especially true in Thao's case, where he was initially there just to check that a child's immunizations were current, but instead subjected the family and their house to a thorough inspection, which revealed doors off hinges, a lack of electricity, and rotting food in the cupboards.

In the county I studied, as in most counties nationwide, emergency response social workers go into the field alone. This is a point of dissatisfaction for the NASW, which suggests that workers would be safer in pairs.[26] If a social worker has reason to believe that a parent is particularly volatile or is likely to present a threat to the worker, he or she will call law enforcement for backup. In those instances, the worker will have to wait—sometimes for more than an hour—for two officers to arrive. Ironically, police practice dictates that armed uniformed police officers always answer domestic complaints in pairs because of the inherent danger domestic violence calls present. Once they arrive, the social worker will enter the house and conduct the investigation while the officers remain in the house, simply making their presence known.

Social workers rely on police presence to escort them into homes where parents have refused to allow them to enter and to inhibit parents who might otherwise threaten or assault the workers. The police officers understand their presence is necessary to allow the worker to investigate alleged abuse and to file the necessary reports should the parent also face criminal charges.[27] However, for the most part they do not perceive that they are there to protect the social workers. In one case I observed where children were placed in protective custody or "PC'd," the police officers left as soon as a family maintenance worker, a high school educated paraprofessional, picked up the children to take them to the county children's receiving home. This left the investigating social worker, who is required to stay after the children are gone to explain to the parent his or her legal rights, alone in the home of a drug-addicted mother whose children had just been removed. It is not difficult to imagine that a parent, perhaps believing he or she had little left to lose, might assault that worker.

County worker safety practices do not meet the safety standards recommended by professional social work organizations. Overall, workers are given the following advice at professional conferences:

- Don't be alone in the office when seeing clients or go on home visits alone.
- Initiate a phone code system whereby a colleague calls ten to fifteen minutes into a session to check in.
- Work out code words that indicate problems.
- Carry a cellular phone.
- Make clients and visitors ring a buzzer to get into the office.

- Work with the local police department to establish a code for emergencies.
- Vary your routes and times when conducting daily business.
- Trust your instincts.
- Take a self-defense class.[28]

Workers with overwhelming caseloads, who frequently work alone and at odd hours, are not able to do these things on a regular basis. In the county I studied, social workers began carrying county-issued cellular phones so they could call supervisors or the police when necessary. They rarely saw clients at their office, which was secured with a buzzer system and guard. Workers are supposed to check in with a supervisor before and after an investigation so their movements can be loosely traced. However, the social workers I observed were assigned to work alone in the field, had no organized or routine access to self-defense classes, and did not receive check-up calls ten to fifteen minutes into an investigation or client meeting.

Social workers try to avoid using their personal cars, which can be traced back to their personal identity or can lead to their being recognized when off duty. Occasionally social workers drop by clients' homes on their way to or from work or on weekends, when working parents are likely to be home. In such instances, they drive their own car. In theory, their license plate numbers are kept confidential by the state department of motor vehicles. However, some workers don't feel safe with parents even knowing what their personal car looks like. Whenever possible, workers drive county-issued vehicles, generic American-made sedans that one child, upon seeing an investigating social worker arrive, called "the FBI car." The social workers' union also owns a few cars that the social workers rotate using; the union cars are usually nicer and more reliable. The county owns the rest of the cars the workers drive, although there are not always enough cars for all the workers on any given day, which forces them to delay their home visits or take their own cars into the field.

Although the availability of cars or the increased use of cellular phones may seem trivial, these issues are central to how social workers understand the context of their work. The scarcity of resources adds to social worker job stress and perceptions of vulnerability. The lack of resources also symbolically communicates a devaluation of their work. In most cases, a parent will not harm the social worker; this fact is of limited relevance. Whether or not the danger is actual or perceived, it affects how workers understand their professional lives. This sense of vulnerability, combined with social workers' perceptions that their work is inherently dangerous, shapes the way in which investigative social work is practiced.

SOCIAL WORK AS STRESSFUL

The perception of their work as dangerous, the hostility they encounter from parents, and the lack of public support for their work make CPS work difficult and stressful. Social welfare scholar Lucy Rey suggests that "awareness and fear of violence may contribute to high stress and potential burnout," noting that 66 percent of social workers in her study had experienced at least one symptom of high work-related stress. However, the greatest challenge to workers is the expectations of the job itself. Most notably, child protection workers must resolve investigations within a narrowly determined time frame—between two hours and ten days—depending on the assessed level of risk.[29] Because children may be in danger, this is a logical requirement. However, the result is that social workers are expected to work far more than a forty-hour workweek to meet this mandate. The short time frames, high volume of cases, and fear of making a wrong decision in a case are significant sources of job-related stress. Illustrating the stressful nature of the work, one CPS office door displayed a cartoon showing a fish in a blender of still water with the text, "You think your life is stressful?" In addition to their ongoing cases, most workers rotate taking evening and weekend emergency calls where they may be summoned at any time of the day or night to investigate allegations of maltreatment that are urgent and can't wait until the next morning or the following Monday.

Despite social workers' desire to help people and protect children, few workers remain on the job for more than a few years because they do not find the work fulfilling. Describing the demoralization of social service providers more broadly, sociologist Michael Lipsky writes, "Large classes or huge caseloads and inadequate resources combine with the uncertainties of method and the unpredictability of clients to defeat their aspirations as service workers."[30] What results is worker burnout. Child abuse policy leaders, concerned with the problems worker burnout presents, advise that

> Burnout is a syndrome of emotional exhaustion, depersonalization, and reduced personal accomplishment. It is a response to the chronic emotional strain of dealing with others who are troubled. Burnout is considered a type of job stress. However, what is

unique about burnout is that the stress is caused by the social interaction between the helper and the client.[31]

The obvious outcome is a high turnover rate among workers. Worker turnover is so common that at the time of my observations, Thao was the second most senior worker in his unit, with just over two years of experience. The high turnover rate among these workers is both a reaction to and cause of the stress. The workers who remain on the job inherit existing cases from the workers who leave, adding to an already overwhelming caseload.

County officials struggle to address the burnout workers experience. The county I studied was unable to fill vacant social work positions, even though funding was authorized to hire more than fifty new full-time workers. Instead, the county discovered that it had exhausted its pool of qualified applicants. Traditionally, being a social worker required an applicant to hold a master's degree in social work (MSW). As counties exhaust their pool of MSW applicants, they are beginning to hire more bachelors-level social workers. The increasing number of workers with less education presents a new challenge in an old battle about the skills needed to be a professional social worker.

The degree to which social work is seen as a profession, with defined professional skills and knowledge base, has been a source of struggle in the field since the profession's inception. In 1915, Abraham Flexner, who most famously defined the boundaries of the elite medical profession in 1910, issued his report stating that social work was not a profession. In his evaluation, "the very variety of situations the social worker encounters compels him to be not a professional agent so much as the mediator invoking this or that professional agency."[32] In many ways, Flexner's findings reflect the early 20th century transition of social work from a male-dominated profession to one in which women assumed leadership positions and proceeded to craft the manner of professional practice. Social work became and remains a female-dominated profession whose central focus on women and children has cost it professional legitimacy, public respect, and adequate resources.[33] Yet efforts to define itself as a profession with specific skills, knowledge base, and research methods reflect a desire to be seen as more authoritative, and in gendered terms, more masculine.

Although social work was able to address Flexner's concerns and establish itself as a recognized profession, this claim has been fragile, and an ongoing source of struggle. Pointing to the importance of reifying its position as a profession, the NASW Code of Ethics identifies a social worker's ethical obligation to strengthen the profession:

Social workers should contribute time and professional expertise to activities that promote respect for the value, integrity, and competence of the social work profession. These activities may include teaching, research, consultation, service, legislative testimony, presentations in the community, and participation in their professional organizations.[34]

As the profession struggles for validation, budget cuts and political controversy over the nature of welfare services—most acute over the past two decades—have challenged the profession and suggested that perhaps workers do not need professional knowledge after all. Recognizing the shortage of workers, NASW has broadly defined social workers as "trained professionals who have bachelors, masters, or doctoral degrees in social work." This definition both accepts the use of bachelors- level workers and reiterates the disciplinary boundaries that require specific professional training and knowledge. Nonetheless, social workers are aware of the public scrutiny that promises "greater accountability." Nicholas Nguyen, an emergency response worker, noted this schism: "social work is a profession that requires a graduate degree but everyone wants to tell you how to do your job." The professional struggles serve as a backdrop to the daily struggles in which social workers engage.

The context of social work shapes how workers do their job and how they interact with those with whom they come into contact, particularly parents. Because social workers perceive their work as dangerous, demanding, and confrontational, they strive to establish their authority early in interactions with parents. By establishing their authority, they can feel more confident that they won't be assaulted, that the interaction will be forthright, and that a parent will work with them to resolve the problems that brought them into the agency's view. In many ways these issues are even more acute for female social workers who may more strongly fear assault or deception by clients and who experience higher rates of burnout. By presenting themselves in a manner that communicates their authority, social workers can feel as though they are being thorough and can confidently face their critics who allege that they are not doing enough. This may also be more relevant to female social workers, who often battle against perceptions of them as "Mary Poppins types" who idealistically offer help to those perceived to be unworthy of such help or to clients who may not take them seriously.

To address these issues, social workers require parents to defer to their authority. By performing deference, parents demonstrate their recognition of the social worker's authority and their desire to comply with the social worker's demands. As other researchers have found to be the case with police officers, social workers expect parents to demonstrate deference, which is perceived as a symbol of subordination. Police officers derive power from weapons, uniforms, and legal permission to physically detain suspects; social workers have none of these resources to perform their policing work, and instead rely on their authority to remove people's children. Workers enter an interaction hoping that parents will trust them and even appreciate their offers of assistance. In essence, social workers hope parents will defer to the worker's good intentions and accept their authority. It is these expectations of deference and subordination, developed in response to the professional challenges of the work, that shape CPS case outcomes. The following chapter describes CPS investigative work and shows how satisfactory demonstrations of deference and subordination determine whether or not children are removed from their homes.

4

EXPECTED PARENTAL BEHAVIOR: THEORIZING SUBORDINATION AND DEFERENCE IN THE INVESTIGATION

James Crockett sighs as he drives a county-issued Ford to the far side of town. Although he doesn't say it, it is clear he is dreading this visit. The report lying on my lap in the passenger seat explains that someone from an elementary school called to report suspected neglect. The children, ages ten, eight, seven, and five years come to school unbathed and in dirty clothes. Other children complain that they smell. The eight-year-old boy complains of a toothache and needs to go to the dentist. I flip to the next page: the report from the state welfare computer. According to the printout, the four school-age children have two younger siblings, ages three and two.

James is a thirty-three-year-old African American social worker who spends one weekend each month—and several weeks each summer—in the Army Reserve. Unlike the other workers I have followed who describe their desire to help children, James explains that he got his Master's degree in social work because becoming a physical therapist, his original goal, took too long and required harder coursework. Cases like this, where material poverty causes child neglect, tend to be the meat-and-potatoes of investigation work. Yet they are often the most frustrating and difficult to manage. Before even stepping foot in the

73

house, James knew that unless there was something glaring, something obviously very wrong, it was unlikely that he could do more than offer services to parents who are largely unable to change their lives.

We arrive on a quiet cul-de-sac where a series of faded yellow apartment buildings stand. It is a hot summer day and the children are playing outside, spraying each other with a hose. A dark-skinned man in white shorts and sandals sits on a low wall and watches them play. As we walk toward him, he stands and takes a few tentative steps toward us. James introduces himself and hands the man his business card. The man seems uninterested in who I am, and with the card in his hand, invites us into his apartment. As we enter, he yells toward the stairs. Lola Reynolds, a twenty-eight-year-old, tall, thin, African American woman, comes downstairs in a T-shirt and jeans with wet hair. She lives there with her six children and Burt Banton, the father of her three youngest. She seems annoyed that we are there, but not anxious; instead her demeanor communicates a familiarity with the process of a CPS investigation. In contrast to Lola's calm, Burt is noticeably nervous; his efforts to appear relaxed are belied by his continual fidgeting with James' card. We four adults, with children slowly gathering around, are all standing in the living room by the small circular kitchen table. Burt notices me looking at an eviction notice on the table. He picks it up, fumbles with it, and then places it on the counter behind him. Later he would tell us that they were being evicted because he broke the mirror off the building owner's truck. The kids remain close. I can't tell if they are nervous by the presence of strangers in their house or if they want our attention. The five-year-old asks his mother if he can give me a paper flower he made at school.

After James works through his standard questions about the children's household routines, Burt announces with some bravado that he has to leave to go fight the eviction. He then systematically kisses each family member one by one; their discomfort communicates that this is more performance than standard practice. James smiles and watches him leave. The papers on James's clipboard tell him that Burt has a lengthy history with CPS for allegations of child endangerment, domestic violence, and drug possession.

Lola and James talk briefly about the things in Lola's life that aren't working. He tells her she needs to take her son to the dentist and she insists she has made an appointment. They exchange a few more words. Then James tells her that he wants to open a case and provide her with in-home family maintenance services. She agrees and James begins the lengthy paperwork. James completes the paperwork, half-listening to Lola, and then after explaining the meaning and expectations of the contract, asks her to sign, which she does. As he completes the form, Lola volunteers that in all likelihood she will eventually leave Burt. She can't yet though because if she does, he'll take the three youngest children "because they have his last name." James gives her a copy of the contract and his business card. He pauses and tells her that "no one can take your kids for no reason." As we get in the car to head to the next investigation, I ask James if perhaps CPS is not the exception.

* * *

The last chapter explored the context in which social workers conduct their work and the content of investigations. As discussed, social workers experience their profession as one that is largely thankless, stressful, and dangerous. As a result, social workers fear making a mistake during an investigation, while less obviously fearing for their own well-being. Sometimes investigations go smoothly, as the one with Lola did. There, she acknowledged James's authority and enrolled in services with a stated desire to change her living situation. At other times, social work investigations are difficult, particularly when children don't cooperate or when parents show signs of aggression.

In this chapter, I have two goals. First, I provide detailed information of how allegations of abuse and neglect come to the attention of CPS and how workers conduct investigations. In doing so, I provide a foundation for looking at how parents and social workers negotiate power in investigations. Social workers, bound by the constraints of their work, must evaluate reports of child maltreatment and decide relatively quickly whether the allegations are credible. In doing so, workers consider statements made by the children themselves, the presence of drugs or, to a lesser extent, alcohol, the condition of the home, and the parents' demeanor. In fact, parental behavior toward the social worker is one of the most important—and least discussed—predictors of whether or not a child is left in the home or removed.

My second goal in this chapter is to show how social workers make decisions in their investigations and how those decisions rely heavily on perceptions of whether parents present themselves as deferential to the social worker during the investigation. To delve into this latter point, I use specific cases, chosen because of their notable similarities as well as differences, to tease out the role of deference in these interactions. In my efforts to cover much ground here, the tone in the chapter noticeably shifts. Nonetheless, I believe that only by understanding the material circumstances and stated goals of the investigation can we understand the more subtle, yet tangible aspects of state efforts to assess potential risk to children.

REPORTERS OF SUSPECTED ABUSE AND NEGLECT

A CPS case begins with a report of abuse or neglect. In California, concerned individuals and/or legally mandated reporters—that is, professionals like social service workers, educators, healthcare workers, child care providers, therapists, or law enforcement officers who work with children and are legally mandated to report suspected child maltreatment to the appropriate agency—call a CPS hotline to report suspected (not certain) child abuse or neglect.[1] There, an intake worker screens the report and assigns it a priority level. Based on the priority level assigned, a case must be investigated within two hours in the most serious instances or within ten days for reports that suggest that children are not in imminent danger; the latter is the more common classification and is the one commonly assigned in neglect cases.[2] An intake worker can also classify a report as unfounded and not refer it for any further investigation,[3] as is the case in 33 to 38 percent of reports nationwide.[4]

About 66 percent of the more than 2.5 million reports filed nationally in 2001 were referred for investigation; the majority relate to neglect.[5] However, many of the cases deemed worthy of investigation are subsequently found to be unsubstantiated and the cases are closed. It is worth noting that even when an allegation is found to be unsubstantiated (sometimes referred to as "unfounded"), the history of the report remains in the social work computer system and can be accessed if future reports are made. Should a future allegation result in children being removed and a case ensuing in the dependency court, the history of reports, even those that were unsubstantiated, will be used to support the current allegation. As an example, I observed a case where there was a history of several past unsubstantiated allegations. During the hearing, the attorney representing the county agency argued that "unsubstantiated doesn't mean it didn't happen."

More than half (56.5 percent) of all referrals made nationally come from professionals who are, with few exceptions, mandated reporters; the remaining 43.5 percent are reported by nonprofessionals, including community and family members.[6] Parents clearly understand the power to report and be reported by others. During investigations, parents often tried to guess who had reported them to CPS and would even call to confront the neighbors, family members, or friends they suspected had reported them, even while the social worker was present. The belief that someone known to the parent had called was so common in low-income areas that when Thao Vue, an investigating social worker, asked one eleven-year-old African American girl if she knew what CPS was, she nodded and explained that it was "when your neighbor calls and says something and then they come and take kids away from their mom."

I suggested in the last chapter that the power to remove a person's children is a source of authority for the social worker. A by-product of this is the less examined perception that because CPS can remove someone's children, the agency can be mobilized by an individual against another individual. Alluding to this dynamic, legal scholar Dorothy Roberts argues that the power CPS wields shapes local perceptions of the agency: "child welfare has a powerful, menacing presence in [poor minority] communities…[and] people sometimes use local child welfare agencies as a way of settling disputes."[7] In my interviews with parents, I frequently heard allusions to this dynamic, which suggested that in communities where resources are limited, CPS can be a powerful weapon. Richie Lyons, a fifty-year-old African American apartment building manager and father involved with CPS, described his power to report others, should he choose to do so:

> I can sit here and say, the girl over in number 22 is mistreating her kids and I can pick up the phone and call CPS and they'll come out here. See what I'm saying? And if they see something that they don't like, they'll take the kids. Regardless if it's something that can be corrected easily or anything. They're just going to take them because they think they can.

Richie's description of this dynamic suggests a local understanding of CPS intervention as a powerful punitive tool in personal relationships. Similarly, Chris Vaughn, a white father who was attempting to gain custody of his daughter, described his participation in making reports against others. He explained,

> I lived in this triangle for a while and it was a CPS triangle. Once one person gets mad at another; like if I was pissed off at you and we were best friends and I had a daughter and you had a daughter, guess what I would do? I'd march home and get on the phone.

Both men's descriptions underscore the recognition that the ability to mobilize CPS against another person is a source of power. Sometimes reports are filed maliciously, as a form of retribution or manipulation, or for personal gain. This important insight came to me when I accompanied Thao to check on a mother and her two young children who were living in a motel. The maternal grandmother reported that her daughter was not adequately caring for the children, that they were frequently left unattended, and that they were not regularly fed. The mother was not at the motel when we went by, but Thao spoke to the motel manager who described the children as appearing well and the mother as seeming appropriate with them. As we left, Thao explained to me that he would check back later, but would most likely close the case. Having spoken to the grandmother who had custody of her daughter's two older children, Thao came to believe that the grandmother wanted custody of the younger two as well and was trying to use CPS to get it.

Nonmandated reporters who make allegations against people whom they know are not the only ones to recognize the potential to utilize CPS power. I followed several CPS workers who were investigating reports of medical neglect made by school nurses; two of the cases involved children who did not have glasses. The nurses, frustrated that the parents were not more responsive to their requests, attempted to force parental compliance by reporting them to CPS. In both instances, the social workers talked to the child and the parent, verified that the child owned glasses or had an appointment to get glasses, and closed the case. Thao, the worker on one of the cases, explained that he would close the case after he verified the appointment with the doctor's office, noting that "this is not a high-risk case. It's not going to put the daughter in a dangerous situation." He explained that "the nurse is using us …which isn't right" and later commented, "people use CPS to enforce what they want. I don't think we should be used that way." The stories at the beginning of this and the preceding chapter each demonstrate the use, and even misuse, of CPS time by school personnel who, lacking other recourse to make parents comply with their recommendations, call CPS to exercise power over parents rather than as an expression of concern that children may face imminent danger. Although lacking glasses, having neglected dental work, or experiencing illness inarguably interferes with children's ability to succeed in school, it does not rise to the level of imminent danger that warrants CPS intervention. For CPS workers who have to ferret out real danger from retribution or other agendas, correctly assessing the dynamics surrounding the origination of reports presents an additional challenge to their already complicated work.

TALKING (WITH) CHILDREN

The entire "child abuse industry," as one county attorney describes it, is based on a desire to protect children from maltreatment. Children as innocent victims provide a rhetorically powerful image in public policy discussions. Sociologist Joel Best notes that "child-victims are not held responsible for their plight. Reformers seek to protect child-victims, both by helping children protect themselves and by cracking down on those who would harm them."[8] Performing a thorough investigation and gathering compelling evidence of maltreatment is necessary for a CPS worker to adequately assess the danger a child is facing. To do this, a social worker charged with investigating abuse must see and talk to the child in question. For an allegation of abuse to be sustained, a child who is old enough to communicate must provide a statement that corroborates the reported abuse, except when nonaccidental injury is so clearly evident that no statement is needed.

Schools are important institutions for CPS work for two reasons. First, teachers and school personnel who are in regular contact with children and more likely to notice signs of maltreatment often call CPS to report suspected neglect or abuse. Second, state law has decreed that CPS workers can gain access to children at school without parental permission,[9] an important advantage since interviewing children away from their homes and parents can lead to more honest accounts of events without the threat of retaliation that parental presence may signal. Despite the advantages that interviewing in the school setting provides, there is no guarantee that a child will disclose abuse to the worker. Traditionally a child's denial of abuse has been envisioned as the by-product of misplaced loyalty or as a sign of fear of his or her parents. What is often overlooked is how children are actors who possess their own understandings of CPS. In many cases, children understand that participating in a CPS investigation will result in removal from their family home, the loss of their possessions, or punishment of their parents. Children who live in communities where CPS's presence is observable understand CPS and its social workers to be their enemy.[10] The following story provides an example of a child who would not assist in her own protection and demonstrates how she, like the eleven-year-old discussed earlier who understood the agency to be the people who "come and take kids away from their mom," had her own perceptions of the agency.

Thao and I met with Haley Smith, an eight-year-old white girl in the second grade, at her school. A teacher reported that her father had come to school the prior week and had been irate; he yelled and threw a bicycle chain at her, but did not hit her. Scared, Haley rode her bike to her grandmother's home where she spent the night. The following day she told teachers, when asked, that she had gotten into trouble. In an attempt to protect her from her father's wrath, teachers began letting Haley out of class ten minutes early each day. They also called CPS.

Thao sat down to interview Haley in the elementary school nurse's office during the school day. This windowless room with a door that closed presented the promise of confidentiality. Rather than addressing the events described by the teachers in the report, Thao attempted to discover how discipline was handled in her home more generally. He asked her what happens when her parents are upset with her. Haley explained that she has to go to her room for ten minutes. Before he could ask his next question, the nurse came in to get something from her desk, apologized, and then left. As the door closed, Thao repeated his last question and Haley explained that she had "to go to her room for five minutes." Then, as though she remembered the inconsistency, she added, "If its really bad, then ten." When asked about the prior week's incident, she denied anything had happened and explained that she had walked home and played video games. When Thao asked whether she had ridden her bike and had gone to her grandmother's house instead of her own, she paused, smirked, and asked, "How do you know that?" Haley's answers alternated between no and maybe. She may have ridden her bike, maybe went home, but maybe she went to her grandmother's. She would answer "no" before Thao was finished asking his questions. She also answered a different partial question by spelling out "no" emphatically, "N-O, N-O, N-O, thirteen times." When I asked how she knew what the question was before he asked it, she said that she knew because she'd been asked before.

Realizing she was not going to cooperate, Thao sent her back to class. He spoke with a couple of teachers about the incident and verified details from the report, but none reported seeing actual physical harm done to her. They recounted the story with the bike chain, explaining that even the teenage aides hid in the office because "the father seemed crazed." They said Haley would change her answers when asked about the bruises on her arm or the situation with her father. When we left, I asked Thao what he would do next. He explained that without a statement from the child, there was little he could do. He also explained that we wouldn't go talk to her parents because doing so could put her at greater risk, and would not likely yield any more information.

Social workers usually strategize their contacts with parents, who are sometimes hostile, in one of two ways. Workers try to see the parent and child on the same day to avoid the child being placed in (further) jeopardy by being the one to tell a parent of the investigation. Alternatively, a worker may elect not to make contact with the parent when the case is going to be closed as unsubstantiated. In Haley's case, there was little doubt that the child had been physically abused. The concern of her teachers and the aides' fear of the father's temper suggested that they had witnessed enough to believe that she was in danger. The girl's experience with social worker interviews suggested that she had been previously referred to CPS. Yet there was not enough evidence available for Thao to believe he could substantiate the allegation and place her in protective custody.

On one hand, it seems illogical that so many adults could believe a child was being physically harmed and yet not intervene. On the other, lacking a child's corroboration, a worse scenario could ensue in which a zealous social worker goes forward with an unverifiable allegation against the child's insistence that the parent did not abuse him or her. These two poles circumscribe the difficulties inherent in CPS investigative work.

As unsatisfying as school-based interviews may be, the situation is worse when school is not in session. Without the anonymity school provides, the workers must go to the house, ask permission (or demand) to speak alone with the child, and absorb the risks to worker and child that a volatile home situation can present. According to social workers, teachers often put off reporting suspected abuse or neglect of their students until the end of the school year. Perhaps in part because they will have reduced contact with the parents and in part because they don't want children to advance to the next grade without having their concerns addressed, the deluge of end-of-the-year reports made by teachers and school personnel makes spring the busiest time for CPS workers.[11]

ASSESSING RISK THROUGH ZERO TOLERANCE FOR DRUGS

A CPS investigative worker's job is to assess the level of risk that children face in their home, with or without obtaining statements from them. Ideally, risk could be assessed before actual abuse occurs, using objective criteria that would be free from worker bias. To this end, counties across the country have begun using risk assessment tools to identify factors that tend to exist in homes deemed unsafe for children. When using these tools, social workers rate or score household characteristics and then total the assigned points, with high scores suggesting an elevated likelihood of child maltreatment. Over the last two decades, risk assessment models have been widely adopted and are used in at least 42 states.[12] There is broad and detailed literature on risk assessment tools, pointing out the strengths and weaknesses of them, which is beyond the scope of the discussion here.[13] In short, risk assessment tools have been developed in response to the broad criticism that CPS becomes involved in maltreatment cases only after abuse or neglect has harmed children—sometimes irreparably. By using these tools, social workers would ideally be able to identify homes where abuse or neglect is likely to take place and thus intervene appropriately. Risk assessment also theoretically provides some level of consistency between social workers. In many ways, the development of uniform measurement tools to assess risk is reminiscent of the goals of the nineteenth century "scientific charity" movement, a professional movement that argued that "charity work…needed to be organized along scientific lines—made more rational and efficient."[14]

At the time I was conducting my fieldwork, the county was attempting to implement some model for assessing risk. In the county I studied, a seventy-four-page report describing risk assessment research and presenting a model was distilled down to six characteristics identified as the most important to consider in investigation. These six signs of risk, widely promoted and posted in most offices in the emergency response unit, are as follows:

- Methamphetamine use in the home
- Child under age five
- Presence of a convicted felon in the home
- Prior CPS history
- Domestic violence
- Failure to comply with a previous case plan

These six factors were adopted as county policy and informed investigative work. Even with the strong emphasis on using risk assessment tools, I never saw a formal instrument scored in the field. Rather, these factors became part of an informal checklist that caseworkers used when evaluating a family. I mention risk assessment here for two reasons. First, the adoption of risk assessment models denotes an expectation that social workers should make every effort to identify potential maltreatment before it occurs. Second, these models created a policy of zero tolerance for parents who use or possess illegal drugs, most particularly methamphetamine. Although drug use is listed as one aspect of risk assessment, it is indisputably the greatest factor in considering parental ability. Any discussion of child protection must include broad consideration of the role of illegal drugs.

The county I studied adopted a zero tolerance policy for illegal drugs, making it one of the strictest counties in the state. Although the county hospital had been drug testing all newborns since the mid- to late 1980s, the zero tolerance policy for CPS investigation was not enacted until 1997, when the county revised its CPS practice, making it more restrictive and less likely to allow children to remain with their parents if questions of risk existed. County officials estimate that up to 80 percent of CPS cases are drug related. This estimate is underscored by the figure that about one-third of all adults who are referred for drug and alcohol treatment in the county are involved in some way with CPS. As such, the zero tolerance policy for drug use has led to a rapid increase in the county's caseload. Between 1996 and 2000, the number of cases in the CPS system doubled, causing this county to have one of the highest per capita rates of foster care placement in the state.

California requires all public hospitals to have a protocol for drug testing newborns.[15] The large county hospital, one of three hospitals in the area that provides labor and delivery services, has an unusual policy of universally screening all newborns for drugs. This is unlike most hospitals in the state that only test newborns in the presence of "suspicion," enforcement of which inevitably reflects race and class.[16] California state law explicitly states that a positive toxicology report in a newborn is on its own not reason to remove a child. However, with the county's zero tolerance policy for parental substance use and the proof of maternal substance use that such test results provide, any baby who tests positive for drugs at birth is almost always placed in protective custody by a designated "pos-tox" CPS worker. This specialized investigative social worker, whose office is physically in the hospital rather than in CPS headquarters, works full time placing pos-tox babies in state custody shortly after birth. Reflecting a belief that drug use alone makes someone incapable of parenting, once a pos-tox newborn is placed in protective custody (or PC'd), all other children in the family are almost always PC'd as well.

Outside of the newborn context, investigations of child neglect or abuse allegations that are not on their face drug related still include an investigation into substance use and criminal history. Usually a parent will deny drug use, even when signs of drug use—residue in ashtrays, the smell of marijuana in the walls and furniture, paraphernalia on the counter—are observable. For the most part, a social worker would have a difficult time substantiating a case based solely on drug use without physical evidence or parental confession. As a result, social workers often attempt to "work an admission" from parents. During the investigation, a worker will ask a parent about any prior arrests or convictions, other adults in the home, and whether they or the other adults in the home use drugs or alcohol. Virtually all parents will deny all substance use. A social worker then might ask, "If I were to ask you to take a drug test right now, would it be clean?" The social worker has no authority to request such a test and cannot legally compel a parent to take one. Nevertheless, during this line of questioning, a parent sometimes offers an excuse or explanation for a positive result to a hypothetical drug test. With that, a social worker may reasonably believe that the parent uses drugs. This answer can sometimes be the deciding factor in determining whether a child should be removed.

State policies around perinatal substance use exist in a larger context of the state policies of a declared "war on drugs" and on those who use them. As discussed in chapter 2, the mid-1980s were marked by new public concern about drug use, particularly crack cocaine in urban areas. Public scrutiny of female drug users who used illegal drugs during pregnancy was particularly harsh, as these women came to be viewed as both antimaternal and as the source of irreparable fetal harm that produced "damaged" children. In the following years, concern about prenatal drug use moved from popular recognition to institutional practice, a process described eloquently by Laura Gomez in *Misconceiving Mothers.*[17] The move to punish drug-related crimes was swift, harsh, and uneven. From 1986 to 1991, there was a 465.5 percent increase in the number of African Americans convicted for drug-related offenses. The number of African American women incarcerated for drug-related offenses increased 828 percent from 1986 to 1991.[18]

People from racial and ethnic minority backgrounds comprise two-thirds of those currently incarcerated. Criminal history, as discussed at length in chapter 7, jeopardizes parents' claim to their children, irrespective of how remote or irrelevant that history may be. For women, the punishments are greater. Women in prison are more likely to be incarcerated for drug-related offenses than are men. As Angela Davis argues of this incongruence, "The woman who does drugs is criminalized both because she is a drug user and because, as a consequence, she cannot be a good mother."[19] Putting this into practice, three-fourths of incarcerated women are mothers, with two-thirds having minor-aged children. This indisputably has placed a significant burden on nonincarcerated family members and the social services system responsible for the care of those children. In addition, because of the dramatic racial disparities in arrests, convictions, and incarcerations, children of color are disproportionately affected by child welfare system policy that so heavily focuses on criminal history and drug use. In the most obvious sense, this can be seen by the identification of felons in the risk assessment tool described above. Yet state ideology remains that parents who commit criminal acts at best provide little or no benefit to children, and at worst are a liability; this philosophy is observable at the ground level of CPS work.

After 1997, county policy reflected the presumption that drug use, most specifically the use of methamphetamine or crack cocaine, was intrinsically incompatible with parenting. Questions about the parenting abilities of a drug user stem from two sources: beliefs about women who use drugs during pregnancy and concerns that drug use interferes with parental responsibility. First, the public attention perinatal substance use has received and the accompanying calls to action point to a widespread belief that women who use drugs during pregnancy are incapable of parenting. The logic goes that a woman who has jeopardized her baby's health in utero has already proven herself to be unfit to mother ex utero. Further, it is easy to believe that a woman who wouldn't abandon drugs while pregnant is not likely to do so after a baby is born. These assumptions have resulted in programs like Barbara Harris's project CRACK, which pays addicts to be sterilized. The organization's website argues, "Women and men who are using or addicted to drugs are often responsible for an extraordinary number of pregnancies (5–10 or more) that they are in no position to take care of." In support of her position, Harris argues, "we campaign to neuter dogs and yet we allow women to have ten or twelve kids that they can't take care of."[20] Harris's statement illustrates the larger belief that drugs and fertility are tightly woven together for poor women and that without intervention they will continue to create a burden for social welfare systems. Although her solutions are extreme, the assumptions they are built upon are more widely held.

The second rationale for a public policy belief that mothering is incompatible with drug use is rooted in a concern that children of drug addicts do not receive adequate supervision and care. As a 1999 report to Congress by the U.S. Department of Health and Human Services (DHHS) explains, "Substance abuse (including both licit and illicit drugs) can impair a parent's judgment and priorities, rendering the parent unable to provide the consistent care, supervision, and guidance children need."[21] Although this is the official statement of a policymaker, research on this issue is mixed, in large part, because of the common causes of maternal substance use and neglect, and thus compromised physical safety. Because many substance-involved mothers are poor, many of the problems identified as resulting from maternal drug use may be confounded by the effects of poverty, and may include malnutrition, higher risk of illness, and limited access to healthcare. In addition, many existing studies of how maternal substance use jeopardizes child well-being examine families who were reported to child protection agencies, and thus may not include families where maternal substance use has not affected child health.[22] Even with these ambiguities of causality, these perceived links between maternal substance use and child abuse or neglect are the basis for policy that automatically removes children who are born to mothers who use drugs and, when possible, incarcerates them so they will remain sequestered from their children.[23]

Most critiques of the public responses to mothers of drug-exposed infants scrutinize the policies because they punish women for their behavior during pregnancy, which represents a threat to reproductive autonomy and unequal criminal liability based on biological sex.[24] Few studies examine whether a drug-using woman actually can adequately care for a newborn after delivery or evaluate programs that might assist such women and their infants. One recent survey, unrelated to drug use, found that "an overwhelming majority of American parents (74 percent) wish they had received assistance in learning how to take care of their newborns."[25] Because most parents feel overwhelmed by their new caregiving responsibilities, concern for the well-being of a newborn with a drug-addicted parent may be well placed, as the parent's coping strategies or judgment might be impaired. Unfortunately, current court practice does not aim to understand whether parental drug use places children in jeopardy beyond that of any new overwhelmed parent. I am not suggesting that parental drug use does not impact parenting. Rather, I am drawing attention to the way that the belief that drugs intrinsically interfere with appropriate caregiving has led to a county policy that does not consider how drugs may differentially impact parenting. Current policy holds that drugs interfere with parenting in all cases, regardless of quantity, use patterns, or individual consumption habits. The zero tolerance policy instead presupposes the inherent incompatibility of drugs and parenting. The way this issue is situated in the larger "war on drugs" is apparent when one considers that alcohol, which is well documented to be destructive to families (as well as fetal formation), is not subjected to a similar zero tolerance ethos.[26]

The outcome of this blanket policy can be tragic, as it was in Robert Davis's case. Robert, a forty-one-year-old African American father of two girls, was admitted to a psychiatric hospital for complications from post-traumatic stress disorder, a condition he reportedly developed after three white men stripped him and locked him in a car for several days, and then set the car on fire. A routine drug test at the hospital was reported as positive, and since Robert and his girlfriend Heather had an open CPS case and were receiving in-home family maintenance services, their two daughters were automatically removed from their custody. Several days later, a hospital technician realized that the test had been read incorrectly and was actually not positive. The error was reported to the court, but by then, CPS workers had assessed that the children faced other risks, including Robert's wavering mental health, and opted to keep them in protective custody. Once in the system, parents are held to a higher standard than at the initial risk assessment level.[27] Under the zero-tolerance policy, no assessment of whether drugs (which turned out to not even be present) affected Robert's parenting was performed before the girls were PC'd. Although social workers later identified other issues facing Robert's family, none rose to the level of imminent danger that would warrant the girls' removal from his custody prior to the reported positive drug test. Yet with this tough stance forcing their entrance into the system, neither Robert nor Heather ever regained custody of their daughters (their case is discussed in greater detail in the next chapter). Indeed, concerns over parental substance use are central to CPS efforts to identify potential risk to children and directly affect a parent's abilities to regain custody from the state.

EVALUATING THE HOME

The condition of the home and its contents is important in evaluating whether children are at risk. Although the condition of the home may not be the sole factor in substantiating allegations of neglect or abuse, the investigating social workers weigh dirty houses heavily against parents. Every visit of a social worker to a home includes an inspection of cupboards and refrigerators for food. This is such a routine part of visits that when Thao went into a home and walked toward the kitchen, the mother yelled, "You did that last time." If the cupboards are bare, parents frequently volunteer that they are about to go shopping. In this situation, a social worker will ask to see money or food stamps. One social worker explained to me that "some people say they have money but really don't have any." This represents one of the few imaginable situations when a poor person will represent himself or herself to a social services agent as having more resources than in reality. This also demonstrates that many parents understand what is necessary to keep the state at bay.

As a short-term solution to a family's lack of food, family service workers—paraprofessional social service workers with less education and authority than professional social workers—can use emergency funds on a one-time basis to buy groceries for the family. After that, families are advised to go to food banks in future emergencies. A longer-term solution is to enroll a family in voluntary family maintenance services, which assist parents in obtaining transportation, better housing, child care, cleaning supplies, public assistance applications, and other referrals or resources. This process provides material resources to families, but it also requires the agency to open an active CPS case; children are left in the home, but are monitored by CPS workers.

Parents who are offered family maintenance services but decline them are likely to be viewed with suspicion or frustration by CPS social workers. In one case, Willow Mason, a Native American mother of a seven-year-old girl who was molested by her teenage cousin, asked Roxanna Villarosa, the investigating social worker, for counseling services for herself. She also agreed that she could benefit from a drug and alcohol assessment and related services. But when Roxanna sat down to complete a family maintenance contract, Willow refused, explaining that she knew a few nightmare CPS cases and she didn't "want to have to have to do anything." Without the obligation to complete services that such a contract embodies, the county will not provide services. After spending more than four hours with Willow, who was eight months pregnant and had relapsed into alcoholism after a long period of sobriety, Roxanna was frustrated. On the one hand, it was admittedly irritating to hear Willow reject needed assistance, while explaining that she wanted to reconcile with her estranged husband who was living with his pregnant girlfriend. On the other hand, Willow's concerns were reasonable, since enrollment in voluntary in-home services also requires agreeing to be surveilled by the state for at least six months. As political scientist Andrew Polsky cautions, "The state has the legal tools to impose client status upon marginalized citizens and the coercive instruments to compel them to remain in that exposed position."[28] For parents like Willow who want assistance, the process of being labeled a bad parent and the knowledge that their parenting will be scrutinized—and potentially deemed inadequate—is a hard pill to swallow.

The stigma parents must accept to receive services is significant. Thao investigated a case in which a teacher reported that a seven-year-old boy in her class was upset because his father had been banging on his front door and threatening his mother, Della Johns, an African American woman in her mid-thirties. When we went to visit their home, the boy and his four siblings were home from school with a skin infection. After discussing the various issues affecting her family, this overwhelmed single mother of five agreed she needed help. Della explained that she had found a hypodermic needle in her yard, likely from a client of the drug treatment day program around the corner, and wanted to move to a different neighborhood. She also explained that she needed a temporary restraining order against her ex-boyfriend. To get help with these issues, she was willing to sign a family maintenance contract. In completing the paperwork, Thao was required to list a reason the family needed services; he checked "general neglect." Reading this on the contract, Della hesitated to sign it. She asked Thao if the general neglect claim reflected badly on her and whether it was necessary. She also asked him whether he believed that her children were really neglected. Thao paused and then said, "Not really, but the condition of the house," which was sparsely furnished and dirty, and the children, who had the aforementioned skin condition, could be classified under neglect, the catchall term when nothing else applies, and he had to put down a reason to give her services. Della explained that she needed the help, but was not happy about being recorded in the system as a neglectful mother. She did sign the contract, and in doing so, Della was able to get some material and legal assistance, and to keep custody of her children. By recognizing that she needed help, or rather, by deferring to the state's definition of her as needing help, she communicated to the social worker that she was basically a good parent who wanted better for her children and was willing to accept assistance to get it. She also voluntarily placed herself in a situation of vulnerability. She is now a parent with an open CPS case file. Like Robert's case above, any future report to CPS will be treated differently.

EXPECTATIONS OF DEFERENCE

In the preceding stories, we can see the important role that parental acknowledgment of social worker authority—essentially deference to that authority—plays. Deference, as defined by Erving Goffman, is the "component of activity which functions as a symbolic means by which appreciation is regularly conveyed *to* a recipient, *of* this recipient, or something of which the recipient is taken as a symbol, extension or agent." Using this definition, Richard E. Sykes and John P. Clark observed the importance of deference in interactions between civilians and police officers:

> [The offender's] very status as a violator implies not only to the officer, but to others, that in some sense he is already guilty, if not of a crime then of failure to display deference toward his fellow citizens. He is then twice obligated; not just to the citizens, but, by showing deference to the officer, he reestablishes himself as someone willing to fulfill his interpersonal obligations and membership in the moral community. For if he refuses deference to the

officer, the symbol of that community's authority, he may be suspected of openly announcing his secession from it: "to be pointedly refused an expected act of deference is often a way of being told that open insurrection has begun" (Goffman 1956, p. 480). The obligation is proportionate to the offense; the greater the violation, the more he must defer in order to establish that he really respects the basic social obligations.[29]

There are useful parallels between the role of deference to the police officer and the CPS social worker. Rather than framing the issue in terms of actual culpability, parents who are investigated by CPS are already stigmatized by the mere investigation. As Mateo Estes, a Latino father in his early twenties, reflects on his own experience of being investigated, he recalls, "I'm in the room, I'm just like, my voice is trembling; it's like I'm nervous...This is not good, this does not look good; it don't sound good, but at the same time I never been through this. CPS was in my house. They got me in my room and asked me what the hell happened to my daughter."

The "crime" parents commit is not simply an offense against fellow citizens, but represents a violation of norms of appropriate parenthood. When a social worker enters a home to investigate, he or she already has reason to believe that the parent has acted inappropriately, in ways incompatible with normative definitions of parenthood. By showing deference to the social worker, the parent communicates that he or she understands what it means to act appropriately and aspires to do so. The adage that knowing you are going crazy is a sign of sanity is a parallel; a parent who recognizes that their family is not functioning appropriately is capable, from the social worker's point of view (and therefore the state's point of view), of change. Accepting help when it is offered is a way for parents to demonstrate that they are appropriate parents, as Della's case illustrates. Parents who do not act with deference, who do not communicate recognition of their own failings, who do not communicate a desire to improve, or who do not agree to the terms required for assistance are perceived to be either in denial or beyond rehabilitation. They are seen as unable to protect or care for their children, which usually results in their children's placement in protective custody.

Social workers' contention that parents must subordinate by showing deference is important for two reasons. First, parents' demonstration of their willingness to perform deference reassures the social worker that he or she will be able to complete the investigation safely. Deference communicates that the parent is not going to attempt to physically harm the social worker. Second, because familial reformation is a core goal of the CPS system, after child protection, deference communicates that a parent is sincere in his or her efforts to improve, making reform seem possible.

In a larger sense, parents who show deference symbolically communicate that they believe that the state is trustworthy and that they long to comply with the expectations of normative parenting so they may become full members of the "moral community" the social worker represents. This very expectation ignores that such membership and the accompanying trust are not equally available to all people. In fact, the experience in many poor communities and communities of color of police indifference, abuse, or lack of judicial justice more generally has left residents with the reasonable assumption that the state does not act in their best interests, and more often presents a liability to their families.[30] From this perspective, a lack of deference is reasonable. Yet social workers' expectations for deference shape the outcomes of their investigations. To further illustrate this process, I identified two cases with many similarities in which parental deference—as a marker of acceptance of the state in a superordinate role—determined case outcome.

Julie Lawrence, a white social worker in her early thirties, investigated allegations of neglect against both Dana Brooks and Jamila Washington. Their homes were in similar condition, though Dana's was dirtier, and Julie proposed family maintenance services in both cases. Yet in the end, Jamila's failure to subordinate herself resulted in her children being removed, while Dana's were left in her care. Following a discussion of these two cases, I examine Candace Williams-Taylor's case. As a professional African American woman with material resources, Candace's case should have resolved quickly. Yet her failure to reunify with her son for more than a year demonstrates the importance of demonstrating deference. These cases, when examined together, demonstrate the role of deference in determining whether or not children are removed from their homes, and how the expectation of deference and interpretations of whether that expectation has been satisfied are filtered through experiences of race, class, and gender—particularly as they shape definitions of good mothering.

Dana Brooks

Early one weekday morning, a white woman walking her dog saw a young child between eighteen months and two years old running around outside near the street with a "diaper that was rotting off." Reportedly his blonde hair was matted, he was filthy, and there was no adult in sight. The woman walked through the apartment complex where he was, knocking on doors; no one answered. The dog walker, a preschool teacher who was a mandated reporter and was trained to report suspected maltreatment, found a ten-year-old boy who said he knew the child and would take him home. The teacher watched the boy take the toddler into an apartment, through a door on which she had knocked earlier. She then called CPS with the address and reported the incident.

A couple of hours later I accompanied Julie, the first "runner" for the day—or social worker responsible for answering the first urgent calls—to the outskirts of town to investigate. Julie was unhappy about the long trek, which consumed time she needed to attend to her other cases, for what she was sure would be a waste of time. A little after 10:00 A.M., we arrived at the apartment complex, parked, and walked to the apartment. Passing a wheelchair and many stray toys, Julie knocked on the door. After several minutes, the same ten-year-old boy who had retrieved the toddler that morning answered the door. He stood in the foyer holding a baby about one-year-old and explained that he was a neighbor and friend of the family. He had been playing video games with Trevor, a dark-haired eleven-year-old boy with a wiry build who remained on the living room floor in front of the television. Trevor looked up and explained that his mother was asleep upstairs. Julie sternly explained that he needed to get her. The friend ran upstairs.

After a few minutes, a young woman came downstairs. Dana Brooks, a nineteen-year-old white woman with an inch of dark roots beneath her long, bleached blonde hair, walked down the stairs expressing irritation and mild hostility. After Julie introduced herself, Dana began ranting about the neighbor who she incorrectly believed had called CPS, insisting that that woman's house was worse than her own. Julie waited for the rant to wane and then we stepped out of the entrance and into the two-level townhouse. It was filthy. Laundry was piled at least three feet high in the small laundry room off the kitchen. Old dried food was caked on the high chair and baby walker. The counters were covered with spoiled food, half-eaten yogurt cartons, dirty dishes, and unidentifiable remnants of former meals. Dana began to explain that she didn't have time to do the dishes, having recently started a job working nights. She added that the mess had just happened the night before.

Julie, lips pursed together and her eyes scanning the room through her wire-framed glasses, turned and began to walk upstairs to the see the two bedrooms. The larger of the two rooms belonged to Dana, her husband, and their two young children, ages one and two years. The smaller bedroom opposite the stairs belonged to Trevor and his thir-teen-year-old sister who was not home, but whose walk-in closet had empty tequila bottles lined up on the shelf and signs professing the vir-tues of LSD on the walls. There were dirty diapers and spoiled food on the floor of the bedroom. As we entered the room, Trevor followed slowly up the stairs. Using his arms, he dragged his small body up the stairs; only then did we realize that the wheelchair outside was his. Trevor, Dana's stepson, had been born with spina bifida and was paralyzed from the waist down. (We learned later that he was also scheduled to have surgery on his kidneys the following month.) Though he could use braces to walk, he hadn't owned crutches or braces in four months while his parents waited for the processing of a public assistance claim for unusual medical expenses. Whereas this likely signified Trevor's family's difficulty navigating state bureaucracy, it also meant in a real sense that Trevor's only means of mobility at home was to crawl.

Julie took Trevor into the bedroom to ask him about his family. While there, Julie and Trevor together changed the diaper of the one-year-old girl, revealing a bright red blistering diaper rash. Trevor explained that he had known Dana since he was seven and that he loved his one-year-old sister and two-year-old brother more than anything. Trevor began to cry, saying that he wanted to stay with his family. He explained that the diapers littering the bedroom floor were his and that he was supposed to take them outside, but didn't. Julie tried to comfort him, reassuring him that he was a kid and that making sure the house was clean was not his responsibility. She explained that her primary concern was to make sure he was okay; Trevor was not reassured. Julie then went to talk to Dana. By now Dana's defenses had crumbled and she was desperate. She explained that she would quit her job or do whatever it takes because she loves her children more than anything. Both begging and ranting, she repeated, "Please don't take my kids."

Julie paused, looked around, and explained that she didn't know what to do. She confronted Dana, explaining sternly that the mess could not have happened overnight and was unacceptable. Dana didn't argue. Julie told Dana to first give the babies a bath and to then start cleaning. She walked her through the house and pointed out what to do first and what was not important. She then said that she would be back in a few hours to check on her progress and to make a decision about whether to remove the children. Julie and I went out to the county car. She turned to me and asked me what I thought; I didn't know. Julie explained that in her view, the mother's denial was the problem. We sat in the car while Julie called her supervisor to discuss the case. They agreed that Julie would leave and come back three hours later. If the condition of the house had improved, she'd return the next week to reassess and then, if the situation remained improved, would enroll the family in services.

A tall, thin white woman who appeared to be in her late thirties and who identified herself as Dana's neighbor came out to the car and tapped on the window. She asked if she could do anything to help Dana, explaining that Dana was inside with the kids in the bath, throwing up in the adjacent toilet. Julie explained that she could not discuss anything with her but that the woman could do anything Dana asked. The woman left and Julie turned to me, sighed, and commented that throwing up was a step backward. She laughed for a moment, revealing her awareness of the angst she was putting this family through and a desire to lighten the sad moment. As we headed off for a long lunch, a rare treat facilitated by our need to return and being so far out of town, Julie explained to me that the case could have gone either way. Dana's willingness to do anything and her fear of losing her children, who she says are "the most important thing in the world," worked in her favor.

We returned three-and-a-half hours later and the house was indisputably better. The children's father Earl, a large-framed white man in his late thirties or early forties, was now home. He apologized to Julie that things had been sliding and promised that it wouldn't happen again. He explained that he was working three jobs and was not the type to get welfare. Dana chimed in to reiterate that she loved the children more than anything. Earl added, "My children are my life." Julie complimented Dana on her progress and told the couple that they needed to childproof the door to prevent the toddler from wandering off again. She then explained to them that she was going to return later in the week to check on them and that if things looked good at that visit, she would enroll them in voluntary in-home services.

On the drive home, Julie reflected on the unusual success of the morning, commenting that it helped that Dana wasn't "system wise" about her rights and how the system works. One week later, Julie returned and provided referrals to family maintenance services. Later, Dana told Julie how much she loved her parenting classes and Earl told Julie that he thought CPS was the best thing that ever happened to them. In completing their services and keeping their children, Dana's family represents one of the unsung victories of the CPS system. Yet, even as social workers like Julie have these triumphs, they also experience failures with other cases. The following case, in which the initial details are similar to Dana's, represents such a failure.

Jamila Washington

A month after that day at Dana's home, I accompanied Julie as she went to investigate the well-being of three girls, ages five years, four years, and nine months. Their mother, Jamila Washington, is a short, heavy-set African American woman with long braids who looks older than her twenty-three years. On this particular day, her right eyeball was filled with blood, the result of having been assaulted by a neighbor the day before. The referral indicated that Jamila had a CPS history in South Carolina and stated that an investigator should bring law enforcement because she was likely to become combative. Julie called the social services agency in South Carolina to ask if law enforcement was really necessary and to gain insight into the family's history. She learned that Jamila and her eighteen-year-old sister, who was currently staying with her, had been raised in foster care in South Carolina and that the sister's parental rights to her own children had recently been terminated. The worker explained that she would have taken custody of Jamila's children, but Jamila moved to California before she could.

We arrived at the house and two uniformed police officers, each in their own patrol car, arrived shortly after we did. One white and one African American, they both quickly introduced themselves before Julie briefed them on what they would be doing while she investigated. Then the four of us walked to the door. When Jamila answered the door and realized what was happening, she was irate. She yelled about knowing her rights and how CPS had no right to come into her house. A social worker, she explained, had been there a couple of months before and had found nothing wrong, so CPS had no right to return. At the police officers' insistence, we entered. Once inside the house, Jamila called her husband, whom she had thrown out the night before (and had previously served jail time for stabbing) to accuse him of calling CPS on her. Although this guess was correct, Julie did not confirm or deny it. This lack of confirmation gave Jamila time to come up with alternate guesses, which led to additional phone calls to accuse other acquaintances of reporting her. Julie and I walked through the one bed-room house while the police officers stood in the living room.

The house was dirty in an unscoured sort of way, but was not in terrible condition, particularly when one considers that there were five people living there. There were stacks of folded clean clothes on the queen-size bed in the bedroom. I followed Julie as she walked from room to room while Jamila continued screaming. Returning to the kitchen, Julie calmly explained to Jamila that one factor in whether her kids were removed was how cooperative she was. Jamila looked at Julie and shouted, "If I don't cooperate with you then you're gonna take my children? That's messed up." Julie ignored this remark and moved to interview the girls, who were sitting quietly on the couch. Julie asked who wanted to talk to her first, and the four-year-old raised her hand. Jamila screamed that no one was going to talk to her kids without her there, as they are only four and five years old. The police officers told Jamila that she could get a lawyer later, but that Julie was indeed going to talk to her children.

I followed Julie and Deja, the four-year-old, into the bathroom. I sat on the toilet as the little girl sat on the edge of the tub and Julie kneeled on the floor in front of her. Deja had lots to say about how she and her sister get "whooped" with a belt when her mom is mad. She showed a gash healing on her left forearm, as well as a few other marks in various stages of healing that, according to Julie, didn't look like belt marks. She mentioned that her sisters also got hit sometimes. In her typically soothing voice, Julie calmly conducted the interview. In the adjacent living room, Jamila continued yelling about "double talk" and "putting ideas in their heads," and about the neighbor who assaulted her and whom she came to believe had reported her.

For the second interview, five-year-old Mahogany came in and sat down on the edge of the tub. Demonstrating that she already understood the ramifications of a CPS investigation, she announced that she didn't want to talk to us and put her fingers in her ears. Jamila continued to yell. Julie calmly asked, "Do you go to school?" With her fingers still in her ears, Mahogany nodded yes, indicating she was listening. As Julie paused to consider how to proceed, Mahogany confidently volunteered, "My mama doesn't whoop me." Julie ignored this statement and instead pursued questions about school, which led to long recitations of the hokey-pokey, colors, numbers, and other first-grade scholastic trivia. When Julie finally asked about what happened the prior night—when her mother and stepfather were fighting—she explained that she didn't want to talk "about nasty stuff." After a few more elementary school details, we all left the bathroom. Mahogany marched over to her mother and proclaimed that she hadn't told us anything and had said that she didn't whoop her. Jamila told Mahogany that she didn't need to lie and that she does get whooped sometimes. Unrewarded for her loyalty, Mahogany sank into the couch next to her sister.

Julie turned to address Jamila, who began yelling again. Julie asked me to take the children into the bedroom, which I did, where we repeatedly read the one book they had and sang songs. The girls proclaimed they liked me. A few minutes later, Jamila's sister entered with Jamila's nine-month-old daughter. She asked the girls what I had asked them and whether I had "planted things." Mahogany self-assuredly stated that she thought I was nice and that she liked me, explaining that we had sung the hokey-pokey and counted. The girls' aunt was not pleased, and after gesturing at my bulging pregnant belly and asking how I would feel if it were my baby, this eighteen-year-old woman began to suck her thumb.

In the other room, Julie offered in-home services to Jamila, who yelled about how she didn't want CPS in her life for six more months, a sign of her knowledge of the system. As Julie began the paperwork, she considered whether Jamila would be any more cooperative with a family services worker, responsible for providing in-home services, than she had been with Julie and two law enforcement officers. Julie stepped outside and called her supervisor, who told her to place the kids in protective custody, or "PC" them, based on the disclosure of physical abuse, the long CPS history of multiple referrals and visits, and the mother's "anger problems," which included a criminal conviction for stabbing her husband. While she called, the five of us left the bedroom and rejoined the two police officers and Jamila in the living room. Julie walked back in and announced that she was taking custody of the children. The nine-month-old baby was only wearing a diaper and Jamila would not say where her clothes were. I grabbed a sleeper from a dresser in the bathroom, but as I walked out I realized that it was too small. As I turned to get a different outfit, Julie told me to forget it, explaining that we needed to go. By now Jamila was howling and screaming. She yelled to Deja as she was being escorted from the house, "I love you, baby, but why'd you have to lie." None of the three girls cried as we left, and after a few minutes of silence in the car, Mahogany asked if we were going to the place with lots of toys.

Similar Circumstances, Different Outcomes

Dana's and Jamila's stories have many similarities, though there are differences as well. Both women were married to the father of their children and both were poor. Both houses were in disarray, although Dana's house was much worse than Jamila's and the allegations in the initial report were more significant in Dana's story. Jamila had a history of violence with her husband (not children), which was not an issue present in Dana's case. Jamila had, as the state defines it, inappropriately disciplined her child, but not to a degree that would necessarily suggest they were in imminent danger. In both cases, Julie wanted to provide in-home family maintenance services, thus suggesting the cases were not significantly different in terms of assessed risk to the children. Yet Dana was able to keep her children while Jamila was not.

In my estimation, their differing willingness to subordinate themselves to the authority of the social worker and show appropriate deference decided their cases. Dana was initially hostile toward Julie. However, she changed tactics relatively quickly and communicated that she would do anything asked of her to keep her children. As someone who had no prior experience with CPS and, according to the background check Julie performed, who lacked a history in the criminal justice system, this was easier for her to do. She either believed that the state was interested in improving her family or was appropriately fearful of the social worker's power to take her children. As a white woman, she also likely could more easily access the vocabulary of good mothering as self-sacrificing (by offering to quit her job or "do anything") and child-centric ("the most important thing in the world"). Doing so did not cost her anything in terms of her sense of self-worth. By deferring, she validated the authority of the social worker, assured her safety, and proclaimed her intentions to meet the expectations placed upon her to be an "acceptable" mother with an acceptable home.

In contrast, Jamila continued to challenge Julie's authority. Julie was willing to enroll Jamila in in-home services similar to the ones offered to Dana, yet Jamila's combative approach to Julie communicated that at best she would complete paperwork as a formality, but would be unlikely to comply in any meaningful sense with the expectations placed upon her. Jamila's insistence that she had used corporal punishment, which she regarded as appropriate, and her unwillingness to subordinate herself to Julie (as Dana had) communicated a rejection of the dominant tropes of motherhood and reiterated her perception that Julie lacked authority. As a woman who had been raised in foster care as a ward of the state and had experienced countless negative state interactions, including incarceration, her resistance to state domination is reasonable, and from her position, even rational. However, in the end, Julie did reestablish her position of power by removing Jamila's three children. (Should Jamila—who did eventually reunify with her children—face future CPS investigations, this experience will likely further her hostility and distrust of the agency.)

Performance of deference is an important aspect of a parent's successful negotiation with CPS workers. From a social worker's perspective, many of these families are not adequately functioning. Poverty, filthy or unsanitary homes, perilous conditions, or signs of physical abuse point to possible dangers these children face. In the social worker's view, parents who fail to acknowledge these unacceptable conditions—who may not even understand what adequate parenting requires—cannot be reasonably trusted to protect their children. Therefore the state, through the social worker, must intervene.

It is important to note that while the state intervenes in situations where children are not receiving adequate care, there are no clear criteria for what is "adequate," since definitions vary with cultural and historical views about children and their appropriate care. In lieu of a formal definition of maltreatment, the state uses a flexible idea of maltreatment that allows for social worker professional judgment and interpretation of cultural standards.[31] Absent a child's obvious physical injury, social workers base their decisions in part on their perceptions of parental behavior, including parents' motivation to change, level of cooperation with the social worker, and perceived future quality of life of the child.[32]

From a parent's perspective, particularly a parent who has had prior negative experiences with other agents of the state—such as probation or parole officers, county welfare eligibility workers, or law enforcement—government intervention is rarely perceived as offering unconditional help. Parents' experiences with CPS are also informed by individual and community understandings of state intervention, meanings that are filtered through experiences of race, class, gender, and culture. Sociologist Elijah Anderson's explication of the "code of the street," that is, "a set of informal rules governing interpersonal public behavior, particularly violence" in inner-city African American communities is useful here. Anderson argues that "the code of the street is actually a profound lack of faith in the police and judicial system—and in others who would champion one's personal security."[33]

Jamila, with her willingness to physically confront her adversaries (including her neighbor and husband) and her willingness to challenge Julie and the police officers around questions of respect and autonomy, suggests that she abides by the code of the street. Because the code of the street provides a system for demonstrating independence and self-sufficiency, system expectations that a parent communicate a need for help violate the tenets of the code. For parents like Jamila who participate in that code system, performing deference might be seen as a sign of weakness, and thus vulnerability. Adding another layer of meaning, Julie's lack of respect for Jamila as a mother may have different meanings—or present a greater offense—to her than it would to Dana, as the importance of both respect and mothering as a source of that respect are differently situated by race, class, community, and local meanings of gender.[34] Indeed, Dana initially tried to appear defiant to Julie, attempting to assert herself as in control of the situation. However, unlike Jamila, she was not inclined to view deference as a personal liability and was quicker to defer to Julie's authority—and to Julie's vision of Dana's better self. Dana quickly acquiesced to Julie and developed a client-provider relationship. However, Julie entered Dana's home without the police and with the assumption that such rapport was possible. In contrast, Julie entered Jamila's home assuming that she would most likely be combative; gaining her cooperation would require some level of threat or coercion, an assumption embodied by the presence of uniformed police officers. In this way, the demand for Jamila's deference was more aggressively sought.

Most of us would agree that a stranger walking into our home, going through drawers and cupboards, voicing their condemnation of our lifestyle, and then taking our children would be infuriating. In most other circumstances, challenging or even assaulting a person who threatens to take our children would be appropriate or even rewarded. Yet when the actor is an agent of the state, being combative is perceived as reflecting a personality flaw, a characteristic that someone is prone to violence; challenging or threatening a social worker only confirms the claim that one is dangerous to one's children and others.

Understanding this, some parents were aware that expressing their feelings of frustration or anger could be a liability in interactions with investigators. For example, Mateo, who did not realize he was being investigated until three days after he took his stepdaughter to the hospital by ambulance for a fractured leg, explains how he suppressed his strong desire to behave combatively after learning his children were being PC'd. Recalling his interaction with the investigating social worker, Mateo states,

> I'm just, I'm filled up with this rage inside when [the social worker] tells me this. [She] walks up to me right here and my mom and [my wife] and she says we're taking your boys into protective custody. And if you get all emotional about it we're taking them right now. These are my babies, and you tell me not to get emotional about my kids? You've known me for all like ten minutes, first time you've laid eyes on my kids, and you're taking them from me. Don't get emotional about it and yet you're taking them? Don't get emotional or we'll take them right now. You're taking them anyway. It was just a major power play and that was her position, that was her ability.

Drawing on this experience, Mateo advises other parents:

If CPS shows up at your door? Go with it, because I wanted to blow up. I wanted to grab the cop by the throat and say, "Give me my children!" I can fight for my children. It's my right as a parent to fight for my kids. Ya know, and if I would have done that, you know that it would have been in the report. "This guy is a freakin' lunatic. Look at this guy."

The expectation that a parent should show deference and cooperate is not subtle. In the aforementioned story, Julie explicitly advised Jamila that her level of cooperation would affect Julie's assessment of risk. In the above passages, Mateo describes his clear understanding that he—or another parent in his situation—is expected to remain calm and demonstrate deference to the social worker's "position." Even as he comprehended this expectation, he also relates the difficulties he had in satisfying them, as it required suppressing his anger, even as he knew it could undermine his ability to present himself as emotionally stable.

Understanding the need to perform deference, the Pacific Justice Institute, a libertarian organization that has filed countless lawsuits against child welfare agencies around the country, offers advice to parents who are under investigation for child maltreatment:

The parent should not lose their friendly demeanor or sound defensive... Parents must not simply hang-up or refuse to cooperate. CPS only needs a "reasonable suspicion" of child abuse (physical or emotional) to temporarily seize children. Consequently, the goal is to negate that reasonable suspicion before CPS has an opportunity to either visit with or take the children.[35]

The expectation of subordination is evident in virtually all CPS cases beyond those mentioned here. As shown in Dana's and Jamila's stories, the willingness and ability to adequately show deference is shaped by parents' experiences of race, class, gender, and history. Here I present another case as a way to better understand how the intersection of social locations alters the meanings of deference. Candace Williams-Taylor is a professional African American woman who resides in a home she owns in an expensive part of town. She is a computer engineer for a major corporation, her boyfriend is a police officer, her sister is a registered nurse, and her cousin is a social worker. Despite these markers of privilege—education, income, social networks of professionals, and prestigious home ownership—she too was held to the same expectation of deference. Intuitively one might expect that Candace's background would facilitate a social worker's ability to view her as an equal and thus expect fewer markers of deference. However, this is not what happened. In the following section I describe Candace's case to show how deference remains central to social worker assessments of risk, even when parents have access to social capital.

Candace Williams-Taylor

One sunny February day, Candace, an African American woman in her mid-thirties, returned home from rollerblading with her two biological sons, Curtis, age seven years, and Zach, age four years, and her adopted son Aaron, age five years. She went out back to sweep the pool, a duty she had neglected for the past month. Often her two younger sons would throw rocks into the pool and either she or her oldest son Curtis would get them out. On that particular day, Candace asked Aaron to put on his swim trunks and fish out the rocks he and Zach had thrown into the pool. She recalled, "I thought, ya know, this water's not cold, it would be a good day to get these rocks out of the pool. So I swept the rocks out to the shallow end of the pool. I knew that Aaron could stand at that end" with the water waist high. "Even though he and Zach both threw the rocks in, I knew that Zach couldn't get those rocks out. So his job was going to be to put the rocks back in their place."

Aaron put on his trunks, complaining that he didn't want to get in the water. Candace told him, "You shouldn't throw the rocks in the pool, so now you have to get the rocks out." After Aaron made a few dunks in the shallow end to pull out rocks, four-year-old Zach also put on his trunks and tried unsuccessfully to help. Unable to reach the rocks, Zach followed Curtis inside to shower; Aaron had one more rock to get and then he was going in as well. Candace held Aaron's ankles loosely as he went down into the water and then she helped him up. Candace recalls,

> This last time he didn't look right. So I immediately took him out, took his trunks off, wrapped him up in his towel and then went into the house and grabbed the phone 'cuz something's not right and I looked at him; his eyes were still open, he was still breathing, he was making this shivering noise. I was looking to see if I needed to do some type of rescue breathing or something like that, but I didn't see anything. And so, I called my sister who's an RN (registered nurse). Couldn't get in touch with her, so then I called my boyfriend who's a police (officer), but is also an EMT (emergency medical technician)…and told him what was happening and he said, "He's having a seizure. Call 911." I can't

get him to stand up. His eyes were open and looking off to the side and I was running the water on him, had the heater on, the little space heater. Okay, this isn't working. I told the other boys to put their clothes on and I just sort of held Aaron until the fire department got there.

The paramedics who responded commented that they noticed a bruise on Aaron's head and decided to take him to a large county hospital where he was eventually admitted through the emergency room. Candace waited for her boyfriend to arrive at her house to watch Curtis and Zach and then drove to the hospital. When she arrived, she asked for her son and was told to wait. A social worker ushered her into a small conference room and said that she could not see Aaron, explaining first that he was being ventilated and later that he was getting a computed tomography (CT) scan. She recounted the story of what had occurred to the social worker and was told to wait. Eventually, after her boyfriend assured her over the phone that she had a right to go find her son, she found a nurse who took her to Aaron, who was still in the emergency room, not on a ventilator, and not getting a scan.

Aaron was admitted to the hospital, photographed, and examined by a doctor. According to Candace, the physician, (who unbeknownst to her was a national expert on drowning), offered four likely explanations for what had caused the seizure, including getting water in his lungs, bumping his head, holding his breath too long, or experiencing the random chance of having a seizure, unrelated to being in the water.[36] According to Candace, when Aaron awoke, he asked, "Mommy? Did I get all the rocks?" stating proudly, "I held my breath for a long time."

Throughout the first day and most of the second of Aaron's hospital stay, Candace was approached by social workers claiming to be following up on the prior worker's interview. According to Candace, each read a statement that they claimed she had made that she had forced Aaron under water. Candace would deny the statement, getting angrier each time. On the second day, a forensic pediatrician—an expert trained to identify abuse—came with the social worker to ask Candace questions, including why she was holding Aaron's ankles. Candace snapped, "Because he asked me to!" and expressed frustration that the doctor's questions showed that he had not looked at Aaron's chart or records. In retrospect, Candace recognized the role this played. She explained, "I was annoyed with him because he was asking about things that I felt he should have known as a doctor by looking at his chart...and he goes, 'well I haven't looked at his CT scan yet' and that really set me off..."

Recognizing how her anger shaped perceptions of her, Candace adds, "If you read some of the [social worker's] reports you'll see that they didn't like my personality at all." Candace admitted that she did not express deference to the police, social workers, or doctors, noting, "I'm just very assertive and I didn't understand that I should be humble and kissing butt at that point. Had I been kissing butt at that point, I wouldn't be here in this situation."

By the evening of the second day of hospitalization, Aaron was better and was sent home with his mother and brothers. The following day, with the boys at school, Candace received a call at work from Detective Parsky of the County Sheriff's Department, explaining that he wanted to come by to see her and would probably bring a CPS worker with him. Unsure of what to expect, Candace called her cousin, herself a CPS worker in another county, to ask for advice. She advised Candace that "they're going to take your kids. Take them out of the house and make sure they're not there when they get there." Candace arranged for her kids to stay with a friend, then called her boyfriend, Kelvin George, who came to meet her at her house as the sheriff and CPS worker arrived. Parsky did not present himself as trustworthy when he asked Candace how she could afford to live in that upper-middle-class neighborhood, nor when he, as Candace saw it, nonverbally communicated his disdain that Kelvin was there. Candace was asked to make another statement, but declined, explaining that a sheriff had already taken her statement. Kelvin interjected that if the sheriff was going to continue to question her, he should advise her of her rights. Sheriff Parsky, a county officer, did not know Kelvin, a plain-clothes city police officer. According to Candace, Parsky turned to Kelvin and asked, "You seem to know so much about the law. How many times have you been arrested?" According to Candace, Kelvin answered, "None. I haven't been arrested at all," but did not identify himself. Parsky, who tried several times to get Kelvin to leave, eventually checked Kelvin's license plates and found out who he was. According to Candace, Parsky grew frustrated and demanded a statement from her, yelling, "I'm going to take your kids!"

Throughout this interaction, Candace's cousin was on the phone listening. She advised Candace, now crying, that she was being harassed and should call 911 to request a supervisor. Candace did, much to the chagrin of Kelvin, but that act—as well as Kelvin's suggestion that Parsky needed to inform her of her rights—only escalated the tension. Each attempt someone made to help Candace assert her rights, a sign of her refusal to defer, worsened the situation. Only when her cousin, a system insider, spoke with Parsky directly on the phone did things calm down. According to Candace, he accepted that she would not make another statement and went over the statement he had, as well as an anonymous report from a neighbor about a heavy-set blonde woman trying to drown a child. (No such woman was ever at their home on the day of the incident or on any other.) Candace calmed down too, and tried to cooperate by discussing the documents Parsky had. Parsky, a stocky white man, reportedly told her "you realize, just because you're talking to me, it won't make a difference if I'm going to take your kids or not." In doing so, he reminded Candace of his power over her.

Finally, the CPS worker who had accompanied Parsky interjected for the first time. She asked whether Candace would ever again use this sort of punishment with her sons. Candace replied that "I would use that again, but I would be more careful." At that point, the worker announced she was taking custody of the children because Candace had inappropriately punished her children in a fashion that jeopardized their safety. Candace was confused and asked, "If my son spills his milk and I tell him to go clean it up and he slips and bumps his head…ya know, I don't understand?" Candace insisted that it was not an issue of punishment, but an attempt at discipline, explaining the difference: "With punishment, you're setting out to hurt, inflict some kind of pain; discipline, you're trying to change something." The social worker was unconvinced. Realizing that she had lost the argument, she convinced the social worker to allow her ex-husband to take all three boys so they would not go to foster care. The worker agreed. Candace's ex-husband kept all three boys for three weeks, during which time Candace was not allowed to see or speak to them. Eventually a judge granted custody of Curtis and Zach to their father, closing their cases. Aaron, their nonbiological sibling, adopted by their mother after their parents' divorce, was sent to foster care.

During this time, Candace hired an attorney and wrote letters to her state assembly representative, information that was described in the sixty-five-page dispositional report submitted by county social workers to the court. Candace explained to me later that the social worker "included that in the report, as if it was a negative. They don't like it when you contact, when you execute, try to execute any constitutional right."

After those first few weeks, Candace decided to try and present herself as more deferential to the social worker, explaining "I called her one time and cried and said 'ya know, I'll do anything to get my sons back.'" Although Candace had come to recognize the importance of deference, her performance was not persuasive. At that late point, Candace's plea was described as both an admission of guilt and a symbol of insincerity. Candace's attorney described the situation: "She is a high-functioning African American woman who, when she finally laid it down, had burned too many bridges."

Candace's case should have, by all accounts, been over within six months. She attended services, had stable housing, had never had a substance abuse problem, and demonstrated her willingness to change. Yet it took twenty months to regain custody of her son; in fact, her reunification was ultimately assisted by court-appointed therapists who recommended allowing Aaron to return to his mother after he was molested in foster care. Although Candace reunited with Aaron, she entered a custody battle for her two other sons in family court, a daunting fight since her entire CPS record, including all court-ordered psychiatric exams, could be used against her by her ex-husband.

Candace's case, which took extraordinarily long to conclude (more than twice as long as Jamila's), demands close examination. In considering her difficulties regaining custody of her son, Candace attributes a great deal to her social location. She explains,

> I think my social status had more to do with it than anything else. Those things combined together, "Oh she's black and she has an education. Oh, we're not going to let her get away with this." If I were an AFDC person, black, white, whatever it would have been different. They would have given them back to me. They wouldn't want them.

Given the remarks Parsky made to her and Kelvin, it is clear that race affected how she was treated. Yet Candace also points to the liability her status as an educated middle-class black woman presented. Indeed, Candace was accustomed to encountering professionals as equals. She did not see the hospital staff or the police as deserving of deference. When Candace arrived at the hospital, having allowed her son to be transported without her while she waited for someone to take her other children, she did not realize that she was already being assessed. Likely the hospital personnel saw a small black boy come by ambulance to the large county hospital without a parent. The limited history of the injury came from the paramedics who routinely develop a sound byte to communicate what little they know about circumstances surrounding the condition of a child they are delivering. It is conceivable that the paramedic explained that they were bringing in a five-year-old boy who had a seizure after being held under water by his mother; the very fact that the hospital social worker was waiting to question Candace supports this hypothesis. When Candace arrived, the hospital staff saw a black woman who did not arrive at the hospital with her child and who might have contributed to his injuries. Their refusal to allow her to see him immediately provided hospital social workers with an opportunity to collect evidence of culpability. Her lack of cooperation likely supported their belief that she was responsible. The mobilization of a forensic pediatrician to Aaron's bedside the following day suggests the staff viewed her, unbeknownst to her, with great suspicion.

Candace's unwillingness to demonstrate deference, or to "be humble and kissing butt" as she describes it, was motivated largely by her belief that she was, as a professional, dealing with other professionals as equals. Even Kelvin's unwillingness to identify himself as a police officer when faced with the insulting suggestion that a black man familiar with the law must be a repeat offender, showed their shared unwillingness to subordinate themselves to the state—and since it is difficult to imagine a white couple receiving similar treatment, their refusal seems warranted. Social theorists have noted that in other encounters, "the higher status actor is not expected to show the same regard as the lower."[37] In Candace's case, one might expect that the similar class locations of Candace, Kelvin, the social worker, and Sheriff Parksy would have allowed them to interact as equals; this was not the case. In fact, in the CPS context social status is not an asset and may, as Candace's attorney suggests, present a liability. In his research on middle-class African Americans, sociologist Joe Feagin suggests that "blacks must constantly be aware of the repertoire of the possible responses to chronic and burdensome discrimination."[38] Here in the CPS context, social class was not an asset that trumped race. In Candace's case, it is difficult to unwind the intersections of race, gender, and class, to evaluate which structures were responsible for which parts of the interaction. Questions of Kelvin's past arrests or of how Candace could afford to live in that neighborhood indicate that Candace and Kelvin were seen primarily as black instead of being perceived as middle class.

Another complicated question is why Candace's education level, financial resources, and knowledge of her rights in the system did not give her an advantage. Much theory has suggested that insider knowledge of how a system operates provides an advantage to the person encountering it.[39] However, in this context, knowledge was not an asset. Both of Candace's attempts to utilize her insider knowledge—through Kelvin's suggestion that she be informed of her legal rights and her social worker cousin's suggestion that she request a supervisor—made the situation worse. Similarly Julie's comment that it helped that Dana was not "system wise" suggests that parents do better in the CPS system when they appear to have less knowledge of the system. Parents who seem uninformed may fare better because knowledge of the CPS system represents experience in it. Parents who seem ignorant of how CPS works communicate to investigators that they are new to the system— not repeatedly reported and investigated—and thus that their fall under the state's gaze is an anomaly. This is, of course, easier for white parents to demonstrate, since police harassment and racial profiling in communities of color grant system knowledge to people of color even before they become parents. Parents who are (or can be perceived as) system strangers must rely on the social worker's knowledge and definitions. As a result, they may demonstrate greater deference solely because they do not have access to competing meanings of state intervention readily available to them. They do not present a challenge to the system.

One aspect of parents' ability to present themselves as competent (or as easy to rehabilitate through services) is to accept the worker's definition of the situation, as Dana and her husband did.[40] In contrast, parents who assert an experientially informed definition of the situation different from the one the social worker has put forward communicate to the worker that they do not accept the social worker's authority and thus do not recognize the gravity of the situation as the worker has defined it. In the eyes of the social worker, this makes the parent a poor candidate for reform. After all, the first step in most treatment programs is to admit you have a problem. For example, Erving Goffman's study of mental patients in psychiatric hospital wards—which he calls the "ward system"—explores how mental hospital patients learn to define themselves in ways that are rewarded. Although a patient might initially try to maintain his self-respect, he will eventually accept an externally applied definition of who he is that matches the institutional expectation. By compromising his sense of self early on, a patient gains privileges within the ward system. "As the person moves up the ward system, he can manage more and more to avoid incidents which discredit his claim to be a human being, and acquire more and more of the varied ingredients of self-respect."[41] To challenge a social worker's assessment of crisis—to minimize one's culpability—is to deny a problem exists.

If Candace had possessed full knowledge of the CPS system, she might have recognized the need to accommodate the social worker and sheriff's definitions and would have gained the ability to manage these consequential interactions. In the ward system, subordinating to the definition of one as insane allows for future freedom from challenges to one's own definition of self. In the CPS system, subordinating to the state's definition of herself as a mother who inappropriately punished her child (not disciplined, as she saw it) would have likely allowed Candace to continue to mother. Of course, as a black woman facing racist remarks from Parsky, Candace quickly understood that she should be distrustful of state agents who clearly were not looking out for her family's best interests. When asked whether or not she would do something like that again, Candace refused to subordinate herself to the state definitions of her. In this instance, Candace's privileged position as a professional with access to cultural capital and material resources was limited by an incomplete understanding of how power is negotiated between state actors and parents. In refusing to provide the required answer about whether she would similarly discipline her child—an answer that would have presumably resulted in her children being left with her—Candace refused the state's vision of her as a failed mother. Because she viewed herself as an equal to the investigators, a position reinforced by her allies who were system insiders, she failed to view herself as subject to the requirements of deference.

MOVING THROUGH THE SYSTEM

I have argued that social workers' desire to establish their authority is one outcome of the context of their work. Dangerous, stressful, and unpopular, social work has left workers afraid for their safety and of making an incorrect decision. As a result, workers adopt a strategy of requiring deference from parents. In the resource-limited and structurally constrained work they perform, deference acts as shorthand: can this family be fixed without anyone being further harmed? Deference communicates that the parent respects the worker's expertise and authority and would like help. Workers rarely fault a parent for needing assistance; after all, the vast majority of workers entered the profession to help others. Parents who reject the worker's assistance by refusing to defer present a challenge to authority, unwillingness to change, and denial that a problem exists. They also communicate a core distrust of the state and a disbelief that its laws and policies are there for their benefit. At its core, the work of CPS social workers is to defend and enforce the rules of parenting prescribed by dominant groups of a larger moral community. In rejecting social workers' authority, parents also communicate that they do not belong—nor aspire to belong—to that community. The outcome of this exchange is that the children of parents who refuse to defer can be assessed as remaining at risk.

The use of deference, while expedient, ignores how it may not be equally tenable for all parents. Deference is less difficult to muster when a parent has a lack of familiarity (or a purported lack of familiarity) with state institutions, particularly criminal justice and CPS itself. For parents who have not experienced state intervention as coercive, restrictive, or punitive, deference is easier. Families in communities with less policing and lower rates of incarceration are more likely to accept state definitions as true and reasonable, and will be more likely to trust the therapeutic expertise of the state. At its most basic, parents whose familiarity with the state extends no further than the Department of Motor Vehicles or the Internal Revenue Service understand the role of deference in navigating a bureaucracy. Providing such deference does not cost the parent much in terms of his or her sense of self. For parents whose experience of the state is that of the criminal justice system or the invasive questioning of welfare eligibility workers (or even growing up in the foster care system as Jamila did), deference means something different. These parents value the self-respect that accompanies fervent self-advocacy; deference then is costly. These situated knowledges are not equally available to all parents, but rather represent larger racial, social, economic, and gender schisms.

On a more basic level, the ability to be seen as deferential may also be differentially situated by ones' resemblance to the ideals of good parenting. Specifically, the vocabulary of good parenting may be more easily accessed by those whose communities it already describes. For example, when Dana's husband described himself as someone who didn't believe in receiving welfare, he was communicating his adherence to dominant definitions of fatherhood as requiring him to be a breadwinner. This is an easier proposition for a white man who does not readily face employment discrimination.[42] In contrast, both Jamila's and Candace's insistence that they were reasonable to corporally punish their children—Jamila by spanking with a belt and Candace by physically requiring her children to retrieve rocks—and their refusal to renounce such practices communicates a style of parenting that differs from that endorsed by the state.

I strongly believe that Julie, the investigating social worker in Dana and Jamila's cases, and her colleagues who I observed are not prejudiced. Rather, they are hardworking, well-intentioned social workers whose jobs demand that they read cues to determine when a child is at risk. Nonetheless, as the enforcers of state definitions of parenting, they prioritize certain cues, most importantly deference, as a way to determine which families can be salvaged with in-home services and which present a real physical risk to the children. In doing so, they inadvertently reproduce the racial inequality that plagues state systems.

The expectation that parents demonstrate their willingness to subordinate themselves through a demonstration of deference saturates each stage of the system. In the investigation stage, there is an expectation that a parent will accept the social worker's authority and definition of the situation. As parents who have lost their children attempt to reunify with them, the expectation of subordination shapes the provision of their services and the perception of their compliance. The next three chapters explore the process by which parents whose children have been removed from their care work to reunite with them. Chapter 8 looks at the end stage of the CPS process and considers how parental subordination defines the moment where a judge decides whether to restore parental rights by returning children to their homes or terminate those rights altogether.

5

REFORMING PARENTS, REUNIFYING FAMILIES

Dan Stephens, a white man in his early thirties, sits down across the table from Melissa Espinosa, a white woman with an exhausted look that makes her seem older than her forty-some years. Dan, Melissa's court-appointed attorney, opens his folder and pulls out the social worker's initial report.

He explains that the allegations in the report are of chronic drunkenness and starts his routine explanation of what will happen at this initial court proceeding, now three days after she was arrested for public intoxication. This arrest caused the police to call social workers, who took custody of two of her daughters (ages twelve and three years) and picked up the third, a seventeen-year-old who had run away and was living with a friend. Although Dan would argue in court that this was hardly "the crime of the century," it was also Melissa's eighth referral to CPS in ten years. It was, however, the only one that resulted in the removal of her children.

Dan stops his explanation of the allegations and turns to Melissa, commenting on the smell of alcohol on her breath. Melissa explains that she had one martini at lunch. Dan tells her to never have alcohol on her breath at court. The court might request drug and alcohol testing.

Melissa asks, with a tone that suggests either sarcasm or frustration, "So it's illegal to drink now?"

Dan replies, "No, its legal. But if you want your kids back, you've got to stop. So you can go out and get loaded, but you won't get your kids back." He also tells her she needs to start going to Alcoholics Anonymous.

Melissa responds, "I don't believe in AA. I can do it all by myself."

Dan reiterates that she needs to go.

Melissa asks, with the sound of disgust in her voice: "Higher power and everything? Is that a requirement?"

Dan retorts, "I'm making it one. If you want your kids back." He tells her she needs to also get copies of sign-in sheets or to get someone to document that she was there. He then resumes going over the report.

Stephanie, her eldest, is almost eighteen. She will be on her own soon. Emma, who is twelve, is reported as crying for her biological father. She wants more time with him. The report says that she also says her mother is a heavy drinker and that there is some history of domestic violence between the adults in the house. Alexandra, age three, is the only child that is legally related to Melissa's long-time boyfriend, Jim Valasquez, a Latino man she has been living with for seven years. He reads more of the report aloud, which quotes Jim Valasquez as saying, "Emma doesn't listen, and doesn't do what she's supposed to. Emma is an asshole."

Dan looks up at Melissa: "Mr. Valasquez doesn't help your case much when he makes statements like these."

Melissa tries to justify the statement by describing Emma's behavior, but Dan cuts her off. With a sigh, he looks up from the papers. This will be "a duck test."

"Meaning?"

"If it looks like a duck, flaps like a duck, and quacks like a duck... Your boyfriend has two DUIs. He has alcohol arrests."

Melissa folds her arms across her chest. "Point blank. What do I need to do to get my kids back?"

"You need to test two to three times a week. They're gonna put you on a random test schedule. One time in the morning, one time at night. It's not real efficient. You can fake it, but you'd be surprised how many people get caught."

Melissa is now angry. "My kids go to school, they are taken care of, they have food. I don't spend my food stamps on dope like my stupid neighbors."

Dan dispassionately explains, "I will argue for return today, but it is unlikely."

As he closes his file, perhaps seven minutes after they sat down, Dan looks at her and says, "I know in my heart you have a very serious drug problem... Anyone arrested for an alcohol problem coming to court with alcohol on her breath has a problem." They stand up and exit. Having concluded what he calls, "reality therapy," he must be ready to go back into court on another case.

* * *

THE CONTEXT AND CONTENT OF SERVICES

Social services are offered to a parent under two circumstances: when a case is opened and the child is left in the home with his or her parents who are given family preservation services (as were Dana and Della in the last chapter), and when a child has been placed in protective custody by the county and a parent is trying to regain custody or to "reunify" with his or her child (as were Candace and Jamila in the last chapter). In both scenarios, the provision of services is guided by federal law that requires states to make "reasonable efforts" to prevent out-of-home placements or to assist in the reunification of children with their parents.[1]

The goal of services, whether the children have remained in or been placed out of the home, is to reduce the identified risk so that children can safely live with their parents. Because the state has determined that a child's family life is unacceptable, a significant reform in parental behavior and family dynamics must occur before the state will relinquish control and entrust the child's material care and legal custody to his or her parents. The state facilitates this transformation by attempting to resocialize parents to behave in ways that are seen as appropriately parental. Essentially the state is attempting to parent parents, and thus has specific goals and expectations for what successful reform looks like.

Philosopher Michel Foucault explains that "it is a normalizing gaze, a surveillance that makes it possible to qualify, to classify and to punish. It establishes over individuals a visibility through which one differentiates them and judges them."[2] As instruments of power, social workers not only surveil the parents who enter the system, but assess whether they are being resocialized, or "disciplined."[3] Here social workers hope that by disciplining parents, they will be remade into adequate ones. In part, this reshaping utilizes degradation ceremonies, in which parents are often demeaned and made aware of their parental failures. As sociologist Erving Goffman writes of the military recruit's experience with degradation rituals,

> … the recruit comes into the establishment with a conception of himself made possible by certain stable social arrangements in his home world. Upon entrance, he is immediately stripped of the support provided by these arrangements. In the accurate language

of some of our oldest total institutions, he begins a series of abasements, degradations, humiliations, and profanations of self. His self is systematically, if often unintentionally, mortified.[4]

Goffman points to the way that military recruits are stripped of their prerecruitment identity and through activities, uniforms, and control of their visitors, are given a new one. Parents in CPS do not reside in an institution that can totally extinguish their prior identity (unless they are in foster care, residential treatment programs, or are incarcerated) and thus the parallel has its limits. Yet the state nonetheless still hopes that by degrading, humiliating, and abasing parents, they can be stripped of their existing concepts of self so that they may build new, more parental selves that will better prioritize care of their children. Once parents receive case plans for reunification, they must complete services, attend visits with their children, and present themselves as responsible people capable of appropriate parenting. Throughout the process, parents are monitored by a family reunification social worker who is responsible for coordinating their services and issuing reports with recommendations for case outcome to the court. The parents' level of cooperation, the content of their therapy sessions, and their punctuality and behavior during visits with their children are all reported to the court and are used to determine whether they should regain their children or lose them permanently. In part, parents are expected to defer to the state's definition of this new self and demonstrate their desire for self-improvement. It is these requirements of deference and subordination, as well as the supervision and time-consuming services, that allow CPS to challenge a parent's current seemingly dysfunctional identity and mortify it. Doing so will, in theory, allow for a more functional parent to emerge.[5]

In interactions with judges, attorneys, and social workers in CPS, parents' success in reunification depends largely on their willingness to accept the state in a parental role and themselves as needing parental guidance. By accepting or deferring to these roles, parents communicate their prioritization of their children and demonstrate a willingness to change. For parents who loathe their current lives, such a performance might be easy to provide. For those who feel the state misunderstands them, a compelling demonstration is more difficult. In this chapter I examine the process by which parents receive services and explore the explicit and implicit content and demands of services. Having provided this context, I show the structural hurdles that keep successful reunification beyond a parent's reach. Beyond structural constraints, parents also strategize their compliance and resistance.

In the latter portion of this chapter, I use three parents' cases as examples of how parents often strategize their own behavior in encounters with the state, sometimes in ways that are counterproductive to their own desires to reunify with their children.

THE RELATIVE RIGHT TO SERVICES

In cases where the state is attempting to prevent out-of-home placement of children, parents receive services from social service agencies. As described elsewhere, services range in focus but generally attempt to address the issues the social worker has identified as presenting potential harm to children. However, the process of receiving services is different when children have been removed from their homes. When children are removed and placed in out-of-home care, a petition is filed with the juvenile court. The case is heard within seventy-two hours, at which time the county presents their petition to the court listing the allegations against the parent(s) and justifying removal of the children.[6] At this hearing, parents can either declare their intent to challenge the allegations and ask the court to set the case for trial, or they can waive their right to a trial and allow the court to review the merits of the petition solely on the reports and supporting documents in the case file. The court uses a "preponderance of the evidence" standard, a low legal standard that attorneys explain to their clients as "50 percent + 1" (or more likely than not), and will frequently find the allegations to be true, with or without a trial. Given the low legal standard, an overwhelming majority of parents waive their right to a trial so they may more quickly begin receiving services. Based on the information in the case, a judge is likely to find the allegations to be true, upholding the petition. Once this has occurred, a parent is considered responsible—often understood by clients unfamiliar with the intricate differences between civil and criminal proceedings as guilty—for the act or acts that brought the family into the system. In most cases, the court will order services after the allegations in the petition are found to be true.

Receiving reunification services is the first step in regaining custody of one's children. The juvenile court orders services for parents to address the identified problems that led to government intervention. For example, a domestic violence incident between two adults in the presence of children would lead to a referral for domestic violence counseling, anger management class, and individual counseling. Inevitably though, a wider array of services is assigned to address other possible issues, even if they are not yet known to be problems. Attorneys who represent parents don't usually object to the additional services.

They commonly refer to cases as examples of how "once you lift a rock, you never know what might crawl out" or point out that the initial allegation that led to the intervention was the "tip of the iceberg." For example, services may be included to address parents' drug addiction, past victimization, history of domestic violence, lack of empowerment or self-efficacy, anger control problems, mental illness, inappropriate parenting strategies, or homelessness. In almost all the cases I observed, parents—now clients—received referrals for drug testing, parenting classes, either anger management classes or a domestic violence support group, thirteen sessions of individual counseling, and housing referrals as needed. I did not witness any instance where parents worked with social workers to design their own service plans, a finding consistent with other observations.[7] Instead, after a judge has ordered services to be directed by a social worker, workers assign services in a somewhat uniform fashion, from the top down.

Although participation in reunification services is necessary to regain custody of one's children, receiving services is not automatic. The 1997 Adoption and Safe Families Act defines a variety of situations in which states are not required to offer reunification services. California adopted these exceptions and added several more, making it among the states with the most reasons to deny services. These exceptions can be grouped into three categories: the severity of acts that brought the family into the CPS system, the behavior of the parent once in the system, and things that are unrelated to the child, but suggest that a parent is unlikely to be an adequate caretaker.

First, if the offense that brought the family into the system is significantly violent, parents or guardians who committed the offense or who "aided, abetted, attempted, conspired, or solicited" the activity are not entitled to services.[8] These activities include, but are not limited to, abandonment, torture, chronic abuse, and sexual abuse of a child or sibling, or the violent assault of a child under the age of five. In many cases, it is likely that the individual who committed such acts may be facing criminal charges or be incarcerated, making reunification services moot. However, the language of the exclusion allows for the denial of services to parents who played some role in the event, even if their culpability does not rise to the level of criminal action.

Second, parents who did or failed to do certain things while already involved with the CPS system are not entitled to services. This includes parents who in the past had their parental rights terminated on a sibling or half-sibling of the child in question; have kidnapped a child or a child's sibling or half-sibling from a foster placement and then refused to return the child to a social worker; or have successfully reunified with some or all of their children in the past, but whose children have again been removed as a result of physical or sexual abuse. Parents or guardians may also be ineligible for services if they have "a history of extensive, abusive, and chronic use of drugs or alcohol" and have resisted prior treatment for this problem, even though the programs identified were available and accessible.[9]

Third, services may be denied because of circumstances that are not directly related to the child, but that are interpreted as signs that the parents are unacceptable caretakers. These include situations in which a parent suffers from a mental disability "that renders him or her incapable of utilizing those services;"[10] has been convicted of a violent felony, particularly when the sentence exceeds the time allowed for reunification under federal law; or when the parents' whereabouts are unknown.[11]

Even when one of the conditions for exception exists, a judge can determine that reunification is in the child's best interest and order services. However, this is less common in cases involving very young children who are seen as likely to be adopted. Instead, juvenile courts are increasingly utilizing the new federal law to deny services to parents. This is often a surprise to parents, particularly ones who had been through the system before the 1997 federal reforms defined such exceptions. Chantelle Carter's case provides an example of how this new judicial prerogative is used, much to the surprise of returning parents.

Forty-year-old Chantelle Carter gave birth to what is known in the system as a "pos-tox" baby, a newborn who tests positive for cocaine at birth because of maternal drug use during pregnancy. According to the report issued to the court, the intake social worker discussed the situation with Chantelle, an African American woman, and relayed, "Mother admits to cocaine and alcohol use since age ten. Says she plans to enroll in Womyn's Treatment Program.[12] Mother recently jailed for ninety days." This baby was the fourth baby born pos-tox to Chantelle; the other three of Chantelle's children were adopted by or are in guardianship with Chantelle's mother. At the initial hearing, the judge denied Chantelle services on the grounds that she had been provided services on three other occasions and reasoned that there was no need to offer more services redundant to the ones that had already failed to help her.

In a meeting before Chantelle's case was heard in court, her attorney man Sam Richman, a white in his early thirties, attempted to explain to her what would happen when they went into court. With the social worker's report and recommendations in hand, he explained that the attorney for the county was going to argue that she should not get services and that he would have a difficult time arguing against that.

He explained that "there is no chance the court or CPS will help you. The judge will not order CPS to give reunification services to you. They might for Scott (the baby's biological father)...CPS will not order you to drug test, to rehabilitation, to parenting classes. But if [your daughter] gets reunification services with Scott, you can do all those things by yourself." To do this, Chantelle would need to find service providers and the means to pay for them. Sam added, "If that doesn't happen, chances of getting the baby back are less than one percent."

For the first time during the meeting, Chantelle looked like she understood the gravity of the situation. She asked, "What do you mean? She's just gone?" Sam answered, "Yeah. She's just gone." He noted that even if Scott did not get reunification services, "you'll still have four months, but in my experience, that's not enough. So your chance is very low... If she was born clean, maybe. But positive, no way." A tear ran down Chantelle's cheek and she sat quietly, looking down. Sam suggested that she should get into drug rehab anyway, particularly if she wanted to continue living in the county and might have additional children. She sat still, said she had no questions, and thanked Sam for his time. As she walked out, Sam turned to me. "She's gonna use tonight."

THE CONTROVERSIAL SYSTEM

The concept of family reunification (or family preservation) services has been controversial since its inception. Debates over whether children are better off being raised by their less-than-ideal natal families or in out-of-home placements are woven through the history of child welfare. In chapter 2, I chronicled the many vacillations between a belief in the superiority of out-of-home placement and an appreciation of children's natal families and communities. This shift reflects the ongoing debate that centers on whether reunification programs are successful, whether children reenter the dependency system, and whether returning children to their parents places them back in dangerous situations. The ideology of family reunification is seen by critics as one that grants too many chances to bad parents, lets children "stagnate" in foster care, and gives children back to parents who will eventually kill them. As Richard Gelles, a former advocate of reunification policy and now strong critic of it, writes, "Again and again, I encountered tragedies that could have been prevented if only we did not embrace the rigid policy of family preservation and family reunification."[13]

Social science research has not resolved questions of the efficacy of family reunification services. A comprehensive federal review of evaluation studies finds that "results of non-experimental studies have been misleading and the findings of controlled studies in these areas are mixed."[14] The long-term success of reunification services is also called into question by studies suggesting that between one-fifth and one-third of children who are reunified with their parents will have repeat contact with the child welfare system.[15]

It is difficult to know whether reunification services can be successful, in large part because they have never been fully attempted. Even when supported in concept, reunification programs have never received adequate resources to provide the full panoply of services that may be necessary for many parents to successfully reunify with and provide a permanent stable home for their children. As social welfare scholar Kristine Nelson notes,

> ...while many times these efforts have included concrete as well as counseling services, they are often too little too late and as such represent a residual approach to social welfare. Even this rather narrow approach to family preservation policy has never been fully implemented since it immediately became subject to the anti-welfare policies of the Reagan/Bush administrations.[16]

The proportion of funding spent on reunification compared to out-of-home placement most easily demonstrates the lack of commitment to reunification and family preservation. In fiscal year 2001, federal funding for foster care was $5.1 billion, with an additional $1.2 billion allocated for adoption assistance, that is, placing children in permanent adoptive homes after their parents' legal rights have been terminated. In comparison, a total of $305 million was allocated to fund Family Preservation and Family Support Services programs that could prevent placing children in out-of-home care. As for monies marked for reunification and other state-sponsored prevention activities, each state is given a base amount of $70,000, with additional funds allocated based on population and state income. In 2001, a total of $292 million was available for distribution.[17] Clearly, adoption is favored over all other possible outcomes for children whose families enter the child welfare system.

One result of resource limitations for reunification has been the strain on social workers, characterized by long hours and large caseloads. The State of California recommends that family reunification workers carry between twelve and fifteen cases each month. In the county I studied, reunification workers seldom carry fewer than thirtyfive to forty cases a month, and often more.[18] When one considers that reunification workers are required to write reports, appear in court approximately five days a month, perform organizational tasks like background research and photocopying, and meet with supervisors, the workload is consistently overwhelming. A reunification worker is required by law to visit a family—including all members involved in a case, even if they are in different residences or placements—at least once each month. Often a social worker with this kind of caseload is unable to do much more than the minimum required.

Although workers spend most of their time visiting families, the bureaucratic side of the job is the most exhausting. As Tom Page, a reunification social worker, once told me, "The number one reason [people leave the job] is the court reports. Most people want to be social workers, not lawyers. Court is very demanding." Yet the importance of those reports is immeasurable. Whether parents receive court-ordered services, whether they are evaluated as succeeding with their services, and in the end, whether they regain custody of their children is largely contingent on the content of those reports.

Recent federal reforms have created additional disincentives to reunification, as discussed in chapter 2. A series of laws passed in 1997 created financial incentives for states to find permanent homes for children away from their parents, including subsidies and tax incentives for adoptive parents or employers who promote adoption, foster homes, and kinship care. Although the 1997 reforms give financial bonuses to states that increase the number of children adopted out of foster care, they do not reward successful reunification of children with their natal families. In fiscal year 2000, the Department of Health and Human Services (DHHS) gave thirty-five such bonuses to states totaling $11 million, with California receiving more than $4 million of those funds.[19] These political and fiscal priorities shape the environment in which parents are attempting to reunify with their children and in which social workers are trying to provide services.

THE EXPERIENCE OF REUNIFICATION SERVICES
"Time Is Moving": Deference to the Process as Soon as Possible

When parents are given a chance to regain custody of their children who have been removed from their homes, the judge will order the county to provide services and ongoing, scheduled, often supervised visits between parents and their children. The judge, following federal and state law, also establishes time frames in which parents must complete their reunification services. Federal law after the 1997 reforms dictates that the case should be resolved within a maximum of eighteen months. Given the volume of services to complete and the significance of the change expected, parents must begin services immediately. Doing so requires them to defer to state authority and the mandates of the process. After the initial hearing, parents' attorneys advise their clients to do whatever their social worker says as quickly as they can. One parents' attorney explained, "I always tell parents to make their social worker their best friend."

One of the initial challenges parents face is overcoming their anger. In addition to the anger they may feel from having a social worker enter their house, go through their cupboards and drawers, and remove their children, parents arrive in court in a subordinate position where they will be described, sometimes inaccurately, in reports to the court. (Details of parents' social or criminal histories or patterns of alcohol or drug consumption are commonly misreported, while many parents feel that descriptions of their homes are embellished.) In the courtroom, attorneys for the parents, children, and county will then argue about whether the parents should get a chance to reunify with their children, what services should be required, how frequent visits with their children should be, and whether these visits need to be supervised. They will also debate which parental faults are greatest and in most need of correction. These conversations occur in the parents' presence, although some parents may not understand much of the highly technical exchange of legal code numbers and acronyms that represent their transgressions. They will not be addressed directly or be allowed to speak until the very end of the hearing; at that point a judge may or may not ask them if they have anything to say. What parents say rarely sways their cases, but may be met with a stern lecture or warning, particularly if they express their frustration or anger.

Routinely the presiding judge will adopt a confrontational stance with parents who protest their innocence after their culpability has been judicially determined, advising them that in light of the seriousness of the allegations, they should move on from questions of responsibility. Parents must perform deference, and expressions of innocence after culpability has been assigned are seen as inconsistent with the state's definition of the situation. For example, in one case, a white couple argued that their house was not filled with animal feces, that their children did not lack food, and that they did not use corporal punishment, as alleged. Judge Thompson, a white man in his forties who I once heard described as "Captain Kirk in a robe," advised them that "time is moving... If you come in here in November saying there's not a big problem, it's all overblown... I'm going to set a hearing for adoption." Setting a hearing for adoption is the final step in a case, following the termination of services. The judge's comment illustrates the view that parents cannot make adequate progress in reforming themselves if they continue to deny that a problem exists.

In another example, the same judge indicated the importance of accepting responsibility to maximize the benefits of services. In this case, a young white woman tested positive for methamphetamine during a prenatal visit when she was six months pregnant; her baby was subsequently placed in protective custody at birth. Her attorney explained that his twenty-six-year-old client "says she drank a spiked drink" at a party and was not a habitual drug user. The judge, clearly irritated, looked at the mother and asked, "Do you know how often I hear that? A lot. You'd do better to be honest than dishonest." The assumption of the therapeutic state is that by being honest and accepting responsibility, parents are able to gain the most from services, thus reducing risk to their children. However, the sense of being misrepresented in court documents, the alienating tone of the proceedings, and the paternalistic lectures they receive all fuel the hostility and sense of indignation that many parents feel, but must suppress. And for the rare parent who might have actually not committed the assigned offense, the mandate that one must accept responsibility to demonstrate progress is unbearable.

Parents who remain angry or fail to accept the court's definition of the problem risk losing services, the last buffer between them and the termination of their parental rights. Knowing that parents must overcome their anger to get along with their social workers and succeed in services, parents' attorneys employ various strategies with their clients. One strategy is to preemptively tell parents not to worry about the content of the social worker's initial report, which describes the allegations that warranted removal of their children. For example, I watched one a parents' attorney, regularly tell parents that the initial report was a "pack of lies" and warn them before they read their copy of the report that had already been submitted to the court that it will make them very angry. Despite his warnings, parents nevertheless are often upset, angered, even furious by the misrepresentation, as can be seen in Leonard's experience.

During an interview with me, Leonard King, a twenty-eight-year-old African American father of a six-month-old girl, voiced his frustration with inaccuracies in the social worker's initial report to the court, which alleged he used drugs. Leonard insisted, "I've never been on drugs. How can you find something that I've never been on? I don't even like cigarette smoke… and then when they say something about [you], you can't do anything about it. You can't sue CPS. They can say anything they want about you on paper and you can't do anything about it."

Dan Stephens, the parents' attorney described at the beginning of this chapter, adopts a more confrontational strategy for addressing parental anger. He explains that a large part of his job in his meetings with parents before the initial hearings is to provide "reality therapy," noting that he tries to work with parents to accept the conditions of their lives and to begin to move forward. In one case, Dan was appointed to represent the mother of a teenage girl who claimed her stepfather molested her. (The mother faced losing her parental rights for failing to protect her daughter, even after the molestation was brought to light.) The mother insisted that her husband had not done it and that her daughter was lying. Dan told her, "I can go in there and call your fourteen-year-old daughter a lying slut. Is that what you want?" Adopting a confrontational manner, he advised his client that she needed to choose between adopting what he called "the lying slut defense" and overcoming her denial to recognize what was happening so she could address it.

Parents who do not overcome their feelings of anger and indignation often struggle in services or fail to begin them all together. Returning to Leonard's story of frustration, we can see how this happens. Leonard appeared in court and faced a report that provided information that he felt was incorrect. Although the presiding judge assured him that she was more concerned about his daughter's safety than the details in the report, he perceived that she weighed those allegations heavily. Frustrated, he explained, "I missed the next court date because I was mad." Although he did attend subsequent hearings, his absence communicated disinterest in his daughter's case or a lack of self-discipline. As such, his anger inhibited his ability to present himself to the court as committed to his daughter and organized enough to meet public responsibilities like court attendance. Given the limited time parents have to regain custody of their children, rejection of the mandates of the court process, including that of deference to the process, can be devastating.

MATERIAL OBSTACLES TO REUNIFICATION

Social workers and court officers expect parents to change by attending and participating in services, and by making larger lifestyle changes, such as immediately abstaining from drugs and alcohol or ending intimate relationships. These expectations also make parental success in regaining custody of their children difficult. While parents struggle to overcome addictions, separate from abusive partners, or learn new parenting skills, a lack of financial or material resources constrain parents who want to reunify. Services are indisputably time consuming, in part by design. By satisfying these cumbersome requirements, parents demonstrate their commitment to their children, as well as their acceptance of their need for services. For many poor parents, the lack of private transportation means relying on time-consuming public transportation. In addition, poor parents who lose public welfare benefits following the removal of their children often face a worsening of their already bleak financial situation, which inhibits their ability to create a safe home environment to which their children can return. This section specifically considers the time bind that reunification services create, not simply in terms of time limits, but also in terms of the large time commitment that services demand. I then examine the ramifications of lost benefits, including subsidized housing and child care or cash grants from the Temporary Aid to Needy Families (TANF) program, demonstrating how, in total, reunification is disproportionately difficult for those without access to material resources.

The Time Bind of Services

Reunification is a full-time job. Whenever parents voice frustration with this aspect of the process—whether to a social worker, service provider, or their own attorney—they are told that they must demonstrate their commitment to reunifying with their children by complying with the court-ordered services. Yet participating in services is cumbersome. One mother's story typifies many parents' descriptions of their efforts to comply and the hurdles they face.

Thirty-five-year-old Latina Susanna Madriz, who lost custody of her infant daughter after her relapse into heroin addiction while receiving in-home services, describes her attempts to satisfy her case plan:

> The first six months I was going through the drug program, which was three days a week and then testing three times a week and then AA [Alcoholics Anonymous] meetings and stuff. And so like I used to tell them, complain to them, I said, "you guys make it seem like every day I wake up, I wake up for you guys"... I don't have time to even take care of my own things 'cuz I'm too busy trying to catch the bus and on top of that, when I was going to individual counseling, he (the social worker) sent me to counseling way out of town, and you see where I live. There's no buses here, so I'd have to walk there. And my appointment was at 11:00. I had to leave here at 8:15, walk there to the bus stop and catch the

bus at 8:36...to get to the mall at 9:10. Catch Bus 68 to the 14th Street railway station, get there at 9:20-something, catch the train to Smithfield and arrive there at 9:59 and then catch Bus 1 to Burdock and Sierra, right there at 10:59, Bus 1 is an hour, and then my session was an hour, from 11 to 12. From 12:00 back, it took me another three hours just to get back here, ya know. So every day I had something to do for them, so how was I able to look for a job and stuff? ... Without transportation?... So I had individual counseling, like I said, which took me the whole day to go to just that one appointment and then I'd get back by 3, 4:00 from the bus. That's if I didn't miss a bus, and I get home exhausted 'cuz I had to walk all this time. So, like I said, it was hard for me to continue to try and keep, to contact the housing, with financial problems and I tried to explain that to [my social worker], but he said, "Oh well. You got to do what you got to do...because you got yourself on CPS." In other words, I was obligated to do whatever it was; if I was dying, I had to walk, ya know, go to this appointment.

Given her limited resources, Susanna's assigned services were overwhelming, time-consuming, and impractical, particularly as one includes transportation and planning time. Her story speaks to the importance of material resources, such as reliable transportation; having access to a car would have saved Susanna as many as five hours each day. Susanna believes that she could have more successfully reached the housing assistance agency or her social worker by phone if she were home earlier, all of which would have contributed to a vision of her as more compliant.

Similarly Alison Hayden, a thirty-two-year-old white mother of four girls, struggled to see her children when they were placed in a neighboring county, about an hour away by car. To see her toddler daughter, Alison relied on the social services agency—subcontracted by the county to supervise the foster placement—to bring the girl to the residential treatment center where Alison lived. As Alison made progress on her case, the court increased her visits from one hour to four hours. However, her reliance on social worker transportation made such visits difficult. She explained that the social worker "keeps saying that it's too far, but she has to look at it from my point of view. I don't have transportation and I didn't ask for them to place her in [the other county]." Alison was also unwilling to request that the agency or county relocate her children, since three of the four were placed together in a foster home. She explained "I'm not asking them to move, because they're comfortable there and they like her, so I'm not going to upturn their life right now, but I just think [the worker's] got to start looking at that more too."

It is worth noting that social workers do not aim to contract with out-of-the-way providers or to place children out of the county. Yet fiscal constraints and a shortage of licensed foster care providers mean that workers take what they can get. Having said that, state requirements of deference and compliance remain the same, irrespective of how these logistics compromise parents' ability to meet them. Although all parents must comply with services, socioeconomic class alters one's ability to do so. The importance of resources should not be underestimated. Having secure housing, reliable transportation to services and visits, the ability to choose your own service providers through private funding or insurance, and self-funded child care remove many obstacles that poorer parents face. Parents with private resources can choose their own service providers, set their own schedule, and engineer their own documentation for submission to the court. Parents who have access to such resources are spared the inefficiencies of public transportation, the often inflexible schedules of low-paid service providers who are contracted with the county, and the difficulties securing referrals from overworked social workers. Although county providers may also evaluate them, parents with access to resources can still supply their own competing evaluations from the counselors or doctors they hire. All these factors provide wealthier families with a significant advantage in maneuvering through the overburdened system. (And as the overburdened system strives to conserve resources, those families are more likely to be cut loose by allowing children to return home.)

In addition to being geographically inaccessible, many parents described their services as sometimes contradictory, overwhelming, and pointless. Frank Ramirez, a forty-four-year-old man of African American and Latino descent, entered CPS when his son Francisco was placed in foster care after testing positive for drugs at birth. Pointing to the contradictory service requirements, Frank told me as he waited for his court hearing, "I've got a [court-ordered] class on Thursday and I'm in conflict with classes right now. I've got anger management and counseling at the same time. I need to change one of them." Frank was attempting to enroll in as many services at the same time as possible so that he could demonstrate his attempt to comply before the next hearing. Shelly Summerland, Frank's thirty-seven-year-old white girlfriend and mother of his child (as well as eight of her own, six of whom were also placed in state custody), described his strategy: "he wanted to get more in before we went back to court because it looks better."

To address this dilemma, Frank adopted a strategy of alternating between attending counseling and anger management, making his attendance at each spotty. Yet he was hesitant to work with his social worker to spread the services out because of his need to leave town for his auto wrecking business. Frank explained,

> …[my counselor] knows how the whole system works. She pretty much knows that I didn't need to come for some of the classes so now, next week I got to go see her and miss anger management… I told her, "Look, I go to class on Thursday and if I come here on Monday," I says "I have no time to go out of town." Because sometimes I like to go out of state to work. So on Thursday or Friday means I have Saturday, Sunday, Monday to go out of town. But when you gonna stick one over here on Monday, one on Wednesday… for me, it's a real headache.

Here, Frank relies on the faulty assumption that his system-wise therapist with whom he seems to have developed rapport was a collaborator in his efforts to modify his case plan. Court-ordered counseling lacks the confidentiality normally granted to a therapeutic relationship; thus Frank's counselor would be required to issue a report detailing the frequency and content of their sessions. Extending the metaphor of state as parent, courts have access to medical and psychiatric records in much the same way parents can access their children's records. Reports of Frank's progress and behavior in therapy, including his poor attendance, are likely to be interpreted by a social worker as a half-hearted attempt at compliance, and thus used as evidence of his lack of sincerity in reunification efforts or his failure to make therapeutic progress. Yet Frank believed that he had adopted a workable strategy. In his mind, he was doing his best to comply while remaining able to keep his business going.

Many parents do not realize that they do not have the authority to modify their case plans without social worker approval, even if the modification looks to the client like a fair trade. Lenicia Watson, an African American woman in her late thirties, who is a former drug addict, fell into this trap. Lenicia completed a residential treatment program in lieu of incarceration two years prior to the CPS case I observed. As this CPS case opened, she was ordered to undergo drug tests three times a week, despite the social worker's assessment that she did not need treatment for substance abuse. After several months of testing negative, she asked to be released from the testing requirement. Jamal Gibran, Lenicia's African American social worker, refused.

Testifying in court, he explained that continuing to test is necessary to stay clean, to "build a track record," and because it "demonstrates a commitment on the part of the parent to prove they are in fact clean." Here, the negative drug tests do not simply demonstrate abstinence from substance use. Rather, as a time-consuming and cumbersome "hoop" through which a parent must jump, drug tests serve as a symbol of a parent's desire to reunify and an accompanying willingness to subordinate to state authority.

When Lenicia began working as a hostess at a large hotel, she was not able to arrange her work schedule to accommodate her testing schedule. On occasions when she missed a scheduled test, she would instead test on the following day. Missed tests, even when made up, are recorded as an "administrative positive." As a result, Lenicia would not be released from testing because each positive result from a missed test was described by her social worker as "a red flag for me." When testifying to the importance of continuing her requirement to drug test, Jamal added, "no matter how she protests, she still in fact doesn't have a squeaky clean record." Frustrated after several months, Lenicia abandoned her efforts to regain custody of her children.

Housing and Public Assistance

Case plans commonly require parents to have appropriate housing before their children can be returned. Inadequate housing is not a legal reason to remove children; however, the bar for minimally acceptable living arrangements is raised once children are wards of the state. To regain custody, parents must provide a home with a separate bed for each child, separate rooms for children and adults, and housing that is, by most measures, safe.[20] Housing arrangements—both in terms of the place and its occupants—need to be approved by the county social worker and often by the social workers who work for the children's attorneys. Though these expectations may seem reasonable, they also present an often insurmountable burden to some parents.[21]

Two competing factors make finding affordable housing quickly very difficult for the CPS parents in my study: the widespread housing shortage in the western United States and the priority that subsidized housing go to families with children. There has been a nationwide decrease in affordable housing, felt most acutely in the western United States and especially in many urban regions of California.[22] According to the Department of Housing and Urban Development (HUD), only 24 percent of very-low-income renters in the West receive assistance, less than in any other region.[23] For example, as of 1997, only 18 percent of very-low-income renter households in the West received housing assistance, compared with an average of 29 percent of very-low-income renters in the other three regions of the country.[24] The turnover rate for public and assisted housing is less than 15 percent per year, exacerbating the shortage of available units. As vacancy rates continue to drop, the most acute shortages are among units with three or more bedrooms, those most often needed by families with children,[25] and most clearly needed by families in CPS who must provide rooms and beds for children to meet the state requirements for reunification.

Even when eligible, finding subsidized or low-income housing is difficult. Once a parent loses legal custody of his or her children, remaining eligible for subsidized or low-income housing is even harder. Eligibility is based on family income per number of family members and having fewer family members alters a parent's eligibility. Although there are no nationally set preferences, giving preference to families with children for the limited available housing is common practice.[26] Parents who don't have custody of their children may not qualify for publicly subsidized housing or may lose existing qualification because their children have been removed.

In addition to the specifics of housing eligibility, when children are removed from the home, welfare-reliant parents lose most or all government cash assistance that the family was using to pay for housing. Most specifically, welfare-reliant parents lose Temporary Aid to Needy Families (TANF).[27] Research indicates that loss of welfare benefits may slow the time to reunification.[28] Without aid, poor parents who were only minimally surviving with their children will find it difficult to secure unsubsidized housing, particularly if it requires a deposit or documentation such as proof of good credit or verification of employment, which many poor parents lack. Although CPS offers referrals for housing assistance and CPS clients' applications are often expedited, HUD estimates that the average wait for subsidized housing nationally is about three years, and is likely worse in the West.[29] Even with CPS assistance, safe and affordable housing is difficult to find. Not surprisingly, one study found that "poverty and economic deprivation, as expressed by inadequate housing, might be the greatest risk from the social environment for successful reunification."[30]

Juan Reyes, a Latino truck driver in his late thirties, fell into this gap. His two daughters and stepdaughter had been in a CPS foster care placement for more than a year. Initially his sister requested that the girls be placed with her, but as she testified in court, "they weren't because my home was not big enough and I didn't have the finances to get a new home."[31] About six months before the hearing to decide whether to terminate services for the parents, Juan felt he needed to separate from his drug-addicted wife Leigh "because I realized she was not going to complete her court order and I was better going with my sister to get the girls." At that point, Juan and his wife separated, although he continued to call her several times a week, and he completed most of his required services.

A remaining barrier to reunification was his lack of housing. Just before his eighteen-month assessment, the hearing to determine if he should receive any further services, he was able to secure a two-bedroom rental in a "hotel for residential living," and planned for his sister to live with him there and provide child care while he worked as an interstate trucker. She testified at that hearing and explained their proposed arrangement: the three girls would get the two bedrooms, she would sleep on a rollaway bed in the living room and her brother would sleep "mostly in his truck. If he wanted to sleep there, he'd sleep on the couch." Although Juan and his sister agreed that this was a temporary solution to their housing dilemma, his sister explained in court that it had taken five months to find this unit because Juan's work history was too short and because of her poor credit history. She added that they did not get assistance from the social worker and did not receive a referral to the county's emergency housing program.

During a recess, Isabel Guzman, a Latina attorney from the office of the county counsel, turned to the young white female county social worker assigned to Juan's case and said mockingly, "I'm going to sleep on the rollaway. He's gonna sleep in the truck. *That's* the stability we're looking for for these girls!" The social worker chimed in. "He calls the mother every two to three days but he can't call me." During closing arguments, Isabel argued against returning the children and continuing services, stating, "Housing is the biggest problem. The father wouldn't be sleeping there, so placement with the aunt seems to be the plan, not the father. He indicated the residence is temporary. He still hasn't obtained permanent housing and he did not contact the social worker who could have helped him." In his ruling, the judge officially terminated Juan's reunification services, allowing the process to move toward assessing whether his daughters would be likely to be adopted. Yet the judge also ordered the county to provide Juan with assistance in finding housing, a move that gave Juan a chance to address this last obstacle before the future of his parental rights would be decided.

Child Care

Although lacking child care is not disastrous while children are in out-of-home care, parents will be asked to describe their plan for child care should they gain custody. Counties usually offer limited spots for subsidized care, but reserve most of them for parents enrolled in welfare-to-work programs. Most urban counties report waiting lists of up to three years for subsidized child care spots. The attorneys for the county or children might argue to delay the child's return home if a parent does not have a reasonable plan for post-reunification care. Chris's struggles demonstrate how future child care can be a stumbling block.

At the time he learned of his daughter Shelby (who had been removed at birth from a woman with whom he had had a fleeting relationship), Chris Vaughn, a thirty-seven-year-old white man, was living with his own mother who did not support his effort to get his daughter. To gain custody of Shelby, Chris needed to find stable housing and make child care arrangements in case she was placed with him. Yet because his daughter was not placed with him, Chris was not able to apply for any publicly funded child care or housing programs. He explained to his attorney, Rebecca Channing, that he was attempting to complete the child care application, including the medical and immunization history forms, but that his daughter's doctor, who only knew her foster mother, would not return his calls. Rebecca warned him that he would need to meet those requirements before the next court date:

> You make damn sure you have housing. You make damn sure you have child care. Because if you don't… All they care about is this little girl…they don't care if you don't have enough time to do everything… You have to do whatever it takes. You have to be creative; you have to be pushy. Whatever it takes to get housing.

Chris confidently reassured her. "I'm not even worried about it because I've come this fucking far."

Chris's inability to secure housing by the hearing date, despite a social worker's testimony that she believed it was likely that he would in the following month, was cited as the reason to terminate his services. His inability to line up a child care spot provided further evidence of his lack of preparedness to be a full-time parent. The termination of his services was followed by termination of his parental rights, which allowed Shelby's foster mother, a single woman in her late thirties or early forties, who had cared for her since birth, to adopt her.

Even when children are returned to their parents, the loss of child care presents a challenge to moving forward. For example, thirty-six-year-old Carla Rizzo faced this dilemma. Carla, a white mother of five, had stopped using drugs long before her children were removed, although she had a lengthy history of CPS investigations dating back to her days of drug use. Her children were removed following an altercation with her drug-addicted ex-husband who she permitted to watch them in her home one evening while she went to work—an inappropriate child care arrangement in the eyes of CPS. Carla, whose children were returned to her (with ongoing monitoring) after only six weeks in state care, faced a dilemma when her children lost their spots at a Head Start program during their foster placement. She explained,

> It took me six months to get my kids back into child care because when they took them they were in full-time child care, and when they took them a lot of things got yanked. So it took me six months to get them back into childcare, which now they're in child care, and we're back to our routine.

Carla was resourceful when it came to navigating referrals, most likely a reason she was able to have her children returned so quickly. She explained her strategy for getting much-needed child care for her four children between the ages of four and seven years. (Her twelve-year-old son does not qualify for the same programs):

> Yeah, well, they had to get a CPS referral. I was getting child care at first because of a CPS referral. And then I started going to school and doing all of these other things like I said, so I kept it going through [a nonprofit program]…because I was working and all this other stuff… Well, now I went in through a different way, so all of that changed. I got a different kind of referral. I got a referral from my welfare worker, but as long as I got them back in child care, because they need that. I don't know if it's so much stability, but they need it and I need it as much as they need it. Because being with the little ones all day long, it's like, God…and now that they're back in daycare I can breathe over here.

In describing her need for child care, Carla alludes to the role such care plays in her own well-being. As a recovering drug addict who has struggled with a history of violent relationships, a resource like safe and affordable child care helps her maintain her sobriety and her sanity. Such services are essential to supporting her efforts to keep her children at home. Further, access to affordable child care would seem an obvious need because her children had been removed when she allowed an inappropriate care provider—their father—to watch them so she could work.

Carla differs from most parents in CPS with regard to the speed with which she regained custody of her children and her willingness to work with social workers to get the referrals she wanted. Parents see social workers approximately once a month, and then once more in court when the worker appears to issue a report and recommendation, often advising against returning children to their parents. Given the criticism parents hear in court from the workers who are supposed to help them, it is understandable that many do not perceive the social worker as an ally in their struggles to obtain needed resources. As a result, parents frequently distrust their social workers, which results in their refusal to utilize referrals or communicate unmet needs to the social worker, who they fear will use the information against them in the next report to the court. Given that social workers also have limited information from their infrequent interactions with parents and reports from service providers, such concerns may be well placed.

This dynamic results in many parents perceiving themselves as being in oppositional relationships with their caseworkers. As Shelly, Frank's girlfriend describes it, "they're not going to work with me; they're going to work against me." Similarly Richie Lyons, a fifty-year-old African American father, recalls the trouble he had with his social worker:

> My worker, me and her, we were at each other. She felt that I wasn't doing enough for her and she harassed the hell out of me. Even after I completed my sixth [and final] drug test, she would have them call me, even at 7:00 in the morning, wake me up and tell me that I had to go test that day and I'm [like] "look, I took all of my tests, I'm not taking one." They're like, "Well, your worker wants you [to]."

Richie challenged the social worker's requests that he felt exceeded the conditions the court had set. Although he recognized and respected the authority of the court, he did not feel the need to subordinate himself to the social worker. Rather, he believed that acquiescing to the worker's demands would not have helped his case:

> Well, ya know what? It's kinda like a Catch-22. Ya know, she can write up things against you, but if she doesn't do certain things, certain things that she said make her look like a damn fool. So she has to do certain things before she can totally incriminate me. And so that means she has to come to my house, she has to make sure, she has to find fault.

Richie understood the power the worker held over him, but also recognized the ways in which she was constrained. Nonetheless, he clearly did not view the social worker as an ally in his bid for his daughter. Few parents spoke about the limits of social worker authority or how they too were constrained by the bureaucratic rules of the state. Instead, many parents discussed the importance of accommodating social workers whose power was perceived to be boundless.

Services and Surveillance

The policy of family reunification has two sides. Even as parents complained about the cumbersome nature of services and the supervision to which they were subjected, many parents identified how CPS involvement can provide much-needed resources to families who are almost always poor. In many cases, CPS provides a place for individuals to explore family dynamics and learn parenting techniques, and offers material assistance with food and housing. As an example, involvement with CPS gives drug-addicted parents priority in overcrowded publicly funded drug and alcohol treatment programs, and the threat of permanently losing custody of children often provides the proverbial "stick and carrot" needed to achieve sobriety. (County drug treatment agencies claim that about one-third of all people who sought treatment in the county were involved with CPS.)

Parents in CPS are expected to demonstrate their subscription to the goals of their state-sponsored improvement. Many parents genuinely aspire to achieve these transformations in their lives and hope to become better parents. Some parents identified ways in which CPS made a positive contribution to their lives. For example, Dana Brooks, the nineteen-year-old mother of two toddlers and the stepmother of two preteens, described in the last chapter, saw her social worker, Julie Lawrence, a week after the initial referral. She gushed that she loved her parenting classes and her husband said that CPS was the best thing that had ever happened to them. Dana's services were successful in preventing out-of-home placement and helped her to acquire skills necessary for raising both toddlers and teenagers.

Carla discussed the positive role of services and the incentive custody of her children provided her in getting off drugs:

> [I had] a drug and alcohol counselor. I bullshitted her for quite a while. Ya know, they know you're gonna relapse, so I just kept like I was an ongoing relapse. And she kinda went for it. But she thought I was testing clean until she talked to (the lab) and they're like, "No, she's never tested clean." And she just said "You

know what? We can't do this. I can't work with someone who's not going to be honest. This is the way we're going to do it." She just finally laid down the law. She said "Look. You've got thirty days, and if you don't clean up we're going to have to take away your kids." And that's when I moved here, and that was over three years ago and I've been clean ever since.

Similar to Carla's experience, Yvonne Platt, a thirty-two-year-old white mother of three, also found the threat of permanently losing her children to be an incentive to stay sober. In reflecting on her nine months of sobriety, she commented on how she has benefited from services and CPS's intervention:

It still is [mostly a good experience], because I'm still learning a lot… I wasn't protecting them. I wasn't protecting myself. Ya know, with all the abuse and stuff and ya know, I wasn't there and things like that, but I won't go back to it… I know I won't, 'cuz it means losing my kids and losing me. I don't want that in my life…I [have a lot to protect] and that's why I won't ever treat my children like that again, because it's all happened for a reason. I don't know what's going to come out of it. My daughter told me, "Mommy, I wish this never happened 'cuz I was a normal kid, I had friends, I went to school." I said, "Look, honestly, I don't [wish that]. [My ex] would still be around, he'd still be abusive, ya know and all that stuff would still be going on."

Dana and Yvonne express a sense of gratitude for the intervention of CPS. Although Carla was frustrated with the intrusion of the state, she recognized the positive outcome to which it led and admitted that her children were treated badly when she was using drugs.

Robert Davis, a forty-one-year-old African American father of two toddler-age girls, is in a different situation. As discussed briefly in the last chapter, his children were removed from his care because he allegedly tested positive for drugs while he had an open case and was receiving in-home services. Although the psychiatric hospital that reported the test admitted in writing that the test results had been read incorrectly, the court felt there were other issues in the home that warranted keeping custody of his children. As such, drug testing was dropped from his case plan and his case continued while his daughters were placed with his mother. Although Robert felt wronged by the process, he acknowledged that he was benefiting from many of his services. He discussed his experiences with court-ordered anger management:

I think the anger management has given me some good skills. Things like time out and it has informed me about things to be on the look out for in relationships. Ya know, certain circles that a family would have that would lead to things like violence… And how to avoid the level, before it gets to the level where they would have a rage of violence. So we would do things like ask your significant other, or things like time out, to become more willing to talk about things that create anger and frustration before it gets to the point where it becomes violent.

Even while recognizing the benefits of services, Robert, like most of the parents with whom I spoke, voiced frustration with the structure and demands of services and the high level of monitoring to which he was subjected. Parents in CPS are under the supervising gaze of the state. As they receive services, their behaviors, actions, and attitudes will likely all be reported back to the court. Parents were often aware of both sides of the CPS coin: the usefulness of services and the supervision that accompanied it. As such, they strategized their interactions with CPS accordingly.

MANAGING STATE POWER: PARENTAL STRATEGIES

Parents are engaged in a dialectic process of both accommodating and resisting the state power that will decide the fates of their families. These processes occur in a variety of interactions, most often with social workers, the state agents with whom they have the most contact. Whereas parents inarguably have less power in defining the situation before them, they are not powerless beings defined by state domination. As Foucault notes, "We're never trapped by power: it's always possible to modify its hold, in determined conditions and following a precise strategy."[32] Parents exercise power in their strategies with social workers and in their choice of whether to defer to their authority. Although they are not free to select the outcomes they most desire, they do make choices about how to best negotiate power within the situations before them. In chapter 4, I demonstrated the importance of deference and subordination in managing the social work investigation. In the reunification process, deference and subordination are equally important. Throughout their encounters with social workers, parents adopt strategies that reflect their relative willingness or refusal to subordinate to the workers or the authority of the state.

Parents' Strategies: Resistance and Accommodation

The CPS system demands deference from parents, signifying their subordination. As Goffman describes, "just as the individual can be required to hold his body in a humiliating pose, so he may have to provide humiliating verbal responses."[33] Instances of what Goffman called "forced deference" are observable in the CPS system. Parents are largely aware of this expectation and often articulated to me how to best maneuver through the system. Richie explains, "All you have to do is pacify the system. They don't care if you're really gaining; all they want to know is that you're performing how they want you to perform."

Alison Hayden, a thirty-two-year-old white mother of four girls, describes how she felt that her social worker, who she felt had previously advocated for her, was now working against her. In describing her social worker's testimony in court, she recalls how her social worker's attitude changed after Alison was arrested for a drug-related offense while she had an open CPS case:

> She just, she kinda kept contradicting herself on the stand. I do believe that she gave up on me because when I was in jail she wasn't talking about reunification for the girls; she just said that I really messed up my case… So that she, she kinda just said that I had to keep it together. And I did. I had one missed drug test. And then there was another time when, my visits are super-supervised, and [the supervising family services worker] made a report saying that I appeared to be under the influence when I wasn't. I had just gotten done testing. And I tried to tell her that, that all she had to do was call the [testing center] and they write the times there, ya know, and she could've checked and backed it up, but she didn't. So when we were in trial they said that, well, the county counsel said that I probably could have went and tested and then used and then went to my visit. And she didn't even work with me to try to, ya know.

Alison's account illustrates powerfully how a social worker's interpretation of parental behavior, separate from a parent's own definition of it, can shape case progress and outcome. Although Alison lived in a residential drug treatment program at the time of the hearing, her recent arrest was interpreted as a lack of commitment to her rehabilitation. With that new definition, Alison's social worker, who had advocated for her, began viewing her behavior with suspicion and arguing against returning her children to her.

Because many parents perceive social workers as adversaries who should be tolerated but not trusted, their strategies reflect this distrust, while acknowledging the need to defer. For example, Barbara Estes, a white mother of three in her mid-twenties entered CPS when her Latino husband Mateo was accused of spiral-fracturing her daughter's leg. She advised, "I think you should cooperate with them. If you don't, [things] are only going to get worse for you." Like Barbara, almost every parent I interviewed said that they would advise parents starting out in CPS to do whatever is asked of them. Robert suggests, "Just don't object to anything that they say. Never argue with them. Stay deep in prayers." Robert explained that part of successful management of social worker interactions required allowing social workers to feel powerful:

> Give them advice such as the fact that as long as they believe or know that they have the upper hand, the chances are much greater for them to get their children back… meaning just they shouldn't be like, well, just humble yourself. If not, you're going to have a lot of problems.

Though parents seem to understand what is expected of them, they do not always choose to accommodate state expectations and instead sometimes strategize their resistance to it, even in ways that may undermine their ultimate goal of reunification. For example, in the passage above, Robert describes his understanding of the deference necessary to successfully manage interactions with social workers. Yet in his own case, he did not "humble" himself or allow the workers to "know that they have the upper hand," as he recommends. In accounting for this inconsistency, he explains, "It's like I don't find myself as an unhumble person. I'm going to call a spade a spade. I mean, that's the way I am. I'm one of the best spade players in the world. You don't expect me to call a diamond a spade." Robert's story reveals his insistence that his definition of the situation was equally valid and thus could not be subordinated to that of the social worker.

In light of the clearly communicated expectation of deference, it is important to explore the reasons parents choose not—or are unable—to fulfill the role expected of them. Reflecting on her own work representing poor clients, Lucy White, an attorney who represented a client she calls Mrs. G. to a welfare appeals board, considered in a compelling essay why her client departed from the script she had prepared for her. Although she had advised her client to present herself to the court in a way she was confident would lead to the reinstatement of her benefits, Mrs. G. provided an entirely different story to the court.

In discussing this departure from the attorney-prepared narrative, White identifies how "a complex pattern of social, economic, and cultural forces underwrote the procedural formalities, repressing and devaluing her voice. ... For a moment she stepped out of the role of the supplicant. She ignored the doctrinal pigeonholes that would fragment her voice."[34]

As with White's client, many of the parents in CPS define their own priorities, even when doing so violates what they know is expected of them. In the CPS context, as in the larger welfare bureaucracy, succumbing to paternalistic expectations is a worthwhile strategy. Yet rather than provide the subordination asked of them, parents often choose to exercise the limited forms of agency available to them. Sociologist William Sewell explains that "agency arises from the actor's control of resources, which means the capacity to reinterpret or mobilize an array of resources."[35] Parents in CPS have limited control of resources. Their ability to exercise agency is bound and constrained by the social structures that surround them. However limited they are, they are nonetheless able to exercise agency by making strategic decisions about their own behavior, involvement, and level of subordination.

To better understand how parents engage with a welfare bureaucracy like CPS, one in which parents lack resources to exercise power, I use the following section to profile three parents involved in three different cases who each described their choice to resist state expectations of subordination to the CPS system and its authorities. Although the one mother and two fathers who are discussed were more articulate about their process of strategizing their behavior than are most parents, these stories provide an opportunity to examine the issues of agency and strategic decision-making in state bureaucracies in which all parents in CPS are engaged. Each of these cases demonstrates how parents attempted to challenge the system and how they narrated their choice to do so, even when they understood that their choices could lead to permanent loss of their children.

Robert Davis Robert, briefly discussed in the last chapter and the preceding sections, is a forty-one-year-old African American father of two toddler-age girls. He and his drug-addicted girlfriend Heather, an African American woman approximately his age, entered the CPS system when, according to Robert, a neighbor who was babysitting his older daughter (at the time his only child) called CPS in retaliation for something Heather had done and claimed the girl had been abandoned. The family was enrolled in in-home services and was close to having their six-month-old case closed when Robert was admitted to a psychiatric hospital. Hospital stays were not uncommon, since Robert

142 • Fixing Families

suffers from post-traumatic stress disorder following an incident he describes as a hate crime, in which three white men stripped him, locked him in the trunk of a parked car for more than thirty hours, and subsequently lit the car on fire. During his brief stay in the hospital, a drug test was reported to the court as positive, a violation of his in-home case plan, and his children were taken into protective custody. The hospital later notified the court that the test had been read incorrectly, but by then there was enough information about other familial issues, including Robert's wavering mental health, to justify out-of-home placement, and the case continued without the drug allegation.

Robert, though functionally illiterate, worked hard to participate in the process of defining his case. In court, copies of reports are distributed to parents, usually handed to them by the court clerk when they check in for that day's hearing. The parent is supposed to read the report and respond to it, advising his or her attorney of inaccuracies before the case is called before the judge. On average, parents' attorneys spend about ten to fifteen minutes with their clients before going into court. This is not enough time to read the report to them or even discuss it in any great detail, a challenge for parents who lack the ability to read it themselves. A parent's attorney can respond to the report verbally in court, but in most cases, if a parent wants items included in the record, they need to submit material in writing to a social worker for inclusion in future reports. For parents like Robert, reviewing reports and preparing written documents is challenging. As an example, on the top of each official court-generated document or report is a header consisting of a series of formatted lines. This block of text provides the date and case number, and identifies the children and parents by social security number and birth date, along with the names of the attorneys who represent them. Rather than word processing the necessary headers, Robert laboriously photocopies, cuts, and pastes those headers from existing court-generated documents to construct his own document. By doing so, he believes his papers look as official as the ones generated by the social workers or attorneys. He explains,

A lot of this paperwork I put together myself even though I can hardly read. I get people to work for me and I still do things like formats and stuff like that. I would graft it onto my paper, like a plain piece of paper and I get somebody to type this stuff all up and I cut it out and tape it down to a paper like so (showing me the paper) and cut out this section and tape it down to a piece of paper. Name of minor, date of birth and stuff like that, and I cut off numbers and stuff like that. And when things change I graft them on there. You don't really want to go through all the stuff that I go through.

He came to the interview with me with his own copy of his case file. As a topic would arise in the interview, he would pull out the correlating document. For example, when I asked if he had been ordered to take a parenting class, he confidently explained, "I completed parenting classes, I passed it. I was the star student. This person wrote a letter" and then he proceeded to search for the letter. His letters of support from friends and service providers were important to him. As he showed me handwritten character references—replete with spelling errors—he had submitted to the court and other documents he had prepared, he seemed proud of his vigilance and frustrated by how laborious participating seemed to be. Of course, parents are not expected to prepare court documents; that is the responsibility of social workers and attorneys. Robert could have at any time given these documents to his attorney, who would have evaluated their relative value to his case and, when appropriate, submitted them to the court. However, to Robert, fully participating in his own legal process—and being perceived as competent to participate—is very important. Even his choice that we meet for our interview in the downtown branch of the public library showed his desire to appear professional and competent, despite his inability to read and lack of formal education. Rather than allowing his attorney to strategize the documents for his case, Robert felt that he needed to perform these duties himself, and in so doing, tried to show legal or professional competence.

Robert is motivated to a large extent by a belief that activism can challenge and change the CPS bureaucracy. He clearly understood the expectations of the system, noting that he would advise other parents to "just humble yourself. I wouldn't advise anyone to go through the hell that I'm going through." Yet when it came to his own case, Robert was unwilling to subordinate himself. When asked why he hadn't been able to follow his own advice, he explained that he was an activist, which indeed he was. Years before, Robert had been involved in an unrelated lawsuit against the state that struck down a ban against victims of crime receiving state-funded resources if they themselves had a past criminal conviction. He was proud of this accomplishment and brought me a copy of the newspaper article about it.

Robert strongly believed that his further activism was necessary to reform the CPS system, which he viewed as deeply flawed. In large part, this view stemmed from a sense of indignation about the way in which he entered the system. Although he had never been asked to drug test or attend treatment services, he did not seem to comprehend that his case was no longer about the misread drug test, but was about his extensive history of mental illness, unstable work and housing, and prior CPS allegations. He never understood why, after the court had received letters explaining that his drug test had been misread (letters he showed me from his file), his case had continued. Nonetheless, he did attend many of his services and separated from his girlfriend Heather, who was still using drugs and not participating in court-ordered reunification services, all positive signs of his intention to reunify with his daughters. However, he never addressed the actual concerns the court was assessing and could therefore not make any significant progress toward reunifying with his daughters.

As a result of these dynamics, he became distrustful of his attorney, who he perceived had failed to fight hard enough. He described his frustration with his court-appointed attorney:

> He done a pretty good job somewhat. But he could have done better, because he never argued the allegations that was brought against me. He done a fine job protecting my rights and then he stopped. I mean a defense is a defense. To protect someone's rights is one thing, but then when there are six allegations or seven allegations and none of them is argued, ya know. That's not a full defense.

Because Robert's case was more than a year old at the time we met, I asked him if it was possible that the allegations were no longer arguable since the case had moved beyond the jurisdictional phase, where the allegations had already been accepted as true. He exasperatedly responded, "How could the judge accept that this test was positive when you have these letters to support it?" He eventually insisted that his attorney, who he came to call "a white devil," be removed from his case. After two years and at least three attorneys, Robert's case ended in the loss of his parental rights of his two daughters, who remained with Robert's mother.

Richie Lyons   Unlike Robert, Richie does not aspire to reform the CPS system. Instead, Richie, a fifty-year-old African American man, believes that resistance to the system's dominance is necessary to succeed. Richie's introduction to CPS came when he was cleaning out his stepmother's house after his father died and found several letters addressed to him from the county juvenile court. The letters explained that he had a daughter, who he had never known about, who was a dependent of the court. Christina, who had been born in jail to a drug-addicted mother, would be freed for adoption if he did not come forward. Though late in the process, Richie came to court and demanded custody of his daughter. He explained, "Yeah, and I went to court. And they thought I was crazy, especially because I have a [criminal] record that probably stands higher than this table." Richie was denied instant custody, but was offered reunification services, which he initially rejected. As he perceived the situation, he had not committed any offense to land in CPS and should therefore not be subjected to the totality of the court process for reunification.

After a month or so, Richie gained the right to visit with his daughter, at that time almost eighteen months old. After she moved through three different foster homes, Richie requested custody of her. Social workers opposed placing her with him. From the social worker's perspective, Richie's extensive criminal history dating back several decades and his lack of cooperation with social workers made him appear to be an unlikely and possibly unsafe full-time single parent of such a young child. In addition, a young healthy child like Christina is likely to be adopted. Richie described his perception of his social workers' attitudes:

> All the workers, even when I first went, the first thing they told me was you don't have a chance with your child because we've got plans for her, she's already up for adoption. I looked at the woman like she was crazy. I was like, I don't know who the hell you think you are but that's my child and I don't give a damn about your plans. And her supervisor was in the room and they gave me a reunification package and I read it and signed it and everything was cool until we got to the point where I had to go to counseling.

Although Richie signed the case plan, indicating his acceptance of it, he refused to attend his services. "I told them, no, I'm not going to them. I'm not doing them. I did not put the child in that position and I do not have a need for those kinds of services and I'm not—So they argued it in court, but they saw it my way." To his credit, Richie was able to negotiate which services he would complete, arguing that he had already completed many of the services while incarcerated. He explained, "Like I told the judge, I've been in the system since I was fourteen years old. I've been through all of that and more. And there's no need for it. There wasn't anything that they could teach me in those classes that I didn't already know." Richie explained that while anger management and financial planning classes were not required in jail, he took them anyway, commenting, "You do what you can and whatever you think will make you look good in their eyes. So it was one of those things. Plus it was a time killer." The judge, a middle-aged white man who was a former probation officer, agreed to a finite number of drug tests and an exemption from certain services based on his completion of those services in prison and jail. To Richie, this was a victory.

Richie believes that a parent can only succeed in CPS when he or she is knowledgeable of the rules of interaction. He notes,

> Like I told [my attorney], this is a game to me. This is nothing but a mind game. This is all a matter of who has the authority to do what and can I use my authority over you and make you accept it. Well, they can't use their authority over me and make me accept it.

Although he is articulate about parents' abilities to challenge state power, he also admits that at some point a parent must choose to pacify those in authority: "Well, you fight them and don't give in a hundred percent, but you have to realize that you have to give in, you have to deal with them. So you give a little. What I gave was the six drug tests and the counseling." Recognizing that his lengthy criminal record would make a judge suspicious of his ability to parent, he rationalized that the drug testing was reasonable and was willing to compromise to provide a finite number of tests, still describing himself as retaining control. Yet when pressed, Richie admits that had the court required additional services, he would have likely attended, but would have continued to refuse to fully participate, explaining that

> it would have just been a thing where I went and spent some time, I wouldn't have paid no attention. I wouldn't have given no damn what they were doing, ya know. I would have just been sitting there waiting for the clock, the time to go by. And for most of the people, that's what they're doing. They just want to get past the stages they need to get to and keep on going.

In this, Richie communicates his willingness to subordinate in body while continuing in spirit to withhold deference to the system goals.

His confidence in his ability to challenge authority comes from more than two decades in and out of the criminal justice system and the paralegal license he claims to have earned while incarcerated. He explains,

They improved me in a lot of ways and they made me more dangerous in a lot of ways. Because now I can take a pencil and paper and fuck them up just as bad as they can me. When I was in the prison system, guards and people didn't mess with me because I knew how to write things up. I could write things up and have them go to a damn psychiatrist... My main thing, with all of them, everybody now, since I'm knowledgeable of the law, is that you should be knowledgeable of what you're getting into. If you don't know what's going on, get a lawyer to give you some laws that you can sit down and read yourself and understand and find out what's going on. Most of the time the lawyers at CPS, the ones they give you, they don't want to fight for you. It's just like having a public defender in a murder trial. They ain't going to do shit for you. And that's how the lawyers are. They're tied up in the system and they're for the system and if you don't know how to buck the system, you're not going to get your children.

Richie did not have any prior experience in the CPS system. Instead, he views the judicial system—from CPS to the criminal courts to civil law—to be monolithic, with the strategy the same. In the end, Richie, who did complete his case plan, succeeded in gaining custody of his daughter. In describing his interactions with the court, he attributes his success to his ability to challenge authority.

Linda Durrant Linda, a thirty-year-old white mother of three, first entered CPS when her first son, Paul, who wasn't growing, was diagnosed as failing to thrive. Although the name of the person who reports a parent to CPS is kept confidential, Linda believes Paul's doctor reported her to CPS to retaliate against her for questioning his orders for a fifth barium swallow and radiological study in three months, which she believed was excessive. A case file was opened and she received in-home services. Less than two years later, Linda's second child, Noah, tested positive at birth for illegal drugs and both children were placed in protective custody. When Linda's case went to court, the attorneys for the county offered her a chance to narrow the focus of her case by concentrating on one or two allegations, with the county dropping the others. This is a common proposal in which the county opts to pursue the stronger allegations for which they have the better evidence—or greater concern—and abandons the lesser claims. Linda explained her perception of this proposal:

The first court attorney that I had told me that if I was to admit to the drugs, they would drop the failure to thrive. First they told me I had no rights, okay, that I had no rights at all. But they told me that if I was to admit to the drugs, then they would drop the failure to thrive. And I said, well that sounds like plea-bargaining to me. And so I went to the library and I read the book, *We Hold the Truth*, about my constitutional rights. And I took a paralegal course. I dismissed this attorney and got another court-appointed attorney. I kept this case open for six years and I refused to do the reunification because I wasn't willing to admit to something that I didn't do.[36]

Dependency hearings are civil matters; thus the notion of a plea bargain is not technically applicable. In this bureaucratic system, parents—who rarely benefit from a trial—routinely waive their right to a trial to determine their responsibility for the allegations and instead agree to allow the court to decide whether the allegations are true based on the records and reports in the case file. In some ways, the process of waiving a trial is its own demonstration of deference to state definitions. In Linda's case, the attorneys likely would have worked out a deal in which she would enter a waiver on the drug offense, which she would be hard-pressed to successfully challenge since the toxicology report on her son's delivery was on file, and the allegations that she caused her son's failure to thrive, a harder claim to substantiate, would be abandoned. Her reunification plan would have included fewer services addressing the failure to thrive issue and instead would focus on drug rehabilitation and parenting. However, Linda did not waive her right to a trial and continued to challenge all the allegations. Even after the court had found the allegations true, she continued to challenge her reunification case plan. When asked if she was ever given a reunification plan, she explains, "Oh, they did, but I refused to sign it. I refused to sign the case plan. I wasn't willing to admit to something that I didn't do. That's not right."

Linda was not popular at the courthouse. Besides changing attorneys at least twice, a process that requires a closed hearing without attorneys present where a judge hears claims of inadequate or incompetent counsel, she challenged every procedure, and by her own account, wrote frequent letters to legislators and public organizations pleading for assistance. Even after her parental rights to her oldest son, Paul, had been terminated, clearing the way for him to be adopted by his paternal aunt and uncle with whom he had been living, Linda continued to challenge the system. She told me that she had brought Paul's case to the attention of the Lieutenant Governor's office, a Democratic state legislator, the National Organization for Women, and the National Association for the Advancement of Colored People (who had their own community-based initiative to examine CPS practice), and was also trying to find an attorney to handle a civil suit against the county. Reflecting on her case, she commented, "They did not like me because I had been fighting them; I got the balls and they didn't like it."

On the day we met, months after her parental rights to Paul had been terminated, but before he had been formally adopted, the county counsel's office called Linda to discuss her case. According to Linda, the attorney complimented her on the brief she had written and offered her "co-kinship" with Paul's aunt and uncle.[37] This is an unusual offer in which she would retain some parental privileges, such as the right to visitation and ongoing contact. Rather than discussing this offer with her attorney, Linda interpreted it as a sign that the county counsel's office was scared that she was going to win her appeal and she declined. The next I heard of Linda, she had finally called her attorney to complain that she was having problems with Paul's aunt and uncle, now his adoptive parents, who were not permitting her to visit.

By the time she had Micah, a third son born to her and her new husband, she was living in a residential church-run drug program. Despite her attempts to resist her case plan, she nonetheless completed many court-mandated services because the treatment program required the same services. As a result, CPS never removed Micah from her and returned Noah with ongoing monitoring. She was able to reunify with Noah, whose case had begun after Paul's and was thus on a separate "track" for reunification. More recently, one of her former attorneys said that she was filing a grievance against him with the state bar.

Activist Parenting and Counterproductivity

Like the vast majority of parents in the CPS system, all three of these parents are poor. All three lacked formal education, material resources, and the accompanying cultural capital that would have allowed them to negotiate the system more successfully. As an example, I observed a case in which a white middle-class man who entered the CPS system because his ex-wife failed to protect their preteen daughter from molestation was awarded custody of his daughter without any required services. I have no doubt that his education and profession—and accompanying stable housing situation and lack of criminal history—allowed him to avoid reunification services in a way Richie could not. Candace Williams-Taylor's husband, an African American professional, discussed in chapter 4, was also able to escape court supervision for his two sons. It is impossible to ignore the ways in which the intersections of race and class affect parents' experiences with CPS. Yet parents' relative successes and failures are not fixed by their status; they are active participants in their own destinies. Parents' situated knowledge comes from their social locations and life experiences, and informs their decisions about how to strategize and manage interactions with the state, as illustrated in each of these stories. In each case, parents attempted to participate in efforts to define them and their treatment needs. Rather than ignore the process completely, as Robert's girlfriend Heather did, each of these parents engaged state actors and the larger process.

In many ways, the parents in these cases embrace a story of themselves as free from culpability. Although Robert was wracked with many problems that made his ability to parent questionable, he focused solely on the misreported drug test. As he was referred for psychological exam after psychological exam, each attempting to determine whether he was sane enough to raise his daughters, he continued to focus on the drug issue, perhaps making him appear less healthy. Similarly Linda was driven by the unsupported allegation that she was responsible for her son's failure to thrive. She believed the pediatrician had made a false report in retaliation for her attempts to question the multiple tests he had ordered and that the county's offer to abandon the allegation proved her innocence.

As a civil court, the CPS system has no notion of judicial guilt or innocence. Rather, the key issue is whether or not the court believes the parent is responsible for the harm that befell a child and how that can be addressed through the ongoing process of reunification services provision and assessment. Linda's unwavering battle over her innocence in a system that has no such term did not serve her well. Her fixation on her innocence allowed her to define herself as a good parent who was wronged; she could then ignore the undisputed fact that she had used drugs throughout her second pregnancy and had delivered a baby who had tested positive for drugs at birth. Richie, who actually was free from culpability, enjoyed the moral righteousness that came with it. He was never asked to explain why he had fathered both Christina and his other toddler-aged daughter, Laquanda, with drug-addicted women, nor why he didn't know about Christina's birth until the court intervened. Instead, he felt entitled to custody of his daughter since he had not personally committed an act that landed her in the system.

Many parents view themselves as innocent or free of culpability. In this way, these three parents are not exceptional. What is useful in their cases is to see how they remained engaged with the court process and articulated their strategies, including their unwillingness to defer. This is in contrast to other parents who felt they were innocent and withdrew from the process completely, or ones like Mateo, the father who denies breaking his daughter's leg, who believes the court was wrong but deferred to its processes and definitions anyway. Many of the parents who do stay engaged while refusing to defer are guided by a belief that they can fully participate in defining the reunification process by challenging procedures or operating within the rules established by the court. They did not necessarily question the nature of the formal legal process; instead, they are concerned with whether the system is operating appropriately, in accordance with the principles of impartial justice to which they subscribe.[38]

Each of the three parents discussed above believed in the model of judicial process: both Linda and Richie described themselves as self-trained paralegals and imagined a future career in the field. Though Robert was not legally trained, he had experienced success in challenging an unfair state policy. As a result, they could each recognize how they were being treated unjustly. Linda explained, "It's like, whatever happened to freedom of speech, ya know? I never threatened anyone's life, I never harmed a child, I never would; I've been accused of things like that, even by my mother... But you're supposed to be innocent until you're proven guilty. Not in this system." Richie boasted of his willingness to call a supervisor when he believed a social worker had overstepped her power by demanding more than what the court ordered, suggesting his acceptance of the bureaucratic hierarchy. Perhaps because of their claims of legal training or experience, all three stayed consistently engaged with the process, with Robert and Linda writing and submitting briefs, letters, and documents. Although they perceived these efforts to be a symbol of their full participation, college-educated and professionally trained lawyers, judges, and social workers—who live in a different socioeconomic world—did not always respect their efforts, nor ascribe credibility to the handwritten letters, rife with grammar and spelling errors.

The stark difference between Richie's case and those of Linda and Robert is that Richie actually succeeded in reunifying with his daughter while the other two did not. Although several factors contributed to these outcomes, one of the most important factors is the difference in their willingness to accept the state's authority. Richie considered the CPS process to be a game, not unlike the power games he played for more than two decades while facing criminal charges or incarceration. Although he spoke of the importance of challenging state power, he also recognized what he needed to do to get what he wanted. Richie did not accept the state as a parental entity that could help parents. Describing his belief that the social workers tried to initially intimidate him into abandoning his bid for his daughter, he explains,

> Nine out of ten people do [what CPS demands] because they don't know how to fight them. Ya know, so nine out of ten people, they tell them, "well you have no more authority to see your child," and they accept that, ya know. And then it's all about you jumping through hoops to see your child. It's like, "I want you to do this, I want you to do that." It doesn't say anything about what you're required to do. It's "I want;" it's a personal thing. It's "this is what I want you to do."

Richie believed that the CPS system was not designed to help parents and perceived it as an adversary in an elaborate chess game; he recognized which pieces he would be willing to sacrifice to win. In the end, at home with his two young daughters, it is clear that he did. He made it through the system with his sense of self intact and with the perception that while he performed the necessary amount of deference, he never truly subordinated to the system.

Linda and Robert's cases ended differently. Both challenged the authority of the state and attempted to participate in the process of defining the situation. Neither was fully successful. Linda was able to regain custody of Noah, who was not as far into the system as Paul, since Paul's case was open long before Noah was born, and she never lost her baby Micah. However, she did lose her parental rights to Paul because of her unwillingness to succumb to the state's definition of her situation. Ironically, CPS was willing to abandon the allegations on Paul altogether (the only child she lost), but with the positive toxicology report on Noah, the state could not abandon their view of her as a problem mother needing rehabilitation. Given that the case lasted six years, the system was to some extent engaging her too, even accepting her unintentional compliance as case progress. On several occasions Linda was offered a way to save face, provided that she defer to the state's authority. In each of these instances, she interpreted the offers as signs of her own efficacy and rebuked them. She truly believed that learning her legal rights and challenging the procedures would somehow allow her to prevail. She then refused her reunification plan outright and did not attempt to comply. When asked to account for her failure to regain custody of Paul, she explained, "It's this whole thing, the lies, there's so much. There's a cover up, there's corruption." She did not recognize any way in which she contributed to her own case failure.

Robert's case is perhaps the saddest of all. Despite his elaborate efforts to participate in the proceedings, he was unable to fully comprehend the nature of his case. Although he laboriously tried to demonstrate competence through his cutting and pasting, he was not able to perform deference. When we met at the library for our interview, he brought with him a video camera with footage of that week's unsupervised visitation so that I could see his daughters. I was also able to see how much he loved them and how central they, and the case, were to his life. As he meticulously organized his court documents, attempting to demonstrate his full participation as an equal, he missed the larger point: the court wanted to know that he was capable of caring for two young children and would not lapse into psychoses that might place them in danger. He never comprehended this, and like Linda, he was unable to strategize compromises in the way Richie did.

REALIZING SYSTEM GOALS: MEANS AND ENDS

Attorneys and system insiders argue that the breadth and depth of surveillance, as well as the totalizing nature of the reunification process, is essential to knowing whether or not risk has been reduced. Without extensive recording of parental behavior, the state would be unable to determine whether a child would be safe returning home. For example, without extensive note-taking during supervised visits, the court would not have known about a father, identified as having "boundary issues," who, during such a visit, paid his daughter five dollars to give him a massage. Another father whose case I observed in court sucked his infant daughter's tongue and licked drool off her chin, also during a court-ordered supervised visit. Indisputably, these fathers can't reasonably be believed to be responsible caretakers. Arguably then, the microscopic management of some parents is appropriate in light of the acts that bring their families into the system. Even if we accept that surveillance is reasonable—or even necessary—there is little reason to believe that parents will passively accept it. Instead, parents often attempt to challenge state control over them. In many cases, parental transgressions—including housing instability; lack of adequate food, health care, or childcare; drug addiction; or even criminal behavior—represent problems perceived by the parents to be beyond their control. Even as they perceive themselves to be of limited responsibility, they usually know that deference is expected of them. As illustrated in the stories above, parents often refuse to provide it, even when it sometimes means losing their children.

Parental resistance frustrates the attorneys who represent the children, the county, and often the parents themselves, although usually for different reasons. Children's attorneys rarely recommend returning children to their biological parents, and instead advocate for new homes with new parents for the children. From their perspective, parents who do not complete services, do not show appropriate deference, and do not try to address the issues that brought them into the system are not appropriate caretakers for their clients. As Andrea Winnow, a children's attorney in her early thirties, explained, "I have to wonder what my client will thank me for when he's twenty-five. Will he thank me for returning him to these parents or finding him a better home?" Noncompliant parents are not perceived as the type to whom a child would be grateful to be returned.

Members of the office of the county counsel hate the volume of cases on which they are filing petitions and the accompanying expense to the system. Joan Billings, a white veteran attorney for the county approaching retirement, is frustrated with the huge amount of money spent on the people who become CPS clients. She notes, "They use child abuse money, criminal justice money, healthcare money...they use ambulances." Describing the disproportionate use of public money with dismal outcomes, Joan sighs: "We pay for them on this end as children and on the other as criminals."

In many ways, these two positions represent state policy around family reunification, and even public assistance more generally. Andrea Winnow's remarks, typical of children's attorneys, embody state fiscal policy that allocates resources for adoption, but not reunification or family maintenance. Joan's comments reflect state ideology that blames poor people for using public resources, even when they do so by becoming incarcerated.

Parents' attorneys almost always argue that children belong with their biological parents, unless the crime against the children is egregious. With an eye on the costs of out-of-home care, they acknowledge that children often fail to thrive when raised in state care and believe that imperfect biological parents who love their children are usually better than care providers who receive a monthly stipend (and there are usually several in children's lives). Yet they too are frustrated by parental resistance.

For parents' attorneys, walking into court to argue that children belong with their parents is difficult when parents haven't made any attempt to comply with court orders. Parents, like Robert and Linda, who profess their innocence, even after the allegations have been substantiated, complicate their attorneys' efforts to advocate for them. The "reality therapy" in which parents' attorneys like Dan engage, or the stern talks parents receive from judges are meant to inspire parental compliance. When Sam directs a client to make the social worker his or her new best friend, he is communicating institutional knowledge that compliance is necessary to succeed in reunification. Some parents remain angry and are never able to satisfy state expectations because they feel indignant that their privacy has been invaded. Although these parents may participate in the proceedings, they choose not to engage with the case everyone else is addressing. Their comments appear irrelevant; they have failed to get over their anger and move on. As such, they are seen as incapable of safely caring for their children.

I have argued that the reunification period is a process of reforming and reassessing parental behavior. Parents who refuse to reform, who resist state control, who refuse to be parented by the state, almost always fail to regain custody of their children. Their lack of deference signifies a lack of parental capability to decision makers. Parents who do not attend court-ordered services stand little chance of reunifying with their children because the system has no other mechanism to assess parental reformation. Parents who do not attend court-ordered visits with their children call their commitment to their children into question. As Monica Giles, a white attorney for the county in her early thirties, considers noncompliant parents, remarks, "I can't understand how parents can't get it together for visits. Maybe because they're not very functional, but if I couldn't get it together for any other service, I would at least make visits." Indeed, whether someone misses visits, regardless of the reason, affects how she and other attorneys are likely to approach a case and the kinds of outcomes for which they will advocate.

Parents may indeed, in many cases, lack the ability—or resources necessary—to "get it together." As noted at the beginning of this chapter, Susanna lacked transportation. Desire to see her daughter did not necessarily help her attend visits, particularly as the visits moved each time her daughter changed foster homes. Similarly Juan's failure to make visits was a byproduct of his attempts to maintain paid employment as an interstate trucker. In this obvious way, class influences who can be perceived as a decent parent. Addressing this, Richie attributes much of CPS's failure to the social distance between service providers and clients. He explains,

The thing about the system is that half of the people in the system don't know where the people that are getting involved in the system are coming from. Ya know, they don't know anything about the ghetto life, as they say. Do you understand what I'm saying?

They don't know that this kid might get up and might not have food in his house everyday and it might not be because mom's on drugs, it might just be because there's not enough money. But they don't have any firsthand experience with these people and that kind of life.

Similarly Gloria Ward, a forty-one-year-old African American mother of two, describes her impression of CPS, also pointing to the difference social distance can make in the relationship between social workers and clients:

It depends on the worker I guess. Each individual worker is different; they go about a situation differently. I think if you've never lived in poverty or in low-income areas, then you don't know what a person goes through that lives there. And I had a worker who actually lived out here and went to school out here and we were really close. She understood what I was going through and things. Ya know, she helped me a lot.

Both Gloria and Richie articulate the importance of their lived experience and the state's devaluing of it. In deferring to state definitions, parents find their own definitions of their lives discarded. For parents whose own definitions resemble those of the state, deference is easier. However, for parents whose concept of self and family differ dramatically from those of the state, deference is harder and more costly. Clearly, the resonance of definitions is shaped by class and race.

Because so many of the families who enter CPS are poor, improving their lives will take more than the limited services they are assigned and longer than the time granted. Yet, even with adequate services, no service strategy, however well-conceived and tested, can substitute for the basics of adequate income, housing, healthcare, education, and public safety.[39] But services do not focus specifically on addressing a lack of material resources. If they did, housing, childcare, and transportation would not be major stumbling blocks to reunification. Instead, the ability to overcome material deprivation becomes further evidence of a parent's commitment to his or her children, a yardstick middle-class parents aren't measured against. Yet the ability to rise above structural limitations, the willingness to ride busses all day to appointments, to continue to drug test despite the lack of evidence that drugs are an issue, all become additional ways parents can demonstrate their commitment to their children and their deference to state goals for their families.

6

COURT-ORDERED EMPOWERMENT AND THE REFORMATION OF MOTHERS IN CPS

Shelly Summerland, a thirty-seven-year-old white woman, sits at the small table in a conference room in the new courthouse. Her attorney, Sam Richman, a white man who is slightly younger, sits across the table. Since her case has been going on for more than eight months, and since she is one of the parents who calls her attorney frequently, she appears comfortable as she discusses her case with him.

Today's hearing is more convoluted than most. She is here so the court can examine the progress she and her boyfriend, Frank Ramirez, have made on their case, which started when their son Francisco tested positive for methamphetamine at birth. When Francisco was placed in protective custody, Shelly's six young daughters were also removed from her custody. (Shelly has eight children from a prior marriage, though only her six young daughters are in state care, since her nineteen-year-old daughter is no longer a minor and her sixteen-year-old son lives at a residential "boy's ranch".) In addition to measuring Frank and Shelly's progress, there are at least two other issues that will be addressed today. Shelly's sister-in-law, who has been providing out-of-home care to two of her daughters, can't take care of them anymore and they need to move to a different relative's house. Shelly's relatives have taken placement of all six girls; however, because Francisco inherited dark skin from his part Cuban and part African American father,

Shelly's family is unwilling to take him. As a result, Francisco lives with Frank's uncle and his girlfriend, though Frank's mother is in the process of applying to become his caretaker. Today's proceeding will reassign Shelly's two daughters to a new home. The third issue of the day is the most complicated. The county will present a petition that Frank molested Shelly's daughters.

Sam explains that the statements of three-year-old Kaylie are the most damning. The other children all say that there is no way Frank did anything. Nonetheless, the children's attorney, Tess Bachmeier, will argue that the court should find the petition true. Sam explains that it is possible the court might find the petition true, based on the preponderance of the evidence, thus accepting that Frank is a predator. He adds that the social worker wrote nice things about Shelly in the report—the same report that supports these new allegations. Shelly shakes her head. "I find it hard to believe, but if the court finds it true, I'll do whatever it takes." Sam tells her that this is the perfect response and encourages her to express that to the judge should the allegations be sustained.

Shelly and Sam agree that they will not oppose the request to move the children from her sister-in-law's to her cousin's, nor will they object to any effort to medically examine her daughters for signs of sexual assault. Their shared goal is to keep the case moving toward reunification. Shelly anticipates the proceeding and laughs, remarking that Tess will not likely cooperate. "You know her."

Sam sighs. "She has been a thorn." It is unclear whether Sam is drawing specifically on Tess's behavior in Shelly's case or remembering his experiences with Tess when they worked for the same firm representing parents—before she changed "sides."

The only thing Shelly wants is for Sam to request unsupervised visits for her. Then she clarifies. "Even if they want me to be supervised, that's fine. I just need more time with them." She currently has one hour a week with each of six children, though she sees them according to placement. This means she sees two daughters at each visit, and then sees Francisco alone. Technically she could see them more if her relatives with whom her daughters are placed agreed to supervise, but thus far they haven't. Shelly complains that they say they don't have time to help with visits. "They won't work with me." Frustrated, she makes it clear that her family resents her relationship with Frank, which she initiated before she had completely separated from her drug-addicted ex-husband.

Sam tells her that she won't get unsupervised visits until the sexual abuse allegation is resolved because she is still living with Frank, now a suspected child molester. Sam suggests that she consider moving out from his apartment and getting a job to support herself. Shelly replies, "That's tough if you've never had a job." She explains that she will also have a difficult time securing housing because, in addition to having no work history, her credit history is terrible. Sam tells her that she can get a referral to emergency housing. Noticing the way Shelly's normally cheerful demeanor is wilting, Sam smiles and tells her that he has "cautious optimism" that she'll get her kids back.

A month later, things are markedly improved. The judge still can't rule on the molestation allegations because he is waiting for the physical evidence report. The social worker wants to refer Shelly to a domestic violence support program, although there is no suggestion that she has been abused. Tess argues that in the interim, Shelly should be ordered to attend "nonoffending sexual abuse counseling," designed to help women better protect their children. The judge shakes his head and explains that he is concerned that Shelly, with her existing services, might become overwhelmed if he were to add nonoffender counseling. Shelly insists that she is okay with it.

The judge also orders Shelly's relatives who are providing care to her children to be more cooperative with her and to facilitate visits. He grants Shelly four hours of visits on the weekend, with discretion over when and if they will be supervised left to her social worker. Frank will have to submit to a psychiatric evaluation before the next hearing date. Most likely, the judge hopes this will ferret out whether the allegations of molestation are true or are the invention of the relatives who hate Frank—and hate Shelly for having a relationship with a black man.

* * *

THE BAD MOTHER IN PUBLIC IMAGINATION AND INSTITUTIONS

Women attempting to reunify with their children are expected to become adequate mothers, in part by conforming to cultural definitions of good mothering that expect mothers to always be available to their children, to spend time with them, guide, support, encourage, correct, love, and care for them physically. Mothers are responsible for the cleanliness of their home environment, are unselfish, and put their children's needs before their own.[1] The dominant ideology of motherhood has been widely critiqued as overly reliant on images of white and middle-class women, as impossible to achieve, and as the basis for criticism of all mothers.[2] However, this construct goes virtually unquestioned in the CPS system. Instead, women in the CPS system are encouraged to embrace tropes that expect mothers to be self-sacrificing, chaste, and able to demonstrate that children are the center of their lives. Because mothers are believed to be naturally or instinctively nurturing, sacrificing, and nonviolent, any deviation from that norm seems "uniquely abhorrent."[3]

Unlike the archetypal good mother, CPS mothers are viewed as bad mothers. By the time they reach the reunification stage, their culpability is no longer in question. As a cultural image, the bad mother may include "those that did not live in a 'traditional' nuclear family; those who would not or could not protect their children from harm; and those whose children went wrong."[4] Law professor Annette Appell writes of CPS mothers specifically, "Bad mothers are the mothers who get caught."[5] Mothers are presumed to be children's primary natural caretakers; as such, they are ultimately responsible for the care of—or failure to care for—their children. As legal scholar Dorothy Roberts observes, "The duty imposed on mothers to protect their children is unique and enormous. Mothers have an immediate and unavoidable duty to care for their children from the moment of birth, if not the moment of conception."[6] Thus many mothers entered the CPS system because of the actions or behaviors of the men with whom they are involved, and the perception that they failed in their duty to protect their children rather than because they actively harmed their children.

Child Protective Services is not only concerned with cases of physical abuse. Many of the problems of home life that lead to CPS intervention— drug use, weapons, nonfamilial adults in the home who may be inappropriate for children, distractions that lead to neglect, or the abuse of the mother in the presence of children—may be instigated by the man in the house. In these cases, CPS holds women responsible for failing to protect their children. (Women may also face criminal prosecution depending on their level of knowledge of the crimes or their participation in them, issues not addressed here.) As active or passive victimizers of their children, mothers in the CPS system are understood to be bad mothers.

Although the assumptions that mothers are primary caretakers make them responsible even when they are not culpable, they also define mothers as fundamentally necessary to child well-being. As such, the court holds that mothers should be assisted in addressing the issues that led to their maternal shortcomings and be reformed if possible. (If reform is not possible, then an alternative should be pursued.)

Whether reform is believed to be possible hinges on the perception of the neglectful or abusive mother who is perceived in two possible ways: "She is either blamed for her individual, autonomous choice to abuse her child, or she is pitied for her victimization and her utter lack of choice."[7] The two roles—abuser and victim—are not equally available to all women at the outset. For example, women who physically abuse or torture their children are rarely viewed as victims, no matter how horrific their own histories or present situation may be, and may not even be offered an opportunity to reunify with their children.[8] Women who use illegal drugs or alcohol during their pregnancies may be perceived as either victim or abuser. On one hand, drug use during pregnancy is often framed as an issue of in utero child abuse; on the other hand, drug addiction is also medicalized and framed as a sign of needed intervention and services. Overall, the perceived egregiousness of the offense shapes how women in CPS are viewed.

When the victim rhetoric is available to mothers in CPS, child abuse professionals—social workers, attorneys, and judges—usually recognize that these mothers have themselves been victimized in the past and do not know how to make good decisions for themselves and their children, especially in their relationships with men. This recognition stems from research and theory that has suggested that women may not be able to protect themselves or their children due to their limited power in the family.[9] Pointing to the connection between mothers' failures to protect their children from harm by others and their own victimization, legal scholar Dorothy Roberts suggests that "maternal failures can only be assessed in the context of mothers' own experience of domestic violence."[10] Not all women who enter the CPS system are battered. Nonetheless, the rhetoric of victimization permeates reunification and creates a perception of CPS mothers as needing help. (This can be seen in the efforts to enroll Shelly in domestic violence support services, despite a lack of evidence that she was abused.) Those who work in CPS often feel sympathy for the women whose children have been removed. Even so, the main goal of the system remains protecting children from their parents. As shown in chapter 5, if parents can be reformed, they can be allowed to parent again. If not, their children will be permanently placed elsewhere. For women who are perceived as victims (and who do not call their victim status into question by resisting efforts to help them), a different expectation for resocialization exists: empowerment.

This chapter looks first at the expectations of all mothers in CPS, focusing on how the CPS system enforces definitions of appropriate mothers as self-sacrificing and chaste, which can be best demonstrated by abstaining from intimate relationships with men. I then examine the discourse of needed empowerment that envelopes mothers who are viewed sympathetically as victims themselves. These women face expectations that they will become empowered in ways recognizable to the court so that they can successfully parent. Thus I show how these mothers must "perform" empowerment, as prescribed by the state, to reunify with their children. By providing this empowerment performance, mothers communicate their acceptance of the state's goals for their rehabilitation, which serves to demonstrate their submission to state authority, another form of deference.

RESOCIALIZING BAD MOTHERS

The court assumes that women must abstain from relationships with men in order to address their family dysfunction and focus on self-improvement. The men who are identified by CPS as unsafe for children have histories of criminal behavior, lack consistent employment, and are likely to be somewhat transient in lifestyle. By focusing on these characteristics, CPS often identifies poor men as "bad men," that is, men whose social or criminal histories shape a view of them as unsafe to be near children. In light of the significant racism in the judicial system and the overrepresentation of poor men and men of color in the criminal justice system, certain men are also more likely to be identified. It is worth noting that if a woman in the CPS system met a man with a white-collar career who was free of a criminal or CPS history, her involvement with him might not be a detriment, and could even be perceived as an asset. In my observations, I never observed a CPS mother with a boyfriend who met these criteria.[11]

Child Protective Services procedures and practices explicitly communicate that mothers should avoid bad men. During the reunification process, a woman is sanctioned if she develops or continues a relationship with a man to whom she is not married. For example, Pam Marsh, a white woman in her late twenties, completed her services and reunified with her son, only to be arrested on an outstanding warrant. At the time of the hearing, she was incarcerated but hoped for an early release. During a hearing to decide where her son should be placed during her incarceration, she argued to the court, "I worked hard to get him back. I've been a good mother to him since I've been sober. After this, I have no other violations." Pointedly, Judge Thompson, a white man in his early forties, asserted, "You need to not just get out of jail. You need to get your boyfriend out of your life. He is not an appropriate person to be around a child." By complying with demands to abandon intimate relationships, women demonstrate that they have prioritized their bond with their children above all others, especially above the romantic relationships that the court believes led them (directly or indirectly) into the system in the first place. This serves to communicate their deference to the system's definitions, even as they represent parenting norms that are situated in meanings of race and class.

In instances where a mother is legally married, particularly when it is to the biological father of her children, the court may support her choice to continue a relationship with him, depending on his perceived level of culpability. However, mothers often find that their cases fare better if they separate from their husbands. This realization is facilitated by the practice of appointing a separate attorney for each parent, since they may have different and competing interests. In virtually all cases, the court communicates that women are better off without men. For example, I observed a case where a child was removed from his mother, Latanya Jones, because his stepfather sold drugs out of their home. Latanya, an African American woman in her late twenties, reportedly allowed her husband to stay at the house, despite court orders forbidding it, following her son's return. The mother came to court and explained that her husband was not living at her house, that he simply came by to visit and only came by when her son was not home. Judge Thompson exploded, stating, "I am not going to play games with you over the meaning of the word '*live!*'" adding that he believed that in fact her husband was sleeping over. The judge, a former probation officer, explained that if there were positive reports from counselors, he would relax the court orders, but if the reports were not positive, "I don't care how long you've been married, I won't allow him there."

The monitoring of mothers' intimate relationships by state officials is not new, and in fact has been part of social work practice since its inception. Illustrating this, social welfare scholar Karen Tice's analysis of early child welfare records shows how social workers in the Progressive Era shifted their focus to become more attentive to issues of women's sexual behavior:

> They revised the long tradition of efforts to rescue and protect indigent and immigrant women that had directed much of the work done in evangelical maternity homes and protective residences for working women. Instead, they focused upon saving society from "morally tainted" women and girls thought to be capable of "infecting its members with a moral evil more hideous than physical disease."[12]

Until recently, welfare workers used a "man-in-the-house rule" to deny women welfare benefits. Under this policy, the presence of a man, sometimes inferred from items, laundry, or shoes, automatically made a home "unsuitable" and was considered evidence that financial need did not exist, irrespective of who the man was, his economic situation, or his relationship to the family. The prohibition against having a man around was enforced by welfare agencies through the use of "midnight raids," unannounced searches of welfare recipients' homes, carried out without a warrant, until the Supreme Court declared them unconstitutional in 1968.[13]

The man-in-the-house policy as a determinant of welfare eligibility has given way to a post-1996 welfare reform policy that promotes marriage as an escape route from public assistance. The 1996 welfare reform act specifically aimed to "encourage the formation and maintenance of two-parent families."[14] More recently, federal law grants hundreds of millions of public dollars to states, localities, and private agencies for programs that encourage marriage.[15] As one federal report on marriage promotion activities explains,

> Recognizing not only changing social forces but also the enduring benefits of marriage, state and local governments, faith-based institutions, non-profit organizations and businesses are developing innovative approaches to promoting safe and stable marriages. These approaches range from changing welfare rules to developing marriage education programs to community organizing and media and education campaigns.[16]

Returning to women's experience in the CPS system, the requirement that women avoid relationships with men contradicts the state goal that women should be married to avoid public assistance. However, because the men in CPS are recognized as neither competent breadwinners nor fathers, they cease to be an asset to women. The presence of men not related to the child—most acutely those with a criminal history involving illegal drugs, violence, or driving under the influence—is seen as an indicator of likely maltreatment. Although the state no longer determines benefits based on women's relationships with men, the presence of men does affect perceptions of risk. As one investigating CPS social worker told me, "We still use the man-in-the-house rule. It's just us now," rather than benefits eligibility workers.

Attorneys, social workers, and judges who are responsible for enforcing a policy that mothers must abstain from relationships with men, do not consider it problematic; rather, such a policy is widely accepted by the players in the system, including parents' own advocates. Sam Richman, a parents' attorney, explains why he believes banning women from dating is reasonable:

It's the 65–35 rule: 65 percent [of the men] are bad news…There are enough good guys that have a couple DUI's or just look scuzzy…There are plenty of decent guys who fall in love with CPS mothers. But overall, I don't think that is a bad rule to have…65 percent are worse than the dads.

Here Sam alludes to the possibility that women in the CPS system may enter relationships with men who pose a risk to them or their children, as in many cases, the children's fathers did. Sam added that mothers "need to take it slow" and that such prohibitions help women to do so. Shirley Dalton's case exemplifies Sam's point.

Shirley, a thirty-one-year-old white woman with eight children by five different African American fathers, received in-home services. In this arrangement, she had an open case file, but her children were not dependents of the juvenile court and had never been out of her care or custody. As part of her case plan, family maintenance workers—pseudo social workers who usually have a high school education—provided Shirley with parenting classes, transportation vouchers, emergency groceries and cleaning supplies, and help with public assistance applications and referrals. They also monitored the home, health, and behavior of her and her children. Typically family maintenance cases are open for six months and if the risk to the children is assessed to be reduced, the case is closed. Parents who are not able to address the issues identified by social workers or whose living situations do not improve (or worsen) during the period of family maintenance usually lose custody of their children.

I first met Shirley in May when I accompanied Thao Vue, an investigating social worker, to her home. He wanted to see whether Shirley had cleaned her house, as discussed at his last visit, and had gotten medical attention for her three-year-old daughter who had burned her arm on the wall-mounted heating unit. When we arrived, the family maintenance worker who had brought over cleaning supplies and had coached her through the scouring process was there. Her four-year-old son slept on the couch, undisturbed by the three adults speaking above him. The three-year-old girl with the burn shyly watched us from her room. Standing in the corner in her underwear, she coyly asked me to help her get dressed. The baby, close to one year old, was picked up and put down by Shirley throughout the visit. As we prepared to leave, Shirley's eight-year-old son, returning home from school, came in and proudly explained to the social worker how he had helped clean the house. Her twelve-year-old daughter walked in a short time later. Shirley's new boyfriend, a thin African American man, likely in his thirties, who was staying with her, was also present. The boyfriend, a man with a known drug-related felony conviction, boasted to the investigating social worker that as money runs low at the end of the month, he helps her out. Yet at the other end of the small house, Shirley confided in me that her boyfriend had only started a job that week and would soon be able to contribute, suggesting that she was financially supporting him and her eight children on her meager public assistance grant.

Shirley failed in-home services in August and her children were placed under intensive supervision, remaining in her home, but under the legal custody of the court with more frequent social worker visits. Finally, they were removed the following April. Social workers identified the ongoing presence in her home of boyfriends like the one described above as the primary reason in-home services failed. At a hearing to address visitation with her children, Andrea Winnow, the children's attorney, opposed granting Shirley unsupervised visits, arguing, "The mother has continued to bring unsuitable men into the house and has been told by social workers repeatedly not to bring unsuitable men into minors' presence, and that has been ignored."

While the judge ordered liberal visitations for the fathers of Shirley's children, he ordered supervised visitations for Shirley "to be arranged and directed" by the social worker. Illustrating the perception of Shirley as unable to refrain from relationships with men, the judge ordered that Shirley's reunification case plan should include services to address "appropriate boundaries, if deemed appropriate by a therapist." Although the cleanliness of her home bounced above and below the social worker's determined line of minimal acceptability, the core issue in Shirley's case was not about her care of her children or home. Rather it was about her unwillingness to exclude men from her life, which was required while under court supervision.

Shirley was most likely overwhelmed while home during the day with four children, all too young for school, and four more when they returned from school. She also seemingly allowed "bad" men to stay with her and her children, including at least one who had been convicted of a drug-related felony, even when she had been cautioned that this would lead to her children being placed in foster care. In doing so, Shirley failed to communicate that she had prioritized her children over her own sexual desires. Yet the underlying reasons for this failure can be viewed in two possible lights. Whether we understand Shirley as someone who made bad choices because she doesn't care about her children, or whether we believe that her own history of victimization has left her without the ability to make good decisions for herself and her children alters our vision for how Shirley should be treated in court. As a poor choice maker, she has proven herself unable to parent. As a victim, she is in need of assistance to learn new skills. Shirley's case would hinge on whether or not she would accept her state-defined need for therapeutic help in learning to set boundaries and communicate a desire to address that issue.

CONTEXTUALIZING MATERNAL SALVATION

The concern that women may not be able to stand up for themselves is rooted to some extent in the successful efforts of feminist organizations and women's advocacy groups to bring domestic violence out of the darkness of American family life. Legal scholar Kate Bartlett argues, "It was the contemporary women's rights movement that generated interest in, and response to, domestic violence as a social issue with severe consequences for many women."[17] These efforts helped to create battered women's shelters and hotlines; reforms in police and prosecutorial practice, including laws that no longer require a victim to press charges; and new legal definitions and psychological understandings of the victim, including the legal recognition of battered woman's syndrome. Battered woman's syndrome describes a constellation of symptoms resulting from chronic abuse and has been used most famously to defend women who eventually kill their batterers. However, the syndrome also contributed to a new understanding of women who live in relationships in which they lack power.

Research has pointed out that many women who are abused have low self-esteem and feel inadequate or helpless in defending themselves or leaving their abusive partner. These women also lack the economic and personal resources to leave, or lack a support system from which to draw strength.[18] Accepting that women could benefit from psychological treatment, one feminist treatment program designed to treat battered women strives to achieve this end by focusing on changing the victim:

> Feminist therapy for battered women does not attempt to change the behavior of batterers, but rather to minimize the violence suffered by the client. When the woman demonstrates… that she intends to stop or diminish the violence against her, the batterer is left with the responsibility to choose whether to stop or continue his violent behavior. By seeking help, a woman increases her strength and power relative to her abuser.[19]

There is little doubt that an overwhelming number of CPS mothers have been victimized at some point in their life. Although the specific rates of abuse among CPS mothers may be unknown, we do know that prior abuse impairs parenting. Research suggests that mothers of sexually abused children are disproportionately more likely to have been abused themselves and that mothers who were sexually abused in childhood are less likely to provide appropriate structure, consistent discipline, and clear behavioral expectations for their children.[20] Other studies suggest that many of the patterns established early in life dictate the kinds of relationships these women are likely to seek out. As such, the prohibition on relationships with men is not entirely illogical. Children who are maltreated are much more likely to have been abused by a boyfriend or stepfather than a biological parent. One study in *Pediatrics* found that "the increased risk of maltreatment death… occurs primarily in households including biologically unrelated adult males and boyfriends of the child's mother."[21] As victims themselves, CPS mothers find—or perhaps, are more likely to be found by—bad men.

Carla Rizzo is an example of a CPS mother who had a propensity for finding abusive men. Carla is a thirty-six-year-old white woman whose five children were removed from her custody following an altercation with her abusive, drug-addicted, Latino husband who is the biological father of the second, fourth, and fifth of her five children. The altercation was approximately the ninth CPS referral for their family. Carla came to recognize her pattern of seeking out bad men while participating in court-ordered counseling, part of her reunification services. In the discussion below, she describes her deep-seated attraction to men who are in trouble with the law.

> I was abused as a child. My mom was an alcoholic and a drug addict and my dad, well, he was also a drug addict, but they split up when I was like three years old. But my mom had a lot of different abusive boyfriends. Before I was even in school, maybe four years old, I can remember pretending I was visiting somebody in prison. I can remember doing that… It's so, I don't know, the word's ironic, and then I progressed from boys' group home to juvenile hall to ya know, to jail to somebody in prison. Ya know, it just progressed like that. And when I look back on all these things, it's like, God, at four years old, before I'm even in school, I'm pretending like I'm in between, like my boyfriend's over here and I'm over here talking to him on the phone…I remember playing like that. It's just, that's what I, it's so strange…and then when I got older it was like I was programmed to be with that

type of man. I would go find guys in a boys' group home and go write them and get to talk to them in that way and it just…oh you're going to prison? Oh, let's write. And ya know, it just went from there.

Like Carla, many mothers who enter the CPS system have spent most of their lives around men who treat them badly. Partly as a consequence, they may not have a sense of their own worth. For example, Jill Wood, a thirty-one-year-old white and Native American woman who was sexually and physically abused as a child by her older brother and later by boyfriends, describes her sense of powerlessness to protect herself and her son:

> I was with this guy who would severely beat us both and the lady downstairs had called the police and CPS and they came and arrested him and they thought I was involved in it too and I had to show them all the bruises on my body. It was really hard for me…I didn't even know what he had done to my son until I was dressing my son for bed that night and my son had bruises all over his body. And you know, when I tried to do something about it, the guy, he really beat me severely, bad. And I felt really hopeless, like there was no hope for me. There was no way for me to escape. And um, and the lady downstairs, I am so grateful to, even though I didn't tell her, she called the police and she called CPS.

As mentioned, CPS officials feel sorry for many CPS mothers—some of whom were themselves wards of the state in their youth—who were left without the guidance to become adequate mothers. However, the primary concern of the system remains protecting current children. As such, sympathy for the mothers is bound by concern for their children. The limits of sympathy for a mother's own victimization can be seen most clearly in the cases of teen mothers in CPS. I observed several cases in which a teenage minor who lived in foster care appeared in court while her own mother's parental rights were terminated, making her a legal orphan. In the cases that immediately followed, the same newly motherless teens were the neglectful mothers facing the loss of their parental rights of their own children. In one tragic case, Kia Bayani, a seventeen-year-old girl of Filipino descent, was placed in foster care after being raped by her mother's boyfriend. The rapist was successfully prosecuted based on genetic testing of Kia's newborn baby. Kia and her baby were placed together in foster care, but Kia would frequently go out with her friends, leaving the baby with the foster mother, who had not agreed to provide child care. As a result, Kia's baby was taken into protective custody for neglect, transforming the teen rape victim into a CPS mother who eventually lost her own parental rights.

This type of case exposes one of the core dilemmas of the CPS system. Though everyone understood the difficulties a teen mother who had been abused would have parenting, protecting her own neglected or abused child becomes the paramount concern for the system. These minor mothers are more likely to come to the attention of CPS because they live in foster care. As foster children, they are supervised by social service professionals who must ensure they are safe. That same "ever-present" social worker, probation officer, or group home leader is also legally responsible for reporting child maltreatment and is often on-hand to witness the young mothers' maternal transgressions. In CPS, the child who was not adequately protected by the system will need to reform into an appropriate mother to keep her own child. Here, Kia is both a victim and victimizer. She may still be seen as a victim, but she is now a victim who must seek reform through self-improvement. As such, she is reduced to the dominant image of CPS mother, and has all the requirements of reunification imposed upon her.

To regain custody of their children, women, including teen mothers, must address their victimization or victim status and become self-efficacious. Recognizing the abusive histories of many CPS mothers, the court believes these women need assistance in learning to stand up for themselves and their children. In an effort to protect children, the court hopes to help their mothers become more self-sufficient and will thus supervise and guide them until they are presumably capable of making good maternal decisions on their own. Since good mothers put their children's needs above their own, demanding that women stay away from bad men, which in some cases means all the men the woman knows, is seen as an important route to becoming self-possessed. A core understanding of these mothers is that without therapeutic help, they are likely to continue relationships with dysfunctional men who will distract them from the self-improvement necessary to regain custody of their children.

PERFORMING EMPOWERMENT

Treatment strategies for those women in CPS who are perceived as worthy and capable of reform require women to deal with their past victimization, low self-esteem, and lack of self-confidence. In doing so, women theoretically gain confidence in their own efficacy and become empowered to make good decisions, which satisfies the state's goal. Empowerment presumes that a "healthy individual" is "self-contained, independent and self-reliant, capable of asserting himself and influencing his environment…and operating according to abstract principles of justice and fairness."[22] Feminist scholar Marion Young defines empowerment as "individual autonomy, self-control, and confidence" as well as "a sense of collective influence over social conditions of one's life."[23] Becoming empowered require individuals to learn to "master their environments and achieve self-determination."[24] In concept, CPS mothers who could become empowered would become self-reliant, self-sufficient, able to protect themselves and their children, and capable of choosing to remain free of bad men. In light of their histories of victimization, empowering women in the CPS system seems a worthwhile goal for reunification services.

However, in a system of bulging caseloads, limited resources, and federal pressure for quicker case resolution, it is unlikely that women with patterns of dependence learned over a lifetime will be cured within the federally mandated time limits. Within six months, parents are asked to demonstrate that they are making significant progress. For women who have long histories of victimization, the limited services provided—a routine package of thirteen sessions of individual counseling, support groups, or short-term drug treatment—are inadequate to address deep-seated interpersonal issues, much less the frequently accompanying substance abuse dependence.[25] Of equal relevance, a mother can more easily demonstrate herself to be self-determined when she has financial resources on which to draw. Thus their very status as poor mothers places efforts to appear empowered even further out of reach.

To be clear, empowering mothers is not the purpose of reunification. Reducing risk to children is the primary goal, and addressing women's lack of empowerment is seen as a way to do that. Potentially, state practices to empower women might even contradict the state's direct interests. A mother that was "self-contained, independent, and reliant," who could exercise "self-control and confidence," might make choices that are not consistent with the state's goals. Empowered clients are also likely to become noncompliant clients. Decisions about whether or not a parent can successfully reunify ultimately depend on issues of deference and subordination; empowering clients could be counterproductive to the state's goals of sending children home.

Rachel Weissman, a forty-year-old white mother, provides an example of how a sense of empowerment can backfire. Rachel's children were removed in large part because of her noncompliance with treatment for her mental illness. After four months of reunification services, Rachel abandoned efforts to regain custody of her two sons. Instead, she allowed her former partner, Elizabeth, to establish guardianship of them, which was consistent with the children's desire.[26] Rachel articulated her experience in terms of an unwillingness to sacrifice her own interests, an expectation of good mothers. In a meeting I observed, Rachel's attorney voiced his concerns about Rachel's future well-being following the conclusion of her case. He explained that she will be alone, no longer having an attorney, the courts, or access to her children, as she had up until then. Rachel assured him that she considered this to be positive:

> I am trying to redefine my life as a human being, not just as someone's mother and an educator. This is the first time in seventeen years…This is the first time in my life I'm taking care of myself. I'm building a life. I'm getting what I want…Children are welcome in my life, but they are not my life.

Rachel's articulation of her choice reflects a sense of empowerment. Her understanding of motherhood and individuality as incompatible captures the reality of the expectations of mothers in the CPS system.

Outside of the reunification context, CPS mothers who were truly empowered could address the social inequalities that they endure. However, they may also question the role of the state in their private family life. They may advocate for themselves in interactions with welfare officials. They may question their lack of resources and opportunity. They may notice that they have been forced to transfer their subordination from men to the state, but have not become independent or self-sufficient. Potentially, empowered clients could even choose to abandon their reunification efforts, as Rachel did. In fact, many clients who choose to abandon efforts to reunify with their children may feel that that strategy presents the greatest opportunity to act in a self-determined way, free from state control. Here, parents in CPS may feel capable of making a strategic choice, even as they lack the ability to exercise control over what they most want: their children. As community psychologist Stephanie Riger suggests, "Many intervention efforts aimed at empowerment increase people's power to act, as an example, by enhancing their self-esteem, but do little to affect their power over resources or policies."[27] Indeed, being empowered and deferring to the state are incompatible.

As such, the goal of reunification services for women is twofold. First, clients must deal with whatever factors have placed a child at risk.

Second, a client should gain a sense of empowerment—increasing her power to act—without jeopardizing the primary goal of reforming her parental behavior, which is to be accomplished in the statutorily determined time frame. What becomes important is that a mother participates in services, develops some skills, and complies with dominant definitions of motherhood. As a woman's self-esteem improves, the court assumes that she will embrace the characteristics of the ideal, self-sacrificing mother. Empowerment is then prescriptive: a woman can only be perceived as successfully empowered if she chooses for herself what the court would choose for her. To be empowered in the context of CPS is to comply. In this way, we can view Rachel, who sounds empowered, as a failure for failing to choose her children over herself. To succeed in reunification, mothers must provide the court with a performance of empowerment, as defined by the state. By providing this performance, mothers satisfy a uniquely gendered expectation of deference.

Sociologist Erving Goffman observed that "when an individual presents himself before others, his performance will tend to incorporate and exemplify the officially accredited values of the society, more so, in fact, than does his behavior as a whole."[28] The successful empowerment performance will show a mother's recognition of the importance of avoiding relationships with men, will demonstrate her unyielding commitment to her children, and will communicate to the court her exercise of independence in a way the court has defined as appropriately maternal. Mothers who fail to perform empowerment will also fail to reunify with their children. The following sections contrast mothers who successfully performed empowerment and mothers who failed to provide a convincing performance.

COURT-ORDERED EMPOWERMENT: SUCCESS STORIES

Audrey Simpson, a nineteen-year-old white woman, entered the CPS system when police executed a search warrant and seized large quantities of drugs and cash that were part of her twenty-seven-year-old live-in boyfriend's side business. At the time of the seizure, she and her boyfriend Miguel Trujillo were arrested and their four-month-old daughter was placed in protective custody. By the time her CPS case came to court, roughly thirty days after her arrest, criminal charges against her had been dropped. In addressing the issues remaining for the dependency court, Karen Klein, the white attorney in her late twenties appointed to represent Audrey's infant daughter, was uncharacteristically sympathetic, explaining that "it appears this mother was dating the wrong person… This is not to say that she isn't to blame; she did have drugs in her home." The judge disagreed with Karen and directed his remarks to Audrey:

> I find it hard to believe you were just dating the wrong man as Ms. Klein said. I find it hard to believe you didn't know… That doesn't mean you use [drugs] and it doesn't mean you aren't a good mother to this child. I would suggest you be given an opportunity to reunify with your child and I want you to take it seriously. I don't think you are totally innocent in this situation.

After the hearing concluded, Karen and I discussed her position. She explained to me that she would "love to be that mother's counselor," and relayed that she had pulled Audrey aside and told her that she needs to "find out who Audrey is…not as a mother, not as a girlfriend" but on her own. As Audrey's daughter's attorney, one would expect that Karen's primary concern would be in Audrey finding out who she is *as* a mother, not on her own. But by adopting the rhetoric of empowerment, Karen takes it for granted that Audrey will discover a greater commitment to mothering once she is free of her boyfriend. She reported that Audrey agreed and that she did not intend to have any more boyfriends.

As Audrey recounted the same conversation to me, she explained that Karen had doubted her resolve to avoid new relationships with men. Audrey explained,

> …Well (my daughter's) lawyer, she's like, "Well, you will, you're just in shock." And I'm like, "No. All I want to do is work and take care of my daughter and that's that." And that's all I do now. I work and come home and take care of her. I don't have time to go out with someone else. I don't see it happening. If it did, it did. But I don't see it happening. I'd feel too guilty towards my daughter. I'd feel too bad bringing other men around.

Audrey provided answers to Karen that indicated she was willing to sacrifice her own social needs for the good of her daughter and that she aspired, for the first time, to provide materially for her child. During her brief incarceration and the accompanying loss of her daughter, and anticipating her boyfriend Miguel's four-year prison sentence, which will culminate in his deportation to Mexico, Audrey discovered that she was capable of rising to this new challenge. She explained,

My mom says, "Audrey, I'm real proud of you. I couldn't have done it, got right out of jail and gotten right out there and got a job. I couldn't have done it." And I did it. I got out of jail and got a job. I never could have left my daughter before and now it's, I just walk out that door and go to work, and it's hard but now it's routine. I mean before I would barely let anyone hold her. It's kind of a big change for me with my daughter.

Audrey's acceptance of her need for independence made her an appropriate mother in the eyes of the CPS system. She convinced Karen—who like most children's attorneys, almost never recommends reunification—that she was reforming. Working full-time demonstrated her commitment to supporting her child, even though it meant leaving her child in day care while she worked, a contradiction that permeates contemporary welfare policy.[29] Nonetheless, Audrey regained custody of her daughter within seven months of the initial removal, with unsupervised visitations granted almost immediately. Audrey's case illustrates how efforts to empower her collapsed into prescriptive definitions of good parenting. Because she accepted these prescriptions, because she deferred to the state, she succeeded in reunifying with her daughter.

Yvonne Platt, a thirty-two-year-old white mother, also provided a compelling performance of empowerment, though she also sincerely aspired to the prescribed transformation. As she describes her lack of interest in developing new relationships, she points to her pattern of entering bad relationships as the underlying reason:

I don't need one. 'Cuz right now I would pick an unhealthy relationship. I'm still in that mode, ya know. Know what I mean? I have to get myself together, my head together, get my kids secure, ya know, before I think about that. It might be years and years before I date or trust somebody. I won't for a long time.

Like Yvonne who identified a pattern of entering relationships with men she believed were poor choices, Carla too identified in the beginning of the chapter her pattern of seeking out bad men. Her case provides another example of the importance of performing empowerment. From the day following the removal of her children, Carla began attending a domestic violence support group and completing all services. She accepted the state's therapeutic vision of her as needing help and worked to reform in the ways prescribed. Carla says she was initially "devastated" when her children were removed. She then almost immediately enrolled in services and began to work to reunify. She recalls,

> Then the day after [they were removed] I went and started getting into parenting class. I did all that before anything actually, actually I, wait, ok, the next day I went and got a restraining order and started the divorce. Then a couple of, then you go three days later is the first court hearing. So I was hoping I'd get them back, but she (the judge) said no, since I had so much history and I'm more or less...I admitted to [the social worker], "Yeah, the day he threw the TV, he was high. I knew he was high.

Carla, who told the social worker that she knew her husband was under the influence of illegal drugs, accounts for her high level of disclosure, by explaining,

> Yeah, I'm not going to lie to people. If they ask me, I don't feel I'm going to get anywhere by lying. So why not be honest, ya know what I'm saying? And not try to hide something because you're going to get caught in the end. So I tried to be honest with them, especially when it comes to my kids. And I told them, "Yeah he was high that day and I made him leave."

Despite the severity of Carla's case—her history of substance abuse, her abusive, drug-addicted husband, and her long history of CPS referrals—she was able to regain custody of her children in six weeks, the shortest amount of time I saw in any of the cases I observed. Carla's success can be accounted for in two ways. First, her self-reported history matched with what the therapeutic state and its helping professionals believed were her issues. She identified her life as unhealthy and herself as a victim of her childhood, in need of help. Carla's willingness to accept the state's definition of her problems showed her desire to change. Indeed, Carla presented herself as forthright by voluntarily seeking out services that showed she not only wanted to comply, but also that she knew she needed help. The second source of Carla's success came in large part because she quickly established distance from her abusive, drug-addicted husband. As a result, she was able to present herself as independent and willing to prioritize her children over men. Carla's willingness to comply was so complete that she immediately evicted her nineteen-year-old stepson from her home as well. Though he was never violent or a danger to the children, she explained that "there was somebody, I don't know if it was a court investigator, somebody said it wasn't a good idea that he be here… I'm the only mother he's ever had, and it was hard. He was workin', he was doing good, and God, it was like, this is just tearing our whole family apart here." Carla, like Audrey, performed well for the courts and quickly reunified with her children.

SEXUAL MOTHERS: REUNIFICATION FAILURES

Many women are not willing to abstain from having relationships while undergoing reunification, thereby communicating their rejection of the state's definition of them as needing help or as needing to aspire to the tenets of state-defined good motherhood. The experience of Maya Wheeler, a white woman in her mid-twenties, illustrates this. Maya entered CPS after the police intervened in a domestic violence incident between her and her African American boyfriend, Joe Cane. Maya has two sons from a prior relationship and one daughter with Joe. Their daughter was born positive for methamphetamine and with many congenital disorders, including microcephaly (a small head in relation to body size), deafness, and possible aphasia (the inability to learn to speak or write). Their daughter's foster parents, who had cared for her since birth, wanted to adopt her. Recognizing their inability to care for a medically needy child, Maya and Joe opted to voluntarily relinquish their parental rights, which Maya hoped would improve her chances of regaining custody of her sons.

Throughout her case, Maya and Joe argued, separated, and reconciled. Because Joe is not biologically related to the boys whose custody was still in question, he was not given a case plan, nor any services. Maya's initial participation in her services was inconsistent, though she eventually began drug testing three times a week and attending parenting classes, as ordered by the court. Maya's attorney warned her that her late efforts might be perceived as "too little, too late" to regain custody of her two-year-old son, whose age allowed for the court to terminate her services in as little as six months, but might help her to regain custody of her older son whose case would continue. In discussing her case progress, Maya's attorney explained that Joe, with whom she was again living, needed to attend services and drug test to demonstrate to the court that he was clean. His only chance for publicly funded testing was through probation, which placed him at increased risk of reincarceration should he test positive. In contrast, should he test positive in the CPS system, his bid for reunification might be jeopardized, but he would not face criminal sanctions. Joe's lack of services, combined with his criminal history and history of domestic violence against Maya, made it impossible for him to demonstrate that he was a positive influence in the home. Despite multiple suggestions to the contrary, Maya refused to leave Joe permanently, even though it cost her permanent custody of her children. Maya's unwillingness to leave her boyfriend was interpreted by the court as an unwillingness to overcome her own weakness and as a failure to prioritize her children. At the same time, the court's strong belief that unrelated men are dangerous to children meant that Joe could not receive the services that would make it possible for Maya to continue a relationship with him while diminishing risk to her children.

For some mothers, the lack of a compelling empowerment performance is not the result of an unwillingness to leave a relationship with an abusive partner. Rather, it reflects structural conditions, which might include cultural barriers, familial expectations, or a lack of resources that prevent it. Although lack of financial resources was not an obstacle, a lack of social and familial support blocked Grace's success. Grace Hang, an eighteen-year-old Hmong woman, met and began dating Pao Leeprecha, an eighteen-year-old Mien man, when they were fourteen. Although she was not planning on becoming pregnant she was also not, as she describes it, planning on not becoming pregnant either. When she did become pregnant at the age of seventeen, her immigrant parents were upset, particularly because she was still in high school and would now be unlikely to continue her education. Four months into her pregnancy, Grace moved in with Pao and his parents "because it was pretty much, it was better if I live with him than my parents, it's the tradition. If you're pregnant it's better if you live with him because it's going to jeopardize my parents' reputation about having a pregnant child in their house." A month later, Grace was "traditionally married," although not legally married, to Pao. Grace explains that the wedding "was unplanned for…it was relatives coming over and talking about it and then saying, we're going to throw the wedding tomorrow." In reflecting on the experience of being informed she would be married, Grace recalls, "I was just shocked, because I was like, whoa, that's too fast. But my parents wanted me to be married if I was going to have a child so I guess it was a good thing."

Following the birth of their son David, Pao and Grace struggled as a couple and fought often. Pao often went out with his friends, and Grace, who was working as a waitress and was often tired when she returned home to care for David, did not. One evening, their routine argument escalated. During the violent altercation, Pao took a marker and wrote on Grace's face and then threw the marker at her, hitting David, who was in her arms. Grace explains that although this was not the first time he had struck her, she called the police that night "because he was hitting me a lot different, very hard… No one was there to stop [it] and so I called the police." When the police arrived, they arrested Pao and placed David in protective custody. After a brief stay in foster care, David was placed with Grace's parents.

Grace's case plan had many contradictions and obstacles. Although the court gave her permission to move in with her parents and David, her parents held her responsible for the events. She explains,

> Oh they're really mad at me because they figure it all started because of me calling the police. I guess it's because they wanted to solve it traditionally, but everything would have followed along the same path. And so I just called the police and they were really mad because that's the thing that I'm going through now, all of the trouble.

When asked what a traditional solution would entail, Grace shrugged. "I don't know. I wouldn't like it, I wouldn't think, because it would have been all of my fault anyway."[30]

Although Grace believed that she and Pao would inevitably continue arguing, she could not envision how she could stay away from him. When asked what she would like her life to look like in two years, Grace's answer demonstrates the intrinsic dilemma she faced:

> I picture living on my own with my kid and I'm not sure if [with Pao], because it doesn't really matter at this point if he's with me or not. Because so many things happen and people go on with their lives, so I mean, if it goes on happy and nothing happens, no arguments, then it would be okay. But to me, it doesn't really matter. Two years from now I can see that my kid will always be with me.

Grace says that she would like "to go back to school so that I can get a better job." However, she is not sure whether she could build the life she would like away from Pao. Although she says that "if I wasn't married I don't think I'd be with him," the cultural definitions of marriage and divorce make it difficult for her to leave him. In Hmong and Mien culture, Grace can only leave a relationship by obtaining a traditional divorce, which requires obtaining the permission of her husband's family. Should she try to live alone without such permission, she would lose the support of her own parents. Her older sister who, with her children, lives with their parents, was permitted to divorce, she explains, "because her husband took off, not her. It was more his fault so my parents took her back. If it was her who took off, my parents wouldn't have taken her back."

In contrast, CPS expects battered women to leave their violent partners to protect themselves and their children. In this way, the court's expectations of maternal empowerment—and ways of evaluating it—are in conflict with the Hmong and Mien cultural expectations of community and family life.

Despite the mixed messages—that she could lose David again should Pao hit her and that she should stay with Pao to maintain her social support—Grace saw value in CPS intervention.

> I kinda think it's a good thing…because it kinda controls me and my kid, brings us together. Because I know what it means to lose my kid…Oh, I've learned a lot of things from this experience. [Like what?] Just pretty much how much my child means to me. Because before I had my child and he was there and I wasn't going to lose him and everything was okay. And I guess after this it's kinda like everything is so hard and there are certain things that I have to do to get him back or certain things that I have to do for this and that…I just realized how much I loved him already, so—it's pretty good…Yeah, 'cuz I think that it's good that I know this now rather than when I'm twenty-five or thirty and have to learn later on what the consequences are and stuff of losing my child, of endangering my child. It's better and I like taking the classes, it's good. At least I have more self-esteem for myself.

In this passage, Grace communicates her acceptance of the therapeutic state's goals for her, even as they remain culturally irrelevant to her situation. In addition, Grace was appreciative of the work her social workers were doing for her, explaining that her family reunification caseworker was especially helpful "because when I came into court I didn't know what was going on and he was telling me everything and answering any questions I had." She was also grateful that her social worker let her move away from Pao's family so she could live with her parents, giving her unlimited access to her son. At the same time, there was little that her social worker could do that would facilitate her permanent exit from her relationship with Pao, except continue to threaten to remove her child should she return to his house.

Mothers who choose to continue relationships with men, though they still wish to reunify with their children, often engage in attempts to hide their relationships. If the court, usually via social workers, discovers a woman's concealment of her relationship, the mother becomes viewed as dishonest and insincere in her attempts to reform and other aspects of her case will be called into question as her credibility is damaged. She also relinquishes her victim status and instead becomes viewed as a selfish mother who has chosen not to transcend her own needs for the good of her children.

Mary Allen's case and its tragic ending illustrate how this plays out. Mary's three children were removed from her custody when her youngest was born positive for methamphetamine. A white woman in her early thirties, Mary did not begin her reunification services until her case was almost a year old, at which point she entered a church-run residential drug treatment program. After completing the program as a model client, Mary stayed on as a group leader and mentor to others. The role gave her a source of positive feedback and a sense of accomplishment. In the program, she met Dennis McCloud, a man with a long criminal history of possession of drugs and paraphernalia and some history of drug dealing. Without telling the program leaders, her social workers, or her attorney, Mary and Dennis were married. While this created an issue for her service providers at the program, it was a crisis for her CPS case. Before the marriage, Mary's children were beginning to have overnight visits with her, an important step in transitioning home. Knowing she was close to having her children placed with her and not wanting to derail that progress, she initially attempted to hide the marriage. She eventually approached her social worker to ask that she give Dennis his own case plan, but the social worker refused, explaining that Mary's case was more than eighteen months old and that she was not willing to start over with someone else. Her marriage and the social worker's accompanying reaction changed Mary's case from one where reunification was likely to one where she was about to lose her children permanently.

The day before the hearing to determine whether she should continue receiving services, Mary filed for a legal separation from Dennis. Her attorney argued on her behalf: "By all accounts, this is a mother who is capable of parenting. She is willing to put aside her relationship with Dennis. She is late but she has done it. She has been very blunt about her relationship since…it came out. She has no intention of reuniting with him." Mary also made this claim, testifying that she separated from Dennis "because my children are first and foremost in importance in my life. I would like my relationship with Dennis to stay permanent, but I want to show to the court that my children come first." She added, "I've made substantial changes. I'm a Christian. I have no grounds biblically to divorce him. I would like this to be a long-term relationship with him, but my children are first…and my own personal life is second." However, both her eleventh-hour statement and clearly visible pregnancy undermined the credibility of this claim.

At the conclusion of the hearing, the judge addressed this issue in his ruling. As he terminated her reunification services, he addressed Mary directly:

> You have done a lot of work, but it's been three years. I can't send them home. You made a fatal error in judgment when you got up to the eighteen-month hearing in March and got involved with and married someone who is clearly inappropriate for these children. He has a long history of substance abuse like their fathers. It is not about now that you're separated.

Mary's involvement with a "bad man" caused her case to unravel. Her willingness to commit energy to a new relationship was perceived as a lack of commitment to her children. Her choice to be with Dennis was interpreted as an indication that she was no longer a victim in need of saving, but instead, a bad mother beyond salvation. The judge remarked,

> You made a poor choice to get involved with a man while you are fighting with what I would assume is everything you've got. It was a poor choice. You've had lots of time and you've come a long way. But even giving you the benefit of what you've done, we don't have time. These children are entitled to go on with their own life. I won't fault [the social worker] for not developing a relationship with Dennis. He shouldn't have been a factor.

Mary did not reunify with her children, who were adopted by their foster parents. Her case, though sad, provides insight into how the therapeutic ideology of the state builds on dominant definitions of mothers as self-sacrificing and chaste to create uniquely gendered expectations of deference during reunification. In the end, Mary failed because she was not able to escape what the court saw as her own dependence on men and she did not place all her energy into her children.

MAKING SENSE OF THE EMPOWERMENT PERFORMANCE

A woman's willingness to avoid relationships with men is a key aspect of performing empowerment, even as doing so places her at odds with other state welfare policies that require her to marry. There is also a problematic disconnect between the goals of child safety and assessments of maternal capability. Although many women need to stay away from the men with whom they are involved, not all men involved with CPS mothers are dangerous to children. In several cases discussed here, a mother's actual ability to care for her children was not central to considerations of her parental capability. Rather her subordination to the mandates of reunification (or lack thereof), which include acceptance of her need for help to achieve independence, determined her case outcome.

A notion that a woman could choose a relationship with a man as an empowered, rational choice is largely lacking in the CPS system. When women are mistreated, particularly when they endure physical violence, yet choose to stay with their violent partners, they often meet with the disapproval of social service providers whose help they need. Typically "a client's choice to stay in a relationship often is interpreted as proof of disorganization and powerlessness, rather than as a sign of her competence and coping."[31] In the CPS context, a woman who chooses to remain in a relationship that is perceived as dysfunctional— or the cause of the family dysfunction—is seen as failing to address her personal weakness, which may threaten child well-being.

A competing narrative of Mary's case might suggest that Mary, after two years in a residential treatment program, felt empowered to begin an equal relationship with a man also in treatment and counseling. However, the court was not interested in assessing the level of egalitarianism in her home life. The only question of concern to the dependency court was whether there was a diminished risk to her children. Her new husband and his lengthy criminal history did not adequately communicate that she had reduced the risk. In this instance, Mary might have *felt* empowered, but in the face of a larger judicial system, she was not truly empowered to make such a decision; in the end, Mary's story provides a powerful reminder that feeling empowered is not the same as being empowered, especially in the CPS system.

It would be irresponsible to argue that mothers have no responsibility to protect their children from harm, particularly when they invited that harm into their children's home because they lack the self-confidence or judgment to recognize the peril their partners present. Many theorists have argued for a broader consideration of how mothers are often battered themselves and are bound by structural constraints that limit their ability to leave abusive men, even as the lives of their children are threatened. The therapeutic model used by the court seems a logical way to address these issues. Even parents' attorneys argue that it does a woman good to be prohibited from establishing a new relationship with a man who is likely to be worse than the one she started with—the one who might have led her into the CPS system. In this light, the intervention of the state is logical, even desirable. However, accepting this policy also requires accepting the diminution of adult women into a subordinate role and leaving them little choice but to adhere to the prescriptions established by the CPS system. Clearly this is a problematic proposition.

In identifying the cases that illustrate the system's prescriptions for empowerment and demands for deference, it became clear that this rhetoric is disproportionately available to white and Asian women, who are perhaps more easily seen as feminine and weak, and thus in need of help. In many of the stories above—those of Shirley, Audrey, Mary, Carla, and Maya—white women identified as needing help were in relationships and had children with men of color. This policy, and its unequal practice, reflects hundreds of years of U.S. history in which white women who engaged in sexual relationships with men of color were seen as damaged, sexually promiscuous, unsuccessful at securing relationships with white men, and even self-loathing. As such, they can easily be seen as needing therapeutic help. Race theorist Ruth Frankenberg points out how the sexuality of men and women of color have been seen as "excessive, animalistic, exotic, in contrast to the ostensibly restrained or 'civilized' sexuality of white women and men."[32] With these cultural constructions as a backdrop, it is easy to identify how men of color are more easily cast as bad men and as predatory to white women and their children. Although African American women, like Latanya, were expected to abstain from relationships with men and to communicate the centrality of their children to their lives, they were not as easily perceived as victims, and instead were more often seen as choicemakers who could choose to pursue or abandon relationships with bad men. They were also more likely to have their credibility called into question.

Because mothers are the presumed primary caretakers and protectors of children, they are held to an exceptionally high standard—one that may be unobtainable for all women.[33] Yet the expectation that mothers are the natural caregivers to children also serves to preserve "the autonomy of mothers and their communities to make mothers principal (although not exclusive) guardians of their children."[34] Though fraught with contradiction, the vision of mothers as intrinsically superior and simultaneously flawed caregivers may be preferable to an alternate one. The perceived importance of biological motherhood serves women well in a system that strives to resolve cases quickly, even when it requires freeing children for adoption. Women—so long as their behavior, resistance, or abuses of their children do not shape a view of them as beyond redemption—are almost always given an opportunity to reunify with their children. Women are also perceived as worthy of rehabilitation because of the perceived importance of the mother–child bond. Without a belief in the sanctity of motherhood, the state could conceivably adopt a practice of viewing mothers as fungible[35] and therefore unworthy of salvation, as is the situation with fathers.

7

BIOLOGY AND CONFORMITY: EXPECTATIONS OF FATHERS IN REUNIFICATION

Dusty Benjamin saunters to the table and pulls out the metal-framed chair. He is wearing a dirty baseball-style jacket with a hole in the sleeve. Sam Richman, a man he has never met before but who will now, as his court-appointed attorney, represent him, sits down across the table without looking up. I walk in behind them, aware that I can smell Dusty's stench from several feet away. Dusty slouches in his seat, with his long thin legs straight out in front of him.

Sam begins working through his standard questions for new clients: does Dusty have any Native American ancestry? Although Dusty doesn't know why he is asked, Sam needs to find out if the provisions of the Indian Child Welfare Act might apply to his case. Dusty shrugs and says he doesn't know, explaining, "I have seizures and lose my memory sometimes."

Sam pages through the initial report, trying to understand the case. Dusty explains that his wife, Marla Chue, says that someone else—her boyfriend Dirk Haigenberger—is the baby's father. I recalled seeing Marla, a young Laotian woman with some kind of cognitive impairment, standing in the lobby with a heavier set white man with a shaved head. I had also seen Dusty, a lanky white man, slide his hand around Marla's waist and call her "Hun." Sam asks if he and Marla are married and whether he lived with her ten months prior, at the time of conception of the now one-month-old baby in protective custody. Upon hearing Dusty say "Yes," Sam begins explaining how being legally married to her makes him the legal father of the infant, Todd.

"Grab a cigar. Congratulations, you're a dad," Sam declares, with some sarcasm. Dusty, who doesn't understand the reference, explains that he likes cigars.

Sam more slowly explains that being married and having lived with Marla makes him the legal father, no matter what Marla says. He asks Dusty whether he wants to pursue custody of the baby, if the court decides Marla cannot take care of him.

Dusty appears to ponder the issue seriously. After a few moments, he explains that he wants to help Marla, but that he doesn't know if he wants custody of the baby, since that would hurt Marla. He also mentions that his own mother, with whom he lives, does not know about the baby. Sam tells him that he needs to call his mother and tell her about Todd. He tries to explain that this is not a matter of "helping" Marla; this is a question of whether he wants to pursue becoming a full-time parent.

Dusty considers the question aloud, following different thoughts as they arise. He has a new girlfriend now. He moved out four months ago, after he found out Marla was cheating on him with Dirk. "She is supposed to be faithful. We're married." He explains, "I just turned my back and took off." He wishes he could get her back, but then again, isn't sure. He again mentions that he has a new girlfriend. Then his thoughts return to Marla. "I used to be able to tickle her and stuff like that... Now she just pushes me away." When I ask him later, he says he would pick Marla over his new girlfriend.

After these ruminations, Dusty meanders back to the matter at hand; he appears uncertain of whether he wants the baby and explains that he has never seen Todd. Sam tells Dusty to think of Todd as his son, and himself as Todd's father. As such, he has the right to visit Todd and participate in his life. Sam suggests that Dusty act like he wants the kid. Dusty says he does. Sam explains that there are responsibilities that come with fatherhood, "like paying child support, and if Todd goes into foster care and gets adopted out, it will have repercussions for future children you may have."

Dusty seems excited about the possibility of being a father. He explains that he has always wanted to have a kid when he was twenty-five years-old. Now he is twenty-five, almost twenty-six. He smiles to himself, and for a moment it appears he believes that this is all part of an adolescent plan coming to fruition. He recalls, "I thought about it when I was eighteen, but I decided I needed to calm down." I ask him what he means and he explains that he wanted to get his seizures under control—with medications, the last three months have been seizure-free—and "be more mature." He takes out a small heart-shaped box and shows us his medications, then stuffs it back in his pocket.

Sam explains that they will go into court shortly to see the judge and provides a brief overview of what will be decided that day. Dusty says that he does not have any other questions, and Sam leaves to see his next client.

* * *

The child welfare system, with policies that appear to be gender neutral, holds unique expectations for men who wish to gain custody of their children—who wish to be full-time fathers. The institution of fatherhood carries its own social significance. More than fifty years ago, feminist theorist Simone de Beauvoir wrote, "The life of the father has a mysterious prestige... It is through him that the family communicates with the rest of the world; he incarnates that immense, difficult and marvelous world of adventure; he personifies transcendence, he is God."[1] Permitted to stay emotionally distant, good fathers have in the last century been the ones who financially supported their wives and children through paid employment (if not through inheritance). It was as breadwinners that men could prove themselves good fathers.[2] In the last two decades, a more modern interpretation of ideal fatherhood has grown to include expectations that men should be emotionally involved with their children and participate in caregiving. However, even with these new expectations, it is primarily through financial support that fathers are evaluated, with other qualities viewed as additional assets.[3] As Kjersti Ericsson notes of assessments of parental capability in the Norwegian child welfare system, "The minimal standard for being a good mother is the ideal, for each shortcoming she slides into the negative. The minimal standard for the father is the detached, old-fashioned model. For each 'modern' achievement, he climbs into the positive."[4] For men who do not (or are not able to) provide financially, particularly those who also do not live with their children, achievement of ideal fatherhood remains elusive. Men who fail to be good providers are labeled in public rhetoric and policy as "dead-beat dads." Although this term reflects the reality that child support payments to single mothers are often low and frequently unpaid, it also symbolically binds financial competence with capable fathering.

No examination of competent fatherhood—in the CPS system specifically or in society more generally—can occur without identifying the ways such definitions are situated within meanings of masculinity. Hegemonic masculinity requires men to have claims to authority, positions of responsibility, and self-control.[5] For the fathers whose children are in CPS custody, these requisite characteristics, often facilitated by professional or financial success, remain out of reach. CPS fathers are disproportionately men of color, frequently have histories of criminal convictions, and have had only limited success in employment, education, intimate relationships, or property ownership. These men are almost all poor or working-class men, and thus lack access to power, authority, and resources as a source of masculine identity. Instead, some of these fathers have defined their manhood through their participation in crime, violence, illegal sources of income, or the "siring" of children outside of committed relationships.[6] Although these activities may have provided a source of masculine competence in their own social worlds, they are devalued and even present a liability in the CPS system. Not surprisingly, this frustrates many fathers, who react with anger or indignation, which, as discussed in chapter 5, further damages their ability to present themselves as fit to father, and may damage the mother's ability to reunify if she does not reject him. Thus professionals in the CPS system aim to manage these "marginalized masculinities" in ways that reduce the risk to children.[7] When possible, this system that strives to reform parents will remake these men into appropriate fathers.

Men are constrained by legal requirements that exclude fathers never married to the mothers of their children. They are also limited by CPS professionals' presumptions about their lack of caregiving abilities, exacerbated by their failure to meet cultural definitions of competent fatherhood. To be perceived as capable of reformation by CPS—the agency responsible for protecting children by resocializing bad parents—fathers in CPS must subordinate themselves to culturally legitimated definitions of fatherhood (and their accompanying meanings of manhood). For men who often feel a sense of hopelessness, the goal of self-improvement, or rather a performance of aspiration for their better future selves, may be difficult to perform. Such a performance, which communicates deference to state definitions and processes, also requires them to relinquish other (less legitimate in the eyes of the court) realms in which they may have experienced validation. If men cannot be quickly and easily reformed—or perceived as such—the system aims to eliminate them from the case as expeditiously as possible.

BECOMING A CPS FATHER

Many fathers enter the CPS system because of the actions of the mothers of their children, with whom they often do not live. One common route is when a baby is born positive for illegal drugs and enters the CPS system at birth. Another common route into CPS for nonoffending fathers is when CPS intervenes because a half- or step-sibling has been abused or molested, in which case protective custody of the child's siblings is automatic. In many of these cases, the men have not directly caused the risk or harm that led the family into the CPS system and may not have even known about it.[8] Yet once the children are placed in protective custody, the court will notify fathers of the proceedings and assess them for possible placement.[9] Despite their lack of offense, many fathers are ruled unsuitable for placement because of their social or criminal history or current living situation. Legally children must be in imminent danger to be removed from their homes by CPS. Once in protective custody, their well-being is the responsibility of the county. Consequently a higher standard exists for returning or placing children than for removing them.[10] After children have become dependents of the court, nonoffending fathers—that is, fathers who are not directly responsible for the harm that led their children into the system—are scrutinized against this higher standard.

The case of Leonard King, a twenty-eight-year-old African American man, provides a useful example. Leonard's six-month-old daughter Leonisha was removed from his girlfriend Traci Mays' custody when she left the six-month-old with her five half-siblings, the oldest of whom was fifteen. Traci's other children had been in CPS custody before Leonisha's birth, following their molestation by their father and the death of one child from what Leonard described as a vitamin overdose—most likely iron poisoning.[11] The current case, in which Leonisha and her five half-siblings were placed in protective custody, began when the social worker responsible for monitoring Traci's children after they were reunited with her conducted an unannounced visit and chose to remove them from what was described as a filthy house. Although Leonard did not live there, he was denied placement of his infant daughter, likely because of a past conviction for drug dealing. Voicing his frustration, he explains,

When they took my daughter, they should have notified me ahead of time and gave me my daughter. They shouldn't have just popped up and taken my daughter and then try to make me out to be someone I'm not. That's a whole lot of mess. CPS is messed up. To me, they messed up…They shouldn't, they shouldn't make the mom or the father suffer because of what the other parent does; see that's one thing I don't like about CPS.

The vocabulary of "reunification" does not really apply to men like Leonard who have never had custody of —or been unified with—their children. Nonetheless, the only mechanism that exists for fathers who are deemed unsuitable but who wish to gain custody of their children is the totality of the reunification services system. For example, Scott Hughes, an African American man in his late thirties, came to court to gain custody of his newborn daughter who tested positive for cocaine at birth, the fourth "pos-tox" baby born to Scott's girlfriend, Chantelle Carter. In keeping with new federal legislation that does not require the county to attempt reunification in situations where parents have not benefited from prior services, Chantelle was not given an opportunity to reunify with her newborn daughter.[12] Although Scott did not have any other children, Tess Bachmeier, a white attorney in her mid-thirties representing the baby, argued in court that Scott should also be denied services. Citing a four-year-old conviction for driving under the influence of alcohol and his failure to complete court-ordered services for that felony, as well as a conviction for driving without a license one year ago, Tess contended that "the father has quite a history of alcohol…and not a lot of respect for court orders." Here Scott, who was not suspected of drug use and had never received family reunification services before, had to fight to establish his right to vie for custody of his daughter.

In addition to his criminal record, Scott's romantic involvement with a woman who was drug addicted was offered as proof that he was not capable of adequately parenting. Pointing to his inability to adequately protect the fetus from drug exposure, Tess continued to outline her position: "Perhaps most concerning is his ambivalence about taking care of his own child…He had knowledge of the mother's substance abuse problem and use during her pregnancy." In his own defense, Scott, who had never lived with Chantelle, said that he had tried to get her to stop using. However, Isabel Guzman, a Latina county attorney—joining with Tess—argued that the fact "that he involved himself with the mother in a fashion that led to the conception of this child" was itself cause for concern. Although he was offered services and visitation with his daughter, his unwillingness to abandon Chantelle eventually led to the termination of his parental rights.

A father who refuses to abandon an abusive or drug-addicted girlfriend, wife, or partner will fail to reunify with his children. But a father's sexual behavior during reunification is not at issue in the same way it is for a mother. As seen in chapter 6, women's sexual relationships indicate a lack of independence or psychological weakness. In contrast, men's sexual relationships represent their capacity to make decisions—good or bad. When a father has a girlfriend without a prior CPS or criminal history, she is often perceived as an asset to his case, especially when she attends visits and services. He may have been living with her and her children without incident, which can provide some promise of a stable home life. However, men who remain in relationships with "bad women" are seen as poor choice makers. For example, Juan Reyes, a Latino truck driver (whose troubles securing housing were discussed in chapter 5) wanted to reunify with his two daughters and stepdaughter. To do so, he needed to abandon Leigh, his drug-addicted wife, who was neither participating in court-ordered services nor drug treatment, and who attended court hearings while self-declaredly under the influence of drugs and alcohol. (As an example of her lack of desire to present herself as attempting reform, her attorney asked her before a court hearing when she last used drugs and alcohol, to which she responded, "What time is it?") Although Juan did eventually separate from Leigh, his hesitance to do so worked against him and nearly cost him his parental rights.

The quality of the partners men choose represents their ability to make responsible decisions—a key aspect of competent masculinity. By having children with women to whom they are not married, men are already suspect, particularly when those women behave in ways that lead to state intervention. Chris Vaughn's case provides an example of this.[13.] Chris, a thirty-seven-year-old white man, had a brief relationship with Erica Finola, a woman he met at a Narcotics Anonymous meeting. After their affair ended, Erica disappeared and was presumed to have relapsed both in her drug addiction and schizophrenia, for which she refused to take her prescribed medications. Approximately one year later, Chris ran into Erica. She informed him that she had given birth to a baby girl that had been taken into CPS custody and that the baby was probably his. Fearful that he would owe child support, Chris hesitated to contact the county and identify himself as the likely father. By the time he did come forward to claim custody of his daughter Shelby—a few months later—the county fought him, insisting that he had come forward too late to qualify for reunification services. The judge eventually awarded Chris a case plan, which included services and scheduled visits with Shelby, that he would have to complete to gain custody of her. Despite Chris's initial victory, he felt it was unjust that he was required to complete services. In an argument with his attorney, Chris bemoaned the cumbersome nature of reunification services. His attorney, Rebecca Channing, retorted, "You went and got a woman pregnant who went and got herself in CPS." In essence, Chris—like Scott, Juan, and other men who impregnate drug-addicted women—was seen as a poor decision maker, and by association, incapable of adequate fathering.

Unlike mothers, who can be perceived as helpless victims who are worthy of pity and in need of guidance, men are presumed to be active agents. Like many of the women in CPS, many men have been victims of violence, neglect, or sexual abuse. Research of the general population estimates that between 4 and 16 percent of males have been sexually abused as children, with as many as 40 percent of the prison population meeting the standard criteria for childhood sexual abuse.[14] Another study found that as many as 69 percent of incarcerated adult male felons reported some form of childhood victimization.[15] As adults, men are much more likely to be the victims of crime than are women.[16] Despite their histories of abuse, there is no rhetoric of victimhood or needed empowerment readily available to men. This is not surprising in light of constructions of masculinity that define victimization as feminizing or as a failure to assert masculine dominance. Instead, attorneys and social workers perceive CPS fathers to be "bad men," regardless of their route into the system or past struggles. Women are seen as victims of their lives and men are perceived as active agents who have created their life circumstances. As such, they must establish that they desire to reform and are worthy of services. This level of deference is difficult for men who are often distrustful of authority, many of whom have only encountered the state as repressive and disciplinary.

MEN'S RELATIVE RIGHT TO SERVICES

Men who are married to the mothers of their children are assumed to be the children's father, unless there is legal documentation to the contrary. However, most of the men who enter CPS were never married to the mothers of their children. Once a man who is not married to the mother of his child at the time of conception or birth comes forward and is identified as someone who is most likely the child's father, he becomes, as far as the court is concerned, the "alleged father." In some cases, there may be multiple alleged fathers. To be entitled to reunification services, an alleged father must become a "presumed father" (or "putative father"),[17] of which there can only be one. The ways a man can establish presumed father status vary slightly from state to state.[18] In California, establishing presumed father status typically requires that men provide the court with some combination of the following documentation:

- A copy of a declaration of paternity, signed at the child's birth (this is a form voluntarily claiming parentage);[19]
- A child support order from the district attorney's office;

- The mother's testimony that he is the biological father, that they lived together at the time of conception, and that she does not believe any one else could be the father; or
- A copy of the birth certificate with the man's name on it. (On its own, the birth certificate does not establish paternity, but does serve as evidence of who the mother believed was the father at the time of birth. However, implementation of the Personal Responsibility and Work Opportunity Reconciliation Act of 1996 requires that unmarried fathers cannot be listed on birth certificates unless they sign a declaration of paternity).[20]

Alternatively, the court can order a paternity test. This genetic test compares the DNA of the alleged father to that of the child in question and determines with 99.9 percent certainty whether the child was conceived from sperm from the alleged father.

Although it would seem simple for an alleged father to provide one of these forms of proof, it is often quite difficult. The case at the beginning of this chapter provides such an example. In that case, a twenty-six-year-old Laotian woman named Marla Chue, who suffers from mental retardation and mild cerebral palsy, was legally married to Dusty Benjamin, a twenty-five-year-old white man who is also cognitively impaired, most likely as a result of a lifetime of severe grand mal seizures. Marla became pregnant and announced that the baby was not Dusty's, but instead belonged to Dirk Haigenberger, a twenty-three-year-old white man who is also impaired, but is the highest functioning of the three. At the time of conception, all three adults were sharing an apartment, but upon learning of the sexual relationship between Marla and Dirk, Dusty moved out.

Jeff Roper, an independent living specialist employed by the county, was assigned to assist Marla and Dirk with the baby. His work included coming to their residence and teaching them appropriate care of the baby, housekeeping, and basic infant safety. Dusty also came over every morning to his former dwelling to "help," though he was told by Jeff that all social services (including those that Jeff provided) were exclusively for Marla and Dirk. Jeff was concerned that Marla and Dirk were unable to keep the infant safe and lacked interest in learning to do so. Within days of the baby's birth, he reported them to CPS. An investigating social worker determined the infant was in imminent danger and placed him in protective custody. The case then went to court.

One of the first tasks for the court was to determine which adults should be eligible to reunify with the infant. Like many states, California presumes that men who are legally married to the mother of their children are the legal fathers.[21] Based on his legal marriage to Marla and their shared residence at the time of conception, Dusty was given the status of presumed father. However, Dirk's appointed attorney, Murray Liebman, a white man in his early fifties, contended that his client, who had signed a declaration of paternity at the hospital at the time of the baby's birth, was legally the father. He argued that according to the statute, that declaration held the same legal power as a court order finding him the father. Unfortunately Dirk could not produce a copy of the document he claimed to have signed. Marla insisted that Dirk was the father and that he too had shared a residence with her at the time of conception. Capturing the murkiness of the competing legal claims, Dusty's attorney explained during a prehearing conference, "The legal term for this is a mess."

As the judge saw it, the obvious solution was to order a paternity test to establish who was actually the biological father. Dirk's attorney argued that the law did not allow the court to order a paternity test when a presumption of paternity existed. Thwarted, the judge explained that he was unsure how to proceed since there were two competing legal presumptions of paternity in this case. Each presumption stemmed from statutes that are meant to be complementary, but were in this instance contradictory. Ending the stalemate, Marla's attorney finally said that his client was willing to request the paternity test, though Marla, who only minimally comprehended the proceedings, never actually voiced the requisite uncertainty, and thus never actually made the request. Nonetheless, once entered on the record, this request overrode all legal presumptions and the paternity test determined that Dirk was in fact the biological father. Dusty became a nonparty to the proceedings.

Most parents in the CPS system are not legally married. Thus paternity almost always hinges on biology. A father who is not genetically related to the child will find it difficult to remain involved in the case. For example, I observed a case in which a man requested reunification services, only to discover that the six-year-old girl he had lived with and raised as his daughter since her birth was not biologically—therefore not legally—his. He was instantly excluded from the process. His parents, who had requested to be considered as relatives for foster placement, were no longer eligible for expedited kinship placement and had to undergo foster care licensing to gain placement of the little girl that they considered their granddaughter. Men in this situation can petition for de facto parent status—that is, recognition that they are parents in fact, even if not in law—but they must demonstrate to the court that their continued involvement is in the best interest of the child.[22] If they were part of the allegation that brought the family into CPS, or if they have a criminal history, there is little to no chance they can demonstrate that their continued involvement is in the child's best interest. Fathers are not seen as essential to children's well-being in the way mothers are, creating a disincentive for the state to include men unless it is legally necessary.

LEGAL CONSTRUCTIONS OF FATHERHOOD

Legal presumptions of paternity have been written into statutes, yet the bulk of their meaning is derived from case law. In general, paternity law in the realm of mainstream family law accomplishes two things: it reifies paternal rights through legal marriage and it identifies who must financially support children. Briefly exploring these legal goals will provide a backdrop to contrast general paternity law with the rules of paternity in the CPS system.

Paternity law has been shaped through a series of lawsuits where men attempted to either assert or renounce their parental rights and responsibilities. One way this has happened has been through a series of unsuccessful lawsuits in which fathers have challenged court orders to pay child support for children who they discover are not genetically theirs. For example, in the 1999 Pennsylvania Supreme Court case of *Miscovich v. Miscovich*, a divorced father proved that he was not the biological father of a son who was born to his wife during their marriage, and thus should no longer be obligated to pay child support.[23] The court rejected his claim, noting that state law does not define paternity as hinging upon genetic testing. Having been married to the boy's mother, state law recognized him as the legal father and the party responsible for supporting his four-year-old son. Most states have similar laws. This is in sharp contrast to CPS, where paternity hinges almost entirely on a genetic relationship.

Paternity law has also been shaped by several cases where fathers who were not married to the mothers of their biological children have been unable to assert their parental rights because the women were married to someone else. In the 1989 case of *Michael H. v. Gerald D.*, the U.S. Supreme Court upheld a law that permitted only a husband or wife to rebut a presumption that a child born during marriage belonged to the husband.[24] Similarly the California Supreme Court refused to allow Jerry K., a biological father, any legal parental rights to a child he conceived with a married woman who was separated from her husband at the time of conception, but who later reconciled with him.[25] Instead, the court upheld the estranged husband's rights to the child. In that case, the majority opinion protected the traditional nuclear family and men's role within it by writing that "a man who wishes to father a child and ensure his relationship with that child can do so by finding a partner, entering into marriage, and undertaking the responsibilities marriage imposes."[26] The language of this decision fleshes out a cultural belief that competent fathers are good providers and should be married to the mothers of their children.

Men are not necessarily excluded from fatherhood without marriage, so long as the mother is not married to anyone else. Other cases have established that unmarried women have no legal right to prohibit men from establishing their rights to paternity of their children. For example, if an unmarried woman is given sperm for the purpose of insemination (without going through a medically licensed intermediary), the man giving her the sperm can make claims of paternity or be obligated to financially support the child, irrespective of any prior agreement to the contrary.[27] Had she been married, the man could assert no such rights because paternity rights would belong to her husband. The California appellate court ruled that this did not present any injustice to the unmarried woman who did not want the sperm donor father to be involved. In their 1986 ruling in *Jhordan C. v. Mary K.*, the court addressed questions of whether "affording protection to husband and wife from any claim of paternity by an outsider denies equal protection by failing to provide similar protection to an unmarried woman." The majority opinion noted that because "a married woman and an unmarried woman are not similarly situated for purposes of equal protection analysis" no such injustice occurred.[28] Again making marriage central to family life, the decision asserts that "the marital relationship invokes a long-recognized social policy of preserving the integrity of the marriage. No such concerns arise where there is no marriage at all." This case, though brought by a woman, again shows how men's ability to exercise their paternal rights is contingent on marital status.[29]

In each of the above cases, the court protected the legal nuclear family. The court not only granted the rights of paternity to married men, but also defined an inescapable responsibility to provide financially for their children. By identifying fiscal responsibility for children as an obligation of legal fatherhood, the state articulates that children are not a public responsibility. This position can be observed in contemporary social welfare policy, which requires women receiving public assistance to identify the fathers of their children to welfare and child support collection agents.[30] In defining children as privately supported and by identifying a single legal father with a responsibility that cannot be renounced, the state protects its own fiscal interests. This political, economic, and ideological construction of fatherhood also reinforces the private patriarchal family as such.

In the CPS system, the state's interests and goals are different, altering the structure of paternal rights. With the primary goal of child safety, the CPS system aims first to reunify children with their parents, when doing so can be achieved quickly. However, a secondary goal is to eliminate parental claims to a child, allowing the court to offer services to fewer people and to free a child for adoption or long-term guardianship sooner, both of which are financially advantageous to the state. It is virtually impossible for fathers to renounce their paternal rights and responsibilities in every other realm of family law, where child support is central. In contrast, in the CPS system, the burden is on a father to establish his paternity in order to gain access to reunification services.

ENCOURAGING ABSENTEE FATHERHOOD

The CPS system advises fathers who come forward to establish paternity that doing so may not be in their best interest. First, parents in CPS may be billed for some portion of the costs of foster care, regardless of whether they succeed in gaining custody of their children.[31] Court documents given to parents at the onset of the case advise:

> TO THE PARENT OR OTHERS LEGALLY RESPONSIBLE FOR THE SUPPORT OF THE CHILD: You and the estate of your child may be jointly and severely liable for the cost of the care, support, and maintenance of your child in any placement or detention facility, the cost of legal services for you or your child by a public defender or other attorney, and the cost of supervision of your child by order of the juvenile court.[32]

While attempting to gain custody of their children, parents also absorb some or all of the costs of services, in addition to the costs of foster care and legal representation, if they are deemed capable of paying. Parents often perceive these costs as an added hurdle to reunification. Mateo Estes, a Latino father in his early twenties, was accused of breaking the leg of his four-year-old stepdaughter, Leanna. He denied causing the spiral fracture and insisted that it was broken when it became lodged between her bed frame and the wall while she was jumping on the bed as he tucked her two-year-old half-brother into his bed in the same room. One proposed solution was for Leanna to undergo an interview at the multidisciplinary interviewing center (MDIC). These centers are staffed by psychologists, social workers, law enforcement officers, and representatives from the district attorney's office who are all present at one location and view a single interview. These centers have grown in popularity nationally, since this "one-stop shop" approach allows for the child to be interviewed only one time (following the initial interviews at the hospital and by social workers) and because the interviewers are considered to be professional and impartial. Though the interview might support his claim that his daughter's leg was broken while jumping on the bed, Mateo felt the costs of the interview would add considerable financial stress.

> They want to do an MDIC on my Lee-Lee, which costs like, which costs like three grand, I was told. And we have to pick that up. And I've borrowed enough from my father. I have to pay my father back five grand (borrowed to hire a private attorney). I can't be tacking on more money on that. I wouldn't ask my family to do that.

Fathers who are not yet identified as legal fathers can avoid these costs by deciding not to participate in reunification. Without establishing legal paternity, they will not be billed. Needless to say, this is an option almost entirely unavailable to mothers.

Also, fathers who come forward assume the risk of failing to reunify, which carries potentially far-reaching consequences. Many counties have adopted federal provisions that allow them to automatically remove other children from parents who have a history of failing to reunify with a child. In such cases, the burden is on the parent to prove that his or her life is substantively different from when the prior CPS case was decided. Although this is a gender-neutral issue, fathers who have not yet established their presumed father status are cautioned that they will need to commit themselves to the process, since failing to reunify can affect their ability to retain legal custody of future children they may have. Mothers, who are easily identified as legal parents, are seldom offered this caution or escape route.[33]

There is a body of literature alleging that fathers are so essential to child well-being that their very absence can explain why some boys engage in criminal activity and accounts for poor outcomes more generally.[34] Those who take this position assume that fathers have a certain level of employability and advocate for men to be married to the mothers of their children. I contend that the dependency court system, a pragmatic institution, views men as potentially more threatening than important. Given the social histories of these men, which often include substance abuse, felony convictions, and nonmarital childbearing, the court does not hold that the presence of the fathers who enter CPS will insulate children against future criminal behavior, nor will it increase their incomes, rates of education, or access to resources. These paternal characteristics also offer little assurance that the children will not face future harm.

WORKING TO REUNIFY

Once a man has established his legal status as the presumed father, he will be assessed for placement of his child. Placement is based on some assessment of risk, drawing on a medley of variables, including employment history, criminal history, history of alcohol or drug use, current housing arrangement, and ongoing social support. During my research, I saw only two cases in which a father gained immediate custody of his children with the court dismissing dependency, meaning they would not even monitor the children in the father's home. In one case, a middle-aged white man who resided in a different state with his current wife was able to immediately gain custody of his preteen daughter who had been molested by her mother's boyfriend. The other was the case described in chapter 4, in which Candace's ex-husband, a middle-class African American man, was able to gain custody of their two biological children when she was accused of inappropriately disciplining a child she had adopted after their separation. Neither man had a criminal history and both were middle-class and employed. Potentially more relevant, both men had been married to the mothers of their children.

The court gives outright custody to few fathers, so most men are subjected to the machinations of the reunification process, whether or not they are directly involved in the harm or risk that led their children into the system. As previously mentioned, once a nonoffending father enters the reunification process, he is treated virtually identically to men who committed an offense against a child. This includes the expectation that he will show deference. Tim Ross, a white man in his early twenties, confronted this expectation. Tim came to court in a bid for his infant son, a child his ex-girlfriend, Lisa Flynn, a white woman in her early twenties, denied was his. Their infant son James became a dependent shortly after birth because Lisa's five-year-old daughter, James's half-sister, had been in protective custody for more than a year after being molested by a male friend of Lisa's. Tim came to court insisting he was James's father and demanded consideration. Although Lisa identified another man as James's father, she indicated that she was not certain. (The other man who received notice from the juvenile court never came forward.) A judge ordered paternity testing, but Lisa's failure to make James available for the test delayed Tim's ability to establish his claim. He became frustrated, an emotion he made known to those with whom he came in contact.

At the next hearing, the family reunification social worker assigned to James's case reported to the court that Tim had been "hostile and aggressive." As the judge asked him about his behavior, Tim stated defensively that he was "just being assertive." The judge informed Tim that should he actually be James's father, the county agency and the court would be in his life for a long time and would make his life more complicated. The judge sternly advised Tim to be cordial. Tim, who had not mistreated the child—not yet even determined to be his child—was asked to defer to the authority of the court and social workers. One might recognize Tim's behavior as consistent with hegemonic masculinity's requirements for aggression, dominance, and self-control. In other situations—including those of his own social world—his behavior might have been rewarded. However, in the context of the system, deference demonstrates an acceptance of state prescriptions and a desire to improve ones self, which are necessary to succeed.

EMPLOYMENT VERSUS COMPLIANCE

Once fathers establish their legal right to participate in reunification, they must prove they can act as children's primary caregivers and be good fathers. Many men understand this to mean that they must first and foremost be good economic providers. The assumption that fathers should be breadwinners rather than nurturers has a long history in public policy. For example, in one 1952 case, the New Jersey State Board of Child Welfare, responsible at the time for administering aid to widows and dependent children, ruled against allowing fathers to collect a Mother's Pension to support and care for their motherless children. The board's statement explained that

> It seems psychologically and socially destructive for a healthy father to willingly surrender his normal role of breadwinner for the purposes of assuming the unfamiliar duties of housekeeper and nursemaid, without damaging his ego and risking the loss of the esteem and respect of his neighbors and friends.[35]

Although welfare policy has changed to grant full-time fathers assistance, social expectations have been slower to shift. To that end, men in

CPS are acutely aware that to be socially competent fathers, they must be good financial providers. For many CPS fathers whose earning potentials are limited by lack of formal education, discontinuous work histories, or prior convictions, appearing to be competent breadwinners is challenging. However, the desire of many men to appear to be good providers distracts them from completing services, which on its own can prevent them from successfully gaining custody of their children.

Parents who try to maintain paid employment often find it difficult to comply with reunification services. Robert Davis, a construction worker, whose case was discussed in chapter 5, described his difficulties: "I just lost a lot of jobs. I'm always on probation [at a new job]. If I were part of the union, they would not have been able to fire me." Yet CPS also made it difficult for Robert to join a union. He explained, "I would be on probation also. And that's one of the things I've been hesitating about, going all the way for the union job, because I would also be on probation when I first started and I don't want to lose that opportunity because I start out on probation and then I get kicked out." When asked if CPS was the reason that he was having difficulty remaining employed, he answered tentatively: "I'm not going to point any fingers. I had to go to parenting classes, I had to go to anger management classes, I have to go to court, I have to go to counseling of some type—that was part of my case file. And each and every one of those things I had in between job hours so I'll let you label that."

Complying with services is even more difficult for parents who work outside of the geographic area. For example, Juan's job created several problems for his case. Juan (whose trouble securing housing was discussed in chapter 5) is a Latino man in his late thirties. His two daughters and stepdaughter were placed in foster care because of general neglect stemming in large part from his wife's addiction to methamphetamine. During the timeframe for reunification, Juan decided he needed a stable job to support his children. Approximately ten months after his case began, he enrolled in a vocational training program to become a truck driver. While in trucking school, his court-ordered visits with his daughters became irregular. When he completed his three-month truck-driver training program, he began driving interstate routes, which also interrupted his visits. When his spotty visitation record was brought up in court, he argued that he often called his social worker and attempted to arrange alternative times for visits or would ask his estranged wife Leigh to arrange the visits for him. In his mind he was making a sincere effort to comply, not realizing that both were poor strategies in light of Leigh's total lack of compliance with her own reunification case plan and his social worker's overwhelming caseload.

Many women struggle to work while participating in reunification, but they seem typically more willing to forego employment to complete their services. In contrast, fathers seem to feel that the best way to demonstrate their ability to parent was to show their ability to financially support their families. (This adherence to a belief in men's need to financially support the family crossed all lines of race, education, and class, although there was admittedly limited variation among the CPS fathers in this study, who were mostly poor or working class.) In the following passage, Richie identifies the way that services interfere with employment to be one of the greatest flaws of the CPS system. In doing so, he privileges the role of the good provider over compliance with other services. He explains,

> Most of the time they make it too inconvenient for the father to even try to get the kids. Half the time, with all of the stuff they want you to go through, you ain't got time to work and go to counseling and money management and anger management and parenting classes. You're doing all of the shit that they want you to do and you ain't got time to work.

Like many other men, Richie did not consider quitting work to focus on reunification, but instead perceived services as a distraction from the real duties of fatherhood.

The judge, guided by social worker recommendations, expects parents to demonstrate their ability to maintain a functional household after reunification; parental employment is a good marker of that. However, employment is less important than completion of the services, as prescribed in a parent's case plan. Without satisfying the case plan, men's employment status or income counts for very little. Addressing this, attorneys sometimes pragmatically suggest that their clients quit work as a way to increase the likelihood of reunification. Parents often ignore this suggestion, as did Chris, who was greatly frustrated with the amount of time his required services demanded. He bemoaned his lack of time for his schoolwork, paid employment, unpaid internship, and daily Alcoholics Anonymous meetings, which were not court ordered, but which had been part of his daily routine for almost a decade. After a hearing, Chris emphatically explained to his attorney Rebecca that he needed more time to complete the requirements of his two-year course in film production. She responded with equal frustration, explaining that he may need to choose between his daughter and his other priorities:

Rebecca: Stop whining, stop whining, stop whining… You might have to choose and you might have to quit… It is a terrible choice, but you might have to do it.

Chris: I can't do it. I can't get back into the program if I take an incomplete. I'd have to do two years over again… The court is creating this!

Rebecca: The court doesn't care about that.

Chris: This is why people go on welfare!

Chris asserts that reunification services interfere with paid employment and thus create a route onto public assistance, which contradicts state goals. This is an astute observation, as federal policy has increasingly defined competent parenting as synonymous with paid employment. As an example of this, Tommy Thompson, as Secretary of Health and Human Services, touted the success of work requirements as a condition of receiving public assistance by stating, "Despite many challenges, TANF families continue to pursue independence for the benefit of themselves and their children." In calling for support for a federal plan to increase the number of hours of work required, he added, "Passage of the President's welfare reauthorization plan will help many more families build a better life. I urge Congress to enact legislation as soon as possible that incorporates the President's principles of work, personal responsibility, and strengthening families." It is difficult to understand how parents' increased absence from their children and children's greater lengths of stay in child care can in any real way "strengthen families." Yet, as Chris observed, Thompson articulated, and many poor families experience, paid employment—even as it pays too little to actually support a family—is rhetorically and culturally synonymous with good parenting.[36] Yet in the CPS system, the prioritization of employment over other services can derail parents' attempts to regain custody of their children.

Although parents identify their own ways of demonstrating competent parenting—including the ability to provide financially for their children—the court holds them accountable for completing the services as laid out by the social worker. The high volume of cases social workers handle translates into practice where case plans are neither flexible, nor negotiable. Although the fathers described above were largely perceived as noncompliant, they were attempting, in a way that made sense to them, to reunify with their children. But in defining their own schedule or priorities, such as prioritizing a job over counseling or drug testing, they allow the state to view them as uncommitted to their rehabilitation. By resisting the prescribed services, parents fail to defer to state definitions and instead communicate that they are unwilling or unable to change to reduce the risk to their children.

PROVING THE CAPACITY TO PARENT

In addition to proving—or performing—commitment to self-improvement, men who want custody of their children must also show that they can provide day-to-day care. To gain custody of their children, fathers must convince social workers and court officers that they cannot only keep their children free from harm, but can adequately meet their daily needs. In addition to the conflicts between paid employment and service completion, men also frequently face skepticism about their ability to serve as primary caregivers. Until the nineteenth century, fathers' claims of ownership of their children, who were seen as an economic resource, were unquestioned. In the late nineteenth century, nurturing and caring for children came to be seen as the responsibility of women, who were perceived to be uniquely qualified to provide it. As childhood evolved into a period of nurture and development, meeting the emotional needs of children became central to decisions about their material circumstance. In situations where parents did not reside together, custody of children was almost always awarded to women. This trend continued as an explicit policy preference through most of the twentieth century. For example, a 1971 Minnesota State Bar Association handbook advised lawyers and judges that "except in very rare cases, the father should not have custody of the minor children. He is usually unqualified psychologically and emotionally."[37]

Reflecting the belief that women were able to provide superior care to young children—a common policy, known as "the tender years doctrine"—young children were to remain with their mothers, unless their mothers were found to be unfit. Welfare historian Mary Ann Mason contends that "the tender years doctrine was never a mother's right; it was a child centered rule. It forced the court to move away from treating children as a property right of their fathers to focusing on the child's need for nurture."[38] In 1979, responding to complaints by alienated fathers, the California legislature adopted a preference for joint custody of children in instances of divorce. Other states followed suit, with at least thirty-five states and the District of Columbia now using a preference for joint custody following divorce.[39] However, the preference for joint custody does not extend to men who were never married to the mothers of their children, the situation of the majority of fathers in the CPS system. Issues surrounding the custody rights of these men have been virtually unexplored in the research and literature on fathers' custody issues, which almost exclusively address the situations of married or divorced men. As such, it is useful to examine the court decisions that have shaped custody rights for fathers who were never married to the mothers of their children to better comprehend the current challenges CPS fathers face.

The first articulation of legal rights for unmarried fathers came in the 1972 case of *Stanley v. Illinois*.[40] Peter Stanley had lived with the mother of his three children on and off for eighteen years, but had never married her. When she died, the children were declared wards of the court and the state attempted to terminate Mr. Stanley's parental rights. Mr. Stanley successfully argued to the U.S. Supreme Court that the state could not assume he was an unfit parent simply because he was unmarried. (The case was then sent back to the Illinois Juvenile Court, where he was declared unfit and permanently lost custody of his children.) Despite Mr. Stanley's failure to keep his own children, the *Stanley* decision established that men are not intrinsically unfit to parent simply because they do not marry the mother of their children.

In 1978 the U.S. Supreme Court further shaped paternal rights for unwed fathers by defining the importance of "a significant parental relationship between the unmarried father and the child." In *Quilloin v. Walcott*, a biological father who had no relationship with his thirteen-year-old son was unable to block his son's adoption by the boy's stepfather, a man who had actively participated in his life since the boy was four years old. In the Court's view, the child's interests were best served by being adopted.[41] Further tying paternity to proof of a significant relationship, the U.S. Supreme Court decided by a 5–4 ruling in *Caban v. Mohammed* (1979) in favor of a man who was challenging a New York law that allowed a woman to consent to the adoption of her child, but did not require the father's consent.[42] The Court reached this decision largely because Mr. Caban had lived with his two children and their mother "as a natural family for several years."[43] (The subtext of this decision is that the families of men who don't live with their children and their children's mothers are unnatural.) In concert, these cases define unmarried fathers' rights and clarify that although failure to marry the mother of one's children does not intrinsically make a father unfit, paternity does require a man to have a relationship of substance with his children. For men married to their children's mother, the presumption is that a significant relationship exists. Unmarried fathers must prove it.

A large body of recent social research demonstrates the ways non-residential or never-married fathers participate in and contribute to their children's lives, even if these ways are informal, inconsistent, or underreported. For example, fathers may bring over diapers, contribute money sporadically, help with bills, or take children out shopping for needed items. This body of work provides important insights into the multiple ways that men, particularly poor and minority men, engage in fathering. However, state practice largely fails to consider these unreported or informal contributions.[44]

Unmarried fathers have gone from having no rights to their children thirty years ago to having some rights. While *Stanley* makes marital status less central to assessments of paternal competence, men who do not marry the mothers of their children are still suspect, a fact that is clear to the fathers in CPS.[45] Many men in CPS feel that images of them as irresponsible, with the tender years doctrine as a backdrop, undermine their claims that they are capable of caring for their children. According to Richie, "For one, they act like fathers don't know how to take care of kids. They act like because you're a man you're not suitable to be taking care of your own children. And as far as thinking-wise, that's an automatic thing for a woman, ya know. But it's not an automatic thing when you think about a man."

Several of the men with whom I spoke discussed how assumptions that women are superior caretakers interfered with their ability to reunify with their children. Robert describes his battle to challenge such assumptions:

> Well, like I was told this morning when I was in conversation with this lady...she was like, "Why don't you let your mother have your children?" And I said, "They're my children; I think I deserve the right to take care of my children." She goes, "Well, they won't let you take care of your children; you're a man." And I've already been told that men are not supposed to raise children by my former social worker. Every time a man makes an attempt to raise a child, people start throwing spears. So it's harder for the man to first get the child so that he can raise the child.

Both Robert and Richie argue that the presumption that women are more capable is unjust. Yet not all the men I interviewed felt that the assumed superior caregiving abilities of women were incorrect. Some men more readily accepted the presumption that parenting comes naturally to women and perceived men's lack of natural aptitude to be an added obstacle. Illustrating this, Chris explains,

Ya know, I don't think it's fair because there are a lot of fathers, I know this one guy who fought for his son and it was a hell of a fight. It's harder for guys because they don't have it built into them. Women, it's like, boom! They're practically born with it. And guys just don't have it. And I'm just starting to find it. And maybe I'll never find it, but I'm going to try to do what I can do to have it happen.

Chris's comment reflects the assumption that parenting comes more naturally to women, while simultaneously arguing that it placed him at an unfair disadvantage; his innate inferiority in parenting is yet another unfair challenge to what he perceives as his patriarchal right to his daughter Shelby. Chris was approached on several occasions by Shelby's attorney, Andrea Winnow, who encouraged him to voluntarily relinquish his parental rights so that Shelby's foster mother could adopt her without a protracted legal battle. Doing so would not only free Shelby for adoption, but would free Chris from the mounting foster care bill.[46] The county counsel and the foster mother's attorney supported this campaign. As Andrea argued for his consent, she attempted to display empathy, commenting, "I know child support is hard for you." Chris replied, "No. *This* is hard for me." Conceivably, Chris could believe that his daughter would be better off with her foster mother because of her superior parenting abilities. Yet Chris vowed to continue his fight for his daughter, stating, "I'm not interested in a compromise. I've come this far."

In addition to the gendered assumptions about them, many men of color, most frequently African American men, felt that racial stereotypes further hindered their attempts to assert their right to parent. They faced images of African American men as dangerous, irresponsible, and predatory, in addition to visions of them as incapable of parenting. African American men have been targeted in the public imagination and in social policy as perpetrators of crime, responsible for high rates of nonmarital childbearing, and as unwilling to support and provide for their children.[47] Further, African American men, while not always explicitly identified as the source of problems, are referenced in policy discussions as "inherently irresponsible, erratic in behavior, and unable to assume the responsibilities of employment or fatherhood."[48] Sensing these prejudices, Robert articulated how he felt these stereotypes reinforced perceptions of him as unable to father: "I've had stereotype. Black man been convicted once before. Black man believed to be hostile. Black man that's not wealthy. Black man that's been involved with a mother who's a controlled substance abuser, sexually. Man does not raise children."

Some men of color articulated their belief that these racialized assumptions actually led to their entrance into the system. Frank Ramirez, a forty-four-year-old man of Cuban and African American descent, entered CPS when his thirty-seven-year-old white live-in girl-friend Shelly gave birth to their son Francisco, who tested positive for methamphetamine. Although Shelly had eight other children from her prior marriage, Francisco was Frank's only child. Shelly's six blonde-haired, fair-skinned daughters who had been living with Shelly and Frank also became dependents of the state, while her sixteen-year-old son, who was attending a residential school out of state, did not (nor did her nineteen-year-old daughter). In discussing their entrance into CPS, Frank identifies race as a factor:

> They look at it from another standpoint. They look at it like here we got this black man with six white girls… I can read people pretty good and before I had this attorney here they were really infringing on seeing me with this woman and these kids. Ya know you could see it. They really wanted to get at me because I'm black and I'm with all of these little white girls. You can see it on people's faces, their attitudes, and stuff.

For many fathers, race, class, and gender come together to form a presumption that they are unfit to father. Their experiences of inequality and of presumed incompetence informs other experiences with the state that then inform their interactions with CPS. Theorist Joan Acker explains, "Gender does not exist in a set of relations that are distinct from other relations, such as those of class or race, but as part of processes that also constitute class and race, as well as other lines of demarcation and domination."[49] While these intersections of inequality shape men's experiences in CPS, they also construct men's experiences in other institutions, including the criminal justice system. This is of particular relevance as criminal histories—affected by the disparate treatment of poor men and men of color in the criminal justice system—interfere with the ability of men to reunify with their children.

BAD MEN AS GOOD FATHERS?

To have their children immediately placed with them, fathers must have little or no criminal history or history of substance use or abuse.[50] In fact, a criminal history for violent or drug-related crimes is one of the most significant hindrances to reunification. According to the Bureau of Justice Statistics, if recent incarceration rates remain unchanged, an estimated one of every twenty persons (5.1 percent) will serve time in a prison during their lifetime. This rate is about eight times higher for men than women. Based on current rates of first incarceration, an estimated 28 percent of black males will enter state or federal prison during their lifetime, compared to 16 percent of Hispanic males and 4.4 percent of white males. Sixty-four percent of state prisoners in 2001 and 63 percent of jail inmates in 1996 belonged to racial or ethnic minorities.[51] In 1996, drug offenders comprised one-third of all persons convicted in state courts, with African Americans comprising more than half of this population.[52] Criminal behavior and parenthood are not mutually exclusive. In fact, drug offenders often have children. Of prisoners with children, 24 percent of parents in state prison and 67 percent in federal prison are incarcerated for drug-related crimes. Of the total inmate population, those who have children are more likely to be incarcerated for drug-related offenses than are prisoners without children. At the same time, approximately 60 percent of children in foster care nationwide are from racial or ethnic minority groups.[53] As a result, the inequalities in treatment of poor men and men of color in the criminal justice system are reproduced in the CPS system where criminal history is a significant litmus test for reunification. Richie, who was incarcerated multiple times between the ages of fourteen and forty, identified the role his criminal history played in undermining his claim to his daughter. Reflecting on the strong opposition he faced, he explained,

> I think a lot... come from, on a man taking care of his kids and certain circumstances, like my circumstances; ya know, I have a hell of a record and I have a lot of shit against me. But me, I don't ever feel that they would believe that I wouldn't do anything to my child. I just think that because of my record and shit they can do this and they were going to do it.

Risk assessment models identify criminal behavior and drug use as intrinsically dangerous to children. Yet these assumptions deserve a closer examination. Does being a criminal make someone a bad parent— or a dangerous parent—by definition? Chapter 4 explored the question focusing on mothers. But this question also lies at the heart of discussions of how CPS fathers should be viewed. Many men in this study were committed to being parents, despite their lengthy criminal records. Yet when entering the CPS system, they found that their criminal records weighed heavily on assessments of their parenting abilities. In Richie's case, a lengthy criminal history interfered with his ability to gain custody of his daughter. He explained, "Yeah, and I went to court and they thought I was crazy, especially because I have a record that probably stands higher than this table." Richie claims that his criminal history included "rape, robbery, violence with guns, assaulting police officers—everything, everything" but explained that "the main thing they were concerned about was that I had two possessions of marijuana on my record." Indeed, under risk assessment, drugs are believed to create a risk to children in their homes, whereas violence against other adults does not necessarily translate into potential harm to children.[54]

Like Richie, many fathers enter dependency court with the identity of "bad man" firmly in place. Criminal history, while relevant, is not utilized in the same way against mothers, who are seen as worthy of reform. For example, Julia Edmonds, a white woman in her late twenties, was brought to court in handcuffs wearing an orange county jail jumpsuit. She had completed reunification, but relapsed into addiction and was again expressing her desire to reunify with her son, who was removed when she was arrested for charges relating to drugs and weapons. She stated that she intended to regain her sobriety and enter a treatment program. When the judge addressed her request for a residential treatment program, he stated, "You probably mean that but you are in jail, facing criminal charges and the loss of your son. These changes will not be easy, but if you don't make these changes [your son] will not be coming home to you." He then turned to the social worker, explaining, "I'm not a drug counselor, but she clearly needs a residential program. She will not be able to do this thing by herself." In contrast, I don't recall ever seeing a father who was in CPS for the second time or who appeared in court in handcuffs being addressed in such an encouraging manner.

Men's criminal history may not bear directly on their ability to father. Richie raised five children with three different women between bouts of incarceration; several of his children went on to college. His last conviction was in 1989, and after his release in 1991, he decided he was finished with criminal activity, explaining, "My mind couldn't accept the confinement like it did when I was younger." At the time Richie learned about nine-month-old Christina, who had been born in jail to Richie's drug-addicted ex-girlfriend, he had sole custody of his three-year-old daughter Laquanda, whose drug-addicted mother, according to Richie, voluntarily gave her to him.[55] Although his criminal behavior predated the births of both girls by at least six years, he argued that the social workers "were treating me like shit at first, I think more because of my record." An unsuitable father on paper, Richie explained why he was not necessarily a bad placement for Christina. "I haven't done anything to my kids, so there was no reason for that [removal]. Ya know, like I told them, they were worried about my record and like I told them, you shouldn't worry about my record. You should look at what I learned from what I done."

Despite Richie's struggle with his reunification and his initial battles with his social worker, he was successful. His attorney explained to me that his case changed direction after the social worker went by his house for an unannounced visit, a strategy that often reveals the proverbial "smoking gun" in an unsuccessful bid for reunification. What she found was a loving, affectionate father at home playing with Laquanda and a few of his grandchildren who were visiting. Upon seeing Richie, an "inappropriate man" engaged in actively appropriate fathering, she began to advocate for him.[56] Christina was returned to Richie shortly thereafter. In addition to the specifics of this case, this story also reveals how easy it was for Richie, as a black man, to exceed the very low expectations his social worker had of him. We can imagine that had a social worker discovered a mother playing with her children, it would not likely have so dramatically swayed her case. However, because unmarried men—especially men of color—are imagined to be incapable of caring for children, Richie was exceptional.

The centrality of drugs and criminal convictions to definitions of adequate parenting also complicate caregivers' abilities to strategize on their children's behalf. For example, Miguel's criminal conviction created confusion for Audrey who, having reunified with her five-month-old daughter after she and Miguel were arrested for drug dealing, was still monitored by social workers. Unlike Audrey, whose criminal charges were dropped, Miguel was convicted of drug dealing. Lacking American citizenship, he will be deported to Mexico upon his release. Because he and Audrey were not legally married, he will have no grounds to challenge his deportation. Nonetheless, Audrey hoped she could sustain a relationship between her daughter and boyfriend, who she regarded as a good father. Audrey agonized over whether she should bring her infant daughter to see Miguel in prison. In fact, she had not been advised against it, but knowing that she was under CPS surveillance, she feared reprisal. Although she was confused about whether she could take the baby to visit, she was most clear about the assumptions of the system:

I don't know if it's okay for me to take her or, I just—they just don't want us to be a family. In their eyes they don't think we're a healthy family…That's really disturbing because I know how much he loves his daughter. How he lived his life and how he made money didn't affect how he treated her, and the way he treated me.

For other caregivers–including relatives who have foster placement—who understand how social workers perceive their charges' parents, deciding and mediating contact and visitation can be risky, particularly if allowing parental visits permits CPS to view these foster parents as also failing to adequately defer to state definitions. Yet care providers or custodial parents like Audrey may quite reasonably believe that allowing their children to maintain a relationship with their fathers is in the children's best interest, even as the state defines their fathers as failures.

In Audrey's story, and in each of the other cases discussed, a distinction can be drawn between men's behavior with their children and men's behavior with the law. Many men who behave criminally are unfit to father. However, their criminal actions do not, on their own, establish that they cannot be appropriate fathers. Rather than using markers of parental qualification, such as criminal history, many fathers identified how the county should have considered other factors. Leonard, who admits to dealing drugs, denies ever using any. He also reports that he has drug tested negatively to the satisfaction of the court for more than three consecutive months. Noting the inaccuracies in the court report and the weight applied to his criminal history, he describes his frustration:

> The first time we went to court, the very first time we go to court, the judge says, "We're not here to go by what's on the report. We're here to go by what's best for the daughter, for the child." And she turned around and went by everything that was in the report. She went straight through it and didn't go by anything else…when they do a background report they should make sure everything is correct, instead of making everything black and white… Everything they go by is in black and white. Everything in life ain't black and white… If they're old enough to be a judge, they should have been through something in life, life experience. You can't learn everything from a book. You've got to learn things from living.

Here, Leonard points to one of the largest failures of the CPS system. In a system where everyone responsible for assessing parental capability is overburdened, social workers frequently lack the time to fully examine the uniqueness of each case. What Leonard describes as "black and white" is a practice of using the presence or absence of a criminal history without a full evaluation of its relevance to parenting.

Some portion of this may be the result of how cases flow through the agency. The investigating social workers who write the petitions and initial reports that detail the reasons the children were placed in protective custody focus almost exclusively on the aspects of parental behavior that justify their decisions to remove the children. Social workers responsible for investigating allegations and determining when to place children in protective custody are fearful of having their decision to remove a child overturned; as a result, there is no incentive to list any of the positives of parenting. As discussed in chapter 5, some of the details may be reported inaccurately, which affects how parents view the agency. For example, Mateo described his perceptions of how the social workers and county attorneys approach a new case: "I say they're dishonest people. I think they're liars, they skew the thing to make their case."

Once the petition is upheld and reunification services are ordered, cases fall to the reunification social workers, whose impressions of parents are first shaped by the initial investigative reports. As such, parents believe social workers are predisposed to view them as damaged and will not be a resource to them. Acknowledging this, Mateo explains,

> On paper, ya know, [the social worker] came and got the report, ya know, and for everything on the report, I would have taken the kids from the original report. If I had read the report, I would have taken the kids too. I would have been over at the house doing the same thing. But you're supposed to be innocent until you're proven guilty. Not in this system. There's no, there's all this energy towards ripping you up, making you look like a piece of crap, writing a story that's not there, but there's no energy towards finding out anything positive.

As mentioned, Mateo was believed to have broken his stepdaughter's leg, though he contends she broke it in a freak accident while jumping on the bed. His description of the system as failing to acknowledge "anything positive" about a parent makes the process even more frustrating, particularly when a man considers himself to be a good father. Ironically, Mateo, a married man with a stable job, was perceived more favorably in the system than are most CPS fathers. As the county counsel, Isabel Guzman, advocated for him in court: "He is a loving, conscientious father who lost his temper and injured his child and is afraid to admit [it] because of the consequences. There is no indication of ongoing anger problems…There is no indication he intended to brutalize this child. It was a rash act…There is no evidence to suggest the mother would not be protective." She then argued that the kids could go home and that Mateo's wife could supervise visits between him and the children. She stated, "There is no doubt that the father is remorseful. Hopefully, he could admit it was an accident in counseling."

Mateo's children went home with his wife Barbara after four weeks in placement with Mateo's parents. Unofficially the case-carrying social worker also told Barbara that Mateo could return home to sleep after the children went to bed, so long as she was present throughout the night and in the morning when they were all together. Allowing Mateo to be home was likely in the family's best interest. Barbara was home alone with three children, with the oldest, only four years old, in a cast from the hip down, relying on a wheel chair to move around their two-bedroom second-story apartment. When she isn't home with the children, Barbara works both weekend days as a clerk in a hardware store. Mateo was probably correct when he stated that this situation was "probably tearing the marriage apart." He described the dynamic in their relationship: "Now Barbara comes home and she's tired and cranky and I ask her what's wrong and I already know the answer."

With Mateo home, Barbara receives some emotional and physical support. Nonetheless, the speed with which this case resolved invites further examination. Most of the cases that enter CPS do not involve broken bones, but rather are the result of neglect that is frequently drug-related. Mateo's case of alleged physical abuse then would seem more extreme, with county officials concerned about future risk to the children. Although Mateo was believed to have physically harmed his stepdaughter, he was not perceived to be a significant risk to her. In contrast to other men whose cases moved more slowly and in which county officials were less optimistic about the father, Mateo communicated that he was, as Isabel stated, "a loving, conscientious father." First, he was married to the mother of his children. (Although Leanna was not genetically his daughter, he had so fully claimed her that she had never been told that he was not her biological father.) As demonstrated in the aforementioned legal cases, marriage communicates responsibility and commitment to family life. Second, Mateo maintained legal employment and had a stable enough job that he was able to take a week off when the case began. In doing so, he communicated his masculine competence and commitment to his family. Undoubtedly this impressed the court officials. Third, although they do not have a great deal of money, Mateo and Barbara were able to borrow money to hire a private attorney, a move that often communicates that a parent is taking the case seriously. Overall, Mateo proved himself to be a competent man who could then be seen as a competent father.

RESOCIALIZING BAD MEN

The CPS system—with its overburdened workers and generic solutions—grants only limited time and ways for men to demonstrate their ability to be caretakers to their own children. To be seen as competent fathers, men must first and foremost perform deference to the court processes. Second, they must defer to the accompanying definitions of reformed fatherhood, which are consistent with expectations of hegemonic masculinity. Many fathers accept the goals of hegemonic masculinity—control, authority, income. They attempt to demonstrate their allegiance to hegemonic masculinity, which they interpret as synonymous with good fathering, by attempting to maintain paid employment or by challenging the frustrating and seemingly irrelevant requirements of the system. In these ways, they could demonstrate how they were autonomous, self-sufficient, and authoritative. However, without demonstrating their deference to system processes and meanings, CPS fathers can not succeed.

For many fathers, the difference between succeeding and failing seemed to hinge on how they viewed the CPS system specifically, and the state more generally. For those who saw CPS as an adversarial system like the criminal justice system, subordination was not perceived to be a viable strategy. Filled with a sense of injustice, some fathers imagined that their "day in court" would be best spent defending their sense of self. By adopting this stance, they fail to perform deference and thus fail to gain custody of their children. Those who understood CPS as another state bureaucracy recognized that deference to the seemingly arbitrary rules and regulations might be the quickest way to have one's needs met. Indeed, these parents also tended to succeed in getting their children. Once again, we see how individual experiences with and understandings of the state shape interactions with CPS, again disadvantaging those who already live under the gaze of the state. In terms of meanings of family, we see that fatherhood is prescriptive, but also fungible. Fathers are not believed to be central to children's well-being in the same way mothers are. As a result, the court—as much an exercise of pragmatism or resource conservation as cultural policing—aims to identify which fathers are worthy (and capable) of rehabilitating and dispense with those who are unlikely to reform. Said differently, when the marginalized masculinities of CPS fathers are imagined to be unmanageable, those men should be cut loose from the CPS apparatus, and in effect, from their children's lives. This is part of the state's effort to act in the best interest of children.

8

BEYOND REUNIFICATION: WHEN FAMILIES CANNOT BE FIXED

It's 10:18 A.M. Susanna Madriz attentively watches the proceedings from her chair, just left of center at the horseshoe-shaped table, a chair she knows well from her frequent appearances during the previous year and a half. Despite the piles of dark hair stacked on her head, her motionless body appears smaller than her 5 foot 7 inch frame. Woody Cortridge, a thin white man with short graying hair, sits beside her. As her attorney, he offers an occasional comment, though in this proceeding he is impotent; he lost this case before it started. The three other attorneys, also seated at the table, speak around Susanna without addressing her or explicitly acknowledging her presence. None of their clients is present: the county has no social worker there today, Susanna's ex-boyfriend—her daughter's biological father—has never participated in the case and is again absent, and Susanna's two-year-old daughter Tiffany has never set foot in the room where her fate will be decided.

The judge, a white woman in her mid-forties, flips through the case file and notes that the anticipated report on the evaluation of the home where Tiffany may go to live is missing. That report will help the judge determine whether or not Tiffany's paternal grandparents will be able to adopt her. Joan Billings, a white woman in her mid-fifties who is the county counsel, requests a continuance for sixty days so the county can complete the evaluation. Karen Klein, a young white woman who is

Tiffany's attorney, seems unfazed that her client's proposed permanent home may not have been evaluated and requests that the day's proceeding to terminate Susanna's parental rights move forward. Woody sees an opportunity, and with some expression of enthusiasm, requests that the entire proceeding be postponed for sixty days. He implores, "If there is a problem with the grandparents, a continuance would give my client a chance to propose other relatives."

The judge pauses, then states that she does not see good cause to delay the proceeding. Each attorney is asked if she or he has anything to add. Someone points out that Susanna only visited Tiffany once in the previous month. No one realizes that Susanna did not visit because she had incorrectly believed that the termination of her reunification services at last month's hearing precluded visitations. Instead, the lack of visits is used to give the impression that she is uninterested in her daughter, which validates the proposed termination of her parental rights. The judge looks down at the table, presumably reading a script that covers all the legal phrases she will need to recite. "The permanent plan for adoption is approved. There is clear and convincing evidence that adoption is appropriate" and that it is in "the best interests of the child" to terminate parental rights.

Susanna does not move. The judge continues to read a statement that generically advises Susanna of her right to appeal the decision and notes the timeline by which an intent to appeal must be filed. The judge looks up and for the first time that day addresses Susanna directly. With a look that communicates as much empathy as efficiency, the judge acknowledges that this is a difficult moment and suggests that Susanna consider writing a note to her child that her social worker can keep in her file for her to read later. In case the family adoption falls through, this will allow her to communicate her family history to her daughter. Susanna nods as a single tear rolls down her cheek. It is 10:26 A.M. and Susanna is no longer Tiffany's mother.

* * *

BEYOND REUNIFICATION

For families whose children have been placed in protective custody, the end of the CPS process is both the most critical and controversial. In all cases, a judge must decide whether a child will live with a biological parent or be permanently placed elsewhere. The judge must also decide whether to terminate "parental rights," that is, a parent's legal rights to his or her child. One legal principle guides this decision: the best interests of the child. The courts and legislature use the concept of "best interests" without clearly defining what it means; in fact, the best interests standard does not provide guidance, but is an intentionally subjective standard. In practice though, the best interests of a child in foster care are defined as met when, at a minimum, the services provided to the child meet his or her needs, that the child is safe from present and future harm, and that the state is working to implement a "permanent plan" for the child as soon as possible.[1] As discussed in the preceding chapters, federal law requires states to make reasonable efforts through the provision of services to prevent the placement of children in foster care, and when that fails, to make it possible for those children to safely return to their home. When children cannot return home to their parents, federal law dictates that they should be provided with permanent and stable homes as soon as possible, be it a long-term foster placement, guardianship with a relative or foster parent, or adoption.[2]

In this chapter I examine CPS case outcomes. First, I lay out the policies, guided by federal statutes that specify time limits, that dictate the end of a case. Next, I show how parents must demonstrate their rehabilitation to the court in order to reunify with their children. Specifically, parents must provide a compelling performance that demonstrates compliance with their case plan, meaningful change, and acceptance of responsibility. The judge will decide whether or not to return children to their parents based on assessments of parental rehabilitation. However, parents' legal rights are not solely determined by parental behavior, but also by the likelihood that the child or children will be adopted by someone else. This last point is not well understood by parents in the system, who largely perceive themselves as the object of scrutiny. I argue that attorneys and social workers all make claims about the relative desirability of the child to advocate for their idealized case outcome, and to thus determine the long-term status of parental rights. The final section considers how court decisions translate beyond the courthouse steps, both in terms of how families—newly formed and dismantled—interpret and rework court orders and how the requirements of deference can extend to new caretakers as well.

TIME RUNS OUT

Parents are allowed a limited amount of time to rehabilitate, and thus regain custody of their children: cases should be resolved within six months for children under the age of three years and within twelve months for older children, though the six-month time limit expanded in 1999 to include children over age three years who have a sibling under the age of three who is also in state custody.[3] When parents are making progress but have not completed their case plans, six more months are routinely given, but by eighteen months, the case should be settled.

At the end of the given period for the provision of reunification services, a judge—drawing heavily on social worker recommendations—will determine whether the parent(s) has been rehabilitated. If the judge decides that a parent has not rehabilitated, reunification will be unlikely and social workers will instead focus on finding the child a permanent home, through adoption, guardianship, or long-term care. These permanent placement options are hierarchically organized, with adoption being the first choice for children who cannot return home.[4] If the parents are believed to be reformed, their children will gradually spend more and more time with them, moving from supervised to unsupervised visits, to whole-day visits that stretch into overnight visits. Should all those visits go well, the children will begin living with their parents again, with social workers monitoring them. If the children remain at home without incident, the case will be closed, allowing the reunited family to live autonomously. Should a parent's behavior or social situation worsen during the supervision period—or if a social worker has lingering concerns about the family's well-being—the social worker can remove the children again and place them back in protective custody. Although the entire legal process begins again, the parents are not necessarily entitled to reunification services.[5] Determining whether a family is making adequate progress toward self-sufficiency and whether the children continue to be safe there is not always easy, particularly as the legislated time limits force a decision.

As an example, Tom Page, an African American social worker in the family reunification division, was responsible for supervising Ruby Jackson. Ruby, a thirty-six-year-old African American mother, was given a ninety-day case plan and supervision after her children were returned to her. Her case plan forbade her from having alcohol or drugs in her home and required her to refrain from all alcohol and drug use, and to maintain a clean home with adequate food. She also needed to complete individual therapy and anger management classes, undergo regular drug tests, and attend Alcoholics Anonymous or Narcotics Anonymous meetings.

Ruby participated in her court-ordered services, but her social worker had concerns about her level of compliance with the totality of her case plan. For instance, when Tom found empty beer cans in a cupboard of her apartment, Ruby explained that she and the children had been collecting cans to recycle for extra money. Although Tom did not believe her, he simply instituted a new ban on collecting alcoholic beverage cans. After leaving a visit, Tom explained, "It upsets me to see how she is and she has the supervision of the court." He stated his belief that her awareness of being supervised kept her just above a line of acceptable behavior and that if he or another social worker could supervise her indefinitely, Ruby could keep her kids. Without supervision, he was unsure how well she'd do. Tom was in a quandary over how to proceed, since he was going to soon face pressure from his supervisor, who was under pressure to abide by legislatively defined time limits, to decide the outcome of the case. He would either need to recommend that the court terminate supervision and allow Ruby to live autonomously or recommend increased monitoring and additional services, with the possibility of again removing her children. Although Tom believed that with continuing supervision she could keep her children, public policy requires that cases be in motion: social workers must either step up or down supervision.

A parent's attorney may request more time when a case comes for review at the end of the legislatively determined time limit of eighteen months. For example, during a hearing to decide whether to terminate his client's services, Mary's attorney questioned Tom, her family reunification worker, about whether he would like more time to work with Mary. (As chapter 6 notes in discussing Mary's failure to perform empowerment, this mother of three was perceived as able to parent and likely to regain custody of her children until she secretly married a man from her drug treatment program.) In addressing whether he would like more time to work with her, Tom explained, "I would like the court to follow the guidelines set forth for all families. If a decision needs to be made in eighteen months, that's what I'd like the court to do." During my ride-alongs with Tom to visit Mary at the church-run drug treatment program's residential "campus" where she lived, and her children at their foster homes, Tom expressed a fondness for Mary and a desire to see her succeed. Nonetheless, he was constantly aware of the time limits that bound both him and his clients. In Mary's hearing he explained, "I believe many parents could eventually come around, but we have to look out for the minors and they need a permanent plan." Tom's assessment of the court's responsibility summarizes both the goal of time limits—to give children a permanent home as soon as possible—and a persistent dilemma—that many parents might be rehabilitated if given more time. Indeed, the length of time a child has spent out of his or her home is the single most frequently used factor in termination of parental rights and provides "a catchall ground for termination…where there is no clear showing of chronic abuse, mental illness, abandonment, or other separate statutory grounds for termination."[6] Thus the inability of many parents to overcome persistent problems—including class-based ones like poverty, homelessness, and drug addiction—within the time allowed, permanently costs them their children.

The policy that allows for such a short time for rehabilitation and reunification is as much pragmatic as harsh. First, one might reasonably argue that the experience of out-of-home placement is qualitatively different for an infant or toddler than for an older child.[7] Twelve months of placement for a child who was placed in protective custody at birth represents the totality of that child's life. For an older child, out-of-home placement is one chapter among many. Second, research suggests that reunification occurs in about half of all cases. When reunification does occur, it is most likely to happen in the first six months.[8] Therefore some would argue that children's chances of returning to their parents decrease after those first six months, while their chances of being adopted or permanently placed also decrease with time. Third, children who are returned to their parents frequently—about twenty percent of the time—reenter the system.[9] The high recidivism of parents in the CPS system encourages many workers to seek adoption for the child as soon as possible rather than seeing the child bounce between the parent and multiple foster care placements until that child is too old to be adopted or is further traumatized.[10] Although these intentions may be noble, enacting policies based on them requires prescient powers; no one can know which children will return and which parents will reunify and escape CPS surveillance permanently. Without such perfect foresight, there may be a tendency to remove and adopt out children, regardless of parental rehabilitation.

DEMONSTRABLE REHABILITATION

Absent the ability to predict future reentry to CPS, social workers and judges decide to return children to their parents and then to withdraw supervision based on an evaluation of parents' level of rehabilitation. This decision, informed by social worker recommendations and attorney's arguments, reflects the state's judgment that a parent can or cannot adequately care for his or her children. In essence, having utilized court-ordered services, the parents must be rehabilitated in ways recognizable to the government officials responsible for protecting children. To demonstrate this, parents must satisfy three requirements to be reunified with their children: be compliant with court-ordered services, demonstrate a benefit from the services, and explicitly accept responsibility for the event or lifestyle that brought the family into the CPS system. Collectively I refer to these practices as *demonstrable rehabilitation*. Demonstrable rehabilitation requires parents to perform their "self-improvement" in a way discernible to the courts and those that inform court decisions. Although demonstrable rehabilitation must be *performed*, this section also shows that parents often internalize the goals the state sets for them. Irrespective of whether or not they accept these goals, in order to gain custody of their children, parents must satisfy all three narrowly defined requirements to demonstrate the ability to parent.

Compliance

Once an allegation of child abuse has been substantiated, parents receive a case plan detailing what they must do to reunite with their children. With few exceptions, parents who do not comply with the services and requirements of their case plan will fail to be reunited with their children.[11] Compliance can be understood as both an attitude, consisting of a willingness or intention to follow prescriptions, and a behavior of actually carrying out the prescriptions. Noncompliant behavior may then reflect "reluctance, reactance, and recidivism characterized by disinterest, refusal to comply, or lack of sustained effort" to follow the recommendations of helping professionals.[12] In the CPS context, failure to complete court-ordered reunification services constitutes noncompliance. In some cases, parents who attend the service but communicate their disdain for the material and refuse to actively participate may also be viewed as noncompliant. The state imagines itself offering parents a chance to improve their lives and to move toward a middle-class standard of family behavior. Therefore compliance is predicated on a belief that the prescribed solution, treatment, or service is rational. In this context, a parent's desire to comply is synonymous with a demonstrated commitment to one's children. Because noncompliance with treatment is seen as irrational, the noncompliant parent is seen as deviant, and as such, perceived as unable or unwilling to parent.[13]

Lisa Flynn's case provides an example of how noncompliance plays out in the CPS arena. Lisa, a white woman in her early twenties, entered CPS in late 1998 when a male friend molested her five-year-old daughter, whom, in the view of the system, she had failed to protect. In March 2000, Lisa's newborn baby James was automatically made a dependent of the court since Lisa had an ongoing CPS case. However, social workers and attorneys agreed to allow Lisa to keep physical custody of James. In this unusual situation, Lisa was both the parent attempting to reunify with her son and the equivalent of a foster parent who cares for a child whose custody belongs to the state. Karen Klein, who as a children's attorney is usually most reluctant to return a child to a parent, commented that while removing custody of James was automatic, she was not terribly worried about him and felt the risk posed by leaving him in his mother's care was minimal. Lisa's blonde hair, fair skin, and appropriate dress may have allowed the attorneys to identify with her more than with parents in other cases. Perhaps the fact that Lisa entered the courtroom breastfeeding James silently communicated her concern for her son's well-being, as the public health campaign of the "breast is best" has suggested.[14] Whatever the reason, everyone seemed uncharacteristically optimistic about Lisa's ability to regain legal custody of her son; having him in her care meant that in many ways she was halfway there.

At the first hearing, the judge ruled that the case could go forward with James remaining in the legal custody of the court, but in the physical care of Lisa. The judge also agreed to order paternity testing for Tim Ross, a white man in his early twenties who was not identified as the baby's father by Lisa or on any document, but who claimed he was. The judge advised Lisa to continue the case plan she had received as part of her daughter's case, which included drug testing, parenting classes, and counseling. Although that case was in its sixteenth month, Lisa had not completed her services, nor had she regained custody of her daughter. The social worker's report stated:

> Mother failed to complete court ordered reunification services designed to help her overcome the problems which led to the initial removal and continued custody of the child's half-sibling. The child's mother has a substance abuse problem from which there is no evidence she has rehabilitated from, which renders her incapable of providing adequate care and supervision for the child in that she failed to comply with court ordered drug testing.

It is important to note that there was no allegation that she was still using drugs. If there had been a strong suspicion that she was, she would have been legally barred from breastfeeding, as many mothers in the CPS system are. Instead, the charge against her was that she had failed to demonstrate her rehabilitation from substance abuse through compliance with court-ordered drug testing. Social workers perceived Lisa as noncompliant in both behavior and attitude; in addition to not participating in her services, she also communicated a lack of respect for the court's vision for her and a general disinterest in rehabilitating.

When Tim, Lisa, and the various attorneys and social workers returned for the next hearing thirty days later, attitudes toward Lisa had changed. Karen stated that "the mother only made herself available last Friday," adding "the child looks well." Isabel Guzman, the county attorney, spoke on behalf of the social worker, explaining, "The mother has been flaky and hard to get a hold of." Isabel requested moving the case to one with "intensive supervision," a legal setback that is usually the last step before a child is removed from a parent's home. The judge explained that to do so, the county would have to file a formal petition for a modification to James's legal status, which was impossible to do that day. The judge addressed Lisa directly and forcefully explained that if she did not cooperate with the social worker, he would remove her baby. She said she understood, explained that there had been a miscommunication, and stated that she was more than happy to cooperate.

As Lisa's case progressed, it only got worse. She left town with James without telling her social worker, a serious offense because she was not the baby's legal custodian. She did not participate in court-ordered services. At each hearing she came to court promising compliance and after each hearing, she became inaccessible to social workers and even her own attorney. In reality, no one believed that Lisa was incapable of caring for her child; had such a concern existed, James would have been removed. However, Lisa's refusal to comply with the court's requirements communicated her lack of respect for the court's authority and shaped an official perception of her as unreliable. Eventually, James was removed from her care.

Tim, whose paternity test proved him to be the biological father, began cooperating with his social worker and satisfying the requirements of his case plan. Upon finding stable housing (away from his own mother, who had her own CPS history relating to Tim's younger half-sibling), James was placed with him. Seven months into the case and only a few months after gaining placement of James, Tim allowed Lisa to serve as their son's day care provider while he worked. When the county learned of this unapproved arrangement, James was placed in foster care.

In thinking through compliance, it is important to note the ways it is relational. For example, failing to follow one's own wishes or desires may make a person fainthearted or weak willed, but not noncompliant. Noncompliance must be because a person refuses to act "in accordance with someone else's wishes, desires, requests, demands, conditions, or regulations."[15] Tim's unwillingness to yield to the will of the state by enforcing the court orders relating to Lisa negated his compliance with court-ordered services. Despite his attendance and participation in services and the social worker's assessment that he was an adequate parent, the court deemed him noncompliant. Given both parents' noncompliance, it is easy for the state to imagine that placing James, a healthy white infant, in a permanent adoptive home would be a better long-term plan than returning him to noncompliant and insubordinate parents who might reenter the system. In reality, no one believed that Tim was unable to parent, just as all parties believed Lisa was essentially able to care for her son. However, assessments of parental ability were, in the end, less important than the failure to comply with the state's requirements, particularly when deciding the fate of an adoptable baby. Again, because noncompliance is deviant, parents who are noncompliant are viewed as deviant parents and will not get their children back.

Meaningful Change

Even when parents have technically complied with services, they must be able to demonstrate to the court that they benefited from the services. As discussed, compliance reflects the behavior and attitude of cooperation and deference to a prescription. In addition to fully participating in services, parents are expected to demonstrate improved lives because of the services. Such improvement must be performed as well as externally validated by a service provider. For instance, Yvonne Platt, a white, drug-addicted mother who was abused as a child, never missed an appointment to drug test, went to all required classes and counseling sessions, and was eager to regain custody of her three children. She enrolled in several courses simultaneously and completed each within the minimum time possible. There was no doubt she complied with her service plan. She accepted the requirements of her case plan and did not seem to mind the demands placed upon her, although she felt impatient for the return of her children, who were not doing well in foster care. Yvonne subscribed to the state's vision of her better self and trusted that the system was committed to her improvement, a sentiment that comes through in her description of her social worker:

> At first I thought she was against me, ya know; I thought she was a real bitch. I told her that I thought she was a hard ass, but then I said what I need is someone like her, ya know, because I never had someone like that in my life growing up, because nobody gave a damn. She's all right. We've talked a couple of times and she's actually changed her tone with me like, and so if she don't recommend, then I'm sure she knows what she's doing.

When Yvonne's case came up for a six-month review, her social worker did not recommend giving her overnight visits or returning her children to her. Instead she voiced concern that Yvonne was completing her services too quickly and was therefore not getting enough out of them. The social worker's report advised the court that Yvonne was not ready to reunify with her children. After the hearing, the worker told Yvonne that she needed to slow down and process the information she was receiving. As Yvonne's appointed attorney, Rebecca Channing, recounted the story to me, she stated exasperatedly, "How can someone do things too quickly? Can you believe this? She is trying too hard!"

Yvonne was compliant with her services and expressed appreciation for the parental role her social worker played, comparing her to the parental figure lacking during her childhood. Despite this, Yvonne's children were not returned to her care for another year. Although she did everything that was asked of her, she was undermined by her inability to demonstrate—or adequately perform—meaningful change as a result of services. It is not entirely clear how Yvonne could have demonstrated her transformation. In a manner that largely relies on intuition, social workers look for signs that parents have gleaned new information that will help them cope differently with the situations that led to the abuse or neglect of their children. In Yvonne's case, it is likely that her social worker wanted to see some expression that reflected therapeutic breakthrough or demonstrated psychological "recovery," and not simply abstinence from drugs and attendance at twelve-step meetings. This would require Yvonne to show her full absorption of the therapeutic ethos and prescribed vision of parenthood. She wanted evidence that Yvonne was transformed.

Most parents who comply but fail to demonstrate benefit from services do not express appreciation for the intervention, as did Yvonne. Some parents may simply lack the ability to process the information from their services in the manner prescribed, making a compelling performance impossible. Erin Nolan's case illustrates this possibility. Erin's case began when her eighteen-month-old son was brought to the hospital for internal injuries, including a bruised liver and ruptured spleen; a healing fracture that had not been treated was discovered upon his hospitalization. Her three-year-old daughter, who had what the social worker described as "impression marks on her arm," was removed as well. Initially Erin, a twenty-five-year-old white woman, and her twenty-seven-year-old white husband, Kyle, explained that they had no idea what had happened. Then they began offering conflicting and changing stories: the baby had stopped breathing and Kyle's amateur attempts at chest compressions caused the injuries; the older child had jumped on the baby; Kyle had his foot on the baby's stomach as he reached for a diaper and his weight unexpectedly shifted. Erin was home, then she wasn't, then she was outside in the yard. Their lack of disclosure frustrated the social worker and judge and led to a slow start for the case. Eventually, Kyle confessed that he had stomped on the baby and was sentenced to eight years in prison for felony child endangerment. He will never be given a chance to participate in reunification services, both because of the severity of his crime and because his sentence will outlast the timeframe in which reunification can legally occur. Erin was offered reunification services only after she admitted she wasn't home at the time the injury occurred and had been lying to protect Kyle.

Erin was described by the social worker in the initial intake report as "indignant and emotional, stating that CPS had no right to keep her children away from her." The subsequent report explained that Erin was going to leave Kyle, who had a history of domestic violence, and that she was ready to cooperate with her social worker. One continuing concern was that Erin did not seem to understand the gravity of what had occurred. At this first hearing, Erin's appointed attorney commented to me that she had that "deer in the headlights look" and that she seemed to be confused by the proceedings. It is possible that Erin was cognitively limited, although no documentation or diagnosis of learning or mental disabilities was brought to the court for consideration. After several months of seemingly not comprehending what was occurring, Erin's attorney and his white female colleague, Kim Karsten, confronted Erin in hopes that she would understand the seriousness of the proceedings. They explained to her that her case was one of the worst cases of child abuse that they had seen, that she had failed to protect her children, and that these court proceedings were significant. Erin reportedly cried and the attorneys felt she finally understood the seriousness of the situation. After this session of what one parents' attorney calls "reality therapy," Erin began cooperating with her social worker, attended all required meetings and appointments, and spoke with her social worker frequently. Her case progressed and she was given unsupervised and overnight visits, usually the last stage before children are returned to their parents. As her case came up for its twelve-month review, the social worker's report indicated that while Erin was meeting all the required services, she did not seem to be benefiting from them. As her attorney explained to me, "The mother has done all of the services and some of the reports are good. But no one is willing to say she gets it."

The ability to demonstrate a benefit from services is largely based on the opinions of helping professionals. If any of the service providers who treated Erin—the mental health counselor, domestic violence support group leader, or parenting class instructor—had been willing to say that she "got it," it is likely that her case would have gone in a different direction. It is difficult for parents to demonstrate reform without this validation. The professional opinion of a therapist (or intern therapist, as is often the case) has an element of subjectivity, which can both capture the nuances of cases and allow for contradiction, with different counselors sometimes reaching opposing positions in the same case. Nonetheless, professional verification of progress carries a great deal of weight, depending on the perceived credibility of the therapist. Lacking this validation, Erin would be responsible for communicating her benefit from services to the social workers and court officials. Erin did not comprehend the transformation that was asked of her, nor could she communicate how she would protect her children in the future. As a result, she could not provide the appropriate performance and was never able to regain custody of her children who were eventually placed in the care of a relative out of state.

Accepting Responsibility

Although compliance and demonstrated benefit from services are essential to parental success, they do not alone ensure that parents will reunify with their children. The third level of demonstrable rehabilitation requires that parents take responsibility for the initial behavior that brought them into the system. The court believes that parents can best demonstrate that they have reduced risk to their children by admitting their previous culpability. Parents are aware of this expectation. For example, Mateo Estes, a young Latino father of two children and one stepdaughter, struggled with how to satisfy the court's requirement that he accept responsibility for breaking his three-year-old stepdaughter's leg, even as he insisted that it was broken while she was jumping on her bed. In the hearing about his case, Isabel Guzman, a Latina attorney for the county, described Mateo in favorable terms, albeit ones that assigned blame. She argued that Mateo "is a loving, conscientious father who lost his temper and injured his child and is afraid to admit [it] because of the consequences." Although this was one of the more generous portrayals I had heard of a father accused of physical abuse, Mateo did not believe that she was an ally to him. He describes his impressions of her and the broader court process:

> Yeah, but in the end I think she's trying to get me to admit to something that I didn't do. Try to be soft and just say, "Oh well. Maybe it was an accident." If it was an accident, I wouldn't get in trouble for it. And I'm not going to admit to it, to being an accident. I didn't do nothin'. That's just the kind of person I am.

> And the hard part is that even the therapist is like, "Mateo, what happened in the room that night?" I'm going to have to lie; I'm going to have to lie to satisfy the judge. I can't say I should've watched my kid closer or I accept what the petition says. I have to flat out say, "I'm sorry I broke my daughter's leg." I can't be sorry.

Here, Mateo communicates his awareness that he must accept responsibility, a particularly daunting expectation if a parent has not actually committed the act for which the court holds them responsible.[16]

Charlie Powell's case provides another, more telling example of how successful reunification often hinges on admission, in addition to compliance and change. Like Mateo, Charlie denied responsibility for the act that led his children into foster care. Charlie, a forty-five-year-old African American father, was brought to the attention of CPS when his longtime girlfriend Lenicia Watson gave birth to a baby who tested positive for illegal drugs. Charlie had custody of their seven other children, ranging in age from three to twelve years, and a social worker came to his home to assess whether the children were safe in his care and whether this new baby could be placed with him. During this visit, a social worker observed a small round mark on the five-year-old boy's back. After taking the child to the hospital for a medical examination, the mark was confirmed by two forensic pediatricians, who specialize in child abuse diagnoses, to be a recent cigarette burn. Charlie was arrested and prosecuted for misdemeanor child endangerment; he pleaded no contest to the charge and served a short jail sentence. Despite his plea, Charlie consistently denied burning his son, and on several occasions voiced doubt that a burn even existed. When asked, Charlie is somewhat evasive about why he pleaded guilty. In some conversations, he intimates—though does not actually state—that he was protecting Lenicia. Most of the time, he explains that he had a bad attorney who negotiated the plea and that as a black man in the criminal justice system, he felt he had little chance to prove his innocence. Charlie's CPS case began after he was released from jail and wanted to regain custody of his children.

Charlie's case began well, as he was quick to comply with court-ordered services. He eagerly attended parenting classes and other required services. After testing negative for twelve consecutive drug tests (and having no known history of drug use), the court agreed to drop testing from his case plan. He earned unsupervised visits rapidly, a sign of progress in a case, but lost them when Lenicia attended a visit without social worker permission. Though Charlie insisted that he and the children accidentally ran into Lenicia at the mall, he was never able to regain unsupervised visits. He attended all required therapy sessions and was reported to be making progress. His first therapist reported that he was doing well and was benefiting from treatment, but had not admitted to burning his son. Jamal Gibran, the social worker responsible for the case, was dissatisfied with that report and referred Charlie to a new therapist with the explicit instruction that Charlie must take responsibility for the burn. Jamal, an African American man, initially referred Charlie to an African American female therapist, which Charlie's attorney believed was done with the hope that as a black woman, she would hold a black man to a higher level of accountability than a white therapist might. When Jamal decided that her support of charlie reflected an inadequate focus in therapy, Charlie was referred to a new therapist. During the court proceeding to determine if Charlie would regain custody of his children or move closer to losing his parental rights, Jamal testified, "I gave the second referral because the comments [the first therapist] made did not address the issues…I thought the father using cigarettes to discipline the minor was the issue." Jamal noted that in his referral to Carmen Ortiz, a Latina who became Charlie's second therapist, he specifically wanted Charlie to address "issues openly, candidly, honestly; to deal with disciplining and torturing his child with cigarettes."

According to Carmen, Charlie "adamantly denied it." The following exchange between Carmen and Jeannie Johnson, the attorney for the county, during the trial demonstrates the explicit expectation that parents must admit responsibility:

Jeannie: Did the father take any responsibility for the cigarette burns?

Carmen: In retrospect, since going through parenting (classes), he felt there were other ways to discipline a child and he no longer felt he needed corporal punishment. He has not admitted to the cigarette burn, but has admitted to using a belt.

Jeannie: Is it fair to say that when a parent is abusive to a child, there is a risk in returning that child to the parent when the parent has not taken responsibility?

Carmen: If he can't identify [with the child], yes.

Jeannie: He has admitted to that?

> Carmen: He has not admitted to [cigarette burns but to] belt marks left on body. He did admit to corporal punishment with his hand and expressed regret for that.

Carmen explained that Charlie, who she said was punctual and well-groomed, spent a great deal of time discussing his plans for parenting in the future. She reflected on their sessions:

> He seemed to know all his children well, including [the one who was burned]. He seemed very motivated to reunify with his children. He seemed willing to show up and participate and do what is required of him…He is making progress in treatment. In the first four sessions, he was closed down…he was fearful of being judged…The last four he has been more open and talked about what he would do if his children were returned… He is open to the therapeutic relationship now. I think he would continue to make progress. He is capable of goals and capable of being a good parent.

She added, "He seemed a sincere, remorseful individual."

One might believe that the testimony of a therapist endorsing Charlie's claim that he was capable of parenting would have been persuasive. Instead, Carmen's statements of Charlie's unwillingness to admit responsibility for the specific event were perceived as a limitation in their therapeutic relationship. Carmen had failed to help Charlie accept responsibility. Thus she could be seen as an ineffectual counselor, making the rest of her professional opinion also of limited value. Jeannie recalled Jamal to the stand to ask him his opinion about Charlie's progress. He explained,

> If he is in therapy and he refuses to deal with the issue…if he failed to acknowledge it, then he is not doing the work in therapy. The kids are at risk because he has not acknowledged or taken responsibility for it…When working with physical abuse and sexual abuse and narcotic users in the past, part of the process is for them to acknowledge the problem to work through it in therapy. These are my concerns…He is going through the motions.

Jamal's testimony suggests that abuse is similar to drug addiction and needs to be treated in the same manner. The role of admission as a sign of therapeutic progress originates in the twelve-step therapeutic model, which advises addicts to "admit to God, to ourselves, and to another human being the exact nature of our wrongs." In this model, recovery requires admission.[17] The therapeutic ethos has become increasingly entrenched in the justice system, saturating legal processes in the civil and criminal systems, and as seen here, permeating the juvenile court system.[18] The role of therapeutic confession as a legal standard in child welfare cases has been endorsed by the state appellate court. In fact, in the 1989 case *Jessica B.*, the California Fifth District Court of Appeals codified this approach. In this case, a father who attended parenting classes and therapy with participation that was "far better than normal" and whose therapist testified that he was making great progress could not regain custody of his daughter until he admitted that he physically abused her to the point where she was left brain damaged. Displaying the role of the therapeutic ethos, the majority opinion explained that the father's "failure to admit fault indicates that he is neither cooperating nor availing himself of services provided."[19] Subsequent cases support the findings in *Jessica B.*, which remains guiding case law. As such, the expectation that parents must admit fault with regret is not just practice, but policy.

In light of this judicially supported legal expectation, Charlie's compliance with services and the therapists' opinions that he was benefiting from services were inadequate; he needed to explicitly admit culpability. In morning calendar call, the half hour preceding the start of court when the attorneys and the presiding judge go over the scheduled cases before clients are present and discuss what each attorney will do in each case as a way of allocating time, the judge asked Charlie's attorney if his client was ready to admit. Charlie's attorney Sam Richman said that his client was ready to take responsibility, hoping that Charlie's willingness to discuss his new understanding of the inappropriateness of corporal punishment would suffice. The judge looked doubtful and facetiously asked Sam, "Wow! A bolt from the blue came down and hit him on the head? That what happened?"

Like his attorney, Charlie was aware of what the court wanted. Yet the knowledge presented a dilemma for both of them. Sam liked his client and wanted to help him get his children back, and Charlie felt trapped by a narrowly defined expectation. Sam wanted to provide the best legal strategy to his client, but he also could not encourage perjury. On the morning of the second day of Charlie's trial to determine whether he would retain his parental rights, Charlie and Sam discussed Charlie's pending testimony. Sam asked whether Charlie thought there would be a better chance of getting kids back if he admitted he burned his son:

Charlie: It's a lie… You want me to lie to get my kids?

Sam: Have you thought about lying to get your kids?

Charlie: No.

Sam: That raises the question about whether you think that if someone did do that, should they get their kids back? You will be asked that on the stand.

Charlie: Do you think that's the best thing to do is to say I burned him?

Sam: No. You tell the truth. If you didn't burn him, don't say you did, because it's a lie. You just get up there and tell the truth.

Had Charlie read the subtext of this exchange and walked into court ready to admit—whether that would be honest disclosure or an insincere performance—he might have regained custody of his children. Such an admission at the proverbial eleventh hour might also have been unsuccessful in light of Charlie's unwillingness to deal with the issue in therapy—to demonstrate the "appropriate remorseful feelings concerning those actions" required by the legal standard set by the appellate court. It is therefore not simply the admission, but the ability to appear sincerely remorseful and, as such, receptive to rehabilitation. Without such an admission, a final refusal to subordinate himself to the therapeutic state, his bid to regain custody of his children was unsuccessful.

DEVELOPING A "PERMANENT PLAN"

Each case discussed thus far shows how parents either succeeded or failed to gain custody of their children based on their capacity to demonstrate rehabilitation. I have described here and in the last two chapters the expectations and stumbling blocks for reunification and have shown how success is largely determined by state perceptions of parental behavior. Failure to reunify, meaning that children cannot return to live with their parents, rests entirely on parents' ability to accept (and perform acceptance of) the prescriptions the state makes for their reform. Although reunification speaks to placement, it does not encompass the status of legal parental rights, nor does it necessarily end parents' relationships with their children. Parental behavior determines whether parents retain or regain custody of their children, whereas final termination of parental rights depends on whether the children are likely to be adopted by someone else or whether adoption is unlikely or inappropriate. When the state believes that a child is unlikely to be adopted, a concept that will be examined further in the latter part of this chapter, there is seemingly no compelling reason to terminate a parent's legal rights, since no one else will assert new parental rights.

A child can never be returned once parental rights are terminated because the biological parent ceases to be legally related to the child. However, in some cases, parental rights are, in essence, suspended. In the immediate, this is similar to terminated parental rights: the child will not be returned to the parent and visitations might end. However, in the long run, there are several important differences. Parents with their legal rights intact may have some contact or decision-making rights over their children. For example, the county might consult with parents about medical decisions, relative placements, or changes in the child's well-being. Parents whose rights have not been terminated, even when they lack custody of their children, can also negotiate for continuing visitation with their children. Perhaps most important, suspended rights can be revisited, while terminated rights are final.

WHEN ADOPTION IS INAPPROPRIATE

As mentioned, federal law dictates that in cases where children cannot return to their biological parents, adoption is the preferred outcome. Thus, even as social workers are providing reunification services to parents, they are also assessing children's adoptability to develop a "concurrent plan." The creation of a federal requirement for concurrent planning of alternative placement options was seen as a way to shorten a child's stay in foster care following parents' failure to reunify. Ideally a child in foster care would be placed in a home with potentially adoptive foster parents, known as "fost-adopts," shortly after being removed from his or her parents. Should reunification fail, the child, enjoying a stable placement with foster parents committed to his or her well-being, would then be formally adopted by those same people shortly after the termination of the biological parents' legal rights. For fost-adopt parents, this requires agreeing to care for and bond with a child who may still return to his or her biological parents, a risk some foster parents who wish to adopt are not willing to assume. Whereas the fost-adopt model works well in some cases, it is not yet perfect at avoiding multiple placements prior to adoption. For example, after four-and-a-half years in placement, 51 percent of the children placed with relatives in kinship care and 79 percent of children in nonkinship placement had been in more than three foster care placements. For children who entered foster care in 2002, 22 percent of those placed with kin and 28 percent of those placed with nonkin had been in more than three placements after only six months in state care.[20]

Children do eventually find their way to potentially adoptive homes. In 2001, there were 107,168 children in foster care, more than half of whom will likely be reunified, and there were about 9,900 adoptions of children from foster care that year. To understand the long-term picture of adoption for individual children, it is useful to examine cohort studies. Of the children who entered care in 1998, 14 percent of those in kinship care and 16 percent of those in nonkinship care were adopted within four-and-a-half years of placement.[21] Of children adopted from the child welfare system in 2002, 47 percent were adopted by foster parents, while 47.5 percent were adopted by family members.[22] The state goal embodied in the promise of the fost-adopt model is for children who are unable to return home to be adopted as soon as possible with as few placements as possible, even if this goal is not always reached.

Parental rights must be terminated before adoption can occur. However, this legal severance is to only occur if there is a substantial probability of adoption. To terminate parental rights, "the state must show that the consequences of allowing the parent-child relationship to continue are more severe than the consequences of terminating that relationship."[23] (This must be determined using a higher legal standard of evidence than the low preponderance of the evidence standard used in the initial proceedings.[24]) In theory, this should not be an issue; officially, all children are presumed to be adoptable. That said, there are specific conditions under which adoption is not considered to be in children's best interests. Under California state law, there are five general conditions under which adoption is deemed inappropriate:

1. The parents or guardians have maintained regular visitation and contact with the child and the child would benefit from continuing the relationship.
2. A child twelve years of age or older objects to termination of parental rights.
3. The child is placed in a residential treatment facility, adoption is unlikely or undesirable, and continuation of parental rights will not prevent finding the child a permanent family

placement if the parents cannot resume custody when residential care is no longer needed.

4. The child is living with a relative or foster parent who is unable or unwilling to adopt the child because of exceptional circumstances that do not include an unwillingness to accept legal or financial responsibility for the child, but who is willing and capable of providing the child with a stable and permanent environment and the removal of the child from the physical custody of his or her relative or foster parent would be detrimental to the emotional well-being of the child.

5. There would be substantial interference with a child's sibling relationship, taking into consideration the nature and extent of the relationship, including, but not limited to, whether the child was raised with a sibling in the same home, whether the child shared significant common experiences or has existing close and strong bonds with a sibling, and whether ongoing contact is in the child's best interest, including the child's long-term emotional interest, as compared to the benefit of legal permanence through adoption.[25]

According to the attorneys, three of these provisions—2, 3, and 4—are not commonly used, nor are they controversial. All attorneys generally accept exception 2, which allows children over twelve years to express their own preference for their relationship, particularly because it applies to children who are likely too old to be adopted. Although twelve years of age is the legal "bright line," some judges will also ask slightly younger children about their preferences for their own long-term care. Exception 3 deals with an unusual situation in which children are assigned to a residential treatment facility; such children are likely to be seen as undesirable to potentially adoptive parents, also making this exception moot.

While potentially controversial, exception 4 was not an issue in the county I studied. This exception is most commonly used in cases where a child lives with a relative who expresses a commitment to the child but an unwillingness to assume the legal identity of parent. Relatives who accept placement of state wards, a practice known as kinship care, commonly establish legal guardianship. For example, I observed one case in which a grandmother explained to the court that although she was wholeheartedly committed to her grandchild, he already had a mother and that she wanted to remain the grandmother. Kinship care is increasingly used in states like California, which legislatively specifies a preference for relative placement over that with strangers. In California in 1997, 48 percent of all children in out-of-home care were placed with their relatives, with some urban counties having as many as 55 percent of their placements with relatives. Kinship care also provides a mechanism to keep children of color in their natal communities, with African American and Latino families disproportionately using kinship care.[26]

It is worth restating that options for permanent plans are hierarchical. Guardianship, that is, the court's appointment of an adult who will have long-term custody of the child, even as the child remains under the supervision of the court, is the preferred permanent arrangement after reunification and adoption have been ruled out. The last resort is long-term placement, a less stable arrangement with less commitment from the caretaker that often leads to residential institutional care facilities, such as group homes. However, in cases where a relative caregiver is unwilling to become a legal guardian and does not wish to adopt, but wants to remain the child's long-term placement, the county will assess whether that relationship and placement are in the best interest of the child.[27]

Exception 5 aims to protect sibling relationships by considering them in placement decisions, even prohibiting adoption when it would cost a child access to those siblings. Because it was only added to law in 2002, its impact is only beginning to be seen. From my observations, attorneys on all sides believed that when possible, siblings should remain together. The only point of controversy is how different attorneys conceptualize the significance of the sibling bond, which must be of some importance to supersede adoption. In these ways, the detailed rules of foster care and adoption allow for significant amounts of judicial discretion, with judges being the ultimate arbiters of what is in the best interest of the child.

IDENTIFYING UNBREAKABLE BONDS

Exception 1 is the most contentious aspect of this law. This clause prohibits termination of parental rights when such an act would be counter to the child's best interest. The law stipulates that "the parents or guardians [must] have maintained regular visitation and contact with the child" and requires evidence that "the child would benefit from continuing the relationship."[28] These can be difficult requirements to satisfy. In the 1994 case of *Autumn H.*, the California appellate court narrowly defined how these conditions could be met. First, a parent must demonstrate that a significant bond or attachment exists that, if terminated, would be detrimental to the child. Second, because the court views a new family through adoption as unequivocally positive—despite the fact that some number dissolve— the bond between the biological parent and child must be strong enough to compete with the benefit promised by adoption. As one appellate decision clarified, "The court balances the strength and quality of the natural parent/ child relationship in a tenuous placement against the security and the sense of belonging a new family would confer." However, if severing the "natural parent/child relationship" would deprive the child of a "substantial, positive emotional attachment," the harm is considered too great to the child and parental rights should not be terminated. The judge must make this assessment.

The state's acceptance that the best interests of a child lay in their level of emotional attachment to a care provider originates in the works of Joseph Goldstein, Anna Freud, and Albert Solnit.[29] In their 1973 book, *Beyond the Best Interests of the Child*, these authors argue that "a child's normal psychological development depends on a secure, uninterrupted relationship with one caregiver—the 'psychological parent.'" Goldstein, Freud, and Solnit's claim that transient foster care had little likelihood of promoting children's emotional well-being was used to launch a "scathing critique of the laws governing foster care" and to advocate broad foster care reform through the 1970s.[30] As discussed in chapter 2, this movement led to the 1980 legislation that required states to make reasonable efforts to reunify children with their parents and generated new sensitivity about the amount of time a child spent in foster care.

Most existing vocabulary and the central assumptions of the child welfare system are derived from the work of Goldstein, Freud, and Solnit.[31] Terms like "bond" and "attachment" are key aspects of that vocabulary. Theories of bonding and attachment originated in research in the 1930s with observations of young geese and other creatures that developed a bond with humans or dogs when their mothers were absent. This research showed that "imprinting, a simple form of infant-to-mother bonding, was...an innate and instinctive process with a specific and predictable developmental window for its occurrence. It was also an essentially unidirectional process."[32] Other research built on these theories, studying long-term outcomes of war orphans, or the behavior of rhesus monkeys separated from their mothers but given wire and cloth surrogates. These studies supported the argument that ongoing nurturing interaction is important for healthy development, with deprivation of a nurturing relationship being damaging.

Studies of bonding in humans increased dramatically in the 1960s and 1970s and led to the creation of the "Strange Situation Procedure." This procedure, designed to be administered to children between the ages of twelve and twenty months, measures an infant's or toddler's level of attachment to his or her caretaker. In the test, a caregiver sits in a playroom while a stranger enters and leaves. Next, the caregiver leaves and reenters. During the combinations of presence and absence of caregiver and stranger, the researchers assess the child's level of distress, attachment, and willingness to explore the room. Using these assessments, the child is classified as secure, insecure avoidant, or insecure resistant. These are imagined to be discrete categories, with children falling into only one. Bonding assessments have been widely adopted as a way to measure whether terminating parental rights would be detrimental to a child. The court routinely orders these assessments after reunification services have been terminated, but before a decision regarding parental rights has been reached, even for children older than the twenty months for which the study was designed.

In addition to their use on children beyond the age for which the tests have been validated, there is also reason to suggest that the test of a child's singular bond may reflect cultural bias—ignoring communities where multiple caregivers may be central to children's lives—and be of limited generalizability. Nonetheless, bonding assessments are accepted as neutral and determinant of a child's emotional state. It is in some ways surprising that bonding assessments are used without significant controversy, despite the lack of consensus among researchers about the accuracy of their findings. However, the use of these assessments can affect case outcomes. As a result, parents' attorneys rarely object to them because they provide a possible last chance to preserve parental rights. County attorneys do not often object, as the assessments may advise their long-term placement strategies. Children's attorneys may object and attempt to argue that there is no reason to believe that a significant bond exists, but the test itself is not questioned. Child psychiatrist David Arrendondo and juvenile court judge Leonard Edwards caution,

> In the context of the family court is the attempt by some experts to use attachment theory to reduce the entire spectrum of human relatedness into a limited number of discrete categories. However useful this approach is for research, it is of limited value in the context of the juvenile and family court—especially when the myriad of special-needs children and families are taken into account.[33]

Even if a bond between parent and child is identified, the bond must be so important that terminating it would be detrimental to the child.

This requires that the bond be more significant than a fondness or affection and must be substantively more than an emotional connection or strong attachment. According to case law, the bond must be explicitly parental. Although the appellate court holds that "interaction between natural parent and child will always confer some incidental benefit to the child," a bond considered to be detrimental should it be terminated must reflect parental caretaking. As one precedent-setting decision described it, "The relationship arises from day-to-day interaction, companionship and shared experiences. The exception applies only where the court finds regular visits and contact have continued or developed a significant, positive, emotional attachment from child to parent."[34]

Parents who lack "day-to-day interaction" with their children because their children were removed from them have great difficulty fulfilling this requirement. In fact, one father challenged this requirement. He argued that this standard renders the exception meaningless, because the very nature of the proceedings removes the possibility for that level of interaction since at the point of assessment, the child is being raised by foster parents.[35] The appellate court rejected this claim and upheld this standard, explaining that this requirement, "while setting the hurdle high, does not set an impossible standard nor mandate day-to-day contact."[36] As a result, parents whose children were removed as babies or as very young children, or whose children have been out of their home for a long time, will have a difficult time meeting this standard.

The level and nature of the parental bond was a significant factor in Lae Rungsang's bid for her five-year-old son Matthew. Lae, a Thai woman in her early thirties, immigrated as a child with her Thai adoptive parents who she says physically and sexually abused her. She ran away from their home when she was seventeen years old and was working as an exotic dancer in New York when she became pregnant with Matthew. According to Lae, Matthew's father began beating her during her pregnancy and she left him. Shortly after Matthew's birth, Lae moved back to California to be closer to her own family. Although her family was initially happy to have her back, their enthusiasm waned and they were only of limited help to her with her son—in part because of their discomfort with him being of part African American heritage. According to court reports, Lae returned to exotic dancing as a source of income before Matthew's birth and continued after. According to social worker reports, she "never bonded" with her son, although Lae reports that she tried to care for him. Feeling overwhelmed and lacking support, Lae called CPS herself in hopes of gaining assistance. At the age of two, Matthew was placed in protective custody and Lae did little to attempt to reunify with him. In the next two years, Lae met Jesus Rivera, a security guard with whom she developed a stable relationship, and became pregnant. When her newborn daughter was automatically removed from her at birth because of Matthew's ongoing case, Jesus worked hard to regain custody of their daughter and inspired Lae to do the same. Together, they completed services and got their daughter back.

Having successfully reunified with her daughter, Lae felt empowered to pursue custody of Matthew, then five years old, despite his long residence in foster care. (Because Matthew entered CPS before the federal reforms were implemented, his case exceeded the current time limits.) The trial to determine the future of Lae's parental rights was lengthy. Matthew had been living with his multiracial gay foster parents, Ben Leighton and Julian Simms, for more than a year and they were committed to adopting him. At the hearing to determine whether to terminate Lae's reunification services and start the process of terminating her parental rights (to free Matthew for adoption), Julian testified about Matthew's perception of his mother. He explained, Matthew "doesn't think his mom takes care of him. It's not her job to help him with his homework. Not her job to help him grow into a great man. That's what Ben and I do. He wants us to take care of him and for Lae to be his friend." Should the court accept the portrayal of her as more playmate than caregiver, she could not establish a claim to a mother-child bond that would protect her parental rights.

DEFINING ADOPTABILITY

It is up to social workers to identify a potentially adoptable home for a child, and it is social workers who ultimately define the relative adoptability of a child, an assessment that is usually codified by judicial determination. Officially, California law states that a child may only be found to be difficult to place for adoption if there is no identified or available prospective adoptive parent for the child for any of three reasons: because of the child's membership in a sibling group; because the child has a diagnosed medical, physical, or mental handicap; or because the child is seven years of age or older.[37] In reality, not all children are identified as equally adoptable, nor are they so easily categorized.

Social workers pursue long-term plans based on their perceptions of the likelihood of success. Whether a child is tracked for adoption or long-term placement relies in large part on whether the social worker perceives the child as adoptable. Thus the perceived adoptability of children determines whether adoption is even pursued. I use the term "adoptability" then to denote a process of assigning value to children based on understandings of their desirability. There is consensus in social welfare research that minority children, most specifically African American children, are less likely to be tracked for adoption. One study found that minority children were 42 percent less likely to exit foster care—through adoption or reunification—after controlling for other factors such as behavioral problems, family characteristics, and level of social services provided.[38] Age is a significant determinant of adoptability. Of the more than 9,000 children adopted from foster care in California in 2001, 55 percent were less than five years old, even though children in this age range constituted only 28 percent of children in foster care in California at the time.[39]

In the final stages of a case, the relative adoptability of a child is a source of controversy in the courtroom. Attorneys make claims on the relative adoptability of the child to influence a case's outcome. The attorney representing the child usually argues that all children are adoptable. Parents' attorneys frequently argue that a child is not adoptable and therefore their clients' parental rights should not be terminated. As one parents' attorney explained to me, "[Children's attorneys] will say that all children deserve a permanent home and then I will say that no child ever gets it." The discussion about the adoptability of a one-year-old boy diagnosed with developmental delay typifies this issue. The child, Cortez, is the son of an African American mother who is mentally retarded, with an IQ reported to be less than 70 and a history of mental illness. The thirty-eight-year-old mother, Joniqua Fields, was initially assigned to live with Cortez in an assisted living home where she would receive instruction and assistance in learning to care for him. However, service providers there quickly deemed her incapable of caring for Cortez, and her services were terminated. Joniqua's father and stepmother, who have custody of her eleven-year-old daughter, wanted guardianship of Cortez. However, the county's goal was to find him a fost-adopt home. Andrea Winnow, the attorney representing Cortez, opposed his placement with his maternal grandparents. During the hearing, she pressed the social worker to explain why an adoptive home had not been identified. The social worker explained, "Because the grandparents are involved. People are not willing to take a child if there is a chance the grandparents could win custody and the child would be taken away." As the mother's attorney cross-examined the social worker, he asked, "Cortez is a client of [a regional center specializing in treating significantly delayed children] with a known psychiatric history of the mother. There is no information on the father. Isn't it possible that Cortez is not adoptable?" The social worker quietly replied, "I don't know."

Behavioral problems are a significant reason a child is seen as unadoptable. In court, attorneys tend to either gloss over or describe in detail children's behavioral problems to justify the claims they are making regarding adoptability. Consensus among attorneys and social workers is that children whose behavior is "out of control" will not be good candidates for adoption. For this reason, Charlie's children, despite some of them being quite young, were all deemed unadoptable. During the hearing to assess the adoptability of his children and thus determine the legal status of Charlie's parental rights, Jamal, the social worker, reported to the court that "the department feels the children are not adoptable…All but [the youngest], because the minors are very troubled. We'd have a tough time getting them adopted." In response, the judge presiding over the case responded disapprovingly, "I have a hard time because I take it that all children are adoptable." Nonetheless, the children were placed in guardianship with their maternal grandmother.

The relative adoptability of children challenges federal legislation—and the notion that all children can be adopted—at its core. In 1996, when he began his campaign to increase adoptions nationwide, President Clinton announced in his radio address that "no child should be trapped in the limbo of foster care, no child should be uncertain about what the word 'family' or 'parents' or 'home' mean, particularly when there are open arms waiting to welcome these children into safe and strong households where they can build good, caring lives."[40] Federal policy also assumes that all children in foster care, children who indisputably need permanent homes, are well suited to join families. Those who suggest otherwise are ridiculed as being antichild or antifamily. In this vein, the politically conservative *Policy Review* published an article explaining that "Liberalism, the self-styled defender of children's welfare, harbors a myth that dehumanizes and threatens countless children every day. It is a myth embodied in a bureaucratic label: 'unadoptable.'"[41]

Like many other accounts from all parts of the political spectrum, the *Policy Review* article relays several stories of love and strength by those who have adopted children who might have otherwise been seen as unadoptable. In fact, there are foster parents who adopt children with significant physical disabilities, medical needs, or psychological problems. In one case discussed earlier, Maya Wheeler, a white mother in her mid-twenties, voluntarily relinquished her parental rights so that her daughter's foster parents could adopt her.[42] Maya's daughter's foster parents desperately wanted to adopt her, despite the fact that she was born positive for methamphetamine, with microcephaly (a small brain in relation to body size), deafness, and possible aphasia (the inability to learn to speak or write). As Maya explained before she turned over custody, "I am leaning towards giving her up for adoption because I know that's what's best for that poor little thing." Although Maya's baby was able to find a secure home, few individuals volunteer for the extra responsibility a child with multiple disabilities brings.

Parents whose children are identified as adoptable are sometimes discouraged from pursuing reunification or are told they have little chance of succeeding. Chris Vaughn's experience provides an example. As discussed in chapter 7, Chris was attempting to gain custody of his infant daughter, Shelby, who had been placed in a fost-adopt home for most of her life. As a white child less than two years old who had been placed with a woman who was committed to her long-term care, Shelby was considered highly adoptable. At court appearances to assess Chris's progress toward gaining placement of Shelby, Shelby's attorney, Andrea Winnow would encourage Chris to voluntarily surrender his parental rights. By doing so, the foster mother would be able to more easily adopt the girl and provide her with the family stability children's attorneys desire for their clients. Andrea assured Chris that if he consented to the adoption, the adoptive mother would allow him to continue to visit. But, she warned him, if he continued to fight Shelby's foster mother, she would be unlikely to allow him to be a part of their life. As she told Chris,

> The more acrimony you have with this foster mother, the more strife, the more she is going to be uninterested in letting you be a part of Shelby's life...I have a vision of what is best for Shelby. It is to stay with this woman who is going to eventually be her mother and for her to have ongoing contact with you...The more you aggravate the foster mother, the less likely that can happen.

Similarly, Richie Lyons describes his conversations with social workers early in his case to gain custody of his daughter Christina, then approximately eighteen months old, as they urged him to abandon his efforts at reunification:

> Before [they gave me placement] they didn't want me to have her, like I said. All the workers even when I first went, the first thing they told me was you don't have a chance with your child because we've got plans for her, she's already up for adoption. I looked at the woman like she was crazy. I was like, "I don't know who the hell you think you are, but that's my child and I don't give a damn about your plans."

Christina and Shelby were considered highly adoptable because of their young age and lack of disabilities, with Shelby having the added asset of having been placed with a fost-adopt mother at birth. As such, both men accurately perceived that social workers and children's attorneys were attempting to convince them that their efforts were futile so they would withdraw from the case.

Examining adoptability is difficult because no research identifies the exact reasons why certain children aren't adopted; discussions of the unadoptable rarely move beyond anecdotes. Some attention and blame falls on social workers, who may differentially identify adoption as the goal for certain children over others. Others acknowledge that limited resources to place children encourage counties to prioritize the children that they believe will be most easily placed for adoption. As the *Policy Review* article points out, it is an unsavory position to say that certain children are not desirable. To do so would be to assign fault to a child because of his or her very victimization, an unpalatable position.

As part of the federal initiative to find adoptive homes for all children who will not return to their parents' homes, state and county agencies employ a variety of strategies. As required by federal law, every state maintains an "adoption exchange" that provides photographs and brief information about children available for adoption. These websites allow visitors to search for an adoptable child by age, race, and the presence or absence of siblings, with the option of excluding specific disabilities provided on a drop-down menu. The search results include photos and descriptions of the children that match the specified search criteria. Sites may also feature prominently on their homepage a particular child who is available for adoption.[43] Counties usually host adoption picnics, where potentially adoptive parents attend an outdoor event and browse for their future child who might be playing with other children, engaging in sporting events, viewing animals at the sponsoring farm or zoo, or snacking on the provided food. Children tend to be on their best behavior and are aware that they are on display; many have attended multiple picnics. Occasionally, counties will secure media coverage to promote adoption. Mimicking the successful animal adoption campaigns of the Society for the Prevention of Cruelty to Animals, county agencies provide photos and descriptions of children who are available for adoption in a "Child of the Week" format on local news programs, radio spots, or newspapers.

Social workers recognize that public funding and policy prioritize adoption. It is imaginable that when a social worker identifies a strong plan for adoption, he or she may invest less energy in developing an aggressive case plan for reunification. After all, a single strong and well-implemented plan may be difficult enough for workers to develop, given their large caseloads and long hours. Whether or not social workers equally prioritize both paths, parents often perceive social workers who have identified adoption of their children as the primary plan to be adversaries in their reunification efforts.

AFTER THE CASE ENDS

Parents who are perceived as being capable of caring for their children without state supervision are the successes of the CPS system. The vast majority of the time, these successful reunifications and closed cases remain invisible to the public. These families may unknowingly be classmates, friends, and co-workers; their prior involvement with CPS will remain unknown so long as they are never again referred to the agency for investigation. Yet it is worth noting that as the court terminates supervision and services, parents may feel liberated, nervous, or both. In these instances, parents are finally empowered to make decisions for themselves and their children without social worker scrutiny. At the same time, they lose services and support on which they may have come to depend. Jill Wood, a thirty-one-year-old white and Native American mother, notes this in describing her feelings about CPS closing her case after her son was returned to her. Although her sponsor in Alcoholics Anonymous has been encouraging her to remain under CPS's supervision so she could receive additional counseling services, Jill recognizes the disadvantages of doing so:

> You know, my sponsor is like, "Well, that's free counseling." I know, but that's another six months that they're in my life and I really want them out of my life. I don't want to have to ask permission to do stuff with my son or, I want to take him out of town. I don't want to have to ask somebody if I can do that. You know, things like that.

In considering what her life will be like without CPS supervision, Jill recognizes both the autonomy she will have and the loss of support:

> It's just, it's just different not having, not to have CPS in your life. Not having to worry about having somebody breathing down your back. It's hard to explain. It's really hard to explain...It's kinda scary. You know. And I won't have them services around anymore. They were offering me a lot of services and um, I won't have that anymore, which is okay because I need to grow up.

Although Jill is relieved to be free to make decisions for herself and her son, she is also nervous about losing the social services on which she has relied. Because Jill's case began before the implementation of the 1997 reforms, CPS had been a part of her life for more than three years. In addition to relying on services, Jill acknowledges that having CPS "breathing down your back" helped to keep her in check. In many ways, Jill accepted the state in a parental role where the state efforts to resocialize her could be seen as parenting her. In this light, Jill's articulation of her need to "grow up" becomes synonymous with living without parental supervision.

For parents who do not reunify with their children, the long-term story is more convoluted. In fact, the moment when adoptability is assessed and a permanent plan is ordered is not the end of the story. Although the odds of finding an adoptive home diminish as the child gets older or changes placements, county social workers are expected to continue looking for adoptive homes for children in long-term care or guardianship. Sometimes they succeed. For example, Lena Burley, a white mother in her late twenties, failed to reunify with her two children, both of whom were less than six years old. As a result of their erratic childhood, both had behavioral problems that made them difficult to place for adoption, despite their young age. Yet after three years of stable placement and counseling services, the long-term placement social workers revisited the case and were able to place the children together in a fost-adopt home. The case came back to court so Lena's parental rights could be terminated. Lena, who was still using drugs and had had no contact with her children in those three years, could not present any argument against it. The judge, who had stated at the hearing to establish their long-term placement that he was "not giving up on those kids," was elated to grant them a permanent home.

To be clear, had Lena come to court with evidence of sustained sobriety and other markers of stability, she may have been evaluated for placement of her children. Her claim for the children would be weighed against the quality of the current placement and her sons' "bondedness" to their current caretaker; again, what is believed to be in the best interest of the children will be decided. A parent whose legal parental rights have not been terminated and whose circumstances have changed (for example, by being released from jail, refraining from substance use, finding stability, or significantly improving his or her life) from the time the case was initially decided can petition for visitation or custody. However, that parent will have to demonstrate to the court that visiting or gaining placement is in the best interest of the child. In a hypothetical case where Lena came to court with evidence of a better home life, she might have been granted visits, but would have had a difficult time proving that the boys would be better with her than in their present stable home.

Parents who do not reunify with their children, but whose parental rights are not terminated, are often allowed to visit their children, even after their reunification services end, so long as the visits are in the best interest of the child, as determined by the court, social workers, foster parents, or other caregivers. If the parent retained legal parental rights because severing a parent-child bond would have been detrimental to the child, such visits would be likely. In some locales, the court may negotiate continued visitation and expectations for consultations with parents in big decisions about the child after the case ends. Increasingly, courts are using mediation services to write agreements about ongoing contact into the final court order. Otherwise, visitation is often left to the discretion of the guardian. Because guardians are sometimes friends or family members of the biological parents, children often have some level of ongoing contact.

COURT ORDERS BEYOND THE COURTHOUSE

Thus far I have focused my discussion on the interactions between the state and the biological parents. It is important to remember that "outcomes" include not only the legal status of parents and children, but also the experiential and familial. Undoubtedly, the ability to permanently remove a child from their parents' custody is the ultimate flexing of the state's muscle. As one journalist noted, "Next to the death penalty, America's courts mete out no justice more final than the termination of parental rights—a permanent break between parent and child."[44] Indeed, there are few other areas in which state action is so potentially complete and devastating. While recognizing the power of the state to legally define familial relationships, it would be naïve to accept that these legal orders determine all familial interactions. As I have argued throughout, parents strategize their interactions with the state, sometimes choosing to resist its prescriptions. Parents are equally likely to resist court orders regarding ongoing contact with their children, if not more so, because they are no longer being considered for custody. In addition, foster and adoptive parents are often willing to trust their own judgment about their charge's best interest over the bureaucratic one communicated by the court.

Children in foster care are frequently—almost half the time—placed with family members. Those foster placements often facilitate ongoing contact with biological parents, which may be an asset to the children.

Sam, Charlie's attorney, speculated that had Charlie's parental rights been terminated, he still would have seen his kids on a regular basis, since they were placed with his girlfriend Lenicia's mother. A comment Lenicia made to me after a hearing supported this theory. Having withdrawn from the court processes that might have allowed her to legally reunify with her children, Lenicia explained, "My daughter is twelve. She is coming home to me soon no matter what." I now realize that she was accounting for her refusal to comply with services, even as it meant abandoning her attempts to formally reunify with her children, because she trusted her place in her children's lives and the unofficial channels that would allow her to preserve those relationships.

Indeed, some biological parents remain in contact with their children, despite court orders that are sometimes to the contrary. If the court discovers this, they may opt to remove the child from that placement and place him or her elsewhere. One study found that "the most common problem contributing to placement disruption in the sample [of kinship placements] was the continued influence of the parent(s)."[45] Foster parents sometimes allow biological parents unsupervised visits, often forbidden by the court. Citing a case report, social welfare scholar Toni Terling-Watt notes that foster parents "have a hard time understanding the seriousness of the allegations and CPS policy concerning the safety plans that they are assigned."[46] With this, we see that the expectations for deference extend to new caretakers. Should they come under the gaze of the state, they too will find that they can lose their foster or adopted children if they communicate a lack of respect for or rejection of state definitions of good parenting.

With that knowledge, caregivers nonetheless strategize their interactions with their children's parents and family members as they see fit, often reworking family relations in new and dynamic ways. The negotiations around custody of Lae's son Matthew illustrate both the potential to reshape these postmodern family relationships and the vulnerability it creates for the adoptive parents.[47] As mentioned, the trial to determine the future status of Lae's parental rights was long and had some of the character of a custody battle, since both Lae and Jesus, and Julian and Ben, wanted Matthew. Julian and Ben had been Matthew's foster parents for more than a year and were committed to adopting him. At the same time, Lae, who had completed her service plan and would have been eligible for reunification had Matthew not been in such a successful and stable placement, was now pregnant with her third child and wanted her children to be together. As the case dragged on, Lae asked Kim Karsten, her attorney, whether this would be the final round. Kim explained that even if she won this court proceeding and retained her legal parental rights, she would not necessarily regain custody of Matthew, who was in a stable, loving home with Julian and Ben. Realizing that her son's future could remain precarious if she continued the fight, Lae asked to meet with Ben and Julian. With attorneys present, Lae explained that she wanted her son to have a permanent secure home; to achieve this she would voluntarily relinquish her parental rights so Ben and Julian could adopt him.

Ben and Julian, a committed gay couple denied the right to legally marry, told Lae that they did not place a great deal of significance in legal definitions of family. As the three adults discussed their hopes for the child that they all loved, the men convinced Lae that they would always regard her as Matthew's mother and wanted her and her children to be active parts of his life. Lae's parental rights were terminated, but Matthew's old and new families have remained in contact, now more than three years after the case ended. Although this may not represent the majority of cases, openness and contact are increasing in post-adoption arrangements.[48]

In Matthew's case, the court blessed Ben and Julian's efforts to maintain contact with Lae and her children. In part, this was because she might have succeeded in gaining placement of him had he not been in a fost-adopt home. Of course, at a hypothetical future time, if Ben and Julian continue to let Lae see Matthew, knowing she had in some way become a danger to him, they would face losing custody of him. In this, adoptive parents who resist court orders or fail to protect their children may endure the state surveillance described throughout this book. With cases like the ones discussed here, we see that as courts build and dismantle legal families through judicial decisions and custody orders, they also give rise to families who exist both inside and outside of the law.

CONCLUSION

Although a constitutional right to become a parent or to refuse to become a parent has been recognized, individuals do not have a constitutional right to raise their own children.[49] Instead, the state has the right to assert control over its citizens and their families. This right is exercised not just when state actors remove children from their parents, but throughout the process of normalizing the parents through the provision of services and evaluating their reformation. Throughout, parents engage these state processes, sometimes cooperating, other times resisting. In total, it is the ability of parents to demonstrate their rehabilitation—either by achieving it or by providing a compelling performance of it—that will determine whether the state is willing to

allow them to again parent. As with other state-mandated perfor-
mances, families who more closely resemble the state prescriptions—even as they reflect meanings of class, gender, and race—are
advantaged.

Although parents' behavior determines whether children will be
returned, it does not on its own determine whether they will retain
their legal parental rights. Instead, that determination is made through
a complex assessment of the nature of the parent-child relationship,
whether children are emotionally bonded to their current caretakers,
and the imagined adoptability of the children in question. This latter
point relies on a speculative assessment of whether the child is desirable to potentially adoptive parents, a factor in part decided by the
social worker's very willingness to try to place the child in such a home.

Even as children find stable homes with new caregivers, many
remain in contact with their parents and biological family members.
New caretakers who choose to pursue these relationships may do so
with the assistance of the court or may choose to do so in violation of
court order. These choices are layered with state expectations that
adoptive and foster parents—like biological parents—will abide by
state definitions of adequate childrearing. The expectation of deference
to state definitions of parenting continues, with some new families
facing reprimand and finding themselves the subject of reformation
attempts. As parents—new and old, biological and social—strategize
their relationships with the state and each other, they reveal the complexities of families and the ways that legal and social families are often
not the same.

9

CONCLUSION

We strive to achieve the well-being of children in our community by protecting children, strengthening families, providing permanent homes, and building community partnerships.

—County CPS mission statement

The core mission of the child welfare system is, by definition, complicated, with inherent contradictions. First and foremost, CPS must protect children, one of the most vulnerable groups in our society. Yet, as the public agency entrusted with protecting children from harm inflicted by their parents or presumed caregivers, CPS must by necessity send its workers to trespass over familial boundaries, and in doing so, further weakens them. CPS is indisputably a powerful arm of the state that can reach across familial boundaries.

Families and their members are not passive recipients of CPS intervention, but instead negotiate case meanings and outcomes with state actors throughout the process. By looking at different critical moments of interaction—investigation, reunification, and case determination—we see that parents' ability to retain or regain custody of their children depends on their capacity and willingness to perform deference and to subordinate to the expectations of the state. This can be seen in investigations when social workers weighed parents' deference heavily when

255

determining which children to remove from their homes. Parents who were willing to defer to the social worker's authority and to commit themselves to doing whatever was necessary to keep their children fared better than parents who challenged social workers' (and by extension, the state's) authority to come into their home—the mythically private realm of family—and tell them what to do with their children.

Once in the system, parents face unprecedented levels of surveillance. Social workers report their own perceptions of parents' attitudes, behaviors, and levels of compliance to the court to affect determinations of whether their clients should be granted custody of their children. Parents are often aware of what the CPS system expects from them and make strategic choices to comply or resist these expectations, even in ways that may be counterproductive to their goals. As shown, parents sometimes refused to participate, or chose not to perform the deference necessary to be seen as rehabilitated. The meanings of deference are situated in parents' experiences of race, class, gender, and community. For parents who have experienced state intervention as punitive, restrictive, or invasive, deference is costlier than it is for parents who find the state to be trustworthy or benignly bureaucratic.

Parents do not always *choose* to resist the services required in their case plan, but sometimes find them difficult to complete. Services are highly prescriptive and often structurally organized in ways that lead to parental failure. Assigned services are sometimes scheduled at overlapping times, in different corners of the county, or at times that interfere with paid employment. Parents with the financial means to hire private service providers are able to coordinate their own services, take leave from jobs without risking dismissal, and engineer documentation to support their bid for their children. In contrast, poor parents who are reliant on county referrals to contracted providers and who likely have more precarious employment and unreliable transportation may find completing services to be difficult, and sometimes even impossible. Case plans often fall short of addressing structural barriers to reunification, such as lack of housing, childcare, transportation, or money for things like food or utilities. In these obvious ways, poor parents are significantly disadvantaged in their efforts to regain custody of their children. For the most part, state actors are not blind to the difficulties parents face in completing services. Rather than simplifying case plans, many social workers and attorneys view complex case plans as an opportunity for parents to prove their commitment to their children and their acceptance of state authority.

The issues encountered by CPS families in this study echo historical themes. Since the profession's inception, social workers have often been perceived as being more like police agents than advocates. This is rooted in the impossible dual roles social workers occupy as gate-keeper to resources and agent of the state. For example, parents who might sincerely desire help moving to safer housing, applying for public assistance, or gaining access to drug treatment are loathe to ask for such help from a social worker since the deficits for which they need help will be documented as risks to their children, with social workers monitoring their family's progress; the threat that they can remove their children always looms overhead. Once they gain referrals, parents become obligated to use those services as prescribed. At this juncture, the parent who wants help becomes the client who must be compliant. Social workers are responsible for executing the state's primary goal: to fix families by resocializing parents. This very goal demands that parents accept a definition of themselves as childlike, needing parental guidance from the paternal state. As a result, social work is intrinsically contentious to parents who may not wish to change in the ways the state prescribes or who reject this definition of themselves. The very nature of this relationship defines social workers as the enemy.

State provision of services to families as a means to rehabilitate them is also not new. Efforts to "help" marginalized families in different historical periods have been discussed at length by others.[1] Historical accounts often identify how the state attempts to help the poor by using coercive measures to force compliance and how these efforts correspond with helping professionals' desire to gain legitimacy. Indeed, the state's gaze has consistently focused on those without power.

Most people who enter social work as a profession do so out of a desire to help others, a motivation that is central to the identity of the profession. The U.S. Department of Labor describes social work as "a profession for those with a strong desire to help improve people's lives. Social workers help people function the best way they can in their environment, deal with their relationships, and solve personal and family problems."[2] Despite these intentions, social workers find themselves stymied by parents' distrust of—and even antipathy toward—them, even as the structure of their work produces that distrust. Richie's comments best communicate this:

> Nowhere in there do they (the social workers) say that we want to help you, ya know? We're going to supply you with certain kinds of counseling and this and that. It's a demand. And to me, I feel that being the system that they are, I think them and the welfare department need to work together so that when families do get in

bad situations they have more social help, ya know? Because CPS only gets involved when it's a threat of taking the kids.

Richie points out that by the time CPS enters the picture, the family is often in peril. He suggests ways that social workers from different agencies could address familial challenges without threatening to remove the children and demanding deference. To get material assistance, parents must subordinate themselves to the state. Perhaps in the most parental way, the state will not give those it views as failed parents the equivalent of a child's allowance without knowing how it will be spent. This ethos that welfare recipients are, at best, irresponsible or, at worst, corrupt, seethes in state welfare policy that has instituted electronic benefit transfer cards that allow state oversight of grocery purchases, that moves toward increasingly restrictive regulations for public housing, including limits on who can stay over in such units, or that disallows assistance for parents with certain criminal convictions, most notably drug-related offenses. With these state policies as a backdrop to CPS work, parental distrust of social workers is well founded.

Many children enter the system with no clear way back out. Most of the parents in the CPS system are poor and are disproportionately African American. The majority of the cases in CPS are based on neglect, largely related to poverty and drug abuse, rather than physical or sexual abuse. The National Child Abuse and Neglect Data System reports that in 2002, 60.5 percent of victims suffered neglect (including medical neglect), while 18.6 percent were physically abused and 9.9 percent were sexually abused. In addition, 18.9 percent of victims were recorded as experiencing "other" types of maltreatment, which includes "abandonment," "threats of harm to the child," and "congenital drug addiction." Of the 113,702 children whose referrals were substantiated in California in 2002, 53 percent were for neglect, 13 percent were for physical abuse, and 8 percent were for sexual abuse.[3] Many of the cases I observed involved medical neglect, lack of supervision, illegal drug use, domestic violence, mental illness, or "parental incapacity," including mental retardation, which is believed to leave a parent unable to adequately care for a child. Middle and upper-class families typically escape the gaze of the state, even when similar parental shortcomings exist, because of the privacy socioeconomic resources provide.

Children do sometimes face real harm in their homes. In 2002, an estimated 1,400 children died as a result of abuse or neglect. (This puts maltreatment on a par with congenital abnormality as the second leading cause of death for children between the ages of one and four years in the United States.)[4] The death of a child in a family with which CPS has been working—as is the case in about 40 percent of such deaths—usually leads to a discernible cry for greater CPS intervention.[5] This can be seen clearly in the cases of Adam and Sarah, discussed in the Introduction. To find more abuse, CPS casts a wider net, and catches even more poverty-related neglect. In the course of investigating these families, the requirements of deference expected during the investigation remain unfulfilled for the reasons discussed. Material and structural barriers that cannot be easily fixed with the limited services provided by the county mix with parental frustration with state expectations to address things they feel are beyond their control. In too many cases, children remain in CPS because their family's circumstances have not noticeably improved and because their parents have failed to accept state prescriptions for their reform.

The role of the state in the private lives of families remains problematic, and varies by social location. Public intervention will likely be experienced as invasive. At the same time, some form of intervention is necessary on behalf of the children who do not receive adequate care (however defined); we cannot dismiss child protection simply as the work of elites against the poor. Instead, research needs to increasingly theorize what levels of intervention are reasonable, and when intervention is necessary, how parents should be able to retain or regain custody of their children. These questions already occupy our collective consciousness, emerging in popular culture[6] and bubbling to the surface in the public outcries that follow each journalistic revelation of another child murder. Within this context, the state, having asserted control over children, needs a clear measure of—or rather a method for measuring— whether a parent is rehabilitated and whether reunification is beneficial. As historian Linda Gordon poignantly states, "If children are to have rights, then some adults must be appointed and accepted, by other adults, to define and defend them."[7]

The current CPS apparatus uses parental subordination and demonstrable rehabilitation to decide whether parents should regain custody of their children. These factors do not provide an accurate basis for generalization. Pointing to the disconnect between assessments of parental ability and parental compliance, legal scholar Dorothy Roberts argues that in CPS,

The issue is no longer whether the child may be safely returned home, but whether the mother has attended every parenting class, made every urine drop, participated in every therapy session, shown up for every scheduled visitation, arrived at every appointment on time, and always maintained a contrite and cooperative disposition.[8]

It is in fact these criteria that act as degradation rituals to discipline parents.

Many of the stories presented here show the disjuncture between compliance and parental capability, in both directions. Some parents fail to reunify with their children, even as CPS officials agree they are likely capable of parenting. This can be seen most clearly in examples of parents like Linda Durrant, who reunify with one child but not another because children end up on different "tracks," with different timetables, because of differences in age or adoptability. Similarly Mary Allen, the mother who secretly married a man from her drug treatment program, had a baby after her parental rights were terminated for her other children. She was allowed to keep the baby, with six months of in-home services, even as she was declared unfit to mother her other children. In contrast, parents like Adam's and Sarah's, discussed in the Introduction, may have attended all required services and even appeared deferential, but in the end continued to be a threat to their children. Adherence to procedural and legal criteria, as constructed, often leads to seemingly illogical results. Further, they ignore the complex web of experiences and knowledge that have been shaped by race, class, gender, sexuality, and history that alter parents' willingness and ability to comply.

GOOD INTENTIONS, POOR OUTCOMES

This system, unlike other points of intersection between the state and individuals, is filled with individuals that are all motivated by a desire to do good. As mentioned, social workers enter the profession out of a desire to help others. Attorneys on all sides of a case are also advocating for what they believe is in the best interest of their clients. Children's attorneys want what is best in the long-term for their clients. For them, this almost always reflects a belief that, whenever possible, children are best served when the state can find them better parents through adoption. With this view, children's attorneys rarely advocate for reunification with biological parents. Also trying to do what they see is best for their clients, parents' attorneys work with their clients in hopes that they will be able to improve their lives and regain their children. These attorneys provide pragmatic suggestions about how to navigate the system and try to best represent to the court their clients' willingness to change, even as it wanes between hearings.

Parents also are largely motivated by good intentions and love for their children. For example, Robert Davis brought a camcorder to his interview with me so I could see the video footage from his recent visit with his two daughters. Lacking a car, he carried this expensive piece of equipment around with him, taping almost all interactions with his daughters so he could see them between visits. I told him how beautiful the girls were and his smile turned to a wide grin when I suggested that the youngest looked like him. Nonetheless, his chronic mental illness raised questions for the court about his parenting ability, questions that remained unsatisfactorily answered by his lack of deference. In another case, Cindy Hayes, a white mother addicted to methamphetamine, demonstrated her concern for her children even as they were being removed. Cindy's case began when an investigating social worker decided to place Cindy's two children, ages three and seven years, in protective custody. Cindy had burned her youngest with a cigarette and later, likely because of the agitation methamphetamine use causes, had picked at his healing wound until it bled again. As the family services worker came to take the kids to the children's receiving home, Cindy, between sobs, insisted on checking whether the county's car seat was installed correctly before allowing her toddler son to be strapped in to it. This act was both ironic and an important reminder that individuals behave in complex and contradictory ways.[9] Here, as Cindy was deemed a danger to her children, she also communicated concern for their safety in an appropriately maternal way.

Robert and Cindy were not good parents by most standards. They can be easily demonized or dismissed as mentally ill and erratic, or as a drug addict who binges while her incarcerated husband is away. Yet there is little doubt that they love their children, even as they fail to adequately care for them. Joan Billings, a veteran county attorney once told me that many parents "love their children, but they love them like they love their television or a puppy." From her view, jaded from more than twenty years in juvenile court, parents don't always conceptualize their children as entities beyond themselves, and may not see them as more than their property (perhaps one of the few things these impoverished parents can actually claim as all theirs). Implicit in Joan's assertion is a belief that some parents love their children without understanding that current parenting norms require parents to place their children's needs above their own. From her perspective, parental anger and resistance remain mechanisms of self-protection, a violation of one of the core premises of middle-class parenting: parents must be self-sacrificing. The cumbersome nature of CPS—with the time-intensive services, complicated schedules, and bureaucratic processes—awkwardly tries to force parents to prove their commitment to their children; if parents will go through all of that, they must be committed to their children. Although we can reasonably wonder whether middle-class parents could pass this test if forced to do so, the simple ability to drive privately owned or leased cars to appointments, scheduled at their leisure, or to rely on a privately funded attorney to screen court documents with more diligence than court-appointed attorneys can spare means that we will never know.

Most parents in this study attempted to address the court's demands, although not always in ways that were recognized as such. Parents who were deemed noncompliant with case plans often attended all court proceedings. Parents (mostly fathers) tried to hold down jobs to prove they could provide for their children upon their children's return home, even as they ignored their required services. Despite their noncompliance, many made personal sacrifices. Many couples separated. For example, Juan Reyes separated from his wife Leigh, whom he adored, because he recognized that her unwillingness to stop using methamphetamine would ruin his chances of regaining custody of their daughters. Others attempted to mobilize the resources they had available. For example, Mateo Estes borrowed money from his parents to hire a private attorney, while Jamila Washington, who was hostile through every stage of the CPS process, went out and proactively found an attorney from the National Association for the Advancement of Colored People, which at the time had a special program designed to monitor CPS's involvement in the African American community and to intervene when possible, to represent her in her efforts to regain custody of her children.

Despite good intentions, efforts to resocialize parents do not usually work as planned. In California in 2001, about 35 percent of children were reunified with their parents after one year in care. A study of the cohort of children who entered foster care in 1998 shows that after four and a half years, 54 percent of those who were placed in kinship care arrangements and 58 percent of those who were placed in nonkin arrangements were reunified with their parents.[10] Although more than half of children will return to their parents, the story is more complicated, particularly for the children, who are easy to lose sight of in discussing parents' experiences. First, it is essential to remember that while four years is a manageable amount of time for adults, it often represents the majority—even entirety—of the life of a child in foster care. Given that the majority of children who are reunified with their parents will be reunified within twenty-four months, policies limiting time toward reunification may be reasonable. Second, many children who are returned to their parents will again enter the CPS system. Children reenter the CPS system after reunifying with their parents in 20 to 37 percent of cases, of which almost 12 percent reenter within twelve months of exiting foster care.[11] In addition to the trauma of again entering foster care and the disruption it causes children, parents whose children reenter are not entitled to additional reunification services.[12] Upon reentering, the new case can move directly toward terminating parental rights.

For these reasons, federal law (ASFA most succinctly) communicates that children should be reunified with their parents as soon as possible, but definitely within twelve months. If this cannot occur, they should be given adoptive or permanent foster homes as soon as possible. This sentiment was communicated in the judge's ruling in one of the cases I observed. As he moved to terminate a mother's parental rights, he reflected,

> It is unfortunate when parents bring children into the world and cannot care for them. It is also unfortunate when parents cannot do what they need to do. I must do what's best for the children, not the parents, not the relatives, not the foster parents. What is easy is to terminate services... These children have a right to permanency. What we do is inappropriate. First, we take them away because the parents are inappropriate. Then we dawdle around for three years. It is not fair to the children.

The judge's remarks make intuitive sense. However, one of the unintended consequences of this law may be that efforts to expedite reunifications are contributing to reentry into state care and the ultimate demise of families. Pointing to this, one federal report found that

> States exhibiting a relatively high percentage of reunifications within twelve months also demonstrate a relatively high percentage of re-entries within twelve months. In contrast, States with a relatively low percentage of reunifications within twelve months also tend to have a relatively low rate of foster care re-entries within twelve months. The consistent finding of a significant correlation between these variables indicates that there is a relationship between reunifications that occur quickly and the rate of re-entry into foster care. This raises concerns about potential unanticipated results of State efforts to expedite reunifications.[13]

The failures of reunification services to help parents regain and maintain custody of their children do not suggest that parents do not need services. Instead, they show that the manner in which services are provided is flawed. Currently parents are offered little or no opportunity to participate in the development of their own case plans. Parents often do not identify the same goals for their own recovery as the state identifies for them and do not always understand that fulfilling the state's requirements—as it demonstrates deference to state values—is what matters most. A more client-centered approach would be an important step in addressing this conflict. Political scientist Andrew Polsky argues that "the notion that citizens must have some space in which to define their concerns in their own language has been subordinated to the premise, drawn from therapeutic discourse, that intervention will leave clients better able in the end to stand on their own two feet."[14] Indeed, parents find not only that their own definitions are irrelevant, but that they are in fact devalued and defined as pathological. From this vantage point, parents must perform acceptance of the goals of state intervention, even as these goals remain foreign in parents' own experiential context. Although I am not arguing against intervention entirely, the lack of a discursive space for parents to define their own priorities and goals has resulted in a system where the tools handed to clients are often not the ones they believe they most need to craft the lives they most desire.

A policy that both acknowledges parents' own desires for their lives and communicates the state's goals in a way that strives to connect the two holds more promise for serving both individual and state needs. A more progressive approach to reunification services would provide services that address the specific aspects of parenting that are lacking, while still granting parents their individuality, even if idiosyncratic. In discussing CPS expectations of mothers, law professor and former dependency attorney Annette Appell argues that "if mothers are the problem, then it is they who must be fixed. To be fixed, however, they must become different women."[15] Parents may never become good parents, but they may become good enough parents, bringing their own unique style to the enterprise. This is all the state has the right to expect. (Should the state seek to give children to "better" homes, rather than adequate homes, virtually all parents would be at risk of losing their children.) Challenging the homogenization of mothers in CPS, Appell argues, "The child welfare establishment too often views [mothers'] lives through a single lens; the textures and perspectives of each mother and her children become invisible or muted."[16] Finding a way to accept parent individuality while also assessing their capacity to care for their children would honor the uniqueness of each family, without jeopardizing child well-being. Sadly, in a culture where the state distrusts poor parents to buy their own groceries, plan their own families, or choose whether or not to marry, allows almost 17 percent of children to live in poverty (85 percent of whom have parents who are employed), and where drug use serves to define a parent's entire worth, such a transformation in approach remains distant.[17]

CPS AND THE ANTIPARENT CULTURE

In writing this book, I struggled to find statistics on rates of successful reunification. In searching for these figures, I was frequently drawn to federal and state reports that promised a discussion of permanency. These data reports use "permanency" as a way to report on rates of adoption and guardianship, not reunification. This is understandable given the spate of recent legislation that created financial incentives for states, individuals, and corporations who facilitate adoptions. However, these policy priorities speak to the antireunification environment that families in the CPS system encounter. Current policy and practice has failed to recognize that children can have permanency in their natal families. Until there is new federal legislation that makes it equally attractive for states to successfully reunify families, until the pendulum swings back, families will continue to lack the resources that are solely directed to other state goals, and will thus remain fractured.

As discussed earlier, public opinion and policy currently assume that biological parents who enter the CPS system—most of whom are poor—are a liability to their children. This ideology reflects a larger culture that assumes poor families are problematic. It is in fact no coincidence that the federal overhaul of child welfare in 1997 followed directly behind welfare reform in 1996 that ended entitlements to public social support and created increasingly coercive conditions for the receipt of even minimal assistance.

Throughout the congressional hearings to pass the ASFA, adoption was identified as the ideal outcome for children in foster care. Dorothy Roberts's description of the proceedings notes that "virtually every mention of biological families was negative, whereas adoptive homes were referred to as loving and stable."[18] The loss of political legitimacy of biological families in poor communities has largely been a success of conservative claims makers who speak of welfare and female-headed households in equally disparaging—and interchangeable—ways. What is desperately needed is a vocabulary to represent the lives of poor families who struggle—sometimes stumbling, sometimes recovering—that communicates respect for their experiences. Recent ethnographies of welfare recipients have helped to craft such a language, but the conversation must also move to the statehouses and popular press to help transform public discourse.[19]

Some portion of this perception comes from the lack of representations of poor families in a positive light. Inclusive is the lack of coverage of CPS successes. Current interpretations of confidentiality laws make it difficult for the media, social workers, or parents themselves to report on system successes. As a result, only the worst possible outcomes of the CPS system are made public. Reunification success stories need to be made publicly available in ways that do not compromise the confidentiality of the families involved. Social workers who remove children speak of their fear of being investigated by their superiors for failing to remove a child who was later beaten or killed. This fear contributes to job stress and inadvertently makes child removal the default outcome. "Better safe than sorry" is rewarded, but there is no credit assigned to workers who succeed in preventing removals or helping families retain their children after reunification. (In fact, for investigating social workers, placing children in state custody often requires less paperwork than does providing well-chosen services.) Creating avenues to publicize the successes of families who received in-home services and improved the care of their children or of the parents who worked hard and reunified with their children would positively affect social worker morale and allow the public to see them less as "baby-snatchers" (or incompetents) and more as the community resources they long to be. It would also provide parents in CPS with a clearer guide and with much needed encouragement. Perhaps most importantly, such a discourse would reshape public perceptions of CPS; rather than being seen as a system that always fails because it grants too many chances to undeserving parents, CPS could be seen as an agency that provides the means to fix families. Transforming media coverage of CPS will matter, but represents only a small ripple in the antiparent current that floods state welfare policy. Yet any efforts that stem the antiparent sentiments that proliferate and that can influence public policy will help.

ADDRESSING SYSTEM FAILURES

The problems in the CPS system emerge from deep structural inequalities erected over time. Solving them will take a wholesale reimagination of the role of the state in poor communities. So long as the state defines its role as that of police agent, the dynamics that lead parents to experience the state as coercive, punitive, and untrustworthy will continue; parent–state interactions in CPS will be haunted by the same dynamics.

Having said that, there are small system tinkerings that might help to improve the experiences of some parents. None of the suggestions detailed below will, by themselves, solve the problems of the CPS system.

Rather, they merely aim to treat the symptoms of a pathological system, to perhaps provide an analgesic to a chronic disease. In the end, larger structural changes will be the only cure for the multiple problems facing the CPS system. Community empowerment, better employment opportunities, affordable housing, high-quality affordable childcare, respectable public education for all children (and adults), drug treatment on demand, healthcare, and readily accessible and affordable family planning services are all necessary to address the variety of issues affecting low-income families who fall under the scrutiny of the state. Until those things happen, these smaller policy changes will only make small improvements in the lives of individual parents and their children.

Social Work Workload

Part of social workers' fear of making mistakes stems from the isolation they experience from working a great number of cases alone. Above all, caseloads should be reduced, which requires greater public allocation of resources. Beyond that, the way in which social work is practiced needs to be examined. One important change would be to allow social workers who currently work alone to work in teams. This change could reduce the isolation workers feel, help them to feel confident when choosing to leave children in their homes (or remove them), and provide some level of mentoring and social support, both of which would directly affect worker retention. Given that CPS workers have a stunningly high turnover rate (you may recall that the second most senior worker in the investigative unit I studied had less than three years experience), this may actually be a cost-effective solution as well.

Giving Voice to Parental Anger

Once their children are removed, parents often feel angry and indignant. Many parents spend several months refusing to cooperate with their social workers, feeling angered and even violated by the experience of having someone enter their home, tell them they are inadequate, and take their children. By the time these parents are ready to participate in services, they are often stunned to find that they have only a few months left to complete their case plan before their children's long-term placement (away from them) will be decided. Providing counselors and anger management instructors to parents on a purely *voluntary* basis within the first seventy-two hours following removal of their children and leading up to their first court appearance could help parents understand the court process and strategize their participation. When investigating social workers place a child in protective custody, they give parents information about their legal rights and obligations to appear in court. It would not be difficult to include additional information about advocacy services available to them. The creation of such services, which would need to be free from the existing requirement that service providers report the content of provider-client interactions to the court, would help parents find ways to express their anger, learn about the court process, and devise ways to advocate on their own behalf that are not detrimental to their long-term goals. Some portion of parents receiving initial intervention might also feel equipped to identify their own service needs before coming to court; this could expedite the reunification process and increase the chances of parent participation.

Access to Advocacy

Parents often need an advocate to help them between court appearances. In many places, children are assigned a court-appointed special advocate (CASA), whose primary responsibility is to make sure children don't fall through the cracks between overworked social workers and transient foster care providers. Having a similar kind of advocate could help parents navigate the multiple bureaucracies and service requirements they face. Many of the parents in CPS lack reliable transportation, functional literacy, and the social skills necessary to fully participate in designing and attending their services as equal partners. An advocate would be a valuable resource to them.

Relevant Services

Some parents will remain noncompliant with services, even if they are given an opportunity to identify their own needs or assistance in addressing them. This reality does not diminish the likelihood that others could perceive intervention as a chance to design the life that they want to live and identify the path to doing so. I have provided multiple examples of parents who did, even with the current system constraints. To facilitate this, service and content eligibility need to be examined. Parents need referrals and access to affordable housing before they reunify with their children. In many of the cases I studied, the ability to secure housing would have enabled a parent to escape an abusive boyfriend, move away from a home shared with a drug dealing partner or family member, and build independence. The period of reunification, when the county is already investing significant financial resources, could potentially provide parents with a chance to find or maintain paid employment without struggling to balance childcare, work, and recent sobriety. Currently, paid employment is discouraged if it interferes with compliance with services. This policy does little to help parents learn to balance multiple responsibilities. There is currently little focus in CPS on helping parents establish and maintain functional lifestyles after reunifying with their children; existing transition services are often limited and inadequate. These dynamics may account for the large number of children who reenter foster care after reunification. In short, the current system sets many parents up for failure by mandating less relevant services and failing to appropriately identify other needs.

THE STATE, FEMINISM, AND THE POLITICS OF PARENTING

By identifying the ways that the therapeutic state aims to resocialize poor and ethnic minority families so they might embrace dominant definitions of parenting, I may have inadvertently suggested that there is no reasonable role for the state in family life. That is not my goal. In fact, state intervention is necessary; without some public mechanism by which children can be protected, children would remain at the mercy of their parents, a terrifying prospect in light of the fact that some parents are indeed hazards to their children. The questions remain: whose community standards should define adequate care of children and what mechanisms should be used to enforce those standards? An accompanying question is, who should be at the proverbial table when such issues are decided?

Such conversations should begin among those who recognize mechanisms by which social inequality persists and who believe that poor families should be recognized as intrinsically valuable in society, as other families already are. With a broad tradition of examining state relationships to family life and well-honed skills for identifying processes that reproduce oppression, feminist scholarship is an ideal place to begin such discussions. Unfortunately feminists have largely resisted a discussion of child maltreatment, which challenges aspects of the domestic violence paradigm that identifies men as abusers and women as victims (as is overwhelmingly the case). Instead, feminist writings often downplay child abuse perpetrated by mothers and instead focus on child abuse as a symptom of patriarchy in the family.[20] The few works that do address the child welfare system skirt around issues of abuse. For example, Annette Appell focuses on "four archetypal 'bad' mothers: the drug user, the mentally impaired woman, the battered woman, and the teenager" in her essay on mothers who are attempting to reunify with their children. Dorothy Roberts's 1999 book chapter exclusively discusses women who fail to protect their children, and her important book on race and child welfare allocates fewer than a half-dozen pages (of more than 276 pages) to child abuse by biological parents.[21] Feminists have identified the structural barriers that shape women's inequality and the cultural contradictions embedded in expectations of motherhood (and fatherhood). Yet, the profound silence around a woman's agency, especially when it may lead to the abuse or neglect of her children, ignores another arena in which to examine the complexities of mothering specifically, and parenthood more generally, as they are experienced by parents, and defined and enforced by the state. In addition, child welfare provides an opportunity to consider the complex ways that children are connected to their parents, while also autonomous from them, including how children may be disadvantaged in their own relationships of power.

The feminist reticence about maternal failure may be in part a reaction to the images of bad mothers that saturate U.S. society. From talk shows and books to news stories and political speeches, women's failures within families are a consistent topic of discussion, critiquing everything from women's sexuality and behaviors in marriage, pregnancy, or childrearing to their very attitudes about motherhood itself. Although definitions of bad mothers—like those of ideal mothers—are indeed socially constructed, their constructed nature does not erase the reality that bad mothers—mothers whose harm to their children represents more than a character flaw—do exist. Yet the proliferation of images of bad mothers as poor, as nontraditional, as members of racial, ethnic, or religious minority communities, as unmarried, or as immoral obscures our ability to differentiate actual abuse from the litany of rhetorical maternal failings. Because so much of mothering is under attack, feminist theorists have needed to defend motherhood itself.

Without an articulate position on actual abuse or neglect, those who critique motherhood specifically and poor parenthood more generally in myriad manifestations of racism and sexism have claimed a discursive space from which to design, promote, and implement punitive policies with little coherent opposition. This lack of organized opposition to the antiparent ethos has allowed CPS policies and practices to be implemented without adequate resources to implement them well, as seen in the overburdened child abuse investigation system, the limited efforts provided for reunification, and the lack of resources committed to providing poor families with some level of material security. Feminist analyses have vigorously defended poor women and argued against excessive state intervention in their lives.[22] These theorists have also demonstrated that class and race do not define parental competence. These are significant contributions. Feminist scholars now need to more rigorously address intersections of the state and family in the child welfare system, even if this requires them to theorize incompetent parents, and acknowledge that in some cases, children are better off away from their parents.

One point of entrance is to build on the work that has already been done. There has been a well-articulated feminist critique of federal welfare reform and the efforts to control reproduction and coerce women into marriage embedded within.[23] Yet there has been little attention paid to the web of contradictory policies that CPS parents, who are largely recipients of public assistance, must endure. For example, women in CPS are penalized for dating or continuing romantic relationships with men, while the federal government funds marriage promotion activities. Families who were receiving TANF lose their grants and access to subsidized housing if their children are removed from their care; yet they cannot reunify with their children without adequate housing or financial resources. Perhaps most ironic, parents are sometimes advised to quit their jobs to focus on their reunification services, even as federal welfare policy demands paid employment above everything, including quality parenting. Adequate examinations of the CPS system must theorize the "state" as a series of interconnected subsystems rather than as a unified power structure.[24] From there, the ways families are pulled in multiple directions by varying rules and regulations can be more fully understood and challenged.

Feminist theory also needs to look critically at fathers' efforts to gain custody of their children, as they present another opportunity to examine gender and familial responsibility within a feminist framework. In the CPS system, many men—largely poor and disproportionately men of color—are attempting to gain the right to become primary caretakers of their children. They often fail because of criminal histories not related to parental ability, stereotypes about men's inability to competently parent, or because their failure to marry the mothers of their children is interpreted as a lack of commitment to those children. The state actively enforces traditional gender roles for both men and women. Feminist theorists have explored gender and custody decisions in the family courts, pointing to ways that men are often advantaged in divorce decrees.[25] In the CPS context, the issue is not about whether custody will be awarded to mothers or fathers. When men fail to reunify with their children, the children who are not deemed adoptable are left in the foster care system; outcomes for children in foster care are dismal. Statistics show that 27 percent of males and 10 percent of females who "aged out" or turned eighteen while in foster care were incarcerated within twelve to eighteen months; 50 percent were unemployed; 37 percent had not finished high school; 33 percent received public assistance; and 19 percent of females had given birth to children. Moreover, 47 percent were receiving some kind of counseling or medication for mental health problems before leaving care; that number dropped to 21 percent after leaving care.[26] Perhaps most depressing is that of the children who exited foster care through emancipation, 36 percent of them entered foster care when they were younger than twelve years.[27] Although foster care cannot be held entirely responsible for these problems, these sad statistics underscore the larger point: there is a great deal at stake.

The gendered experiences of men and women in CPS illustrate how the state polices gender and demands conformity. Looking at these experiences provides a valuable opportunity to analyze gender and power within the family and between the state and family. Sociologist Carole Joffe notes that "feminist theoretical writing [during the second wave of feminism] saw the place of women in the family as critical to an understanding of the larger political situation of women."[28] With this background, feminists are logically positioned to engage with child protection policy.

LOOKING FORWARD TO POSTMODERN POST-CPS FAMILIES

To successfully engage with the child welfare system requires feminist theorists and activists to focus on two fronts. First, many of the flaws in existing policy need to be addressed and remedied. These include but are not limited to investigations by overburdened social workers who work alone, inadequate reunification services, the conflation of compliance with parental capability, and the catch-22s that expect parents to secure resources like subsidized child care, healthcare, or housing while lacking custody of the children that would make such an application possible or that expect them to maintain employment while attending services during regular work hours. Doing so would help to ensure that parents are given every opportunity to care for their children.

Second, there must be recognition that in some cases, parents cannot adequately care for their children, no matter how many services they receive. (With improvements in service provision and CPS practice, there would be fewer of these cases than there are currently.) It is important to recognize that in some situations, children are better off without their biological parents. In such cases, we need to find ways to advocate for the best alternative outcomes possible. This would include honoring and supporting adoptive families, encouraging quality foster care, and creating ways to support children and parents who may need to mourn each other's loss, even as that separation represents the best outcome in a terrible situation.

Sociologist Judith Stacey suggests that "like post-modern culture, contemporary Western family arrangements are diverse, fluid, and unresolved...our families today admix unlikely elements in an improvisational pastiche of old and new."[29] Nowhere can the postmodern family condition be more clearly observed than in the families that are reformed and reshaped by the CPS system. Many parents who do not reunify with their children remain close to their own parents or extended biological families, many of whom have custody of their children, throughout their lives. In other cases, adoptive parents—both relatives and nonrelatives—develop and maintain relationships with their children's biological family. Although the practice of open adoption continues to be an evolving process for most adoptive families, one study found that as many as one in five children adopted from foster care has contact with a biological relative.[30]

Outside of continuing relationships with biological family members, new families are formed through state intervention. In fact, foster care and adoption are increasingly becoming avenues by which gay men and lesbians become parents.[31] In addition, many working-class families utilize adoption from foster care as an affordable alternative to private adoption. Currently the CPS system relies heavily on narrow definitions of parenthood, based almost exclusively on biology. Feminists, too, in a defense of parenthood often under siege, have adhered to the superiority of reunification between biological children and parents over all other outcomes in the CPS system, while simultaneously celebrating a diversity of family forms in other realms. These suppositions should now be brought together in a cohesive discussion that identifies the ways state intervention promotes dominant meanings of family, while also recognizing the plethora of families that emerge from that very same state intervention. New definitions of family that consider the familial role of those who provide care and accept responsibility for children have been theorized elsewhere.[32] These ideas need to be integrated into considerations of the CPS system. The child welfare system presents a rich opportunity to explore both the meanings of state intervention in the family as well as new forms of the family— fluid, diverse, and unresolved—that emerge.

APPENDIX: METHODS

This is an ethnography of the child welfare system in one northern California county and the individuals and families who interact within it. I intentionally never name this county in an effort to protect the anonymity of those whose stories are recounted here. In some ways, the very structures of the system help me to ensure their anonymity: thousands of parents cycle through the CPS system each year, and once out of the system, most change addresses or even cities. Attorneys move in and out of different roles in the court, and social workers too frequently leave their posts. I verified this last point unintentionally; about one year after I completed my fieldwork, I tried to call the social workers I had followed to say hello and to ask a few more questions about their work. By the time I called, about half the workers I had followed had already left this field office and their new replacements knew little about where they had gone. Despite these structural means by which individuals who have been in the CPS system are hard to find, I have nonetheless attempted to do everything in my power to protect their identities.

This book is based on multiple sources of data: participant observations with social workers, observations of confidential court proceedings in the dependency branch of the juvenile court, formal interviews with parents, informal interviews with social workers and attorneys, and content analysis of court reports and documents. Although my years of committee work performed before my formal data collection began (described below) are not specifically excerpted as data, the information gained there indeed provided the soil from which this project grew. In addition, because CPS policy is often motivated by and responded to in news coverage, I collected newspaper articles about CPS in the years preceding and during my formal data collection. The hundreds of articles I collected allowed me to better understand the public perceptions of the agency and how that impacts the agency itself. In this appendix, I try to account for how I became interested in child welfare, describe how I collected data, and provide information about the parents in my study. In addition, I reflect on the unique experience of being pregnant during portions of my data collection and point to the ways it facilitated or altered my access to data and the unique insights the experience yielded. In the end, I hope my efforts represent the intentions of all the players in this system, while also pointing to the ways in which the system is doomed to fail the families it aims to fix.

BECOMING A CHILD ABUSE RESEARCHER

My entrance into studying CPS came when I was appointed to a county CPS oversight committee—organized by the county department of health and human services—and then joined a child abuse prevention committee—a community-based advisory board—in a neighboring county; I served on each for two years. Studying child abuse and the systems that respond to it was not my goal at the time. Rather, I began my committee work as someone who had studied the growing trend of cities and counties prosecuting pregnant women for their behavior while gestating, which mostly focuses on, but was not limited to, drug use. Child welfare agencies, following the prosecutorial trends, were beginning to place greater attention on perinatal drug use, so I thought observing CPS agencies would provide a greater understanding of this issue, including how agencies conceptualize women's autonomy. At that time, I imagined this would be useful background for my intended research focus on state management of reproduction.

I should say a bit about my fascination with state reproductive law and policy, an interest that developed in the early to mid-1990s at a time that I consider to be one of a national obsession with issues related to procreation. That period witnessed the increasing use of reproductive technologies and accompanying controversy, which included questions about the legality of surrogacy contracts, custody battles over frozen embryos, and the high costs of the technologies with often low rates of success. There were also problems relating to the management or mismanagement of the materials for in vitro fertilization: embryos implanted in the wrong women, doctors substituting their own sperm for that of the intended father, and uncertainty about what to do with abandoned pre-embryos. At the same time some were struggling to achieve and define parenthood through technology (and the courts), others were defining—sometimes claiming, sometimes denouncing—parenthood with different technology, namely paternity testing. At the time, it seemed that television talk shows had come to rely on episodes that pointed to the complicated meanings of parenthood. A staple was the recurring setup where a woman who expresses uncertainty about who the genetic father of her child might be invites two or more men on air to be tested. Montell, Jerry, Ricki, Jenny, and their brethren seemed to revel in the suspense as they announced which man was the "real father," with little regard for who may have been performing the duties of real fatherhood. These shows reflected increasing public anxiety about nonmarital childbearing and new laws requiring women to name their children's fathers for the purpose of child support collection. At the same time, poor women and women of color found themselves facing criminal prosecution or "protective incarceration" for acts ranging from drug use during pregnancy to failing to follow medical advice about pregnancy management. All of this was set against the backdrop of decreasing access to legal abortions caused by a combination of legislative and judicial action, the murders of abortion providers, the declining numbers of physicians trained to provide abortions, and the absorption of public health care facilities into Catholic ones. These dilemmas of reproduction were not just in the public consciousness; they also reflected the increasing role of the state in regulating reproduction.

My decision to sit on these child welfare committees was a pivotal one. Committee service to the first county provided access to high-ranking agency administrators and to drafts of policies under development or in varying stages of reform, while my work with the second county helped me understand expressions of community concern about child maltreatment and the role of nonprofit agencies in addressing them. The first county—the one that is the subject of this book—was actively revamping its agency practice to reduce the likelihood of another child fatality like Adam's, whose death seemed to have single-handedly launched these reforms. Through these meetings, I came to see child protection work as fertile ground to explore my interests in reproductive rights. Of particular interest to me was the legal disconnect between rights and privileges: individuals have a constitutionally guaranteed right to bear children, but are not assured the right to raise them, which is somehow deemed a privilege to be granted by the state. Further, I could articulate the flaws of public policy that prioritized fetal rights over those of adult women. However, my thoughts were not as clear when I considered state policy involving actual children, with full rights of personhood. The CPS system was in fact the ideal realm to explore what I came to see as the other end of the same continuum.

COLLECTING DATA

In the county-sponsored committee, I came to know senior CPS administrators who were supportive of my desire to study the workings of their agency. After submitting a proposal and participating in the county "ride-along" program, which allowed committee members—as well as other interested citizens, including medical students, physicians, and other health service workers—to observe CPS social workers performing their work, I began collecting data. In the initial phase of data collection, I observed two kinds of social workers: emergency response workers and family reunification social workers. My fieldwork with them allowed me a view into their professional worlds: I followed social workers and observed their work as they determined whether to remove children from their homes, enrolled parents in services, and developed their recommendations for the court. Workers discussed their decisions with me and explained their reasoning. I observed virtually all social worker interviews of children, parents, and other relevant parties, known as "collateral contacts" (which include teachers, school nurses, health care providers, and concerned relatives) and watched almost all social worker inspections of homes. I also watched discussions between social workers and their professional allies, which included supervisors, police officers, and other social workers. On occasion, I was also present when a child was removed from parental custody because a social worker decided the child faced imminent danger.

My observations of social workers were in one investigation unit, that is, one field office among several in the county. The office is comprised of several dozen caseworkers, five support staff members, a social worker supervisor, a unit supervisor, and approximately six family maintenance workers who provide assistance to social workers and clients. Family maintenance workers are paraprofessionals who usually have a high school education, in contrast to professional social workers, who, in the county I studied, hold a minimum of a bachelor's degree in social work and often a master's degree in social work. It is important to note that this is not the case in a great many places, where members of the workforce often lack specific training in social work or lack a master's degree.

At the beginning and end of each day and between cases, I spent a great deal of time talking with the various agency employees and was known in the office. In the four months I was in the emergency response unit, I followed several different social workers into the field and on occasion accompanied family maintenance workers, though the bulk of my observations were with five full-time social workers. Thao Vue was the second most senior investigating worker in the office—with slightly more than two years on the job—and as a result, he was assigned by the agency supervisor to be the first person I observed. As a Hmong immigrant, he is considered a special skills worker, having cultural and language skills for working with the county's large Laotian, Mien, and Hmong communities. During the month or so I spent with Thao, I learned a great deal about the agency generally and the challenges of working with the Southeast Asian community specifically. However, I had not attended any emergency calls and had not seen any cases that Thao felt warranted placing children in protective custody. Thao felt this was anomalous and suggested that I follow other social workers, particularly those serving as "the first runner of the day." The first runner in the emergency response unit is the social worker who, for that day, is responsible for investigating cases that have been deemed emergent and therefore must be investigated within two hours of being reported. (When the first runner is called out, the second runner moves up the list and fields the next call. Answering these emergent calls takes precedence over their other cases, which still must be completed within the time specified by the intake worker.)

Following Thao's suggestion, I began following several other workers. Roxanna Villarosa, a Latina who was a child services worker in New York City before coming to California, was a native Spanish language speaker and thus brought cultural and language skills for working with the county's Latino community, many of whom were Mexican immigrants. I also observed Kevin Slybrooks, a former police officer who became disabled from law enforcement after he was shot in the line of duty. Kevin is openly gay and is considered a special skills worker because of his extensive knowledge of issues relating to HIV/AIDS and related community resources. As an example of how his skills are utilized, I once accompanied Kevin on a call where a woman reported that her grandchildren's mother was allowing the children to hug and be close to their father (the reporter's son) who was dying of an AIDS-related illness. She also alleged the children's mother refused to have the children tested for HIV. Kevin went to the house, met the children and their mother, found out which services she had accessed (and knew her counselors at a county AIDS outreach project by name), helped her complete a housing application, and closed the case as unsubstantiated. In addition to working as a full-time social worker, Kevin also provides sensitivity training on gay and lesbian issues to law enforcement officers.

In addition to those three special skills workers, I spent a great deal of time with two other emergency response social workers: Julie Lawrence, a white Catholic lesbian had recently transferred into CPS from Adult Protective Services, another county agency, and James Crockett, an African American man who became a CPS worker after finishing college on the GI bill. James claims he chose social work because the graduate program in social work required less time than one in physical therapy, his original goal, and had a high degree of job security. James had been with the agency for more than a year, Julie and Roxanna had been on the job less than six months, and Kevin had been there less than three months when I began following them.

Several months after I began observing workers in the emergency response unit, I also began accompanying a family reunification worker; I spent one day a week for four months with him. The family reunification unit's work is quite different from that of the emergency response unit. The reunification workers are responsible for executing court orders for services and visits, evaluating foster care placements and parental progress toward reform, and making recommendations to the court. Thomas Page, an African American man, had been working in the family reunification unit for about eight years. He was well liked and well respected by other workers, supervisors, and by parents' attorneys, who told me they were happy when their clients were on Tom's caseload. With Tom, I observed supervised visits between children and parents, visited biological parents and foster parents in their homes, and observed Tom's discussions with the children he supervised in state custody. Unlike investigative social work, reunification work requires the social worker to maintain a continuous relationship with the family. As such, we often visited the same family multiple times in a variety of settings. Tom, like all the social workers I followed, was exceedingly generous with his time and seemed most willing to explain case background, decisions, and broader agency policy and practice to me.

My day following social workers almost always began at 8:00 A.M. and usually ended between 4:30 and 6:00 P.M., although they occasionally ran later—once as late as 2:00 A.M. When I arrived at the field office in the morning and was "buzzed" in through the electronically locked doors by a security guard, the social workers had almost always been there for at least an hour before I arrived and often stayed several hours after I left. I never met a social worker who did not take work home or work on weekends.

Initially social workers were unsure how to treat me, an uncertainty that arose in part because of my familiarity with senior agency supervisors. This was clear to me on one particular day, early in my fieldwork, when I came to the office to meet Thao. Thao was in a meeting with senior administrators from county headquarters (which often seemed worlds away from this field office) who were asking him questions about a former case of his. In that case, Thao had helped a Vietnamese woman and her son move out of the home of the mother's abusive boyfriend. After completing services and maintaining a safe residence away from the boyfriend, Thao closed the case. About six months later, Thao learned that the mother had reconciled with her boyfriend who proceeded to drive his car—with her son strapped in—into a river. Thao now had to justify his decision to close the case and leave the child, now deceased, with his mother. As he came out of his meeting, the senior agency supervisor recognized me and we exchanged greetings, alerting Thao to my status as more than the usual interested community observer or student researcher.

To my good fortune, social workers accepted that I was not going to report their actions to the countywide administration and integrated me into their work days. During investigations, I sometimes read maps and navigated as we found our way to the homes and schools of the children they were charged with protecting. I learned which forms needed to be available in each situation and often had them ready when we arrived. Because social workers in this county almost always work alone, they often seemed grateful for my presence as a lunch companion, navigator, or sounding board. This acceptance gave me insight into the context and content of their work, as workers freely discussed their cases with me; it also implicated me in the practice of policing families. This was most clear on one occasion when Roxanna was investigating an allegation that a ten-year-old girl had been molested by her adult brother. As Roxanna walked through the small house, checking each room, I heard the mother say something that indicated that she knew her son was molesting her daughter. In our discussion in the car on the way back to the office, I asked Roxanna what she made of the remark. At that point, it became clear that Roxanna had not heard it. Yet in writing her report that justified placing the girl and her two younger sisters in protective custody, Roxanna included the statement. Later, the social work supervisor and Roxanna each credited me with providing the proverbial smoking gun in the case. Obviously in a moment like that, and more subtly when I was generically asked what I would do if it were my investigation, I was aware how thin the line was between observer and participant.

A couple of months after I began my observations of social workers, I was granted a court order to observe confidential juvenile court proceedings. A copy of the order was distributed to all five county juvenile court judges who were hearing child welfare cases and all attorneys who worked regularly in the dependency branch of the juvenile court. The order established that attorneys were permitted to discuss cases with me and to assist me in understanding them. It also stated that I would face contempt charges should I reveal identifying information about any child in the system. By distributing the order and clarifying the terms, my entrance into this closed world was easier than I could have hoped. When I introduced myself to courtroom staff and attorneys, people often knew who I was. I was required to do little to explain why I was permitted to be there and attorneys seemed to feel comfortable discussing case specifics with me.

The juvenile court is small and intimate, with a handful of people staffing most cases there all day, but it is disorienting and intimidating at the same time. Between each case, the bailiff clears the courtroom so that the only people in the gallery are those directly involved in the case or those who work for the system. Attorneys move in and out of adjacent conference rooms where they meet their clients, while parents who are waiting for their case to be called wait in the hallways. Cases fly through quickly and attorneys who already know each other discuss cases in abbreviations and code both during and between proceedings. As I heard one attorney agree to abandon the B1 allegation, but insist on pursuing the D, or when there are no objections on the 387, but the 342 petition must go forward, I was reminded that I was a stranger in a strange land. I also knew that this culture could not be easy for parents, who spend only minutes in the courtroom for every day I spent. When I began my courtroom observations, I attended court, watched court proceedings, and sometimes sat in on meetings between parents and their attorneys. I jotted down everything I could and went home to look up the legal codes that were referenced in shorthand. Yet over time I began to understand the flow of cases, the statutory requirements, and the esoteric vocabulary of the proceedings.

With that increased understanding, I started to follow specific cases over time by attending the next scheduled hearing in a particular case, as announced at the conclusion of the last. (Of course, sometimes the case would be rescheduled, unbeknownst to me, and I would miss it.) I also began interviewing parents. Initially parents' attorneys referred parents whose cases they thought were interesting or would be informative for me. Often I was able to meet with attorneys and examine background materials or would receive an explanation of the case history. As my confidence grew, I began approaching parents in the courthouse and asking if they would be willing to talk with me about their experiences. Whenever possible, parents asked their attorneys if it was safe to talk to me. In all instances, they were assured that I was bound by court order to keep whatever they told me confidential.[1] Parents seemed to accept this and oftentimes in interviews or conversations confided information to me that may not have been available to the court or their own attorneys. In all, I interviewed twelve mothers and nine fathers. Interviews were tape-recorded and transcribed and participants were assigned pseudonyms. Overall, I had very few parents decline my request for an interview. Seven of the twenty-one interviews were conducted in a conference room at the courthouse. Because they were there waiting for their case to be called anyway, the interview was not an inconvenience and might have even given them something to do while they waited.

When I interviewed parents outside of court, I would either go to their homes or meet them at a public place of their choosing, which included meeting someone at a drug-testing site so we could walk together to a nearby coffee shop, meeting at restaurants near their homes or places of employment, or meeting at a public venue like a public library. Once in a while, these meetings highlighted class differences between my interviewee and myself. For example, ordering at a nearby Starbucks, while second nature to me, was noticeably foreign to one woman who finally asked me for guidance. At other times, the fact that I could drive to our appointments highlighted their lack of transportation. At other times, these meetings and their chosen locations erased social distance, like when an African American man in his forties and I discovered we both adored the same greasy-spoon pancake house, or when I could meet them at a preferred place of their choosing, making them the expert. In general, I was more likely to interview women in their homes (as was the case with seven mothers and two fathers) and slightly more likely to interview men at the courthouse (two mothers and five fathers). In part, this was based on convenience; fewer men had stable housing where they felt they could be confidentially interviewed. It also reflects the fact that I conducted more interviews with fathers later in my data collection, at a time when my comfort with the courthouse and its spaces that promised confidentiality had increased.

I do not recall feeling uncomfortable with my interviewees or concerned for my safety during interviews, with the exception of one instance when I was observing a meeting between a father and his attorney in my first weeks of courthouse data collection. The father, a white man in his early thirties was brought to the courthouse from the county jail in handcuffs, having been arrested for repeatedly having sex with his fourteen-year-old daughter, beginning when she was twelve years old. Meetings between incarcerated parents and their attorneys are not held in the usual conference rooms, but instead in a small room off a long corridor, staffed by several sheriffs, in the back of the courthouse. In this particular case, the man's attorney, noting his new client's level of agitation, suggested that I leave. Although I was never in any actual danger, it was the one time I recall feeling intimidated by a parent—and the first time I recognized that some parents should never be allowed near their children again.

While few parents declined to be interviewed, there were two who expressed interest but were not interviewed. One mother scheduled an interview at her home and then was not there. She also rescheduled the interview and again was not home. One father asked me to meet him at the location of his court-ordered visit with his daughter; when I arrived, his girlfriend, who was not participating in reunification efforts, apologized and then explained that he would not be able to speak to me while the father who had agreed to be interviewed stood silent. The interviews followed a pretested interview schedule consisting of semistructured open-ended questions. Questions covered various aspects of the parents' lives before and after CPS intervention, often even before they were parents. Topics included their childhood, reproductive choices, partners, substance use, criminal histories, court processes, and experience with and opinions of CPS. However, by virtue of having open-ended questions, parents usually led the interview by choosing the topics and telling the stories they felt were most pertinent to my attempts to understand the experience of living under the watchful eye of CPS and the dynamics that led them there.

THE PARENTS

This book is based largely on the experiences of sixty-two parents, involved in forty-seven cases, whose children were removed by CPS. Of these sixty-two parents, all of whom are biologically related to the children in question, thirty-nine are mothers and twenty-three are fathers. This count does not include other adults who played integral roles in cases, such as stepparents, domestic partners, foster parents, or grandparents, though they are discussed throughout the book. It also does not necessarily include the other biological parent in a case, since I might have had little or no contact with one parent, while having extensive contact with another. Although I saw hundreds of cases in court and fifty or so more during my fieldwork with social workers, I am drawing most significantly on these sixty-two parents with whom I had multiple contacts at critical moments in the CPS process. With all but seven of these sixty-two parents, I did two or more of the following:

- Was present at the initial investigation with an emergency response worker
- Followed the case with a family reunification social worker
- Observed a meeting between parent and attorney
- Observed the initial detention hearing in court
- Observed subsequent court hearings
- Conducted, tape-recorded, and transcribed an in-depth interview with the parent
- Discussed the case, case history, or case progress with a social worker
- Discussed the case history or progress with an attorney
- Reviewed limited or redacted case materials or reports

I have included seven parents—five mothers and two fathers—with whom I had one prolonged contact: a long recorded interview, in-depth initial investigation, sometimes resulting in removal of their children, or lengthy court proceeding or trial that yielded detailed information about a case's history or progress.[2]

Parents ranged in age from seventeen to fifty years, with most parents' ages evenly distributed between eighteen and forty-one years. Of the thirty-nine mothers, twenty-one are white, eleven are African American, four are Asian, two are Native American (both having some white heritage), and one is Latina. Of the twenty-three fathers, eleven are white, seven are African American, three are Chicano or Latino, one is Asian, and one is both Latino and African American. Understanding the racial landscape of parents in the CPS system is difficult since administrative data are collected about the race of children, not parents. It is also incorrect to assume that the children are the same race or ethnicity as their parents. Illustrating this, about half of the twenty-one white mothers in this study have children who were fathered by men of color; thus their children would likely be counted as children of color in administrative data.

The parents whose stories constitute the bulk of this book became part of this work in some ways by happenstance: their case was in an early stage, allowing me to follow it over time; their proceedings were ongoing with additional hearings scheduled; they were willing to talk with me; they were assigned an attorney who felt comfortable referring them to me; I happened to be present when a social worker placed their children in protective custody; their cases came to court after I saw their children removed, making it possible for me to observe various stages in the process with the same family; or I happened by chance to be in court on multiple occasions when their case was heard. After leaving the field in May 2000, I combed through my field notes to identify those parents with whom I had had multiple points of contact and identified them for coding and analysis. The cases I saw only once were also coded, and were used to identify patterns and trends that my primary cases illustrate.

My goal was to include as many parents as was feasible. Thus there was little effort to purposively "sample." Both because of this recruitment strategy and the total dearth of information about the parents who enter CPS, I have no real way to know how representative the parents I studied are of the larger CPS population. Yet I do know that because I gained access to parents who attended court proceedings or were in some way engaged with efforts to reunify with their children, I can say little about the parents who never formally attempt to regain custody of their children. I did make a few attempts to access this group through community-based drug treatment programs or other nonprofit agencies, but found it difficult to identify them. It is difficult to study parents who no longer have children, as they appear on the outside to be the same as those who have never had children. These parents' absence in this book is a source of frustration for me, since their perspective would reveal information essential to understanding the policing of families and parental strategies within it. But many of the issues that made these parents unwilling or unable to regain custody of their children—drug addiction, homelessness, or mental illness—also make them invisible. And their invisibility—including basics like their lack of a state-known address—makes them difficult to access.

I was unable to financially compensate the parents who participated; however, whenever possible, I bought them coffee or meals or brought cookies or snacks to their homes. Despite these limited forms of compensation, I believe that in general the parents who were interviewed gained something from the process. In interviews, parents were able to organize a narrative of their experience and gained an interested audience, not commonly found in the CPS process, where their own advocates may have only minutes to spend with them. When asked, I offered my insights on successful cases that I had observed, which I hoped they could use to make strategic decisions in their own cases. On occasion, I read and interpreted court reports for parents whose reading comprehension skills were such that they were not able to make sense of the documents themselves. Once, a parents' attorney told me that he and his colleague joked that I was their best lawyer, explaining that often after talking to me, their clients had a better understanding of the system. In these ways, I provided a service that no one else in the system had the time to provide. Often parents expressed appreciation and appeared happy to see me in court at the next hearing, sometimes even asking in advance if I would be there. Indisputably, I took more from the parents and professionals in the CPS system than I was able to return. In no way do I mean to imply otherwise. Nonetheless, I believe that my presence often positively affected parents and that I sometimes became a temporary advocate, or at the very least, a momentary cheerleader. Although I usually wanted to see the parents succeed, I also try in the narratives of the parents to provide a nuanced view of them, with full acknowledgement of the things that have placed them under state scrutiny.

I had exceptional access to the dependency court and larger child welfare system in this one county. For example, on at least three occasions, I gained knowledge from one system player in one part of the process that was valuable to another player, but that I could not disclose. In one case, a social worker told me he was planning to recommend that the court terminate services to the parent, usually the last procedural stop before the legal termination of parental rights. I was following that case in court and knew that the attorney would need to modify his strategy in light of that forthcoming recommendation, but I could not disclose any information to the attorney before the social worker's report was formally issued. Similarly, when I met with parents, I could not tell them what their social workers were planning to do in their cases or tell them which aspects of their ongoing behavior or lifestyle were an issue for the social worker. In a complicated case that went on for about two years, I knew the case from more sides than did anyone else. With Tom, I had visited the youngest two children's foster home, attended court-ordered supervised visits between these foster parents and the half-sibling of their charges who was placed elsewhere, and had been to the residential drug treatment program where the biological mother was living. I attended court hearings, discussed the case with social workers and attorneys, and talked to the foster parents and their attorneys outside of hearings. By the end of that case, many of the seven parties' attorneys (representing one biological mother, two biological fathers, two sets of foster parents, the county, and the children) had moved on or been transferred to other cases; only the mother's attorney had been on the case as long as I.

I attended court three to five days a week for nine of thirteen months. The four months I was not in court are the months immediately before and after the birth of my son. During those months, I was in touch with several parents' attorneys and received updates on cases I was following. For three years after completing my fieldwork, I would still talk to parents' attorneys once a month or so to ask about the progress and outcome of cases still pending. Although I no longer follow cases so closely, parents' attorneys occasionally call or e-mail when a case I followed is revisited or when a parent I know reenters the system and is again part of their clientele.

PREGNANT PAUSES IN FIELDWORK

I did a little more than half of my data collection while I was pregnant. I started fieldwork with social workers at the beginning of my second trimester, adding my courtroom observations a month or two later. I continued in court until my eighth month of pregnancy, and then returned about two and a half months after my son was born and continued my fieldwork for another five months. Although I have reflected on the implications of this in greater detail elsewhere, I feel it is also important to account for how the experience affected my data collection and analysis here.[3] When I began my fieldwork with social workers, I tried to hide my pregnancy under baggy clothing. In doing so, I imagined myself to be less marked or less visible to those I was observing.[4] Midway through, I was no longer able to conceal my pregnancy and thus my pregnancy became part of the discussions I had with those I studied. Many social scientists have examined how embodiment impacts research and how fieldwork as an embodied experience is also interactive. As Carol Warren and Jennifer Hackney explain, "We peer through our own flesh to see the other, and we present our own flesh to the other while we are engaged in the act of observation—and this embodiment has consequences for our research."[5] It was perhaps the experience of being observed and interpreted as a pregnant woman that I most feared. I was afraid my pregnancy would influence my access to information, that it was in some way cruel to be pregnant as I attended the removal of other people's children, or that others, not just social workers or attorneys, but the parents themselves, would judge my pregnancy and behavior while pregnant (like CPS parents endure) and that this would limit my ability to collect data. What I could not have predicted was the myriad ways that my own pregnancy was an important source of data, both in terms of more viscerally understanding the experience the public gaze pregnancy and children elicit and in terms of the unique information being pregnant yielded.

Pregnant bodies are public. People feel comfortable touching a pregnant woman, commenting on her size, evaluating her behaviors, and dispensing advice or predictions.[6] I intensely hated that aspect of pregnancy, the invasive nature of how others projected meaning onto me and felt free to expound on the correct way to be pregnant, endure childbirth, or raise children. Although irritating from the perspective of a pregnant woman, such behavior also involves a high level of disclosure, for which I was grateful as a fieldworker. As people commented on reproduction, they were also revealing a great deal about the ideologies and expectations employed.

I was surprised to find that among the professionals in CPS, there was a sense of enthusiasm for my pregnancy. Being pregnant allowed me entrance into conversations in court (a realm comprised mostly of people who had children or were expecting), helped bailiffs and other courtroom gatekeepers remember me from week to week, and provided some level of credibility with parents who largely distrust childless social workers and attorneys, who they view as unable to fully understand their experiences. Attorneys told me about their own pregnancies or children, asked to see pictures after my son was born, or told me about their nieces and nephews with great affection. Yet I was aware of how their interest in my pregnancy lay in stark contrast to the reproduction of parents in CPS.

In observing this difference, I came to understand how CPS professionals defined a culture of normative reproduction among "people like us," while defining the nonnormative reproduction of clients of the CPS system. This ethos can be seen in current welfare policy that aims to more aggressively modify poor people's behavior, with reproduction being central among "the pathologies to be curtailed by new regulations."[7] Targeting poor women's reproduction directly, welfare reform requires poor women to work instead of caring for their babies and grants states the right to deny aid to children whose mothers were receiving assistance at the time of their births, a policy known as a family cap. These twin provisions articulate a definition of normative reproduction that reflects a belief that good parents exercise individual restraint, financial independence (best achieved through heterosexual marriage), and that childbearing is a reward for hard work.

As mentioned, parents in the CPS system are almost all poor, with a significant portion receiving public assistance. They are also disproportionately from ethnic minority backgrounds. Consistent with the rhetoric of welfare reform, the pregnancies of CPS clients are met with a sense of dread and disapproval. Like the logic of the family cap, CPS officials are frustrated when the parents they perceive as failing to adequately care for their existing children bear more children that they imagine they will also likely neglect or abuse. County policy, informed by the 1997 federal law, requires that all babies born to parents who have had open CPS cases or who have failed to reunify with other children be assessed; an assessment that almost always results in their removal from their parents at birth. As a result, child welfare system insiders see these new babies as an inevitable burden to the state, which translates into increasing caseloads for courts and social workers. In contrast, my status as a professional middle-class white woman exempted me from suspicion that I would ever add to their caseload.

Researching families while pregnant was not without issues. Although my pregnancy was not the liability I anticipated, I nonetheless chose early on to conduct interviews with parents only during the early stages of my pregnancy, before it could be physically observed, and after the birth of my son. As a result, there were some parents I observed in court but did not interview whose cases would have enhanced my study. I also missed whatever information my pregnancy might have yielded in those interviews. In addition, the physicality of pregnancy created unique challenges in fieldwork. I had to use the restroom more than most participant-observers. Given that I was often riding in cars with social workers, my bathroom breaks required my subjects to accommodate me. I was also prone to nausea. In other field settings, this might not have been an issue. However, the nature of this project required me to enter homes where rotting food, powerless refrigerators, piles of dirty diapers, and unspeakable odors proliferated; on at least one particularly pungent occasion, I had to step outside before the investigation was complete.

Even with these physical limitations, and the ways they necessitated accommodation, pregnancy was not the obstacle I had anticipated. In fact, one of the greatest lessons I learned came in my recognition that most informants I encountered in the course of my fieldwork—both parents and CPS personnel—seemed unconcerned about my pregnancy; while they sometimes expressed interest, they did not perceive my pregnancy to be out of place in the public world. For the majority of the courthouse workforce, who are in their late twenties to early forties in age, pregnancy was a fact in their lives and the lives of their friends and colleagues. For the parents I studied, reproduction was a prerequisite to entering the system. Willow Mason, a Native American mother who was eight months pregnant when her daughter was molested, asked me about my pregnancy while Roxanna investigated her daughter's well-being. She mentioned how grateful she was that the agency had sent women to her home and seemed happy to engage me around our shared pregnant state. On one occasion, I recall feeling self-conscious about being pregnant while visiting a residential drug treatment facility that was largely occupied by parents whose children had been removed by CPS. I imagined that my pregnant body accompanying a social worker assigned to check up on a resident would make the residents feel resentful. As the social worker knocked on the door, a female resident passing by smiled and congratulated me on my pregnancy. It struck me as strange that a woman who I perceived as having so many obstacles in her life would congratulate me, someone I imagined she would interpret as a compatriot of those who had taken much from her. I was both moved and humbled by her gesture and also increasingly aware of the complex webs of social meaning that we share and that divide us.

Being pregnant in the field meant being gendered. Of course, we are always gendered in the field, even when we are not aware of its role in our interactions. Yet I was particularly aware of how my body invoked awareness of my gender, my sexuality, and my marital status. With the aforementioned conversations about my pregnancy came inquiries about other aspects of my family life. In addition to marking my gender and (pending) familial status, pregnancy also altered perceptions of the kind of woman I was. Until then, I was accustomed to being seen as a short brunette researcher whose student status made others willing to explain things. In describing her experience of doing fieldwork on fetal surgery, Monica Casper reflected on how being "a young graduate student, a persona greatly enhanced by being both female and blonde" facilitated rapport with some informants. She noted that some informants "responded to my gender in interesting ways, often volunteering information in a sort of flirtatious, boastful fashion which I was undoubtedly supposed to receive in the appropriate doe-eyed manner."[8] My experiences of conducting fieldwork before being pregnant more closely resembled Casper's. In past research projects where I interviewed men, I found that my interest in men's lives and my willingness to hang on their every word could be mistaken for romantic attraction. However, by being pregnant, I was no longer sexualized in a way that invited flirtation. In this project, my pregnancy seemingly stripped away my sexuality, erecting a barrier between my male informants (who during my pregnancy were attorneys, judges, social workers, and fathers) and me that alleviated much of the awkwardness I had experienced in other projects. However, I likely lost out on some of the information that is offered during flirtation in the field.

When asked whether she could have done the study that led to *Families We Choose* had she not been lesbian, Kath Weston replied, "No doubt, but then again, it wouldn't have been the same study."[9] Similarly I have no doubt that I could have conducted a study on this topic had I not been pregnant, but I believe it would have likely yielded some different data. Indeed, performing research while pregnant not only provided me access and credibility, but it provided a level of insight I had not anticipated and did not recognize until I was out of the field. When I began studying child abuse and the systems charged with responding to it, I was childless. By the time I completed this book, I was the mother of two children. In the course of that transformation in my own family and identity, I was sometimes cautioned that having children would make my research topic too difficult to study. Having children, I was warned, would change me. These forecasters were half right. Indeed, my experience of pregnancy and subsequent parenthood changed my thinking about many of the issues endemic to the CPS system, but not in the way those who had advised me had predicted. Rather than feeling outrage and disgust with bad parents, I instead can more easily imagine how it would feel as a parent to have the state's gaze upon me. Even now, several years after leaving the field, I will be picking up toys or washing dishes and will suddenly imagine scenes where CPS comes into my house and investigates me. I look around my kitchen where breakfast dishes may only get cleared in time for dinner or open a sparsely stocked refrigerator only to realize we are out of state-defined essentials like bread, milk, and eggs. I wonder if a new, overly cautious social worker would believe me when I say that I am planning on going to the store tonight, or that the bruises my children so often sport are only the marks of a happy active childhood. I know that our failure to install childproof locks under the sink would be judged poorly. How does a routine diaper rash or my daughter's long, often-matted hair look through the eyes of a new social worker, eager to do his or her best under stressful circumstances? Would I remember to demonstrate appropriate deference while someone goes through my drawers and cupboards? I have learned what the public gaze feels like from my own experience with pregnancy and have seen it deployed as I walked into houses with the authority of the state, silently thinking to myself that they were only a little worse than my own. These insights played an indelible role in this project.

BIBLIOGRAPHY

Abramovitz, Mimi. Regulating the Lives of Women: Social Welfare Policy from Colonial Times to the Present. Boston: South End Press, 1988.

Adoption and Safe Families Act of 1997, P.L. 105-89 (November 19, 1997).

Albert, Vicky. "Identifying Substance Abusing Delivering Women: Consequences for Child Maltreatment Reports." Child Abuse & Neglect 24, no. 2 (2000): 173–83.

Albert, Vicky N., and Richard P. Barth. "Predicting Growth in Child Abuse and Neglect Reports in Urban, Suburban and Rural Counties." Social Service Review 71, no. 1 (1996): 58–82.

Alcoholics Anonymous: The Story of How Many Thousands of Men and Women Have Recovered from Alcoholism, 2nd ed. New York: Alcoholics Anonymous World Services, 1955.

Alliance for Non-Custodial Parents. "Joint Custody Laws in the U.S. Alliance for Non-Custodial Parents, 2003." Available at http://www.ancpr.org/joint_custody_laws_in_the_united.htm.

Alter, C. F. "Decision-Making Factors in Cases of Child Neglect." Child Welfare 64, no. 2 (1985): 99–111.

American Civil Liberties Union. "Coercive and Punitive Governmental Responses to Women's Conduct During Pregnancy." New York: American Civil Liberties Union, 1997.

American Journalism Review. "Covering Child Abuse (Report on the Conference on 'Rethinking the Blame Game: New Approaches to Covering Child Abuse')." American Journalism Review, September 1997: S1–13.

Anderson, Elijah. Code of the Street: Decency, Violence and the Moral Life of the Inner City. New York: W.W. Norton & Co., 2000.

———. Streetwise: Race, Class, and Change in an Urban Community. Chicago: University of Chicago Press, 1990.

Appell, Annette R. "Increasing Options to Improve Permanency: Considerations in Drafting an Adoption with Contact Statute." Children's Legal Rights Journal 18, no. 4 (1998): 24–51.

———. "On Fixing 'Bad' Mothers and Saving Their Children." In "Bad" Mothers, edited by Molly Ladd-Taylor and Lauri Umansky. New York: New York University Press, 1998.

Arad, Bilha Davidson. "Parental Features and Quality of Life in the Decision to Remove Children at Risk from Home." Child Abuse & Neglect, 25, no. 1 (2001): 47–64.

————. "Predicted Changes in Children's Quality of Life in Decisions Regarding the Removal of Children at Risk from Their Homes." Children and Youth Services Review 23, no. 2 (2001): 127–43.

Ards, Sheila D., Samuel L. Myers, Jr., Allan Malkis, Erin Sugrue, and Li Zhou. "Racial Disproportionality in Reported and Substantiated Child Abuse and Neglect: An Examination of Systemic Bias." Children and Youth Services Review 25, no. 5/6 (2003): 375–92.

Arredondo, David E., and Leonard P. Edwards. "Attachment, Bonding, and Reciprocal Connectedness: Limitations of Attachment Theory in the Juvenile and Family Court." Journal of the Center for Families, Children and the Courts 2, no. 1 (2000): 109–27.

Ashe, Marie, and Naomi Cahn. "Child Abuse: A Problem for Feminist Theory." In The Public Nature of Private Violence: The Discovery of Domestic Abuse, edited by Martha A Fineman and Roxanne Mykitiuk. New York: Routledge, 1994.

Atkinson, Leslie, and Stephen Butler. "Court-Ordered Assessment: Impact of Maternal Non-Compliance in Child Maltreatment Cases." Child Abuse & Neglect 20, no. 3 (1996): 185–90.

Azar, Sandra T., and Corina L. Benjet. "A Cognitive Perspective on Ethnicity, Race, and Termination of Parental Rights." Law and Human Behavior 18, no. 3 (1994): 249–68.

Azar, Sandra T., Corina L. Benjet, Geri S. Fuhrmann, and Linda Cavallero. "Child Maltreatment and Termination of Parental Rights: Can Behavioral Research Help Solomon?" Behavior Therapy 26, no. 4 (1995): 599–623.

Badgett, M. V. Lee, and Nancy Folbre. "Assigning Care: Gender Norms and Economic Outcomes." International Labour Review 138, no. 3 (1999): 311–26.

Baker, Ken. "I Want My Kids Back: Fighting Child-Sex Charges and Alcoholism, Comedian Paula Poundstone Is Out to Clear Her Name and Reunite Her Family." US Weekly, July 23 (2001): 54–55.

Barbell, Kathy, and Madelyn Freundlich. Foster Care Today (Casey Family Programs National Center for Resource Family Support, 2001); available at http://www.casey.org/cnc/policy_issues/foster_care_today.htm#IndianChildWelfare.

Barnett, Ola W., Tomas E. Martinez, and Mae Keyson. "The Relationship Between Violence, Social Support, and Self-Blame in Battered Women." Journal of Interpersonal Violence 11, no. 2 (1996): 221–33.

Barth, R. P. "After Safety, What Is the Goal of Child Welfare Services: Permanency, Family Continuity or Social Benefit?" International Journal of Social Welfare 8, no. 4 (1999): 244–52.

Barth, R. P., and M. Berry. Adoption and Disruption: Rates, Risks and Resources. New York: Aldine de Gruyter, 1988.

Barth, Richard P., Mark E. Courtney, and Vicky N. Albert. From Child Abuse to Permanency Planning: Child Welfare Services Pathways and Placements. New York: Aldine de Gruyter, 1994.

Bartholet, Elizabeth. Nobody's Children: Abuse Neglect, Foster Drift, and the Adoption Alternative. Boston: Beacon Press, 1999.

Bartlett, Katherine T. Gender and the Law: Theory, Doctrine, Commentary. Boston: Little, Brown & Co., 1993.

Bates, Sanford. "Should a Father Have a Mother's Pension? (Originally Published in July 1952 in this Journal)," Public Welfare 51, no. 1 (1993): 12.

Beaucar, Kelley O. "State Bill Would Protect Caseworkers: Two Workers Would Go on Potentially Dangerous Home Visits." NASW News, February 2000.

Begus, Sarah, and Pamela Armstrong. "Daddy's Right: Incestuous Assault." In Families, Politics, and Public Policy, edited by Irene Diamond. New York: Longman, 1983.

Bernard, Jessie. "The Good Provider Role: Its Rise and Fall." In Diversity and Change in Families: Patterns, Prospects, and Policies, edited by Mark Robert Rank and Edward Kain. Englewood Cliffs, NJ: Prentice Hall, 1981.

Berrick, Jill Duerr. "When Children Cannot Remain Home: Foster Family Care and Kinship Care." Protecting Children from Abuse and Neglect 8, no. 1 (1998): 72–87.

Berrick, Jill Duerr, and Ruth Lawrence-Karski. "Emerging Issues in Child Welfare." Public Welfare 53, no. 4 (1995): 4–12.

Berrick, Jill Duerr, Barbara Needell, Richard P. Barth, and Melissa Jonson-Reid. The Tender Years: Toward Developmentally-Sensitive Child Welfare Services for Very Young Children. Oxford: Oxford University Press, 1998.

Berrick, Jill Duerr, Barbara Needell, and Meredith Minkler. "The Policy Implications of Welfare Reform for Older Caregivers, Kinship Care, and Family Configuration." Children and Youth Services Review 21, no. 9/10 (1999): 843–64.

Besharov, Douglas, and Karen Baehler. "Introduction." In When Drug Addicts Have Children: Reorienting Child Welfare's Response, edited by Douglas J. Besharov. Washington, DC: Child Welfare League of America, 1994.

Best, Joel. Threatened Children: Rhetoric and Concern About Child-Victims. Chicago: Chicago University Press, 1990.

Blankenhorn, David. Fatherless America: Confronting Our Most Urgent Social Problem. New York: Harper Collins, 1996.

Blum, Linda. At the Breast: Ideologies of Breastfeeding and Motherhood in the Contemporary United States. Boston: Beacon Press, 1999.

Bonavoglia, Angela. "The Ordeal of Pamela Rae Stewart." Ms Magazine, July/August 1987: 92–95, 196–204.

Boney-McCoy, Sue, and David Finkelhor. "Psychosocial Sequelae of Violent Victimization in a National Youth Sample." Journal of Consulting and Clinical Psychology 63, no. 5 (1995): 725–36.

Boots, Shelley Waters, and Rob Green. "Family Care or Foster Care? How State Policies Affect Kinship Caregivers." Washington, DC: Urban Institute, 2001.

Bordo, Susan. Unbearable Weight. Berkeley: University of California Press, 1993.

Boris, Eileen, and Peter Bardaglio. "The Transformation of Patriarchy: The Historic Role of the State." In Families, Politics, and Public Policy: A Feminist Dialogue on Women and the State, edited by Irene Diamond. New York: Longman, 1983.

Bourgois, Philippe. In Search of Respect: Selling Crack in El Barrio, edited by Mark Granovetter. Cambridge: Cambridge University Press, 1995.

Brace, Charles Loring. "Child Saving: The Children's Aid Society of New York. Its History, Plan, and Results." In History of Child Saving in the United States; National Conference of Charities and Corrections; Report of the Committee on the History of Child-Saving Work to the Twentieth Conference, Chicago, June 1893, ed. National Conference on Social Welfare, Committee on the History of Child-Saving Work. Montclair, NJ: Patterson Smith, 1971.

Brooks, Devon, Richard P. Barth, Alice Bussiere, and Glendora Patterson. "Adoption and Race: Implementing the Multiethnic Placement Act and the Interethnic Adoption Provisions." Social Work 44, no. 2 (1999): 167–78.

Brooks, Devon, and Sheryl Goldberg. "Gay and Lesbian Adoptive and Foster Care Placements: Can They Meet the Needs of Waiting Children?" Social Work 46, no. 2 (2001): 147–57.

Brownfield, Paul. "A Comic in Trouble, an Image Rewritten: No Matter How the Paula Poundstone Case Turns out, One Thing Is for Sure: Thanks to a Scandal-Hungry Media, the Comedian's Life, and Career, Will Never Be the Same," Los Angeles Times, July 10, 2001.

Bureau of Justice Statistics. "Criminal Offender Statistics." Washington, DC: Department of Justice, 2001.

——. "Sourcebook 2000." Washington, DC: Department of Justice, 2000.

Bureau of Labor Statistics, Occupational Outlook Handbook. Washington, DC: U.S. Department of Labor, 2002.

California Department of Alcohol and Drug Programs. "Substance-Exposed Infants (Senate Bill 2669) Fact Sheet." Sacramento: California Department of Alcohol and Drug Programs, 2001.

California Welfare and Institutions Code section 361.5, 2001.

Canedy, Dana. "Case of Lost Miami Girl Puts Focus on an Agency." New York Times, May 3, 2002: A19.

Cash, Scottye J. "Risk Assessment in Child Welfare: The Art and Science." Children and Youth Services Review 23, no. 11 (2001): 811–30.

Casper, Monica. "Feminist Politics and Fetal Surgery: Adventures of a Research Cowgirl on the Reproductive Frontier." Feminist Studies 23, no. 2 (1997): 232–63.

Center for Reproductive Law and Policy. "Punishing Women for Their Behavior During Pregnancy." New York: Center for Reproductive Law and Policy, 2000.

——. "U.S. Supreme Court Affirms Right to Confidential Medical Care." CRLP Press, March 21 (2001): 1.

Center for Social Services Research. "California Children's Services Archives: Child Abuse Referral Highlights from CWS/CMS." Berkeley: University of California at Berkeley, 2003.

——. "California Children's Services Archives: Child Welfare Foster Care Exits Over Time from CWS/CMS." Berkeley: University of California at Berkeley, 2003.

——. "California Children's Services Archives: Foster Care Placement Stability from CWS/CMS." Berkeley: University of California at Berkeley, 2003.

Chasnoff, Ira J. "Drugs, Alcohol, Pregnancy, and the Neonate: Pay Now or Pay Later." JAMA, Journal of the American Medical Association 266, no. 11 (1991): 1567–68.

Chasnoff, Ira J., Dan R. Griffith, Scott MacGregor, Kathryn Dirkes, and Kayreen A. Burns. "Temporal Patterns of Cocaine Use in Pregnancy: Perinatal Outcome." JAMA, Journal of the American Medical Association 261, no. 12 (1989): 1741–45.

Chasnoff, Ira J., Harvey J. Landress, and Mark E. Barrett. "The Prevalence of Illicit-Drug or Alcohol Use During Pregnancy and Discrepancies in Mandatory Reporting in Pinellas County, Florida." New England Journal of Medicine 322, no. 17 (1990): 1202–6.

Cheal, David. Family and the State of Theory. Toronto: University of Toronto Press, 1991.

Cherlin, Andrew J., and Frank F. Furstenberg, Jr. "Stepfamilies in the United States: A Reconsideration." Annual Review of Sociology 20 (1991): 359–81.

Children's Bureau. "Adoption Data." Washington, DC: Washington, DC: Administration for Children and Families, 2003.

Chiriboga, C. A. "Fetal Alcohol and Drug Effects." Neurologist 9, no. 6 (2003): 267–79.

Christoffersen, Mogens Nygaard, and Keith Soothill. "The Long-Term Consequences of Parental Alcohol Abuse: A Cohort Study of Children in Denmark." Journal of Substance Abuse Treatment 25, no. 2 (2003): 107–16.

Clinton, Bill. "The President's Radio Address." Weekly Compilation of Presidential Documents (1996): 2512–15.

——. "Proclamation 7048—National Adoption Month, 1997." Weekly Compilation of Presidential Documents (1997): 1726.

Cohen-Schlanger, Miriam, Ann Fitzpatrick, J. David Hulchanski, and Dennis Raphael. "Housing as a Factor in Admissions of Children to Temporary Care: A Survey." Child Welfare 74, no. 3 (1995): 547–63.

Collier, Ann Futterman, Faith H. McClure, Jay Collier, Caleb Otto, and Anthony Polloi. "Culture-Specific Views of Child Maltreatment and Parenting Styles in a Pacific-Island Community." Child Abuse & Neglect 23, no. 3 (1999): 229–44.

Collins, Patricia Hill. Black Feminist Thought: Knowledge, Consciousness, and the Politics of Empowerment. New York: Routledge, 1991.

Coltrane, Scott. "Changing Patterns of Family Work: Chicano Men and Housework." In Shifting the Center, edited by Susan Ferguson. Mountain View, CA: Mayfield Publishing, 1998.

Comanor, William S., and Llad Phillips. The Impact of Income and Family Structure on Delinquency: Working Paper. University of California-Santa Barbara, 1998; available at http://www.econ.ucsb.edu.

Connell, R. W. Masculinities. Berkeley: University of California Press, 1995.

Connolly, Deborah R. Homeless Mothers: Face to Face with Women and Poverty. Minneapolis: University of Minnesota Press, 2000.

Conrad, Peter. "The Meaning of Medications: Another Look at Compliance." Social Science in Medicine 20, no. 1 (1985): 29–37.

———. "Types of Medical Social Control." Sociology of Health and Illness 1, no. 1 (1979): 1–11.

Cook, Jeanne F. "A History of Placing-Out: The Orphan Trains." Child Welfare 74, no. 1 (1995): 181–98.

Coontz, Stephanie. The Way We Never Were: American Families and the Nostalgia Trap. New York: Harper Collins, 1992.

Corsaro, William A. The Sociology of Childhood. Thousand Oaks, CA: Pine Forge Press, 1997.

Costin, Lela B. "Cruelty to Children: A Dormant Issue and Its Rediscovery, 1920–1960." Social Service Review 66, no. 2 (1992): 177–99.

Courtney, Mark, and Yin-Ling Wong. "Comparing the Timing of Exits from Substitute Care." Children and Youth Services Review 18, no. 4–5 (1996): 307–34.

Courtney, Mark E., Irving Piliavin, Andrew Grogan-Kaylor, and Ande Nesmith. "Foster Youth Transitions to Adulthood: A Longitudinal View of Youth Leaving Care." Child Welfare 80, no. 6 (2001): 685–717.

Cox, Major W. "Make Adoption Policies Colorblind." Montgomery Advertiser, January 13, 1994.

Congressional Quarterly Researcher. "Foster Care Reform." Washington, DC: Congressional Quarterly, 1998.

Crume, T., C. DiGuiseppi, T. Byers, A. Sirotnak, and C. Garrett. "Underascertainment of Child Maltreatment Fatalities by Death Certificates, 1990–1998." Pediatrics 102, no. 2 (2002): e18.

Curran, Laura, and Laura S. Abrams. "Making Men into Dads: Fatherhood, the State, and Welfare Reform." Gender & Society 14, no. 5 (2000): 662–78.

Dalton, Susan. "Nonbiological Mothers and the Legal Boundaries of Motherhood." In Ideologies and Technologies of Motherhood: Race, Class, Sexuality, Nationality, edited by Helena Ragone and France Winddance Twine. New York: Routledge, 2000.

Davis, Angela. "Race and Criminalization: Black Americans and the Punishment Industry." In The House That Race Built, edited by Waheema Lubiano. New York: Vintage Books, 1998.

———. Women, Race and Class. New York: Vintage Books, 1983.

deBeauvoir, Simone. The Second Sex. New York: Vintage Books, 1974.

DHHS. "Adoption Excellence Award Recommendations for the Year 2001." Washington, DC: Administration for Children and Families, 2001.

———. "Adoptions of Children with Public Child Welfare Agency Involvement by State." Washington, DC: Children's Bureau, 2001.

————. "The AFCARS Report." Washington, DC: Department of Health and Human Services, 2001.

————. "AFCARS Report: Preliminary FY 2001 Estimates as of March 2003." Washington, DC: Department of Health and Human Services, 2003.

————. "Better Outcomes for Children—The Child and Family Services Reviews." Washington, DC: Department of Health and Human Services, 2000.

————. "Blending Perspectives and Building Common Ground: A Report to Congress on Substance Abuse and Child Protection." Washington, DC: Department of Health and Human Services, 1999.

————. "Child Maltreatment 2001." Washington, DC: Department of Health and Human Services, 2003.

————. "Child Maltreatment 2002." Washington, DC: Department of Health and Human Services, 2004.

————. "Child Welfare Outcomes 1999: Annual Report." Washington, DC: Department of Health and Human Services, 2001.

————. "Child Welfare Outcomes 2001: Annual Report to Congress. Safety, Permanency, Well-Being." Washington DC: Department of Health and Human Services, 2004.

————. "HHS Awards Adoption Bonuses." HHS News, September 10 (2001).

————. "Nurturing Fatherhood: Improving Data and Research on Male Fertility, Family Formation, and Fatherhood." Washington, DC: Federal Interagency Forum on Child and Family Statistics, 1998.

————. "Strengthening Healthy Marriages: A Compendium of Approaches: Draft." Washington, DC: Department of Health and Human Services, 2002.

Dohan, Daniel. The Price of Poverty: Money, Work, and Culture in the Mexican American Barrio. Berkeley: University of California Press, 2003.

Donzelot, Jacques. The Policing of Families. New York: Pantheon, 1979.

Dorsey, Tina, Marianne Zawitz, and Priscilla Middleton. "Drugs and Crime Facts." Washington, DC: Office of Justice Programs, 2001.

Dunn, Jennifer L. "Innocence Lost: Accomplishing Victimization in Intimate Stalking Cases." Symbolic Interaction 24, no. 3 (2001): 285–313.

Edin, Kathryn. "Few Good Men." American Prospect, January 3 (2000): 26–27.

Edin, Kathryn, and Laura Lein. Making Ends Meet: How Single Mothers Survive Welfare and Low-Wage Work. New York: Russell Sage Foundation, 1997.

Ehrenreich, Barbara. Nickel and Dimed: On (Not) Getting by in America. New York: Henry Holt & Co., 2002.

Eistenstein, Zillah. The Female Body and the Law. Berkeley: University of California Press, 1988.

Elshtain, Jean Bethke. "Antigone's Daughters: Reflections on Female Identity and the State." In Families, Politics, and Public Policy, edited by Irene Diamond. New York: Longman, 1983.

Ericsson, Kjersti. "Gender, Delinquency and Child Welfare." Theoretical Criminology 2, no. 4 (1998): 445–59.

Evan B. Donaldson Adoption Institute. "Open Records, 2003." Available at http://www.adoptioninstitute.org/policy/intro.html.

Fadiman, Anne. The Spirit Catches You and You Fall Down: A Hmong Child, Her American Doctors, and the Collision of Two Cultures. New York: Farrar, Straus, and Giroux, 1997.

FDA. P94-18, "Childhood Iron Poisoning," press release. Rockville, MD: Food and Drug Administration, 1994.

Feagin, Joe. "Changing Patterns of Racial Discrimination? The Continuing Significance of Race: Anti-Black Discrimination in Public Places." American Sociological Review 56, no. 1 (1991): 101–16.

Field, Tiffany. "Attachment and Separation in Young Children." Annual Review of Psychology 47, no. 1 (1996): 541–61.

Fineman, Martha Albertson. The Neutered Mother, the Sexual Family and Other Twentieth Century Tragedies. New York: Routledge, 1995.

Focus on the Family. "Focus on the Family Defends Parents' Right to Discipline," 2002; available at http://www.family.org/welcome/press/a0021264.cfm.

Fondacaro, Karen M., and John C. Holt. "Psychological Impact of Childhood Sexual Abuse of Male Inmates: The Importance of Perception." Child Abuse & Neglect 23, no. 4 (1999): 361–69.

Foucault, Michel. Discipline and Punish: The Birth of the Prison. New York: Vintage Books, 1995.

———. Power/Knowledge: Selected Interviews and Other Writings, edited by Colin Gordon. New York: Pantheon Books, 1980.

Frame, Laura. "Suitable Homes Revisited: An Historical Look at Child Protection and Welfare Reform." Children and Youth Services Review 21, no. 9–10 (1999): 719–45.

Frankenberg, Ruth. White Women, Race Matters: The Social Construction of Whiteness. Minneapolis: University of Minnesota Press, 1993.

Frasch, Karie, Devon Brooks, Jennifer Reich, and Leslie Wind. "Enhancing Positive Outcomes in Transracial Adoptive Families." Berkeley: University of California at Berkeley, Social Work Education Center, 2004.

Frasch, Karie M., Devon Brooks, and Richard P. Barth. "Openness and Contact in Foster Care Adoptions: An Eight-Year Follow-up." Family Relations 49, no. 4 (2000): 435–47.

Friedan, Betty. The Feminine Mystique. New York: W.W. Norton & Co., 1963.

Gadsen, Vivian L., and Ralph R. Smith. "African American Males and Fatherhood: Issues in Research and Practice." Journal of Negro Education 63, no. 4 (1994): 634–48.

Gambrill, Eileen, and Aron Shlonsky. "Risk Assessment in Context." Children and Youth Services Review 22, no. 11–12 (2000): 813–37.

Gelb, Joyce. "The Politics of Wife Abuse." In Family, Politics, and Public Policy: A Feminist Dialogue on Women and the State, edited by Irene Diamond. New York: Longman, 1983.

Gelles, Richard. The Book of David: How Preserving Families Can Cost Children's Lives. New York: Harper Collins, 1996.

Gelles, Richard, and Claire Pedrick Cornell. Intimate Violence in Families. Thousand Oaks, CA: Sage Publications, 1985.

Gerson, Kathleen. "Dilemmas of Involved Fatherhood." In Reconstructing Gender, edited by Estelle Disch. Mountain View, CA: Mayfield, 1997.

Gilder, George. Wealth and Poverty. New York: Basic Books, 1981.

Giles-Sims, Jean. "Current Knowledge About Child Abuse in Stepfamilies." In Family Violence: Studies from the Social Sciences and Professions, edited by James M. Makepeace. New York: McGraw-Hill, 1998.

Gilliom, John. Overseers of the Poor: Surveillance, Resistance, and the Limits of Privacy. Chicago: University of Chicago Press, 2001.

Glisson, Charles, James W. Bailey, and James A. Post. "Predicting the Time Children Spend in State Custody." Social Service Review 74, no. 2 (2000): 253–280.

Goffman, Erving. Asylums: Essays on the Social Situation of Mental Patients and Other Inmates. Garden City, NY: Anchor Books, 1961.

———. The Presentation of Self in Everyday Life. New York: Anchor/Doubleday, 1959.

Golden, Olivia A. "Testimony on the Final Rule on Federal Monitoring of State Child Welfare Programs by Olivia A. Golden, Assistant Secretary for Children and Families, U.S. Department of Health and Human Services." Washington, DC: Department of Health and Human Services, 2000.

Goldman, Juliette D. G., and Usha K. Padayachi. "Some Methodological Problems in Estimating Incidence and Prevalence in Child Sexual Abuse Research." Journal of Sex Research 37, no. 4 (2000): 305–14.

Goldstein, Joseph, Anna Freud, and Albert Solnit. Before the Best Interests of the Child. New York: Free Press, 1979.

———. Beyond the Best Interests of the Child. New York: Free Press, 1973.

———. In the Best Interests of the Child: Professional Boundaries. New York: Free Press, 1986.

Gomez, Laura E. Misconceiving Mothers: Legislators, Prosecutors, and the Politics of Prenatal Drug Exposure. Philadelphia: Temple University Press, 1997.

Gordon, Linda. "Family Violence, Feminism, and Social Control." In Women, the State, and Welfare, edited by Linda Gordon. Madison: University of Wisconsin Press, 1990.

———. Heroes of Their Own Lives. New York: Penguin Books, 1988.

———. Pitied, but Not Entitled. Cambridge, MA: Harvard University Press, 1994.

Gough, David. "Defining the Problem." Child Abuse & Neglect 20, no. 11 (1996): 993–1002.

Hagan, John. "The Everyday and the Not So Exceptional in the Social Organization of Criminal Justice Practices." In Everyday Practices and Trouble Cases, edited by Austin Sarat, Marianne Constable, David Engel, Valerie Hans, and Susan Lawrence. Chicago: Northwestern University Press, 1998.

Hancock, LynNell. Hands to Work: The Stories of Three Families Racing the Welfare Clock. New York: William Morrow-Harper Collins, 2002.

Hand, Jennifer Ayres. "Note: Preventing Undue Terminations: A Critical Evaluation of the Length-of-Time-out-of-Custody Ground for Termination of Parental Rights." New York University Law Review 71, no. 5 (1996): 1251–300.

Haney, Lynne. "Feminist State Theory: Applications to Jurisprudence, Criminology, and the Welfare State." Annual Review of Sociology (2000): 641–66.

Hanigsberg, Julia E., and Sara Ruddick, eds. Mother Troubles. Boston: Beacon Press, 1999.

Haugland, Bente Storm Mowat. "Paternal Alcohol Abuse: Relationship Between Child Adjustment, Parental Characteristics, and Family Functioning." Child Psychiatry & Human Development 34, no. 2 (2003): 127–47.

Hays, Sharon. Cultural Contradictions of Motherhood. New Haven, CT: Yale University Press, 1998.

———. Flat Broke with Children. New York: Oxford University Press, 2003.

Hoffnung, Michele. "Motherhood: Contemporary Conflict for Women." In Women: A Feminist Perspective, edited by Jo Freeman. Mountain View, CA: Mayfield, 1989.

Hohman, Melinda M., and Rick L. Butt. "How Soon Is Too Soon? Addiction Recovery and Family Reunification." Child Welfare 80, no. 1 (2001): 53–67.

Holland, Sally, and Jonathan Scourfield. "Managing Marginalised Masculinities: Men and Probation." Journal of Gender Studies 9, no. 2 (2000): 199–211.

Hollinger, Joan Heifetz. "A Guide to the Multiethnic Placement Act of 1994, as Amended by the Interethnic Adoption Provisions of 1996." Washington, DC: American Bar Association Center on Children and the Law, National Resource Center on Legal and Court Issues, 1998.

———. Response to CWLA "Analysis" of Uniform Adoption Act (Kevin McCarty, 1997); available at www.webcom.com/kmc/adoption/law/uaa/hollinger.html.

Hollingsworth, Leslie Doty. "Symbolic Interactionism, African American Families, and the Transracial Adoption Controversy." Social Work 44, no. 5 (1999): 443–53.

Holm, Soren. "What Is Wrong with Compliance?" Journal of Medical Ethics 1993, no. 19 (1993): 108–10.

Horejsi, Charles, Cindy Garthwait, and Jim Rolando. "A Survey of Threats and Violence Directed Against Child Protection Workers in a Rural State." Child Welfare 73, no. 2 (1994): 173–179.

House Ways and Means Committee, "2000 Green Book. Section 11: Child Protection, Foster Care, and Adoption Assistance." Washington, DC: U.S. Government Printing Office, 2000.

Hubner, John, and Jill Wolfson. Somebody Else's Children: The Courts, the Kids, and the Struggle to Save America's Troubled Families. New York: Crown Publishers, 1996.

HUD. "General Information on Subsidized Housing." Washington, DC: Department of Housing and Urban Development, Multifamily Housing Division, 2001.

———. "HUD's Public Housing Program: Common Questions." Washington, DC: Department of Housing and Urban Development, 2001.

———. "Rental Housing Assistance—The Crisis Continues: The 1997 Report to Congress on Worst Case Housing Needs." Rockville, MD: Department of Housing and Urban Development, Office of Policy Development and Research, 1997.

———. "A Report on Worst Case Housing Needs in 1999: New Opportunity Amid Continuing Challenges." Washington, DC: Department of Housing and Urban Development, Office of Policy Development and Research, 2001.

Hunter, Andrea G., and James Earl Davis. "Hidden Voices of Black Men: the Meaning, Structure, and Complexity of Manhood." Journal of Black Studies 25, no. 1 (1994): 20–40.

Inkelas, Moira, and Neal Halfon. "Recidivism in Child Protective Services." Children and Youth Services Review 19, no. 3 (1997): 139–61.

Jacobs, Mark D. Screwing the System and Making It Work: Juvenile Justice in the No-Fault Society. Chicago: University of Chicago Press, 1990.

Jellinek, Michael S., J. Michael Murphy, Francis Poitrast, Dorothy Quinn, Sandra J. Bishop, and Marilyn Goshko. "Serious Child Mistreatment in Massachusetts: The Course of 206 Children Through the Courts." Child Abuse & Neglect 16, no. 2 (1992) :179–85.

Joffe, Carole. "What Abortion Counselors Want from Their Clients." Social Problems 26, no. 1 (1978): 112–21.

———. "Why the United States Has No Child-Care Policy." In Families, Politics, and Public Policy, edited by Irene Diamond. New York: Longman, 1983.

Johnson, Jennifer. Getting by on the Minimum: The Lives of Working-Class Women. New York: Routledge, 2002.

Johnson, John M., and Kathleen J. Ferraro. "The Victimized Self: The Case of Battered Women." In The Family Experience, edited by Mark Hutter. Boston: Allyn & Bacon, 2000.

Jones, Loring. "The Social and Family Correlates of Successful Reunification of Children in Foster Care." Children and Youth Services Review 20, no. 4 (1998): 305–23.

Jones, Richard Lezin. "Report Says 13 of Child Agency's Cases Died of Abuse or Neglect." New York Times, February 12, 2003, Late Edition – Final, sect. B, p. 5, col. 2.

Jump, Teresa L., and Linda Haas. "Fathers in Transition." In Changing Men: New Directions in Research on Men and Masculinity, edited by Michael Kimmel. Newbury Park, CA: Sage Publications, 1987.

Kaminer, Wendy. I'm Dysfunctional, You're Dysfunctional. Menlo Park: Addison-Wesley, 1992.

Kapp, Stephen A., Thomas P. McDonald, and Kandi L. Diamond. "The Path to Adoption for Children of Color." Child Abuse & Neglect 25, no. 2 (2001): 215–29.

Kelley, Tina, and Leslie Kaufman. "McGreevey Plan Would Help Agencies Protect Children." New York Times, February 3, 2003, Late Edition – Final, sect. B, p. 5, col. 1.

Kennedy, Joseph P. "Introduction of the Adoption Incentives Act of 1995." 141 Congressional Record E1383. U.S. House of Representatives: Congressional Record—Extension of Remarks, 1995.

Kirp, David L. Learning by Heart: Aids and Schoolchildren in America's Communities. New Brunswick, NJ: Rutgers University Press, 1990.

Kline, Marlee. "Complicating the Ideology of Motherhood: Child Welfare Law and First Nation Women." In Mothers in Law: Feminist Theory and the Legal Regulation of Motherhood, edited by Martha Albertson Fineman and Isabel Karpin. New York: Columbia University Press, 1995.

Klingemann, Harald. "'To Every Thing There Is a Season'—Social Time and Clock Time in Addiction Treatment." Social Science and Medicine 51, no. 8 (2000): 1231–40.

Korbin, Jill E., Claudia J. Coulton, Heather Linstrom-Ufuti, and James Spilsbury. "Neighborhood Views on the Definition and Etiology of Child Maltreatment." Child Abuse & Neglect 24, no. 12 (2000): 1509–27.

Krane, Julia, and Linda Davies. "Mothering and Child Protection Practice: Rethinking Risk Assessment." Child & Family Social Work 5, no. 1 (2000): 35–45.

Kurz, Demie. For Richer, for Poorer: Mothers Confront Divorce. New York: Routledge, 1995. ———. "Women, Welfare, and Domestic Violence." In Whose Welfare?, edited by Gwendolyn Mink. Ithaca, NY: Cornell University Press, 1999.

Ladd-Taylor, Molly, and Lauri Umansky, eds. "Bad" Mothers: The Politics of Blame in Twentieth-Century America. New York: New York University Press, 1998.

Ladner, Joyce. Mixed Families: Adopting Across Racial Boundaries. New York: Anchor Press/ Doubleday, 1977.

Lamb, Michael E. "The History of Research on Father Involvement: An Overview." Marriage & Family Review 29, no. 2–3 (2000): 23–43.

Lareau, Annette. "Invisible Inequality: Social Class and Childrearing in Black Families and White Families." American Sociological Review 67, no. 5 (2002): 747–76.

———. Unequal Childhoods: Class, Race, and Family Life. Berkeley: University of California Press, 2003.

Lasch, Christopher. Haven in a Heartless World: The Family Besieged. New York: W.W. Norton & Co., 1995.

League of Women Voters of California. "League of Women Voters of California, "Juvenile Justice in California, Part II: Dependency System. Facts & Issues." Sacramento: League of Women Voters of California, 1998.

Leichtentritt, Ronit D., Bilha Davidson-Arad, and Yochanan Wozner. "The Social Work Mission and Its Implementation in the Socialization Process: First- and Second-Year Students' Perspectives." Social Work Education 21, no. 6 (2002): 671–83.

Lerman, Robert, and Elaine Sorenson. "Father Involvement with Their Nonmarital Children: Patterns, Determinants, and Effects on Their Earnings." Marriage & Family Review 29, no. 2–3 (2000): 137–158.

Leschied, Alan W., Debbie Chiodo, Paul C. Whitehead, Dermot Hurley, and Larry Marshall. "The Empirical Basis of Risk Assessment in Child Welfare: The Accuracy of Risk Assessment and Clinical Judgment." Child Welfare 82, no. 5 (2003): 527–40.

Lindgren, Ralph, and Nadine Taub. The Law of Sex Discrimination. Eagen, MN: West Publishing, 1993.

Lipsky, Michael. Street-Level Bureaucracy: Dilemmas of the Individual in Public Services. New York: Russell Sage Foundation, 1980.

Littell, Julia, and John R. Schuerman. "A Synthesis of Research on Family Preservation and Family Reunification Programs." In A Part of the National Evaluation of Family Preservation Services. Washington, DC: Department of Health and Human Services, 1995.

Lombardi, Chris. "Justice for Battered Women." The Nation, July 15 (2002): 24–27.

Lowenhaupt-Tsing, Anna. "Monster Stories: Women Charged with Perinatal Endangerment." In Uncertain Terms: Negotiating Gender in American Culture, edited by Faye Ginsburg and Anna Lowenhaupt-Tsing. Boston: Beacon Press, 1990.

Lyle, Charles Gene, and Elliott Graham. "Looks Can Be Deceiving: Using a Risk Assessment Instrument to Evaluate the Outcomes of Child Protection Services." Children and Youth Services Review 22, no. 11–12 (2000): 935–49.

Macdonald, Grant, and Frank Sirotich. "Reporting Client Violence." Social Work 46, no. 2 (2001): 107–14.

Madriz, Esther. Nothing Bad Happens to Good Girls: Fear of Crime in Women's Lives. Berkeley: University of California Press, 1997.

Maluccio, Anthony, and James K. Whittaker. "Learning from the "Family Preservation" Initiative." Children and Youth Services Review 19, no. 1/2 (1997): 5–16.

Mansbridge, Jane J. Why We Lost the ERA. Chicago: University of Chicago Press, 1986.

Marsiglio, William, Paul Amato, Randal D. Day, and Michael E. Lamb. "Scholarship on Fatherhood in the 1990s and Beyond." Journal of Marriage and the Family 62, no. 4 (2000): 1173–1191.

Marsiglio, William, Randal Day, and Michael E. Lamb. "Exploring Fatherhood Diversity: Implications for Conceptualizing Father Involvement." Marriage & Family Review 29, no. 4 (2000): 269–94.

Mason, MaryAnn. The Custody Wars: Why Children Are Losing the Legal Battle and What We Can Do About It. New York: Basic Books, 2000.

———. From Father's Property to Children's Rights: The History of Child Custody in the United States. New York: Columbia University Press, 1994.

Mathias-Williams, Rachel, and Nigel Thomas. "Great Expectations? The Career Aspirations of Social Work Students." Social Work Education 21, no. 4 (2002): 421–35.

McCormick, John. "Chicago Hope: How a Judge Bucked the System by Putting Children First." Newsweek March 24 (1997): 68.

McKinnon, Catherine. "Sex and Violence." In Gender Inequality: Feminist Theories and Politics, edited by Judith Lorber. Los Angeles: Roxbury Press, 1998.

Meddin, B. Y. "Criteria for Placement Decision in Protective Services." Child Welfare 63, no. 4 (1984): 367–73.

Miccio, G. Kristian. "A House Divided: Mandatory Arrest, Domestic Violence and the Conservatization of the Battered Women's Movement." Houston Law Review 42, no. 2, (2005): 237–323.

Michel, Sonya. Children's Interests/Mothers' Rights: The Shaping of America's Child Care Policy. New Haven, CT: Yale University Press, 1999.

Millett, Kate. "Beyond Politics: Children and Sexuality." In Pleasure and Danger: Exploring Female Sexuality, edited by Carole S. Vance. London: Pandora, 1984.

Mink, Gwendolyn. "The Lady and the Tramp: Gender, Race, and the Origins of the American Welfare State." In Women, the State, and Welfare, edited by Linda Gordon. Madison: University of Wisconsin Press, 1990.

———. "Welfare Cant." Crossroads, March (1995): 2–6.

Mink, Gwendolyn, and Rickie Solinger, eds. Welfare: A Documentary History of U.S. Policy and Politics. New York: New York University Press, 2003.

Morton, Thomas D., and Marsha K. Salus. "Supervising Child Protective Services Caseworkers: Increasing Job Satisfaction and Preventing Burnout." Rockville, MD: Department of Health and Human Services, Administration for Children and Families, Administration on Children, Youth, and Families, National Center on Child Abuse and Neglect, 1994.

Mumola, Christopher. "Incarcerated Parents and Their Children." Washington, DC: Bureau of Justice Statistics, 2000.

Murphy, Patrick T. Wasted: The Plight of America's Unwanted Children. Chicago: Ivan R. Dee, 1997.

Murray, Charles. "The Coming White Underclass." Wall Street Journal, October 29 (1993).

National Association of Social Workers. "Code of Ethics of the National Association of Social Workers." Section 5. Social Workers' Ethical Responsibilities to the Social Work Profession, Subsection 5.01, Integrity of the Profession, 1999.

———. "Safety Guidelines." Boston: NASW, Committee for the Study and Prevention of Violence Against Social Workers, 1996.

National Clearinghouse on Child Abuse and Neglect. "Child Abuse and Neglect Fatalities: Statistics and Interventions." Washington, DC: Administration for Children and Families, 2004.

———. "Foster Care National Statistics: April 2001." Fairfax, VA: National Clearinghouse on Child Abuse and Neglect, 2001.

Needell, B., D. Webster, S. Cuccaro-Alamin, M. Armijo, S. Lee, B. Lery, T. Shaw, W. Dawson, W. Piccus, J. Magruder, S. Ben-Poorat, and H. Kim. Child Welfare Services Reports for California. University of California at Berkeley Center for Social Services Research, 2004; available at http://cssr.berkeley.edu/CWSCMSreports.

Needell, Barbara, Stephanie Cuccaro-Alamin, Alan Brookhart, and Seon Lee. "Transitions from AFDC to Child Welfare in California." Children and Youth Services Review 21, no. 9–10 (1999): 815–42.

Needell, Barbara, Daniel Webster, Stephanie Cuccaro-Alamin, and Michael Armijo. "Performance Indicators for Child Welfare Services in California: 1997." Berkeley: University of California, Berkeley, Center for Social Services Research, 1998.

Nelson, Barbara. Making an Issue of Child Abuse. Chicago: University of Chicago Press, 1984.

Nelson, Kristine E. "Family Preservation—What Is It?" Children and Youth Services Review 19, no. 1/2 (1997): 101–18.

Nelson, William A. "The New Inquisition: State Compulsion of Therapeutic Confession." Vermont Law Review 20, no. 4 (1996): 951–99.

Neubeck, Kenneth J., and Noel A. Cazenave. Welfare Racism. New York: Routledge, 2001.

Newhill, Christina E. "Client Violence Toward Social Workers: A Practice and Policy Concern for the 1990's." Social Work 40, no. 5 (1995): 631–36.

Newman, Katherine S. No Shame in My Game. New York: Russell Sage Foundation/Vintage Books, 1999.

Noble, Amanda. "Law, Medicine, and Women's Bodies: The Social Control of Pregnant Drug Users." PhD dissertation, University of California, Davis, 1992.

Noble, Amanda, Dorie Klein, Elaine Zahnd, and Sue Holtby. "Gender Issues in California's Perinatal Substance Abuse Policy." Contemporary Drug Problems 27, no. 1 (2000): 77–119.

Nolan, James L. The Therapeutic State. New York: New York University Press, 1998.

Nurse, Anne. Fatherhood Arrested. Nashville, TN: Vanderbilt University Press, 2002.

Oates, Kim R., Jennifer Tebbutt, Heather Swanston, and Deborah Lynch. "Prior Childhood Sexual Abuse in Mothers of Sexually Abused Children." Child Abuse & Neglect 22, no. 11 (1998): 1113–18.

O'Connor, Stephen. Orphan Trains: The Story of Charles Loring Brace and the Children He Saved and Failed. New York: Houghton-Mifflin, 2001.

PACE. "Remember the Children: Mothers Balance Work and Child Care under Welfare Reform." Berkeley: Graduate School of Education-PACE, 2000.

Pacific Justice Institute. "Parents' Rights to Discipline in California." Pacific Justice Institute, 2003; available at http://www.pacificjustice.org/resources/articles/focus.cfm?ID=ART750858607.

———. "When Child Protective Services Calls." Pacific Justice Institute, 2002; available at http://www.pacificjustice.org/resources/articles/focus.cfm?ID=ART513510669.

Padilla, Laura. "Intersectionality and Positionality: Situating Women of Color in the Affirmative Action Dialogue." Fordham Law Review 66, no. 843 (1997): 843–929.

Pager, Devah. "The Mark of a Criminal Record." American Journal of Sociology 108, no. 5 (2003): 937–75.

Paltrow, Lynn M. "Criminal Prosecution Against Pregnant Women: National Update and Overview." American Civil Liberties Union Reproductive Freedom Project, 1992.

Patton, William Wesley. "Child Abuse: The Irreconcilable Differences Between Criminal Prosecution and Informal Dependency Court Mediation." University of Louisville Journal of Family Law 31, no. 1 (1992): 37–64.

Pearce, Jeremy. "Taking on a Troubled Agency." New York Times, January 26 (2003), NJ 1.

Pecora, P. J., J. K. Whittacker, and A. N. Maluccio. The Child Welfare Challenge: Policy, Practice, and Research. New York: Aldine de Gruyter, 1992.

Peddle, Nancy, Ching-Tung Wang, Javier Diaz, and Robert Reid. "Current Trends in Child Abuse Prevention and Fatalities: The 2000 Fifty State Survey." Working paper 808. Chicago: Prevent Child Abuse America, 2002.

Peled, Einat, Zvi Eisikovits, Guy Enosh, and Zeev Winstock. "Choice and Empowerment for Battered Women Who Stay: Toward a Constructivist Model." Social Work 45, no. 1 (2000): 9–25.

Pelletier, Melissa. "U.S. Parents Want Help with Newborns: Lack of Experience and Skill Seen as Reason for Increased Child Abuse and Neglect." Press release. Washington, DC: Prevent Child Abuse America, 1999.

Petchesky, Rosalind Pollack. Abortion and Woman's Choice: The State, Sexuality, and Reproductive Freedom. Boston: Northeastern University Press, 1990.

Pfohl, Stephen J. "The 'Discovery' of Child Abuse." Social Problems 24, (1977): 310–23.

Piven, Francis Fox, and Richard A. Cloward. Regulating the Poor: The Functions of Public Welfare. New York: Vintage Books, 1993.

Polikoff, Nancy D. "Gender and Child-Custody Determinations: Exploding the Myths." In Families, Politics, and Public Policy, edited by Irene Diamond. New York: Longman, 1983.

Polsky, Andrew J. The Rise of the Therapeutic State. Princeton, NJ: Princeton University Press, 1991.

Popenoe, David. "A World Without Fathers (Consequences of Children Living Without Fathers)." Wilson Quarterly 20, no. 2 (1996): 12–30.

Quadagno, Jill. The Color of Welfare: How Racism Undermined the War on Poverty. Oxford: Oxford University Press, 1996.

Ragin, Charles C. "Introduction: Cases of 'What Is a Case?'" In What Is a Case? Exploring the Foundations of Social Inquiry, edited by Charles C. Ragin and Howard S. Becker. Cambridge: Cambridge University Press, 1994.

Rank, Mark. Living on the Edge: The Realities of Welfare in America. New York: Columbia University Press, 1994.

Reich, Jennifer A. "Investigating Child Abuse Investigations." In Sourcebook of Family Theory and Research, edited by Vern L. Bengtson, Alan C. Acock, Katherine R. Allen, Peggye Dilworth-Anderson, and David M. Klein. Thousand Oaks, CA: Sage Publications, 2004.

———. "Pregnant with Possibility: Reflections on Embodiment, Access, and Inclusion in Field Research." Qualitative Sociology 26, no. 3 (2003): 351–66.

Reinarman, Craig, and Harry G. Levine. "Crack in Context: America's Latest Demon Drug." In Crack in America: Demon Drugs and Social Justice, edited by Craig Reinarman and Harry G. Levine. Berkeley: University of California Press, 1997.

Renzetti, Claire M. Violent Betrayal: Partner Abuse in Lesbian Relationships. Thousand Oaks, CA: Sage Publications, 1995.

Rey, Lucy. "What Social Workers Need to Know About Client Violence." Families in Society 77, no. 1 (1996): 33–39.

Rich, Adrienne. Of Woman Born: Motherhood as Experience and Institution. New York: W.W. Norton & Co., 1976.

Richards, Keith N. Tender Mercies: Inside the World of a Child Abuse Investigator, rev. ed. Washington, DC: Child Welfare League of America, 1998.

Riger, Stephanie. "What's Wrong with Empowerment." American Journal of Community Psychology 21, no. 3 (1993): 279–92.

Rinfret-Raynor, Maryse, and Solange Cantin. "Feminist Therapy for Battered Women: An Assessment." In Out of the Darkness: Contemporary Perspectives on Family Violence, edited by Glenda Kaufman Kantor and Jana L. Jasinski. Thousand Oaks, CA: Sage Publications, 1997.

Roberts, Dorothy. Killing the Black Body: Race, Reproduction, and the Meaning of Liberty. New York: Vintage Books, 1997.

———. "Mothers Who Fail to Protect Their Children." In Mother Troubles: Rethinking Contemporary Maternal Dilemmas, edited by Julia E. Hanigsberg and Sara Ruddick. Boston: Beacon Press, 1999.

———. Shattered Bonds: The Color of Child Welfare. New York: Basic Civitas Books, 2002.

———. "Welfare's Ban on Poor Motherhood." In Whose Welfare?, edited by Gwendolyn Mink. Ithaca, NY: Cornell University Press, 1999.

Rose, Susan J. "Reaching Consensus on Child Neglect: African American Mothers and Child Welfare Workers." Children and Youth Services Review 21, no. 6 (1999): 463–79.

Rose, Susan J., and William Meezan. "Variations in Perceptions of Child Neglect." Child Welfare 75, no. 2 (1996): 139.

Rosenthal, J. A. "Outcomes of Adoption of Children with Special Needs." Adoption 3, no. 1 (1993): 77–88.

Rosner, David, and Gerald Markowitz. "Race, Foster Care, and the Politics of Abandonment in New York City." American Journal of Public Health 87, no. 11 (1997).

Ross, Jane. "Parental Substance Abuse: Implications for Children, the Child Welfare System, and Foster Care Outcomes," GAO/T-HEHS-98-40. Washington, DC: General Accounting Office, 1997.

Roth, Julius. "Some Contingencies of the Moral Evaluation and Control of Clientele: The Case of the Hospital Emergency Service." In The Sociology of Health and Illness: Critical Perspectives, edited by Peter Conrad and Rochelle Kern. New York: St. Martin's Press, 1994.

Rothman, Barbara Katz. Recreating Motherhood: Ideology and Technology in a Patriarchal Society. New York: W.W. Norton & Co., 1989.

Rubin, Lillian. Families on the Fault Line: America's Working Class Speaks About the Family, the Economy, Race, and Ethnicity. New York: Harper Collins, 1994.

Ruscio, Ayelet Meron. "Predicting the Child-Rearing Practices of Mothers Sexually Abused in Childhood." Child Abuse & Neglect 25, no. 3 (2001): 369–87.

Sawicki, Jana. Disciplining Foucault: Feminism, Power, and the Body. New York: Routledge, 1991.

Schene, Patricia A. "Past, Present, and Future Roles of Child Protective Services." Protecting Children from Abuse and Neglect 8, no. 1 (1998): 23–38.

Scheper-Hughes, Nancy. Death Without Weeping: The Violence of Everyday Life in Brazil. Berkeley: University of California Press, 1992.

Schmidt-Tieszen, Ada, and Thomas McDonald. "Children Who Wait: Long Term Foster Care or Adoption?" Children and Youth Services Review 20, no. 1/2 (1998): 13–28.

Scott, Ellen, Andrew London, and Nancy Myers, "Dangerous Dependencies—The Intersection of Welfare Reform and Domestic Violence." Gender and Society 16, no. 6 (2002): 878–97.

Scott, Ellen K., Kathryn Edin, Andrew S. London, and Rebecca Joyce Kissane. "Unstable Work, Unstable Income: Implications for Family Well-Being in the Era of Time-Limited Welfare." Journal of Poverty 8, no. 1 (2004).

Segal, Lynn. Slow Motion: Changing Masculinities, Changing Men. London: Virago Press, 1990.

Sewell, William. "A Theory of Structure: Duality, Agency, and Transformation." American Journal of Sociology 98, no. 1 (1992): 1–29.

Shanley, Mary L. "Fathers' Rights, Mothers' Wrongs? Reflections on Unwed Fathers' Rights and Sex Equality." Hypatia 10, no. 1 (1995): 74-103.

Shapira, M., and R. Benbenisty. "Modeling Judgments and Decisions in Cases of Alleged Child Abuse and Neglect." Social Work Research and Abstracts 29, no. 2 (1993): 14–19.

Shlonsky, Aron, and Eileen Gambrill. "The Assessment and Management of Risk in Child Welfare Services." Children and Youth Services Review 23, no. 1 (2001): 1–2.

Shoop, Julie Gannon. "Marriage Trumps Biology in California Paternity Fight." Trial 34, no. 7 (1998): 18–21.

Siegel, Loren. "The Pregnancy Police Fight the War on Drugs." In Crack in America: Demon Drugs and Social Justice, edited by Craig Reinarman and Harry G. Levine. Berkeley: University of California Press, 1997.

Silverman, Arnold. "Outcomes of Transracial Adoption." In The Future of Children: Adoption, edited by Center for the Future of Children. Palo Alto, CA: The David and Lucile Packard Foundation, 1993.

Skocpol, Theda. Protecting Soldiers and Mothers: The Political Origins of Social Policy in the United States. Boston: Harvard University Press, 1992.

Smolowe, Jill. "Adoption in Black and White: An Odd Coalition Takes Aim at the Decades-Old Prejudice Against Transracial Placements." Time August 14 (1995): 50–51.

Snell, Tracy, and Danielle Morton. "Women in Prison: Survey of State Prison Inmates, 1991." Washington, DC: Bureau of Justice Statistics, 1994.

Solinger, Rickie. "Race and 'Value': Black and White Illegitimate Babies, 1945–1965." In Feminist Frontiers IV, edited by Laurel Richardson, Verta Taylor, and Nancy Whittier. New York: McGraw-Hill, 1997.

Solkoff, Scott Michael. "Judicial Use Immunity and the Privilege Against Self-Incrimination in Court-Mandated Therapy Programs." Nova Law Review 17, no. 3 (1993): 1441–94.

Spraggins, Johnnie David Jr. "African American Masculinity: Power and Expression." Journal of African American Men 4, no. 3 (1999): 45–72.

Stacey, Judith. Brave New Families: Stories of Domestic Upheaval in Late Twentieth Century America. New York: Basic Books, 1991.

———. In the Name of the Family: Rethinking Family Values in a Postmodern Age. Boston: Beacon Press, 1996.

Stearns, Cindy A. "Breastfeeding and the Good Maternal Body." Gender and Society 13, no. 3 (1999): 308–25.

Stein, Theodore J. Child Welfare and the Law, rev. ed. Washington, DC: CWLA Press, 1998.

Sterett, Susan M. Public Pensions: Gender and Civic Service in the United States, 1850–1937. Ithaca, NY: Cornell University Press, 2003.

Stiffman, Michael N., Patricia G. Schnitzer, Patricia Adam, Robin L. Kruse, and Bernard G. Ewigman. "Household Composition and Risk of Fatal Child Maltreatment." Pediatrics 109, no. 4 (2002): 615–21.

Stuart-Macadam, Patricia, and Katherine A Dettwyler. Breastfeeding: Biocultural Perspectives on Breastfeeding. New York: Aldine de Gruyter, 1995.

Sudnow, David. "Normal Crimes: Sociological Features of the Penal Code in a Public Defender Office." Social Problems 12 (1964): 255–76.

Sykes, Richard E., and John P. Clark. "A Theory of Deference Exchange in Police-Civilian Encounters." American Journal of Sociology 81, no. 3 (1975): 584–600.

Tannen, Deborah. "Marked Women, Unmarked Men." In The World Is a Text, edited by Jonathan Silverman and Dean Rader. Englewood Cliffs, NJ: Prentice Hall, 2002.

Terling, Toni. "The Efficacy of Family Reunification Practices: Reentry Rates and Correlates of Reentry for Abused and Neglected Children Reunited with Their Families." Child Abuse & Neglect 23, no. 12 (1999): 1359–70.

Terling-Watt, Toni. "Permanency in Kinship Care: An Exploration of Disruption Rates and Factors Associated with Placement Disruption." Children and Youth Services Review 23, no. 2 (2001): 111–26.

Testa, Maria, Brian M. Quigley, and Kenneth E. Leonard. "Does Alcohol Make a Difference? Within-Participants Comparison of Incidents of Partner Violence." Journal of Interpersonal Violence 18, no. 7 (2003): 735–43.

Thomas, William I. On Social Organization and Social Personality. Chicago: University of Chicago Press, 1966.

Thompson, Tommy. "HHS Announces Decline in TANF Caseloads." HHS News, December 2 (2003).

Tice, Karen. Tales of Wayward Girls and Immoral Women. Urbana: University of Illinois Press, 1998.

Time. "Father Makes Two: Unmarried Men Who Raise Their Children Are One of the Fastest-Growing Groups in America." Time, November 19 (2001).

Tong, Rosemary. Feminist Thought: A Comprehensive Introduction. Boulder, CO: Westview Press, 1989.

"Toogood Pleads Guilty." St. Joseph County Prosecutor's Office, February 14 (2003).

Trattner, Walter. From Poor Law to Welfare State: A History of Social Welfare in America, 5th ed. New York: Free Press, 1994.

Trillin, Calvin. Family Man. New York: Farrar, Straus, and Giroux, 1998.

U.S. Census Bureau. "State and County Quickfacts." Washington, DC: U.S. Census Bureau, 2002.

Vidaeff, A. C., and J. M. Mastrobattista. "In Utero Cocaine Exposure: A Thorny Mix of Science and Mythology." American Journal of Perinatology 20, no. 4 (2003): 165–72.

Voss, Kim. The Making of American Exceptionalism: The Knights of Labor and Class Formation in the Nineteenth Century. Ithaca, NY: Cornell University Press, 1993.

Walker, Lenore. The Battered Woman. New York: Harper & Row, 1979.

Walkowitz, Daniel J. "The Making of a Feminine Professional Identity: Social Workers in the 1920s." American Historical Review 95, no. 4 (1990): 1051–75.

Walton, John. "Making the Theoretical Case." In What Is a Case? Exploring the Foundations of Social Inquiry, edited by Charles C. Ragin and Howard S. Becker. Cambridge: Cambridge University Press, 1994.

Warner, Joe. "An Initial Assessment of the Extent to Which Risk Factors, Frequently Identified in Research, Are Taken into Account When Assessing Risk in Child Protection Cases." Journal of Social Work 3, no. 3 (2003): 339–63.

Warren, Carol A. B., and Jennifer Kay Hackney. Gender Issues in Ethnography, 2nd ed. Thousand Oaks, CA: Sage Publications, 2000.

Weber, Max. "Bureaucracy." In From Max Weber: Essays in Sociology, edited by H. H. Gerth and C. Wright Mills. New York: Oxford University Press, 1946.

Weeks, Robin, and Cathy Spatz Widom. "Self-Reports of Early Childhood Victimization Among Incarcerated Adult Male Felons." Journal of Interpersonal Violence 13, no. 3 (1998): 346–62.

Weinger, Susan. Security Risk: Preventing Client Violence Against Social Workers. Washington, DC: NASW Press, 2001.

Weitz, Rose. The Sociology of Health, Illness, and Health Care. Belmont, CA: Wadsworth Publishing, 1996.

Wells, Kathleen, and Shenyang Guo. "Mothers' Welfare and Work Income and Reunification with Children in Foster Care." Children and Youth Services Review 25, no. 3 (2003): 203–24.

Wells, Susan J., John D. Fluke, and C. Hendricks Brown. "The Decision to Investigate: Child Protection Practice in 12 Local Agencies." Children and Youth Services Review 17, no. 4 (1995): 523–46.

West, Cornel. Race Matters. New York: Random House, 1994.

Weston, Kath. Families We Choose: Lesbians, Gays, Kinship. New York: Columbia University Press, 1991.

———. "The Virtual Anthropologist." In Is Academic Feminism Dead? Theory in Practice, edited by The Social Justice Group. New York: New York University Press, 2000.

Wexler, Richard. Wounded Innocents: The Real Victims of the War Against Child Abuse. Buffalo: Prometheus Books, 1995.

White, Lucy. "Subordination, Rhetorical Survival Skills, and Sunday Shoes: Notes on the Hearing of Mrs. G." In Feminist Legal Theory: Readings in Law and Gender, edited by Katherine Bartlett. Boulder, CO: Westview Press, 1991.

Whitehead, Barbara Dafoe. "Dan Quayle Was Right." The Atlantic April (1993): 55.

Wilkes, Michael S., and Richard L. Kravitz. "Medical Researchers and the Media: Attitudes Toward Public Dissemination of Research." JAMA, Journal of the American Medical Association 268, no. 8 (1992): 999–1004.

Williams, Joan. Unbending Gender: Why Family and Work Conflict and What to Do About It. London: Oxford Press, 1999.

Wilson, Melvin, and Jeanne Brooks-Gunn. "Health Status and Behaviors of Unwed Fathers." Children and Youth Services Review 23, no. 4/5 (2001): 377–401.

Woodhouse, Barbara Bennett. "Making Poor Mothers Fungible: The Privitization of Foster Care." In Child Care and Inequality: Re-Thinking Carework for Children and Youth, edited by Francesca M. Cancian, Demi Kurz, Andrew London, Rebecca Reviere, and Mary Tuominen. New York: Routledge, 2002.

Yoest, Charmaine Crouse. "No Child Is Unadoptable." Policy Review, January–February, no. 18 (1997): 13–16.

Young, Iris Marion. "Punishment, Treatment, Empowerment: Three Approaches to Policy for Pregnant Addicts." Feminist Studies 20, no. 1 (1994): 33–58.

Zelizer, Viviana A. Pricing the Priceless Child: The Changing Social Value of Children. New York: Basic Books, 1985.

Zuckerman, Barry. "Effects on Parents and Children." In When Drug Addicts Have Children, edited by Douglas J. Besharov. Washington, DC: Child Welfare League of America, 1994.

NOTES

Chapter 1

1. All cases described in this chapter use pseudonyms to protect the identity of the county and its employees and clients.
2. For examples of the critique of reunification policies, see Elizabeth Bartholet, *Nobody's Children: Abuse Neglect, Foster Drift, and the Adoption Alternative* (Boston: Beacon Press, 1999); and Richard Gelles, *The Book of David: How Preserving Families Can Cost Children's Lives* (New York: Harper, 1996).
3. Adoption and Safe Families Act of 1997, P.L. 105-89 (November 19, 1997). The specifics of this bill are discussed in detail in chapter 2.
4. I call the agency CPS because it provides a generic marker, references the name many agencies used before changing their names as part of broader reforms, and because it denotes the agency goal. It is worth noting that in other counties and locales, child welfare agencies are also known as the Department of Children and Families, Family Services, Social Services, Children and Family Services, Children's Services, Department of Youth and Family Services, DFS, DCFS, DCS, DSS, DYFS, as well as many other labels and acronyms.
5. For a discussion of the history of race and racism in welfare see Sharon Hays, *Flat Broke with Children* (New York: Oxford University Press, 2003); Kenneth J. Neubeck and Noel A. Cazenave, *Welfare Racism* (New York: Routledge, 2001); and Jill Quadagno, *The Color of Welfare: How Racism Undermined the War on Poverty* (Oxford: Oxford University Press, 1996).
6. Social service research often identifies common characteristics of families who enter the CPS system. For example, for a study of the relative effectiveness of services provided to families in the system, see Toni Terling, "The Efficacy of Family Reunification Practices: Reentry Rates and Correlates of Reentry for Abused and Neglected Children Reunited with Their Families," *Child Abuse & Neglect* 23, no. 12 (1999); and Susan J. Wells, John D. Fluke, and C. Hendricks Brown, "The Decision to Investigate: Child Protection Practice in 12 Local Agencies," *Children and Youth Services Review* 17, no. 4 (1995). See also Loring Jones, "The Social and Family Correlates of Successful Reunification of Children in Foster Care," *Children and Youth Services Review* 20, no. 4 (1998); Julia Littell and John R. Schuerman, "A Synthesis of Research on Family Preservation and Family Reunification Programs," in *A Part of the National Evaluation of Family Preservation Services* (Washington, DC: Department of Health and Human Services, 1995); Anthony Maluccio and James K. Whittaker, "Learning from the 'Family Preservation' Initiative," *Children and Youth Services Review* 19, no. 1/2

(1997); and Kristine E. Nelson, "Family Preservation—What Is It?," *Children and Youth Services Review* 19, no. 1/2 (1997). For an evaluation of the long-term outcomes for families after state intervention, see Jennifer Ayres Hand, "Note: Preventing Undue Terminations: A Critical Evaluation of the Length-of-Time-Out-of-Custody Ground for Termination of Parental Rights," *New York University Law Review* 71, no. 5 (1996); Moira Inkelas and Neal Halfon, "Recidivism in Child Protective Services," *Children and Youth Services Review* 19, no. 3 (1997); and Ada Schmidt-Tieszen and Thomas P. McDonald, "Children Who Wait: Long Term Foster Care or Adoption?," *Children and Youth Services Review* 20, no. 1/2 (1998). For examples of works that argue for or against greater intervention, see also Bartholet, *Nobody's Children*; Gelles, *The Book of David*; John Hubner and Jill Wolfson, *Somebody Else's Children: The Courts, the Kids, and the Struggle to Save America's Troubled Families* (New York: Crown Publishers, 1996); Patrick T. Murphy, *Wasted: The Plight of America's Unwanted Children* (Chicago: Ivan R. Dee, 1997); and Richard Wexler, *Wounded Innocents: The Real Victims of the War Against Child Abuse* (Buffalo: Prometheus Books, 1995).

7. See Stephanie Coontz, *The Way We Never Were: American Families and the Nostalgia Trap* (New York: Harper Collins, 1992).

8. Calvin Trillin, *Family Man* (New York: Farrar, Straus and Giroux, 1998). For a discussion of variations in child maltreatment definitions, see David Gough, "Defining the Problem," *Child Abuse & Neglect* 20, no. 11 (1996): 993; Susan J. Rose, "Reaching Consensus on Child Neglect: African American Mothers and Child Welfare Workers," *Children and Youth Services Review* 21, no. 6 (1999); and Susan J. Rose and William Meezan, "Variations in Perceptions of Child Neglect," *Child Welfare* 75, no. 2 (1996). See also Ann Futterman Collier et al., "Culture-Specific Views of Child Maltreatment and Parenting Styles in a Pacific-Island Community," *Child Abuse & Neglect* 23, no. 3 (1999); and Jill E. Korbin et al., "Neighborhood Views on the Definition and Etiology of Child Maltreatment," *Child Abuse & Neglect* 24, no. 12 (2000). For an examination of class differences in parenting, see Annette Lareau, "Invisible Inequality: Social Class and Childrearing in Black Families and White Families," *American Sociological Review* 67, no. 5 (2002).

9. Christopher Lasch, *Haven in a Heartless World: The Family Besieged* (New York: W.W. Norton & Co., 1995), 4. See also Jacques Donzelot, *The Policing of Families* (New York: Pantheon, 1979).

10. The notion of parental sacrifice is situated in a concept of family as both an integrated unit that works as a collective and a constellation of individual members with sometimes competing rights and needs. As early as the nineteenth century, theorists on family life began arguing that the family should be studied as "a unit of interacting personalities" (i.e., Lasch, *Haven in a Heartless World*, 35). Consistent with this approach, the burdens of parenthood have been addressed in great detail. Women face overwhelming expectations of family life and are gradually transformed into an overburdened wife or mother, as argued, for example, by Simone deBeauvoir, *The Second Sex* (New York: Vintage Books, 1974) and Betty Friedan, *The Feminine Mystique* (New York: W.W. Norton & Co., 1963). At the same time, men struggle with expectations to be both good providers and involved fathers (see Jessie Bernard, "The Good Provider Role: Its Rise and Fall," in *Diversity and Change in Families: Patterns, Prospects, and Policies*, eds. Mark Robert Rank and Edward Kain (Englewood Cliffs, NJ: Prentice Hall, 1981); Scott Coltrane, "Changing Patterns of Family Work: Chicano Men and Housework," in *Shifting the Center*, ed. Susan Ferguson (Mountain View, CA: Mayfield Publishing, 1998); and Kathleen Gerson, "Dilemmas of Involved Fatherhood," in *Reconstructing Gender*, ed. Estelle Disch (Mountain View, CA: Mayfield Publishing, 1997). For both genders, these cultural expectations of ideal

parenting often exceed individual capability. As overwhelming parental expectations continue to grow, there is an accompanying assumption that being a good parent requires sacrificing one's own needs for the sake of one's children.

11. See Viviana Zelizer, *Pricing the Priceless Child: The Changing Social Value of Children* (New York: Basic Books, 1985). Zelizer's work points to the early role of social reformers who worked to enact child labor laws and compulsory education regulations in shaping the very meanings of childhood.

12. There are gradations within this proposition ranging from more public resources for families to wages for domestic work to the dismantling of nuclear family forms. See Rosemary Tong, *Feminist Thought: A Comprehensive Introduction* (Boulder, CO: Westview Press, 1989). On domestic violence, see Joyce Gelb, "The Politics of Wife Abuse," in *Family, Politics, and Public Policy: A Feminist Dialogue on Women and the State*, ed. Irene Diamond (New York: Longman, 1983). On publicly funded child care, see Sonya Michel, *Children's Interests/Mothers' Rights: The Shaping of America's Child Care Policy* (New Haven, CT: Yale University Press, 1999). On access to safe and affordable abortion, see Rosalind Pollack Petchesky, *Abortion and Woman's Choice: The State, Sexuality, and Reproductive Freedom* (Boston: Northeastern University Press, 1990). On the near passage of the Equal Rights Amendment, see Jane J. Mansbridge, *Why We Lost the ERA* (Chicago: University of Chicago Press, 1986). On affirmative action programs in education and employment, see Laura Padilla, "Intersectionality and Positionality: Situating Women of Color in the Affirmative Action Dialogue," *Fordham Law Review* 66, no. 843 (1997). These works provide examples of rich areas of research that illustrate the role of the state in facilitating gender equity.

13. As an example, see Jean Bethke Elshtain, "Antigone's Daughters: Reflections on Female Identity and the State," in *Families, Politics, and Public Policy,* ed. Irene Diamond (New York: Longman, 1983).

14. Angela Davis, *Women, Race and Class* (New York: Vintage Books, 1983); Dorothy Roberts, *Killing the Black Body: Race, Reproduction, and the Meaning of Liberty* (New York: Vintage Books, 1997).

15. Francis Fox Piven and Richard A. Cloward, *Regulating the Poor: The Functions of Public Welfare* (New York: Vintage Books, 1993), 167.

16. Quoted in Mimi Abramovitz, *Regulating the Lives of Women: Social Welfare Policy from Colonial Times to the Present* (Boston: South End Press, 1988), 314.

17. David Cheal, *Family and the State of Theory* (Toronto: University of Toronto Press, 1991), 83.

18. According to the federal Food and Nutritional Service, the sponsoring federal agency and part of the Department of Agriculture, the Supplemental Nutrition Program for Women, Infants and Children, better known as the WIC program, "serves to safeguard the health of low-income women, infants, and children up to age 5 who are at nutritional risk by providing nutritious foods to supplement diets, information on healthy eating, and referrals to healthcare."

19. Women utilizing domestic violence resources face scrutiny from service providers (Einat Peled et al., "Choice and Empowerment for Battered Women Who Stay: Toward a Constructivist Model," *Social Work* 45, no. 1 (2000)), police, and prosecutors (Jennifer L. Dunn, "Innocence Lost: Accomplishing Victimization in Intimate Stalking Cases," *Symbolic Interaction* 24, no. 3 (2001)), and can result in CPS intervention for engaging in domestic violence (Chris Lombardi, "Justice for Battered Women," *The Nation*, July 15 (2002), 24).

20. Adoption and Safe Families Act of 1997, P.L. 105-89, § 101(B).

21. Andrew Polsky, *The Rise of the Therapeutic State* (Princeton, NJ: Princeton University Press, 1991), 3.

22. Peter Conrad, "Types of Medical Social Control," *Sociology of Health and Illness* 1, no. 1 (1979), 1. Therapists are seen as able to determine who is sick and who is sicker, that is, who is ill and needs treatment and who is beyond salvation. Crime dramas like *Law and Order* frequently use the forensic psychologist to help district attorneys make sense of how to best prosecute those who commit acts of violence. Such assessments of the accused allegedly elucidate intent, comprehension, and motivation. Similarly attorneys, judges, and social workers in the child welfare system rely on assessments of parents because a deviant parent's potential for rehabilitation is central to the system's operation.

23. Polsky, *The Rise of the Therapeutic State*, 4. See also James L. Nolan, *The Therapeutic State* (New York: New York University Press, 1998). The popularity of television and radio characters who apply "Dr." in front of their first names (i.e., Phil or Laura) to communicate approachability and professionalism illustrates the widespread acceptance of the therapeutic ethos. Similarly shows like *The Sopranos* and movies like *Analyze This* show how the use of therapy is no longer stigmatizing.

24. Wendy Kaminer, *I'm Dysfunctional, You're Dysfunctional* (Menlo Park, CA: Addison-Wesley, 1992), 31.

25. Polsky, *The Rise of the Therapeutic State*, 4.

26. Michel Foucault, *Discipline and Punish: The Birth of the Prison* (New York: Vintage Books, 1995), 184.

27. The definition of the situation was described by William I. Thomas, *On Social Organization and Social Personality* (Chicago: University of Chicago Press, 1966).

28. Several legal scholars have voiced concerns that these proceedings violate the Fifth Amendment right against self-incrimination and legal requirements for due process. See William A. Nelson, "The New Inquisition: State Compulsion of Therapeutic Confession," *Vermont Law Review* 20, no. 4 (1996); William Wesley Patton, "Child Abuse: The Irreconcilable Differences Between Criminal Prosecution and Informal Dependency Court Mediation," *University of Louisville Journal of Family Law* 31, no. 1 (1992); and Scott Michael Solkoff, "Judicial Use Immunity and the Privilege Against Self-Incrimination in Court-Mandated Therapy Programs," *Nova Law Review* 17, no. 3 (1993).

29. Section 107 of the Child Abuse Prevention and Treatment Act Amendments of 1996 (P.L. 104-235) requires that each state include "provisions and procedures requiring that in every case involving an abused or neglected child which results in a judicial proceeding, a guardian ad litem, who may be an attorney or a court appointed special advocate (or both), shall be appointed to represent the child in such proceedings" (42 U.S.C. 5106a)(2)(A). In theory, a private attorney could represent the children; however, I have never seen such a case. In addition, some locales do not use attorneys as representatives. This county did.

30. These firms also, although less often, represent dependents, foster parents, or other participants in the dependency process.

31. David Sudnow, "Normal Crimes: Sociological Features of the Penal Code in a Public Defender Office," *Social Problems* 12 (1964), 264.

32. Ibid., 262.

33. It is worth noting that the proceedings sometimes become more formal in the rare cases where an outside attorney has been retained by a parent.

34. The foster care rates in California are high, not necessarily because of entrance rates, but because of slow exit rates. See "The AFCARS Report" (Washington, DC: U.S. Department of Health and Human Services, Administration for Children and Families, 2001). For data, see "State and County Quickfacts" (Washington, DC: U.S. Census Bureau, 2002).

35. For a discussion of this issue, see Dorothy Roberts, *Shattered Bonds: The Color of Child Welfare* (New York: Basic Civitas Books, 2002).

36. Data are taken from the U.S. Census Bureau and a community report card issued by the state.

37. Questions of racial overrepresentation are difficult to fully understand, with little agreement on how to define overrepresentation. Recent research has suggested that children of color may not be as dramatically overrepresented as initially reported, since some studies failed to differentiate rates in the community. As an example of efforts to better understand the meanings of overrepresentation of children of color in child welfare systems, see Sheila D. Ards et al., "Racial Disproportionality in Reported and Substantiated Child Abuse and Neglect: An Examination of Systemic Bias," *Children and Youth Services Review* 25, no. 5/6 (2003). Note that the total percentages in my figures are greater than 100 percent because percentages were rounded up.

38. California state law explicitly discourages agencies from using the presence of drugs as grounds for child removal; however, it has been implemented differently. This law and its interpretations are discussed in chapter 2.

39. I make this statement based on my reading of other theoretical and empirical work discussing child protection work in other locales.

40. Understanding exactly how many of the parents are poor is difficult, as is estimating the number of CPS families who are also recipients of—or are poor enough to be eligible for—public assistance. Barbara Needell et al. found that of the 63,768 children entering AFDC between 1990 and 1995 in ten California counties that were followed, within five years of AFDC entry, 27 percent of children had child abuse referrals, 22 percent had child abuse investigations, 8 percent had child welfare cases opened, and 3 percent were placed in foster care (Needell et al., "Transitions from AFDC to Child Welfare in California," *Children and Youth Services Review* 21, no. 9–10 (1999)). However, in estimating the number of families in the system that are or have been recipients of public assistance, the number is much higher. Needell's preliminary analysis of children in supervised foster care (which does not include children receiving in-home services) who were from families that were eligible for income maintenance programs suggests "that about 2/3 of the children in foster care were from families who were eligible." According to one of her collaborators, this figure is believed to be an underestimate because of missing data and criteria which she was unable to account for, but which might have increased the number of children in her sample who would have been eligible. Examples of informative works on families in poverty include Kathryn Edin and Laura Lein, *Making Ends Meet: How Single Mothers Survive Welfare and Low-Wage Work* (New York: Russell Sage Foundation, 1997); Barbara Ehrenreich, *Nickel and Dimed: On (Not) Getting by in America* (New York: Henry Holt & Company, 2002); Jennifer Johnson, *Getting by on the Minimum: The Lives of Working-Class Women* (New York: Routledge, 2002); Katherine S. Newman, *No Shame in My Game* (New York: Russell Sage Foundation/Vintage Books, 1999); Ellen Scott, Andrew London, and Nancy Myers, "Dangerous Dependencies: The Intersection of Welfare Reform and Domestic Violence," *Gender and Society* 16, no. 6 (2002). However, these works do not explore the prevailing problems many of the families I studied face in addition to material poverty.

41. In the efforts to "reform" welfare, stories of mothers who sold food stamps, denied having access to other monies, or who in some way used public funds in ways seen as illegitimate were used. Similar stories are used to turn public support away from other publicly funded programs, including those providing healthcare, housing, and even child care.

42. As an example, see Wexler, *Wounded Innocents*.

43. Marie Ashe and Naomi Cahn, "Child Abuse: A Problem for Feminist Theory," in *The Public Nature of Private Violence: The Discovery of Domestic Abuse*, eds. Martha A. Fineman and Roxanne Mykitiuk (New York: Routledge, 1994), 167.

44. Linda Gordon, "Family Violence, Feminism, and Social Control," in *Women, the State, and Welfare*, ed. Linda Gordon (Madison: University of Wisconsin, 1990), 182.

45. Gordon, *Heroes of Their Own Lives* (New York: Penguin Books, 1988), 8.

46. Donzelot, *The Policing of Families*, 153–54.

47. See Roberts, *Shattered Bonds*, as well as the entire issue of *Children and Youth Services Review*, vol. 25, no. 5/6 (2003) for discussions of race in the child welfare system.

48. For a discussion of case analysis, from which I found inspiration if not exact methodological prescriptions, see Charles C. Ragin, "Introduction: Cases of 'What Is a Case?'" in *What Is a Case? Exploring the Foundations of Social Inquiry*, eds. Charles C. Ragin and Howard S. Becker (Cambridge: Cambridge University Press, 1994), 1. See also John Walton, "Making the Theoretical Case," in *What Is a Case? Exploring the Foundations of Social Inquiry*, eds. Charles C. Ragin and Howard S. Becker (Cambridge: Cambridge University Press, 1994), 121.

49. I took this call to action from Gordon, *Heroes of Their Own Lives*. Gordon's historical work provided me with a model of how feminist scholarship can provide theoretical analysis, complete with nuanced portrayals that are true to the subjects of inquiry. (See especially p. vi.)

50. Total percentages are greater than 100 percent because numbers were rounded up to the next round number. Eliminating specific figures also serves to disguise the details of the county.

Chapter 2

1. According to sociologist Joel Best, "social constructionists argue that conditions must be brought to people's notice in order to become social problems" (Best, *Threatened Children*, 11). I adhere to a similar vision of social problems and the accompanying meanings of claims making.

2. Joel Best, *Threatened Children: Rhetoric and Concern About Child-Victims* (Chicago: Chicago University Press, 1990); and Barbara Nelson, *Making an Issue of Child Abuse* (Chicago: University of Chicago Press, 1984).

3. Linda Gordon, *Heroes of Their Own Lives* (New York: Penguin Books, 1988); Andrew J. Polsky, *The Rise of the Therapeutic State* (Princeton, NJ: Princeton University Press, 1991); Karen Tice, *Tales of Wayward Girls and Immoral Women* (Urbana: University of Illinois Press, 1998); and Walter Trattner, *From Poor Law to Welfare State: A History of Social Welfare in America*, 5th ed. (New York: Free Press, 1994).

4. Gordon, *Heroes of Their Own Lives*, 28.

5. Polsky, *The Rise of the Therapeutic State*, 32.

6. The child savers had close ties with the temperance movement and identified alcohol use as being a particular threat to child well-being. Both movements grew out of the social purity campaigns, which opposed drinking and prostitution; as such, alcohol was inextricably linked with sexual promiscuity and immorality. This political connection and ideological commonality allowed child protection efforts to move forward without objection. Gordon suggests that the "emphasis on the drink, and the envisioning of cruelty to children as something that 'they'—the immigrant poor—did, never 'us'—the respectable classes—allowed even anti-feminist moral reformers to include wife-beating within their jurisdiction...Similarly, child protection agencies were able to prosecute many incest cases without offending anti-feminists" (Gordon, *Heroes of Their Own Lives*, 20).

7. Linda Gordon, "Family Violence, Feminism, and Social Control," in *Women, the State, and Welfare*, ed. Linda Gordon (Madison: University of Wisconsin, 1990), 179.

8. Gordon, *Heroes of Their Own Lives*; Polsky, *The Rise of the Therapeutic State*; Trattner, *From Poor Law to Welfare State: A History of Social Welfare in America*; and Kim Voss, *The Making of American Exceptionalism: The Knights of Labor and Class Formation in the Nineteenth Century* (Ithaca, NY: Cornell University Press, 1993).

9. William A. Corsaro, *The Sociology of Childhood* (Thousand Oaks, CA: Pine Forge Press, 1997); and Gordon, *Heroes of Their Own Lives*.

10. Trattner, *From Poor Law to Welfare State*, 111.

11. Gordon, *Heroes of Their Own Lives*; David Rosner and Gerald Markowitz, "Race, Foster Care, and the Politics of Abandonment in New York City," *American Journal of Public Health* 87, no. 11 (1997); and Trattner, *From Poor Law to Welfare State*.

12. Stephen O'Connor, *Orphan Trains: The Story of Charles Loring Brace and the Children He Saved and Failed* (New York: Haughton Mifflin, 2001).

13. Jeanne F. Cook, "A History of Placing-Out: The Orphan Trains," *Child Welfare* 74, no. 1 (1995), 182.

14. Ibid.

15. Ibid.

16. Charles Loring Brace, "Child Saving: The Children's Aid Society of New York. Its History, Plan, and Results," in *History of Child Saving in the United States; National Conference of Charities and Corrections; Report of the Committee on the History of Child-Saving Work to the Twentieth Conference, Chicago, June 1893*, ed. National Conference on Social Welfare, Committee on the History of Child-Saving Work (Montclair, NJ: Patterson Smith, 1971), 3.

17. For informative analyses of the policy of placing out, see Cook, "A History of Placing-Out;" O'Connor, *Orphan Trains*; and Trattner, *From Poor Law to Welfare State*.

18. Polsky, *The Rise of the Therapeutic State*. See, in particular, p. 32.

19. Mary Ann Mason, *From Father's Property to Children's Rights: The History of Child Custody in the United States* (New York: Columbia University Press, 1994); Polsky, *The Rise of the Therapeutic State*, 32.

20. Polsky, *The Rise of the Therapeutic State*, 32.

21. Ibid., 39.

22. Ibid.

23. Ibid., 40.

24. Lela B. Costin, "Cruelty to Children: A Dormant Issue and Its Rediscovery, 1920–1960," *Social Service Review* 66, no. 2 (1992), 180.

25. Gordon, *Heroes of Their Own Lives*; Mason, *From Father's Property to Children's Rights*; and Polsky, *The Rise of the Therapeutic State*.

26. Trattner, *From Poor Law to Welfare State*, 118.

27. Many explanations for the decline in placing out have been offered, including "the initiation of new ways of coping with industrialization, the recognition of environmental factors as the cause for some social problems, and the reforms of the Progressive Era, including compulsory school attendance and child labor laws" (Cook, "A History of Placing-Out," 185). Some states felt that juvenile delinquents were dumped in their states and passed laws requiring the CAS to post bonds to protect the state from future support or prohibited placement of "criminal, diseased, insane, or incorrigible children in their states" (Mason, *From Father's Property to Children's Rights*, 80). These changes may also have altered placement rates. In addition, charitable aid to single mothers and the emergence of social work as a profession, "which focused on new methods for working with impoverished children and families," have been offered as explanations for the decline (Cook, "A History of Placing-Out," 185).

28. Gordon, "Family Violence, Feminism, and Social Control," 179.

29. Mason, *From Father's Property to Children's Rights*, 88.

30. Tice, *Tales of Wayward Girls and Immoral Women*, 48.

31. Ibid, 48.

32. For a discussion of how the professionalization of social work reflected both efforts to create a collective institutional identity that marked them as different than their clients, as capable of managing a male ethos of dispassion in professional work, and as remaining feminine and willing to defer to male leadership, see Daniel J. Walkowitz, "The Making of a Feminine Professional Identity: Social Workers in the 1920s," *American Historical Review* 95, no. 4 (1990).

33. Linda Gordon, *Pitied, but Not Entitled: Single Mothers and the History of Welfare* (Cambridge, MA: Harvard University Press, 1994), 40.

34. Mason, *From Father's Property to Children's Rights*, 90.

35. Trattner, *From Poor Law to Welfare State*, 216.

36. Funds to Parents was initially passed in Illinois in 1911. By 1919, 39 states and the territories of Alaska and Hawaii had provisions to support children in their homes (Mason, *From Father's Property to Children's Rights*, 92).

37. Gwendolyn Mink, "The Lady and the Tramp: Gender, Race, and the Origins of the American Welfare State," in *Women, the State, and Welfare*, ed. Linda Gordon (Madison: University of Wisconsin, 1990), 109. See also Susan M. Sterett, *Public Pensions: Gender and Civic Service in the United States, 1850–1937* (Ithaca, NY: Cornell University Press, 2003) for a discussion of relative meanings of citizenship within the welfare state and the complexities that led to this pension program. See Mason, *From Father's Property to Children's Rights*, and Gordon, *Pitied, but Not Entitled*, for discussions of eligibility and discrimination within programs.

38. As of 1996, this program became Temporary Aid to Needy Families (TANF).

39. Patricia A. Schene, "Past, Present, and Future Roles of Child Protective Services," *Protecting Children from Abuse and Neglect* 8, no. 1 (1998), 27.

40. See Laura Frame, "Suitable Homes Revisited: An Historical Look at Child Protection and Welfare Reform," *Children and Youth Services Review* 21, no. 9–10 (1999), for a discussion of these entwined programs.

41. Mason, *From Father's Property to Children's Rights*, 93.

42. Ibid., 99.

43. Frame, "Suitable Homes Revisited," 722. Demie Kurz, "Women, Welfare, and Domestic Violence," in *Whose Welfare?*, ed. Gwendolyn Mink (Ithaca, NY: Cornell University Press, 1999), provides an important reminder of the role of welfare in aiding women who wish to leave marriages.

44. Gordon, *Heroes of Their Own Lives*.

45. Costin, "Cruelty to Children," 190.

46. Ibid., 193; for a discussion of the lack of public interest, see also Nelson, *Making an Issue of Child Abuse*.

47. Stephen J. Pfohl, "The 'Discovery' of Child Abuse," *Social Problems* 24 (1977).

48. Nelson, *Making an Issue of Child Abuse*, 45.

49. Pfohl, "The 'Discovery' of Child Abuse," 319.

50. Best, *Threatened Children*; Richard Gelles, *The Book of David: How Preserving Families Can Cost Children's Lives* (New York: Harper Collins, 1996); and Nelson, *Making an Issue of Child Abuse*.

51. Jill Duerr Berrick and Ruth Lawrence-Karski, "Emerging Issues in Child Welfare," *Public Welfare* 53, no. 4 (1995).

52. Nelson, *Making an Issue of Child Abuse*, 12.

53. Ibid., 107.

54. Ibid., 108.

55. Best, *Threatened Children*. Here Best discusses the rates of qualification for federal funds, though it is not clear when states created and supported child protection agencies. Mimi Abramovitz suggests that the 1967 amendments to the Social Security Act "strengthened the ability of welfare departments to remove children from the home." These amendments also articulated, for the first time since the Mother's Pension was created, that some children might be better off in foster homes or institutions than in their own homes (Abramovitz, *Regulating the Lives of Women*, 338). Andrew Polsky points to reorganizations in federal welfare bureaucracy that required states to separate their aid and service functions by 1972 as contributing to the modern organization of child protection. The result of these changes was the consolidation of "all those with casework skills, including assistance caseworkers and child protection personnel" being grouped together in a single office (Polsky, *The Rise of the Therapeutic State*, 193). Despite various federal legislative initiatives, CAPTA represents the clearest effort to both require and fund child protection.

56. Sociologist Joel Best suggests that while physicians tended to narrowly focus on the problem of physical abuse, child welfare professionals promoted a broader definition of child maltreatment: "battering had few defenders, [so] it offered a basis for consensus" and allowed for an expansion of meaning (Best, *Threatened Children*, 69). Child abuse evolved to include physical, sexual, emotional, and verbal abuse. In addition, child maltreatment came to include the damage caused by parents who withhold affection; fail to supervise children; belittle, criticize, or yell at their children; and those who fail to meet children's material needs.

57. In 1975, Title XX of the Social Security Act was passed, which provided states with funds to use for social services for low-income individuals. This act potentially could have allowed states to provide broad-based emergency funds and services to prevent out-of-home placements. However, funds were not used this way; by 1979, approximately 75 percent of "child welfare monies were devoted to foster care rather than to services to support or preserve families" (Schene, "Past, Present, and Future Roles of Child Protective Services," 29).

58. Gelles, *The Book of David*.

59. Congressional Quarterly Researcher, "Foster Care Reform" (Washington, DC: Congressional Quarterly, 1998), 14.

60. Goldstein, Freud, and Solnit, *Beyond the Best Interests of the Child* (New York: Free Press, 1973); Goldstein, Freud, and Solnit, *Before the Best Interests of the Child* (New York: Free Press, 1979); and Goldstein, Freud, and Solnit, *In the Best Interests of the Child: Professional Boundaries* (New York: Free Press, 1986).

61. As a result, the psychological parent rule can be used to argue against removing children from their parents and to argue for expanded rights for foster parents, including the right to keep a child in their care. The model suggests that if a child is not significantly bonded to their present caregiver, he or she will not be significantly damaged by having that relationship permanently severed. Therefore the child's best interest is not jeopardized through the termination of that relationship.

62. David E. Arredondo and Leonard P. Edwards, "Attachment, Bonding, and Reciprocal Connectedness: Limitations of Attachment Theory in the Juvenile and Family Court," *Journal of the Center for Families, Children and the Courts* 2, no. 1 (2000); and Jennifer Ayres Hand, "Note: Preventing Undue Terminations: A Critical Evaluation of the Length-of-Time-out-of-Custody Ground for Termination of Parental Rights," *New York University Law Review* 71, no. 5 (1996).

63. Sandra T. Azar and Corina L. Benjet, "A Cognitive Perspective on Ethnicity, Race, and Termination of Parental Rights," *Law and Human Behavior* 18, no. 3 (1994); and Tiffany Field, "Attachment and Separation in Young Children," *Annual Review of Psychology* 47, no. 1 (1996), 542.

64. Arredondo and Edwards, "Attachment, Bonding, and Reciprocal Connectedness;" and Sandra T. Azar et al., "Child Maltreatment and Termination of Parental Rights: Can Behavioral Research Help Solomon?," *Behavior Therapy* 26, no. 4 (1995).

65. Arredondo and Edwards, "Attachment, Bonding, and Reciprocal Connectedness," 113.

66. Joyce Ladner, *Mixed Families: Adopting Across Racial Boundaries* (New York: Anchor Press/Doubleday, 1977); and Rickie Solinger, "Race and 'Value': Black and White Illegitimate Babies, 1945–1965," in *Feminist Frontiers IV*, eds. Laurel Richardson, Verta Taylor, and Nancy Whittier (New York: McGraw-Hill, 1997).

67. Quoted in Arnold Silverman, "Outcomes of Transracial Adoption," in *The Future of Children: Adoption*, ed. Center for the Future of Children (Palo Alto, CA: The David and Lucile Packard Foundation, 1993), 106.

68. Leslie Doty Hollingsworth, "Symbolic Interactionism, African American Families, and the Transracial Adoption Controversy," *Social Work* 44, no. 5 (1999).

69. See www.cwla.org for their organizational mission.

70. Major W. Cox, "Make Adoption Policies Colorblind," *Montgomery Advertiser*, January 13, 1994.

71. *Miller v. Youakim*, 44 U.S. 125, 99 S. Ct. 957 (1979).

72. Jill Duerr Berrick, Barbara Needell, and Meredith Minkler, "The Policy Implications of Welfare Reform for Older Caregivers, Kinship Care, and Family Configuration," *Children and Youth Services Review* 21, no. 9/10 (1999).

73. Shelley Waters Boots and Rob Geen, "Family Care or Foster Care? How State Policies Affect Kinship Caregivers," (Washington, DC: Urban Institute, 2001).

74. Under ICWA (P.L. 95-608), child welfare agencies must identify American Indian children, including the child's tribal ancestry and relationship to one or more federally recognized tribes and then notify the child's tribe and the Indian parent or custodian of any scheduled court proceedings that could result in the child being placed out-of-home or in the termination of an American Indian parent's legal rights. If the tribal membership is not known, the court must give notice to the Bureau of Indian Affairs. See Kathy Barbell and Madelyn Freundlich, *Foster Care Today* (Casey Family Programs National Center for Resource Family Support, 2001); available at http://www.casey.org/cnc/policy_issues/foster_care_today.htm#IndianChildWelfare. For a discussion of the law itself, see Theodore J. Stein, *Child Welfare and the Law*, rev. ed. (Washington, DC: CWLA Press, 1998).

75. Adoption Assistance and Child Welfare Act of 1980, P.L. 96-272 (June 17, 1980).

76. In the class action suit *Suter v. Artist M. et al* (1992), parents alleged that the Illinois Department of Children and Family Services had failed to make reasonable efforts to reunify them with their children. In this case, the U.S. Supreme Court ruled that the AACWA requires states to submit a plan with certain criteria to the Secretary of Health and Human Services for approval. However, the court ruled that the law does not "contain any guidance for how to measure 'reasonable efforts'" and therefore cannot be enforced, except by the Department of Health and Human Services (DHHS), in terms of adherence to the submitted plan (503 U.S. 347, 112 S. Ct. 1360).

77. Jane L. Ross, Director, Income Security Issues, Health, Education, and Human Services Division, testified to Congress that the foster care population increased dramatically between 1985 and 1995, with parental substance abuse involved in a large number of cases." See "Parental Substance Abuse: Implications for Children, the Child Welfare System, and Foster Care Outcomes," GAO/T-HEHS-98-40 (Washington, DC: General Accounting Office, 1997), 5.

78. Most authors identify 1986 as the start of the crack epidemic. See Douglas Besharov and Karen Baehler, "Introduction," in *When Drug Addicts Have Children: Reorienting Child Welfare's Response*, ed. Douglas J. Besharov (Washington, DC: Child Welfare

League of America, 1994); and Craig Reinarman and Harry G. Levine, "Crack in Context: America's Latest Demon Drug," in *Crack in America: Demon Drugs and Social Justice*, eds. Craig Reinarman and Harry G. Levine (Berkeley: University of California Press, 1997).

79. Reinarman and Levine, "Crack in Context," 1.

80. As an example of this rhetoric, the description by two social welfare scholars in the preface of their book notes, "Since 1986, when crack cocaine first hit inner-city streets, drug use has become a fixture in the lives of many low-income families and in the neighborhoods where they live. Each night brings new stories of crime and senseless violence. Less visible, but just as serious, is the abuse and neglect of children caused by parental drug addiction. More than alcohol, and more than heroin, crack cocaine threatens the well-being of hundreds of thousands of children, especially African-American children" (Besharov and Baehler, "Introduction," ix).

81. Amanda Noble et al., "Gender Issues in California's Perinatal Substance Abuse Policy," *Contemporary Drug Problems* 27, no. 1 (2000), 79.

82. Laura E. Gomez, *Misconceiving Mothers: Legislators, Prosecutors, and the Politics of Prenatal Drug Exposure* (Philadelphia: Temple University Press, 1997), 14. Here Gomez provides an excellent discussion of the frames that were used to create a public policy response to crack use, particularly when used by women.

83. Ibid., 3.

84. Rosalind Pollack Petchesky, *Abortion and Woman's Choice: The State, Sexuality, and Reproductive Freedom* (Boston: Northeastern University Press, 1990), xiii.

85. For examples of the medical effects described, see Ira J. Chasnoff et al., "Temporal Patterns of Cocaine Use in Pregnancy: Perinatal Outcome," *JAMA, Journal of the American Medical Association* 261, no. 12 (1989); and Barry Zuckerman, "Effects on Parents and Children," in *When Drug Addicts Have Children*, ed. Douglas J. Besharov (Washington, DC: Child Welfare League of America, 1994).

86. Loren Siegel, "The Pregnancy Police Fight the War on Drugs," in *Crack in America: Demon Drugs and Social Justice*, eds. Craig Reinarman and Harry G. Levine (Berkeley: University of California Press, 1997), 255. The actual impact of crack cocaine remains unclear. Although it is clear that amphetamine and cocaine use during pregnancy leads to increased risk of miscarriage, preterm birth, and low birth weight, the longer-term effects of perinatal substance use have been acknowledged to have been initially overestimated. As A. C. Vidaeff and J. M. Mastrobattista suggest, "Fetal cocaine exposure has proven to be an area of medicine that has generated more heat than light. Although many reports associate cocaine with a variety of isolated structural anomalies, there is no detectable syndromic clustering, raising doubts about a real causal association or a specific teratogenic action" ("In Utero Cocaine Exposure: A Thorny Mix of Science and Mythology," *American Journal of Perinatology* 20, no. 4 (2003), 165). In addition, it is difficult to separate out the effects of drugs from those of other substances known to cause negative fetal outcomes, including alcohol and cigarette smoke (C. A. Chiriboga, "Fetal Alcohol and Drug Effects," *Neurologist* 9, no. 6 (2003)). Vidaeff and Mastrobattista suggest that what is needed are "innovative approaches to assure that the myths conjured up about 'crack babies' are replaced with reliable, high-quality scientific data" ("In Utero Cocaine Exposure", 165).

87. Gomez, *Misconceiving Mothers*, 22. See also Vidaeff and Mastrobattista, "In Utero Cocaine Exposure."

88. An editorial in the *Journal of the American Medical Association* by Ira J. Chasnoff, one of the first researchers to identify the medical conditions affecting crack-exposed babies, advocated early intervention in pregnant addicts' lives, epitomizing this sentiment. Ira J. Chasnoff, "Drugs, Alcohol, Pregnancy, and the Neonate: Pay Now or Pay Later," *JAMA, Journal of the American Medical Association* 266, no. 11 (1991). Laura

Gomez (*Misconceiving Mothers*) compellingly argues that the relationship between fetal protection and child abuse became blurred.

89. Amanda Noble, "Law, Medicine, and Women's Bodies: The Social Control of Pregnant Drug Users" (PhD dissertation, University of California, Davis, 1992). Noble provides an informative discussion of how these laws were implemented and used.

90. Lynn M. Paltrow, "Criminal Prosecution Against Pregnant Women: National Update and Overview" (American Civil Liberties Union Reproductive Freedom Project, 1992).

91. Center for Reproductive Law and Policy, "Punishing Women for Their Behavior During Pregnancy" (New York: Center for Reproductive Law and Policy, 2000).

92. Ira J. Chasnoff, Harvey J. Landress, and Mark E. Barrett, "The Prevalence of Illicit-Drug or Alcohol Use During Pregnancy and Discrepancies in Mandatory Reporting in Pinellas County, Florida," *New England Journal of Medicine* 322, no. 17 (1990).

93. Center for Reproductive Law and Policy, "Punishing Women for Their Behavior During Pregnancy." Center for Reproductive Law and Policy, "U.S. Supreme Court Affirms Right to Confidential Medical Care," *CRLP Press*, March 21 (2001).

94. For a discussion of what problems this law aimed to address, how it was developed, and how it has been implemented differently in different counties with mixed results, see Vicky Albert, "Identifying Substance Abusing Delivering Women: Consequences for Child Maltreatment Reports," *Child Abuse & Neglect* 24, no. 2 (2000). See also Center for Reproductive Law and Policy, "Punishing Women for Their Behavior During Pregnancy"; Gomez, *Misconceiving Mothers*; and Noble et al., "Gender Issues in California's Perinatal Substance Abuse Policy."

95. Abandoned Infants Assistance Act, P.L. 100-505 (October 18, 1988).

96. Ryan White, a hemophiliac who received blood products as part of his treatment, was thirteen- years old in 1984 when he was told he had contracted human immuno-deficiency virus (HIV). His battle to remain in school and to destigmatize AIDS were nationally known and resulted in several television movies, public benefits, various charities, public education campaigns, and federal funding for carework. See David L. Kirp, *Learning by Heart: AIDS and Schoolchildren in America's Communities* (New Brunswick, NJ: Rutgers University Press, 1990).

97. National Clearinghouse on Child Abuse and Neglect, "Foster Care National Statistics: April 2001" (Fairfax, VA: National Clearinghouse on Child Abuse and Neglect, 2001).

98. Jill Smolowe, "Adoption in Black and White: An Odd Coalition Takes Aim at the Decades-Old Prejudice Against Transracial Placements," *Time*, August 14 (1995), 50.

99. Brooks et al., "Adoption and Race: Implementing the Multiethnic Placement Act and the Interethnic Adoption Provisions," *Social Work* 44, no. 2 (1999), 169.

100. *Congressional Record* 4726–4727. By March 28, 1995, the bill had been read twice and referred to the Committee on Finance, where it remained. (104th Congress; 1st session, 104s. 637.)

101. The original bill was the Family Educational Rights and Privacy Act, P.L. 103-382 (42 USC 622). On August 20, 1996, President Clinton signed the Small Business Job Protection Act of 1996 (P.L. 104-188). Section 1808 of the act is entitled "Removal of Barriers to Interethnic Adoption." According to a DHHS statement, "The section affirms and strengthens the prohibition against discrimination in adoption or foster care placements." This amendment creates a requirement that states adopt plans for compliance and delineates penalties for noncompliance applicable to both states and adoption agencies. In addition, it repeals Section 553 of MEPA, which in essence removes the language that allowed "permissible consideration," a provision that had allowed federally funded agencies to consider the cultural, ethnic, or racial background of the child and the capacity of the prospective foster or adoptive parents to

meet the needs of a child as one of a number of factors used to determine the best interests of a child. The Office of Civil Rights was also brought in to help with enforcement. For a discussion of the law, see also Joan Heifetz Hollinger, "A Guide to the Multiethnic Placement Act of 1994, as Amended by the Interethnic Adoption Provisions of 1996" (Washington, DC: American Bar Association Center on Children and the Law, National Resource Center on Legal and Court Issues, 1998).

102. "Testimony on the Final Rule on Federal Monitoring of State Child Welfare Programs by Olivia A. Golden, Assistant Secretary for Children and Families, U.S. Department of Health and Human Services," February 17, 2000 (Washington, DC: Department of Health and Human Services). Accessed online at http://www.hhs.gov/asl/testify/t000217b.html.

103. 929 F. Supp. 662, 670 (S.D.N.Y. 1996).

104. This clarified a 1989 case, *DeShaney v. Winnebago County Dept. of Social Services* (489 U.S. 189; 109 S. Ct. 998; 103 L. Ed. 2d 249), in which a mother unsuccessfully sued a child protection services agency for not intervening before her son's father beat him so badly that he was left retarded. In that case, the U.S. Supreme Court did not find the state to be at fault.

105. 929 F. Supp. 662, 676 (S.D.N.Y. 1996).

106. Bill Clinton, "The President's Radio Address" (Weekly Compilation of Presidential Documents, 1996), 2513.

107. According to a June 30, 1995, speech by Joseph Kennedy II, introducing the Adoptions Incentives Act of 1995, 180 of the Fortune 1000 companies at the time had established corporate programs to financially assist employees who were adopting children to help cover adoption-related expenses. Kennedy, "Introduction of the Adoption Incentives Act of 1995," *Congressional Record* 141, E1383 (1995).

108. Camp-Kennelly Adoption Promotion Act of 1997, H.R. 867 (January 7, 1997).

109. Adoption and Safe Families Act of 1997, P.L. 105-89 (November 19, 1997).

110. Jill Duerr Berrick et al., *The Tender Years: Toward Developmentally-Sensitive Child Welfare Services for Very Young Children* (Oxford: Oxford University Press, 1998). Here they argue that if parents do not begin efforts to reunify within the first six months, they are less likely to reunify than those who do, making such a law seem reasonable.

111. DHHS, "Adoption Excellence Award Recommendations for the Year 2001" (Washington, DC: Administration for Children and Families, 2001); DHHS, "HHS Awards Adoption Bonuses," *HHS News*, September 10 (2001).

112. DHHS, "Adoptions of Children with Public Child Welfare Agency Involvement by State" (Washington, DC: Children's Bureau, 2001).

113. PACE, "Remember the Children: Mothers Balance Work and Child Care Under Welfare Reform" (Berkeley, CA: Graduate School of Education-PACE, 2000).

114. Theda Skocpol, *Protecting Soldiers and Mothers: The Political Origins of Social Policy in the United States* (Boston: Harvard University Press, 1992), 538.

115. See Barbara Bennett Woodhouse, "Making Poor Mothers Fungible: The Privitization of Foster Care," in *Child Care and Inequality: Re-Thinking Carework for Children and Youth*, eds. Francesca M. Cancian et al. (New York: Routledge, 2002).

Chapter 3

1. Keith N. Richards, *Tender Mercies: Inside the World of a Child Abuse Investigator*, rev. ed. (Washington, DC: Child Welfare League of America, 1998), 2.

2. Ronit D. Leichtentritt, Bilha Davidson-Arad, and Yochanan Wozner, "The Social Work Mission and Its Implementation in the Socialization Process: First- and Second-Year Students' Perspectives," *Social Work Education* 21, no. 6 (2002); and

Rachel Mathias-Williams and Nigel Thomas, "Great Expectations? The Career Aspirations of Social Work Students," *Social Work Education* 21, no. 4 (2002).

3. Dorothy Roberts, *Shattered Bonds: The Color of Child Welfare* (New York: Basic Civitas Books, 2002), 74.

4. DHHS, "Better Outcomes for Children—the Child and Family Services Reviews," (Children's Bureau, Department of Health and Human Services, 2000) Accessed on-line, pages unavailable.

5. DYFS is an acronym for Department of Youth and Family Services, the child protection agency in New Jersey. First quote is from Richard Lezin Jones, "Report Says 13 of Child Agency's Cases Died of Abuse or Neglect," *New York Times*, February 12, 2003; second quote is from Tina Kelley and Leslie Kaufman, "McGreevey Plan Would Help Agencies Protect Children," *New York Times*, February 3, 2003.

6. *Calabretta v. Floyd*, 189 F.3d 808, 28–29 (9th Cir. 1999).

7. Michael S. Wilkes and Richard L. Kravitz, "Medical Researchers and the Media: Attitudes Toward Public Dissemination of Research," *JAMA, Journal of the American Medical Association* 268, no. 8 (1992), 999.

8. Daniel J. Walkowitz, "The Making of a Feminine Professional Identity: Social Workers in the 1920s," *American Historical Review* 95, no. 4 (1990). Walkowitz offers a useful discussion of the negative ways in which early social work was represented in the popular press. He argues that efforts to professionalize social work inspired representations of social workers in popular fiction as unfeeling and hardened, having lost the ability to nurture. Citing Sinclair Lewis' 1933 book, *Ann Vickers*, he quotes, "Rather than the nurturing expected of Good Mothers, she finds twentieth century charity obsessed with record keeping and puritanical notions of need" (pp. 1068–9). Embedded in these representations is disdain for social work's professionalization (in terms of the payment of salaries that replaced volunteer work and the adherence to specialized knowledge) and bureaucratization (in terms of consistent procedures) because of its toll on femininity.

9. For a sample article about Rilya Wilson, see Dana Canedy, "Case of Lost Miami Girl Puts Focus on an Agency," *New York Times*, May 3, 2002. The Toogood case is discussed in a press release from the St. Joseph County Prosecutor's Office in "Toogood Pleads Guilty" (February 14, 2003).

10. Paul Brownfield, "A Comic in Trouble, an Image Rewritten: No Matter How the Paula Poundstone Case Turns out, One Thing Is for Sure: Thanks to a Scandal-Hungry Media, the Comedian's Life, and Career, Will Never Be the Same," *Los Angeles Times*, July 10, 2001.

11. Ken Baker, "I Want My Kids Back: Fighting Child-Sex Charges and Alcoholism, Comedian Paula Poundstone Is out to Clear Her Name and Reunite Her Family," *US Weekly*, July 23, 336, 54–55, 2001.

12. "Covering Child Abuse (Report on the Conference on 'Rethinking the Blame Game: New Approaches to Covering Child Abuse')," *American Journalism Review*, September 1997, S2.

13. John Hubner and Jill Wolfson, *Somebody Else's Children: The Courts, the Kids, and the Struggle to Save America's Troubled Families* (New York: Crown Publishers, 1996), xiii.

14. I was able to gain a similar court order to secure access for this research, although confidentiality issues are different as I have changed all identifying information in a way journalists typically do not.

15. Ashe and Cahn, "Child Abuse: A Problem for Feminist Theory," in *The Public Nature of Private Violence: The Discovery of Domestic Abuse*, eds. Martha A. Fineman and Roxanne Mykitiuk (New York: Routledge, 1994), 190.

16. Maxwell Bloomfield quoted in Eileen Boris and Peter Bardaglio, "The Transformation of Patriarchy: The Historic Role of the State," in *Families, Politics, and Public*

Policy: A Feminist Dialogue on Women and the State, ed. Irene Diamond (New York: Longman, 1983), 83.

17. Focus on the Family, "Focus on the Family Defends Parents' Right to Discipline," http://www.family.org/welcome/press/a0021264.cfm; and Pacific Justice Institute, "Parents' Rights to Discipline in California," http://www.pacificjustice.org/resources/articles/focus.cfm?ID=ART750858607.

18. Susan Weinger, *Security Risk: Preventing Client Violence Against Social Workers* (Washington, DC: NASW Press, 2001).

19. NASW, "Safety Guidelines" (Boston: NASW, Committee for the Study and Prevention of Violence Against Social Workers, 1996), 1.

20. Christina E. Newhill, "Client Violence Toward Social Workers: A Practice and Policy Concern for the 1990's," *Social Work* 40, no. 5 (1995); and Lucy Rey, "What Social Workers Need to Know About Client Violence," *Families in Society* 77, no. 1 (1996).

21. Grant Macdonald and Frank Sirotich, "Reporting Client Violence," *Social Work* 46, no. 2 (2001); and Rey, "What Social Workers Need to Know About Client Violence." Both studies point to the difficulties in measuring such incidents. Percentages reported are rounded to the nearest whole number.

22. Charles Horejsi, Cindy Garthwait, and Jim Rolando, "A Survey of Threats and Violence Directed Against Child Protection Workers in a Rural State," *Child Welfare* 73, no. 2 (1994).

23. Richard E. Sykes and John P. Clark, "A Theory of Deference Exchange in Police-Civilian Encounters," *American Journal of Sociology* 81, no. 3 (1975), 584.

24. For a discussion of issues relating to performing fieldwork while pregnant, see the appendix of this work and Jennifer A. Reich, "Pregnant with Possibility: Reflections on Embodiment, Access, and Inclusion in Field Research," *Qualitative Sociology* 26, no. 3 (2003).

25. See *Calabretta v. Floyd*, 189 F.3d 808 (9th Cir. 1999).

26. Kelley O. Beaucar, "State Bill Would Protect Caseworkers: Two Workers Would Go on Potentially Dangerous Home Visits," *NASW News*, February 2000.

27. Typical charges include child endangerment and weapons or drug possession charges. Police will also sometimes intervene when parents have outstanding warrants.

28. Beaucar, "State Bill Would Protect Caseworkers."

29. These time frames are likely California-specific and may be different in other localities.

30. Michael Lipsky, *Street-Level Bureaucracy: Dilemmas of the Individual in Public Services* (New York: Russell Sage Foundation, 1980), xii.

31. Thomas D. Morton and Marsha K. Salus, "Supervising Child Protective Services Caseworkers: Increasing Job Satisfaction and Preventing Burnout" (Rockville, MD: Department of Health and Human Services, Administration for Children and Families, Administration on Children, Youth, and Families, National Center on Child Abuse and Neglect, 1994) accessed on-line. Pages unavailable.

32. Walter Trattner, *From Poor Law to Welfare State: A History of Social Welfare in America*, 5th ed. (New York: Free Press, 1994), 258.

33. Walkowitz, "The Making of a Feminine Professional Identity," points to the ways in which female social workers were poorly paid "because of the presumption female staff had men to support them" (p. 1070) and struggled to shape the profession as one deserving respect while also striving to maintain something uniquely woman-like about their work. In my own research, I observed an office where the office director and unit supervisors were women, as were about half of the social workers. Of the men I observed, most were men of color. The one white man I followed in my research was gay, and thus faced limits in his own access to systems of hegemonic masculine privilege. See Appendix I for a more detailed discussion of my data collection and observations.

34.   NASW, "Code of Ethics of the National Association of Social Workers," http://www.naswdc.org/pubs/code/code.asp.

Chapter 4

1.   Laws requiring these professionals to report "knowledge of or a reasonable cause to believe a child is being neglected or physically or sexually abused" were passed by all fifty states by 1968. The development of these policies is discussed at length in chapter 2.

2.   Time limits also vary by agency. According to the Children's Bureau, "most States have established time standards for initiating the investigation of reports and monitor whether the investigations commence within the priority time standards required. High-priority reports usually require an immediate response from CPS (within 3 to 24 hours). Reports not considered high priority are classified as needing a response from within a few days to within a few weeks." Based on data from twenty states, the average response time from report to investigation in 2000 was fifty-four hours. DHHS, "Child Maltreatment 2001" (Washington, DC: Department of Health and Human Services, Administration on Children, Youth and Families, 2003).

3.   Reports may not be investigated if the victim is older than the age specified in state law, if the reporter provides insufficient or incomplete information, or state law does not cover the allegation made. Theodore J. Stein, *Child Welfare and the Law*, rev. ed. (Washington, DC: CWLA Press, 1998).

4.   According to DHHS, in 2001, CPS agencies nationwide received about 2.7 million referrals concerning approximately 5 million children. Of those reports, about 32.7 percent (an estimated 870,000) were screened out. This was less than in 2000, when 38.3 percent of referrals, or 1,070,000 reports, were screened out. Stated in reverse, the agencies "screened in"—or chose to investigate—67.3 percent (an estimated 1,789,000) of referrals (compared to 61.7 percent or 1,726,000 in 2000). The rate of screened-out referrals per 1000 children in the population was 11.9 (compared to 14.8 in 2000), while the rate of screened-in referrals was 24.7 (compared to 23.9 in 2000). DHHS, "Child Maltreatment 2001." Of the 9,485,676 children age 0 to 17 years in California, 544,739 had a child abuse referral in 2002 (57.4 children per 1000), and 115,600 (or 20 percent) of these children had their referral substantiated (12.2 children per 1,000). Referrals were ruled inconclusive 21 percent of the time and were ruled unfounded in 29 percent of the cases. Barbara Needell et al., *Child Welfare Services Reports for California* (University of California at Berkeley Center for Social Services Research, 2004).

5.   DHHS, "Child Maltreatment 2001." DHHS, "Child Welfare Outcomes 1999: Annual Report" (Washington, DC: U.S. Department of Health and Human Services, Administration for Children and Families, Administration on Children, Youth and Families, and the Children's Bureau, 2001).

6.   The three most common sources of reports were education personnel (16.2 percent), legal or law enforcement personnel (15.6 percent), and social services personnel (15.1 percent). According to DHHS, sources of reports from nonmandated reporters include parents, other relatives, friends and neighbors, alleged victims, alleged perpetrators, anonymous callers, and other sources not categorized. "Anonymous or unknown" and "other" report sources accounted for the largest number of reports in the nonprofessional category at 13.7 and 8.9 percent, respectively. The number of reports made by nonprofessional sources decreased three percentage points from 1997 to 2001, with a concomitant increase in professional sources. (DHHS, "Child Maltreatment 2001.")

7.   Dorothy Roberts, *Shattered Bonds: The Color of Child Welfare* (New York: Basic Civitas Books, 2002), 75.

8. Joel Best, *Threatened Children: Rhetoric and Concern About Child-Victims* (Chicago: University of Chicago Press, 1990), 5.

9. Penal Code § 11174.3(a) states that "whenever a representative of a government agency investigating suspected child abuse or neglect or the State Department of Social Services deems it necessary, a suspected victim of child abuse or neglect may be interviewed during school hours, on school premises, concerning a report of suspected child abuse or neglect that occurred within the child's home or out-of-home care facility."

10. Roberts, *Shattered Bonds*. She offers a useful discussion of community experiences with child welfare agents. See most particularly chapter 5.

11. Although teachers are mandated reporters, many may not decide that their students are in danger until they have had substantial contact with them. Teachers also strategize when to report maltreatment. Child welfare work is not evenly distributed throughout the year, both in terms of the seasonality of investigation and because workers are busier sending children home during the summer months. Vicky N. Albert and Richard P. Barth, "Predicting Growth in Child Abuse and Neglect Reports in Urban, Suburban and Rural Counties," *Social Service Review* 71, no. 1 (1996); and Richard P. Barth, Mark E. Courtney, and Vicky N. Albert, *From Child Abuse to Permanency Planning: Child Welfare Services Pathways and Placements* (New York: Aldine de Gruyter, 1994).

12. Bilha Davidson Arad, "Parental Features and Quality of Life in the Decision to Remove Children at Risk from Home," *Child Abuse & Neglect* 25, no. 1 (2001).

13. See Aron Shlonsky and Eileen Gambrill, "The Assessment and Management of Risk in Child Welfare Services," *Children and Youth Services Review* 23, no. 1 (2001) and the accompanying special issue of *Children and Youth Services Review* on risk assessment in child welfare. See also Scottye J. Cash, "Risk Assessment in Child Welfare: The Art and Science," *Children and Youth Services Review* 23, no. 11 (2001); Eileen Gambrill and Aron Shlonsky, "Risk Assessment in Context," *Children and Youth Services Review* 22, no. 11–12 (2000); Julia Krane and Linda Davies, "Mothering and Child Protection Practice: Rethinking Risk Assessment," *Child & Family Social Work* 5, no. 1 (2000); Alan W. Leschied et al., "The Empirical Basis of Risk Assessment in Child Welfare: The Accuracy of Risk Assessment and Clinical Judgment," *Child Welfare* 82, no. 5 (2003); Charles Gene Lyle and Elliott Graham, "Looks Can Be Deceiving: Using a Risk Assessment Instrument to Evaluate the Outcomes of Child Protection Services," *Children and Youth Services Review* 22, no. 11–12 (2000); and Joe Warner, "An Initial Assessment of the Extent to Which Risk Factors, Frequently Identified in Research, Are Taken into Account When Assessing Risk in Child Protection Cases," *Journal of Social Work* 3, no. 3 (2003).

14. Walter Trattner, *From Poor Law to Welfare State: A History of Social Welfare in America*, 5th ed. (New York: Free Press, 1994), 94.

15. Chapter 2 provides a discussion of this legal mandate and the policy issues surrounding it.

16. SB 2669, California legislation that requires drug testing was passed without funding. As a result, counties have implemented the law in varying ways. In 1992 and 1994, the effectiveness of the implementation of SB 2669 was evaluated. In 1992, 34 of 49 counties surveyed had developed protocols; however, the majority of counties reported that the implementation of protocols by hospitals was inconsistent. Reasons cited included a lack of funds, liability concerns, and resistance among private physicians whose clientele are primarily white and middle class. In 1994, hospital perinatal nurse managers and county social and health services personnel were surveyed. The follow-up study again found inconsistent utilization of protocols. Although 69 percent of the responding counties had protocols that would identify perinatal substance

exposure, only 33 percent of the counties indicated their hospitals routinely followed the protocol guidelines. In addition, 50 percent of hospital nurse-managers believed that substance abuse treatment resources were not available for women giving birth in their communities. In addition, the study indicated that screening and assessment is more thorough and consistent in public hospitals than in private hospitals. California Department of Alcohol and Drug Programs, "Substance-Exposed Infants (Senate Bill 2669) Fact Sheet" (Sacramento: California Department of Alcohol and Drug Programs, 2001).

17. Laura E. Gomez, *Misconceiving Mothers: Legislators, Prosecutors, and the Politics of Prenatal Drug Exposure* (Philadelphia: Temple University Press, 1997).

18. See Sentencing Project (www.sentencingproject.org). See also Tracy Snell and Danielle Morton, "Women in Prison: Survey of State Prison Inmates, 1991" (Washington DC: Bureau of Justice Statistics, 1994).

19. Angela Davis, "Race and Criminalization: Black Americans and the Punishment Industry," in *The House That Race Built*, ed. Waheema Lubiano (New York: Vintage Books, 1998), 275.

20. As of 2004, CRACK (Children Requiring a Caring Kommunity) was renamed "Project Prevention: Children Requiring a Caring Community." The tone of the rhetoric, which in its latest incarnation refers to empowering drug addicts, has changed, but the program remains the same.

21. DHHS, "Blending Perspectives and Building Common Ground: A Report to Congress on Substance Abuse and Child Protection" (Washington, DC: Department of Health and Human Services, 1999).

22. Amanda Noble et al., "Gender Issues in California's Perinatal Substance Abuse Policy," *Contemporary Drug Problems* 27, no. 1 (2000).

23. The county I studied did not prosecute for perinatal substance use. However, other locales have attempted such prosecutions. These attempts, resulting in U.S. Supreme Court review, shape perceptions of drug-using mothers nationwide and affect state responses in subtle ways. See note 24 for examples of such prosecutions and policies.

24. ACLU, "Coercive and Punitive Governmental Responses to Women's Conduct During Pregnancy" (American Civil Liberties Union, 1997); Angela Bonavoglia, "The Ordeal of Pamela Rae Stewart," *Ms Magazine*, July/August 1987; and Center for Reproductive Law and Policy, "Punishing Women for Their Behavior During Pregnancy" (New York: Center for Reproductive Law and Policy, 2000).

25. Melissa Pelletier, "U.S. Parents Want Help with Newborns: Lack of Experience and Skill Seen as Reason for Increased Child Abuse and Neglect," press release (Washington, DC: Prevent Child Abuse America, 1999), 1.

26. There is a huge body of literature examining the relationship between alcohol and familial demise, with a large focus on violence. For example, see Mogens Nygaard Christoffersen and Keith Soothill, "The Long-Term Consequences of Parental Alcohol Abuse: A Cohort Study of Children in Denmark," *Journal of Substance Abuse Treatment* 25, no. 2 (2003); Linda Gordon, *Heroes of Their Own Lives* (New York: Penguin Books, 1988); Bente Storm Mowat Haugland, "Paternal Alcohol Abuse: Relationship Between Child Adjustment, Parental Characteristics, and Family Functioning," *Child Psychiatry & Human Development* 34, no. 2 (2003); and Maria Testa, Brian M. Quigley, and Kenneth E. Leonard, "Does Alcohol Make a Difference? Within-Participants Comparison of Incidents of Partner Violence," *Journal of Interpersonal Violence* 18, no. 7 (2003).

27. This is discussed in greater detail in chapter 5.

28. Andrew J. Polsky, *The Rise of the Therapeutic State* (Princeton, NJ: Princeton University Press, 1991), 4.

29. Quoted in Richard E. Sykes and John P. Clark, "A Theory of Deference Exchange in Police-Civilian Encounters," *American Journal of Sociology* 81, no. 3 (1975), 588–89.

30. Several urban ethnographies or detailed explorations of the experiences of poor people of color with the police demonstrate the lack of police and legal justice available. For a few excellent examples, see Elijah Anderson, *Code of the Street: Decency, Violence and the Moral Life of the Inner City* (New York: W.W. Norton & Co., 2000); Daniel Dohan, *The Price of Poverty: Money, Work, and Culture in the Mexican American Barrio* (Berkeley: University of California Press, 2003); and Roberts, *Shattered Bonds*.

31. For a discussion of this issue, see the Introduction of this book and Ann Futterman Collier et al., "Culture-Specific Views of Child Maltreatment and Parenting Styles in a Pacific-Island Community," *Child Abuse & Neglect* 23, no. 3 (1999); David Gough, "Defining the Problem," *Child Abuse & Neglect* 20, no. 11 (1996), 993; Jill E. Korbin et al., "Neighborhood Views on the Definition and Etiology of Child Maltreatment," *Child Abuse & Neglect* 24, no. 12 (2000); Susan J. Rose, "Reaching Consensus on Child Neglect: African American Mothers and Child Welfare Workers," *Children and Youth Services Review* 21, no. 6 (1999); and Susan J. Rose and William Meezan, "Variations in Perceptions of Child Neglect," *Child Welfare* 75, no. 2 (1996). For a discussion of the role of workers' perceptions of future quality of life, see Bilha Davidson Arad, "Predicted Changes in Children's Quality of Life in Decisions Regarding the Removal of Children at Risk from Their Homes," *Children and Youth Services Review* 23, no. 2 (2001).

32. For the role of motivation to change, see C.F. Alter, "Decision-Making Factors in Cases of Child Neglect," *Child Welfare* 64, no. 2 (1985). For cooperation with social workers, see Sandra T. Azar and Corina L. Benjet, "A Cognitive Perspective on Ethnicity, Race, and Termination of Parental Rights," *Law and Human Behavior* 18, no. 3 (1994); B.Y. Meddin, "Criteria for Placement Decision in Protective Services," *Child Welfare* 63, no. 4 (1984); and M. Shapira and R. Benbenisty, "Modeling Judgments and Decisions in Cases of Alleged Child Abuse and Neglect," *Social Work Research and Abstracts* 29, no. 2 (1993). See Michael Lipsky, *Street-Level Bureaucracy: Dilemmas of the Individual in Public Services* (New York: Russell Sage Foundation, 1980) for a discussion of how social workers and other street-level bureaucrats interpret and enact their work.

33. Anderson, *Code of the Street*, 33 and 34.

34. Meanings of motherhood are different for women of different racial, ethnic, and class positions. For examples of this issue, see Patricia Hill Collins, *Black Feminist Thought: Knowledge, Consciousness, and the Politics of Empowerment* (New York: Routledge, 1991); and Annette Lareau, *Unequal Childhoods: Class, Race, and Family Life* (Berkeley: University of California Press, 2003).

35. Pacific Justice Institute, "When Child Protective Services Calls" (Pacific Justice Institute, 2002), http://www.pacificjustice.org/resources/articles/focus.cfm?ID=ART513510669.

36. Candace told me who her physician was. I am the source of the information that he is a national expert who has written pediatric textbook chapters on management of near-drowning victims.

37. Sykes and Clark, "A Theory of Deference Exchange in Police-Civilian Encounters," 589.

38. Joe Feagin, "Changing Patterns of Racial Discrimination? The Continuing Significance of Race: Anti-Black Discrimination in Public Places," *American Sociological Review* 56, no. 1 (1991), 115.

39. Elijah Anderson, *Streetwise: Race, Class, and Change in an Urban Community* (Chicago: University of Chicago Press, 1990); Mark D. Jacobs, *Screwing the System and Making*

It Work: Juvenile Justice in the No-Fault Society (Chicago: University of Chicago Press, 1990); and Max Weber, "Bureaucracy," in *From Max Weber: Essays in Sociology*, eds. H.H. Gerth and C. Wright Mills (New York: Oxford University Press, 1946).

40. See William I. Thomas for a larger discussion of the meanings of the "definition of the situation." Thomas, *On Social Organization and Social Personality* (Chicago: University of Chicago Press, 1966).

41. Erving Goffman, *Asylums: Essays on the Social Situation of Mental Patients and Other Inmates* (Garden City, NY: Anchor Books, 1961), 166–67.

42. Devah Pager, "The Mark of a Criminal Record," *American Journal of Sociology* 108, no. 5 (2003) provides evidence of employment discrimination based on race, as well as the differential impact of criminal conviction on employability.

Chapter 5

1. The Adoption Assistance and Child Welfare Act of 1980 and the Adoption and Safe Families Act of 1997 both have this requirement. See chapter 2 for details. This chapter focuses more heavily on cases in which services are provided to parents whose children are placed outside the home, although there are some dynamics and issues common in both scenarios.

2. Michel Foucault, *Discipline and Punish: The Birth of the Prison* (New York: Vintage Books, 1995), 184.

3. Discipline is a term set out most usefully by Jacques Donzelot, *The Policing of Families* (New York: Pantheon, 1979); and Foucault, *Discipline and Punish.*

4. Erving Goffman, *Asylums: Essays on the Social Situation of Mental Patients and Other Inmates* (Garden City, NY: Anchor Books, 1961), 14.

5. Service providers commonly have expectations of the normative client role. Research has shown that abortion providers want their clients to acknowledge "the morally problematic nature of abortion" [Carole Joffe, "What Abortion Counselors Want from Their Clients," *Social Problems* 26, no. 1 (1978): 113], district attorneys prosecute stalking cases differently depending on how they view the victim [Jennifer L. Dunn, "Innocence Lost: Accomplishing Victimization in Intimate Stalking Cases," *Symbolic Interaction* 24, no. 3 (2001)], and physicians make treatment decisions differently depending on their perceptions of a patient's "worthiness and legitimacy" [Julius Roth, "Some Contingencies of the Moral Evaluation and Control of Clientele: The Case of the Hospital Emergency Service," in *The Sociology of Health and Illness: Critical Perspectives*, eds. Peter Conrad and Rochelle Kern (New York: St. Martin's Press, 1994), 311].

6. Time listed is in court hours and days, and thus excludes weekends and hours when the court is not operating.

7. Annette R. Appell, "On Fixing 'Bad' Mothers and Saving Their Children," in *"Bad" Mothers*, eds. Molly Ladd-Taylor and Lauri Umansky (New York: New York University Press, 1998).

8. California Welfare and Institutions Code (2001).

9. Parents must have resisted treatment during the three-year period immediately prior to the current CPS allegation or "have failed or refused to comply with a program of drug or alcohol treatment described in the caseplan" on at least two prior occasions. California Welfare and Institutions Code.

10. This must be based on two psychological examinations. See Jeremy Pearce, "Taking on a Troubled Agency," *New York Times*, January 26, 2003.

11. This statute applies to cases where parents' whereabouts are unknown after "a reasonably diligent search has failed to locate the parent or guardian." California Welfare and Institutions Code.

12. Treatment program names, service providers, and locations have all been changed to preserve the anonymity of the participants.
13. Gelles, *The Book of David: How Preserving Families Can Cost Children's Lives* (New York: Harper Collins, 1996), 9–10.
14. Julia Littell and John R. Schuerman, "A Synthesis of Research on Family Preservation and Family Reunification Programs," in *A Part of the National Evaluation of Family Preservation Services* (Washington, DC: Department of Health and Human Services, 1995).
15. Barbara Needell et al. found that about 20 percent of children reenter CPS, while Toni Terling found that 37 percent of children reunited with their parents reenter the child welfare system within 3½ years. Needell et al., "Performance Indicators for Child Welfare Services in California: 1997" (Berkeley: University of California at Berkeley, Center for Social Services Research, 1998); Terling, "The Efficacy of Family Reunification Practices: Reentry Rates and Correlates of Reentry for Abused and Neglected Children Reunited with Their Families," *Child Abuse & Neglect* 23, no. 12 (1999). It is worth noting that the meaning of child reentry is complicated by the very use of prior CPS history as a sign of risk, thus increasing the likelihood of subsequent removal.
16. Kristine E. Nelson, "Family Preservation—What Is It?," *Children and Youth Services Review* 19, no. 1/2 (1997), 104.
17. Foster care funds are available for monthly payments to foster care providers on behalf of foster children and vary in amount and form from state to state. Adoption assistance funds are available for one-time payments for the costs of adopting children, as well as to provide monthly subsidies to adoptive families for the care of the children (who are eligible for welfare under the former Aid to Families with Dependent Children program or for Supplemental Security Income). These amounts also vary from state to state. In addition, these funds can be used by states to assist with agency administrative costs, including costs associated with child placement, case management, training for staff, foster parents, and adoptive parents, foster and adoptive parent recruitment, or other relevant expenses. Family Support Services, often provided at the local level by community-based organizations, typically are activities that help families alleviate crises that might lead to out-of-home placements of children. They help to maintain the safety of children in their own homes, support families preparing to reunify or adopt, and assist families in obtaining other services to meet multiple needs.
18. In many places, social workers face much larger caseloads. For example, in the reports following the death of Faheem Williams in New Jersey in early 2003, social workers reported that they sometimes carried as many as one hundred cases at a time.
19. DHHS, "HHS Awards Adoption Bonuses," *HHS News*, September 10 (2001).
20. As with most aspects of case assessment, social workers determine what constitutes safe housing. Though this is a subjective determination, such an assessment would likely consider whether the residence was free of structural damage—including exposed wiring, leaky plumbing, or damaged walls or floors—but might also include its location in areas free of violent crime and gunfire, or distance from drug treatment centers or halfway houses.
21. One study from Canada found safe family housing to be an issue in 18.4 percent of the 957 child welfare cases surveyed where children were taken from their parents' care. The authors suggest that in light of the cost of foster care, a reexamination of housing policy is in order. See Miriam Cohen-Schlanger et al., "Housing as a Factor in Admissions of Children to Temporary Care: A Survey," *Child Welfare* 74, no. 3 (1995).

22. HUD, "A Report on Worst Case Housing Needs in 1999: New Opportunity Amid Continuing Challenges" (Washington, DC: Department of Housing and Urban Development, Office of Policy Development and Research, 2001), 2.

23. Ibid., 7.

24. HUD, "Rental Housing Assistance—The Crisis Continues: The 1997 Report to Congress on Worst Case Housing Needs" (Rockville, MD: Department of Housing and Urban Development, Office of Policy Development and Research, 1997). The HUD Office of Policy Development and Research defines "worst case housing needs" as "unassisted renters with incomes below fifty percent of local area median (those with 'very low' incomes) who pay more than half of their income for housing or live in severely substandard housing." HUD, "A Report on Worst Case Housing Needs in 1999," 2. According to HUD, "as has been the pattern for the past decade, very-low-income renters were most likely to have severe problems [in the West], with worst case conditions troubling 36 percent of very-low-income renters and 48 percent of unassisted very-low-income renters. Despite high rates of unmet problems observed in the West, only 24 percent of very-low-income renters in the West receive assistance, less than in any other region." HUD, "A Report on Worst Case Housing Needs in 1999," 7.

25. HUD, "A Report on Worst Case Housing Needs in 1999," 10.

26. HUD, "HUD's Public Housing Program" (Washington, DC: Department of Housing and Urban Development, 2001).

27. Federal law permits states to pass laws allowing parents to keep some level of benefits for up to 180 days if their children are removed from their care and placed in the child welfare system. California passed such legislation in 2001, after data collection for this project concluded.

28. Kathleen Wells and Shenyang Guo, "Mothers' Welfare and Work Income and Reunification with Children in Foster Care," *Children and Youth Services Review* 25, no. 3 (2003).

29. HUD, "General Information on Subsidized Housing" (Washington, DC: Department of Housing and Urban Development, Multifamily Housing Division, 2001).

30. Loring Jones, "The Social and Family Correlates of Successful Reunification of Children in Foster Care," *Children and Youth Services Review* 20, no. 4 (1998), 305.

31. Typically housing is not a significant hurdle in kinship placements, which does not require biological family members to meet the same requirements as licensed foster parents. However, in this case, the aunt's understanding of why she was denied placement of her two biological nieces and one teenaged step-niece was that her housing in a one-bedroom apartment was inadequate.

32. Quoted in Jana Sawicki, *Disciplining Foucault: Feminism, Power, and the Body* (New York: Routledge, 1991), 25.

33. Goffman, *Asylums: Essays on the Social Situation of Mental Patients and Other Inmates*, 22.

34. Lucy White, "Subordination, Rhetorical Survival Skills, and Sunday Shoes: Notes on the Hearing of Mrs. G," in *Feminist Legal Theory: Readings in Law and Gender*, ed. Katherine Bartlett (Boulder, CO: Westview Press, 1991), 415, 417.

35. William Sewell, "A Theory of Structure: Duality, Agency, and Transformation," *American Journal of Sociology* 98, no. 1 (1992), 20; see also Michel Foucault, *Power/ Knowledge: Selected Interviews and Other Writings*, ed. Colin Gordon (New York: Pantheon Books, 1980).

36. Linda's case began prior to the passage of the 1997 federal reforms that created more stringent timelines.

37. Co-kinship is not a legal term, but reflects Linda's understanding of this option. She is actually referring to a provision in California kinship adoption legislation that

allows for nonbinding contracts known as kinship adoption agreements that specify the amount and degree of contact between birth parents and adoptive parents.

38. This is not dissimilar to the Progressive Era belief in the neutrality of the courts, discussed in chapter 2.

39. Anthony Maluccio and James K. Whittaker, "Learning from the 'Family Preservation' Initiative," *Children and Youth Services Review* 19, no. 1/2 (1997); and P.J. Pecora, J.K. Whittaker, and A.N. Maluccio, *The Child Welfare Challenge: Policy, Practice, and Research* (New York: Aldine de Gruyter, 1992).

Chapter 6

1. Marlee Kline, "Complicating the Ideology of Motherhood: Child Welfare Law and First Nation Women," in *Mothers in Law: Feminist Theory and the Legal Regulation of Motherhood*, eds. Martha Albertson Fineman and Isabel Karpin (New York: Columbia University Press, 1995), 120. See also Sharon Hays, *Cultural Contradictions of Motherhood* (New Haven, CT: Yale University Press, 1998).

2. See Deborah R. Connolly, *Homeless Mothers: Face to Face with Women and Poverty* (Minneapolis: University of Minnesota Press, 2000); Martha Albertson Fineman, *The Neutered Mother, the Sexual Family and Other Twentieth Century Tragedies* (New York: Routledge, 1995); Julia E. Hanigsberg and Sara Ruddick, eds., *Mother Troubles: Rethinking Contemporary Maternal Dilemmas* (Boston: Beacon Press, 1999); Molly Ladd-Taylor and Lauri Umansky, eds., *"Bad" Mothers: The Politics of Blame in Twentieth-Century America* (New York: New York University Press, 1998); Adrienne Rich, *Of Woman Born: Motherhood as Experience and Institution* (New York: W.W. Norton & Co., 1976); Dorothy Roberts, *Killing the Black Body: Race, Reproduction, and the Meaning of Liberty* (New York: Vintage Books, 1997); Barbara Katz Rothman, *Recreating Motherhood: Ideology and Technology in a Patriarchal Society* (New York: W.W. Norton & Co., 1989); Karen Tice, *Tales of Wayward Girls and Immoral Women* (Urbana: University of Illinois Press, 1998).

3. Connolly, *Homeless Mothers: Face to Face with Women and Poverty*, 40. See also Anna Lowenhaupt-Tsing, "Monster Stories: Women Charged with Perinatal Endangerment," in *Uncertain Terms: Negotiating Gender in American Culture*, eds. Faye Ginsburg and Anna Lowenhaupt-Tsing (Boston: Beacon Press, 1990); and Nancy Scheper-Hughes, *Death Without Weeping: The Violence of Everyday Life in Brazil* (Berkeley: University of California Press, 1992).

4. Ladd-Taylor and Umansky, eds., *"Bad" Mothers*, 3.

5. Annette Appell, "On Fixing 'Bad' Mothers and Saving Their Children," in *"Bad" Mothers*, eds. Molly Ladd-Taylor and Lauri Umansky (New York: New York University Press, 1998), 357.

6. Dorothy Roberts, "Mothers Who Fail to Protect Their Children," in *Mother Troubles: Rethinking Contemporary Maternal Dilemmas*, eds. Julia E. Hanigsberg and Sara Ruddick (Boston: Beacon Press, 1999), 31.

7. Marie Ashe and Naomi Cahn, "Child Abuse: A Problem for Feminist Theory," in *The Public Nature of Private Violence: The Discovery of Domestic Abuse*, eds. Martha A Fineman and Roxanne Mykitiuk (New York: Routledge, 1994), 172. See also Barbara Bennett Woodhouse, "Making Poor Mothers Fungible: The Privitization of Foster Care," in *Child Care and Inequality: Re-Thinking Carework for Children and Youth*, eds. Francesca M. Cancian et al. (New York: Routledge, 2002).

8. As discussed in chapters 2 and 5, the federal Adoption and Safe Families Act delineates circumstances in which states are not obligated to attempt reunification.

9. Joyce Gelb, "The Politics of Wife Abuse," in *Family, Politics, and Public Policy: A Feminist Dialogue on Women and the State*, ed. Irene Diamond (New York: Longman,

1983); Richard Gelles and Claire Pedrick Cornell, *Intimate Violence in Families* (Thousand Oaks, CA: Sage Publications, 1985); Linda Gordon, *Heroes of Their Own Lives* (New York: Penguin Books, 1988); John M. Johnson and Kathleen J. Ferraro, "The Victimized Self: The Case of Battered Women," in *The Family Experience*, ed. Mark Hutter (Boston: Allyn & Bacon, 2000); Maryse Rinfret-Raynor and Solange Cantin, "Feminist Therapy for Battered Women: An Assessment," in *Out of the Darkness: Contemporary Perspectives on Family Violence*, eds. Glenda Kaufman Kantor and Jana L. Jasinski (Thousand Oaks, CA: Sage Publications, 1997); and Roberts, "Mothers Who Fail to Protect Their Children."

10. Roberts, "Mothers Who Fail to Protect Their Children," 33.

11. Candace, discussed in chapter 4, may provide an exception. Her police officer boyfriend theoretically should have been an asset to her case. However, it is likely that because he was not of a higher socioeconomic level than her, he did not contribute in any specific way. Further, as an African American man, he was presumed to be a liability by the investigating social worker and sheriff.

12. Tice, *Tales of Wayward Girls and Immoral Women*, 30. Internal quotes are from Vida Hunt Francis, a 1906 charity worker.

13. Francis Fox Piven and Richard A. Cloward, *Regulating the Poor: The Functions of Public Welfare* (New York: Vintage Books., 1993); and Walter Trattner, *From Poor Law to Welfare State: A History of Social Welfare in America*, 5th ed. (New York: Free Press, 1994).

14. Personal Responsibility and Work Opportunity Reconciliation Act of 1996, P.L. 104-193, § 401, 3.

15. One example is H.R. 4, the Personal Responsibility, Work, and Family Promotion Act of 2003, passed by the House of Representatives in February 2003, which provided $300 million annually for grant making to programs that promote marriage.

16. DHHS, "Strengthening Healthy Marriages: A Compendium of Approaches: Draft" (Washington, DC: Department of Health and Human Services, Administration for Children and Families, 2002).

17. Katherine T. Bartlett, *Gender and the Law: Theory, Doctrine, Commentary* (Boston: Little, Brown & Co., 1993), 529–30.

18. For examples on the difficulties women face in leaving battering relationships, see Lenore Walker, *The Battered Woman* (New York: Harper & Row, 1979); Demie Kurz, "Women, Welfare, and Domestic Violence," in *Whose Welfare?*, ed. Gwendolyn Mink (Ithaca, NY: Cornell University Press, 1999); Ellen Scott, Andrew London, and Nancy Myers, "Dangerous Dependencies—The Intersection of Welfare Reform and Domestic Violence," *Gender and Society* 16, no. 6 (2002); and Ola W. Barnett, Tomas E. Martinez, and Mae Keyson, "The Relationship Between Violence, Social Support, and Self-Blame in Battered Women," *Journal of Interpersonal Violence* 11, no. 2 (1996).

19. Rinfret-Raynor and Cantin, "Feminist Therapy for Battered Women," 233.

20. Kim R. Oates et al., "Prior Childhood Sexual Abuse in Mothers of Sexually Abused Children," *Child Abuse & Neglect* 22, no. 11 (1998); and Ayelet Meron Ruscio, "Predicting the Child-Rearing Practices of Mothers Sexually Abused in Childhood," *Child Abuse & Neglect* 25, no. 3 (2001).

21. Michael N. Stiffman et al., "Household Composition and Risk of Fatal Child Maltreatment," *Pediatrics* 109, no. 4 (2002), 618–19. See also Jean Giles-Sims, "Current Knowledge About Child Abuse in Stepfamilies," in *Family Violence: Studies from the Social Sciences and Professions*, ed. James M. Makepeace (New York: McGraw-Hill, 1998) and Gelles and Cornell, *Intimate Violence in Families*, for a discussion of women who repeatedly enter relationships with men who are likely to batter them.

22. Stephanie Riger, "What's Wrong with Empowerment," *American Journal of Community Psychology* 21, no. 3 (1993), 280. Stephanie Riger uses male pronouns deliberately to point to the ways these expectations suggest a male-centered worldview.

23. Iris Marion Young, "Punishment, Treatment, Empowerment: Three Approaches to Policy for Pregnant Addicts," *Feminist Studies* 20, no. 1 (1994), 48.

24. Einat Peled et al., "Choice and Empowerment for Battered Women Who Stay: Toward a Constructivist Model," *Social Work* 45, no. 1 (2000), 15.

25. Addressing time necessary for services is difficult. As Harald Klingemann points out, "Societal values—lack of time in affluent societies—and a general acceleration in the fields of communication, consumption, work and leisure are mirrored in the treatment system. Recovery as a long-lasting learning process stands in sharp contrast to the "quick fix." Klingemann, "'To Every Thing There Is a Season'—Social Time and Clock Time in Addiction Treatment," *Social Science and Medicine* 51, no. 8 (2000). Generalizing from other studies on treatment provides an indication that more than the services provided are needed. For example, Hohman advocates for a minimum of six months of drug treatment, with many programs requiring 90 meetings in 90 days, for drug-addicted parents in reunification. Melinda M. Hohman and Rick L. Butt, "How Soon Is Too Soon? Addiction Recovery and Family Reunification," *Child Welfare* 80, no. 1 (2001). Toni Terling identified factors such as the inability to change after prior interactions with CPS, substance abuse, parents' inability to address their problems, and a lack of social support as causes for families' reentrance into CPS. Terling, "The Efficacy of Family Reunification Practices: Reentry Rates and Correlates of Reentry for Abused and Neglected Children Reunited with Their Families," *Child Abuse & Neglect* 23, no. 12 (1999). Other studies have found that at least three months of intensive services were far more successful than routine services. Kristine E. Nelson, "Family Preservation—What Is It?," *Children and Youth Services Review* 19, no. 1/2 (1997).

26. Lesbianism was not an issue in this case, with Elizabeth, a white middle-class woman, actually perceived as an asset to Rachel's initial bid for her children. As the chapter suggests, a relationship with a man is often a greater liability to a woman's case than is an intimate relationship with another woman. This may be due to beliefs that lesbian relationships are more egalitarian and do not contain domestic violence issues. See Claire M. Renzetti, *Violent Betrayal: Partner Abuse in Lesbian Relationships* (Thousand Oaks, CA: Sage Publications, 1995). It is important to note that because this research was conducted in California, I may have observed a higher level of tolerance for gay and lesbian relationships than is present in other states where a mother's lesbianism alone may make her unfit in the eyes of the court.

27. Erving Riger, "What's Wrong with Empowerment," 282.

28. Goffman, *The Presentation of Self in Everyday Life* (New York: Anchor/Doubleday, 1959), 35.

29. Kathryn Edin and Laura Lein, *Making Ends Meet: How Single Mothers Survive Welfare and Low-Wage Work* (New York: Russell Sage Foundation, 1997); and Dorothy Roberts, "Welfare's Ban on Poor Motherhood," in *Whose Welfare?*, ed. Gwendolyn Mink (Ithaca, NY: Cornell University Press, 1999).

30. For a discussion of Hmong culture and family structure, see Anne Fadiman, *The Spirit Catches You and You Fall Down: A Hmong Child, Her American Doctors, and the Collision of Two Cultures* (New York: Farrar, Straus, and Giroux, 1997).

31. Peled et al., "Choice and Empowerment for Battered Women Who Stay," 16. See also G. Kristian Miccio, "A House Divided: Mandatory Arrest, Domestic Violence and the Conservatization of the Battered Women's Movement," *Houston Law Review* 42, no. 2, 237–323 (2005). Deborah Connelly provides an interesting discussion of working with clients who choose to remain with an abusive partner from the perspective of the service provider. Connolly, *Homeless Mothers: Face to Face with Women and Poverty.*

32. For a discussion of race and sexuality, see Ruth Frankenberg, *White Women, Race Matters: The Social Construction of Whiteness* (Minneapolis: University of Minnesota

Press, 1993); Patricia Hill Collins, *Black Feminist Thought: Knowledge, Consciousness, and the Politics of Empowerment* (New York: Routledge, 1991); Cornel West, *Race Matters* (New York: Random House, 1994). For an excellent discussion of black women's sexuality, see Collins, *Black Feminist Thought*. It is impossible to ignore the ways that the sexuality of women of color is tied to rhetoric of welfare and poor women's childbearing. See Roberts, *Killing the Black Body*, as one shining analysis of this issue.

33. Feminist scholars have suggested that the ideal motherhood is unobtainable; see Hanigsberg and Ruddick, eds., *Mother Troubles: Rethinking Contemporary Maternal Dilemmas*; Ladd-Taylor and Umansky, eds., *"Bad" Mothers*. For a discussion of how women are seen as failing as mothers through employment or lack of employment see Michele Hoffnung, "Motherhood: Contemporary Conflict for Women," in *Women: A Feminist Perspective*, ed. Jo Freeman (Mountain View, CA: Mayfield, 1989; Lillian Rubin, *Families on the Fault Line: America's Working Class Speaks About the Family, the Economy, Race, and Ethnicity* (New York: Harper Collins, 1994); and Joan Williams, *Unbending Gender: Why Family and Work Conflict and What to Do About It* (London: Oxford Press, 1999). For a discussion of women's reliance on public assistance as a source of perceived maternal failings, see Mimi Abramovitz, *Regulating the Lives of Women: Social Welfare Policy from Colonial Times to the Present* (Boston: South End Press, 1988); Edin and Lein, *Making Ends Meet*; Linda Gordon, *Pitied, but not Entitled* (Cambridge, MA: Harvard University Press, 1994); Piven and Cloward, *Regulating the Poor*; and Roberts, "Welfare's Ban on Poor Motherhood." For consideration of how mothers' sexual relationships outside of marriage or lack of sexual relations within marriage define failed mothering, see Fineman, *The Neutered Mother, the Sexual Family and Other Twentieth Century Tragedies*; and Tice, *Tales of Wayward Girls and Immoral Women*. For a discussion of failed mothers and child maltreatment, see Appell, "On Fixing 'Bad' Mothers and Saving Their Children." For a discussion of the role of women's behavior during pregnancy, see Center for Reproductive Law and Policy, "Punishing Women for Their Behavior During Pregnancy" (New York: Center for Reproductive Law and Policy, 2000); Laura E. Gomez, *Misconceiving Mothers: Legislators, Prosecutors, and the Politics of Prenatal Drug Exposure* (Philadelphia: Temple University Press, 1997); Amanda Noble et al., "Gender Issues in California's Perinatal Substance Abuse Policy," *Contemporary Drug Problems* 27, no. 1 (2000); and Lynn M. Paltrow, "Criminal Prosecution Against Pregnant Women: National Update and Overview" (American Civil Liberties Union Reproductive Freedom Project, 1992). For a discussion of mothers who fail to breastfeed, see Linda Blum, *At the Breast: Ideologies of Breastfeeding and Motherhood in the Contemporary United States* (Boston: Beacon, 1999); and Cindy A. Stearns, "Breastfeeding and the Good Maternal Body," *Gender and Society* 13, no. 3 (1999). Maternal failings are ubiquitous and even include women's emotional ambivalence about mothering. Rich, *Of Woman Born: Motherhood as Experience and Institution*.

34. Roberts, "Mothers Who Fail to Protect Their Children," 34.

35. Woodhouse, "Making Poor Mothers Fungible." Here she argues that the Adoption and Safe Families Act of 1997, which deemphasizes family reunification and instead aims to move children out of state care and into adoptive homes reflects a view of motherhood as fungible. I agree with Woodhouse's analysis of this legislation, as discussed in chapter 2. However, this new law has not yet entirely transformed cultural views on mothers as necessary. Instead, I observed judges and attorneys interpreting the law as a way to eliminate dangerous mothers, while providing an opportunity to resocialize mothers viewed as victims. This differs greatly from the view of fathers who are not married to the mothers of their children. These men are

indeed considered unnecessary and are even viewed as an obstacle to be overcome. This issue is discussed in detail in chapter 7.

Chapter 7

1. Quoted in Lynn Segal, *Slow Motion: Changing Masculinities, Changing Men* (London: Virago Press, 1990), 27.
2. Jessie Bernard, "The Good Provider Role: Its Rise and Fall," in *Diversity and Change in Families: Patterns, Prospects, and Policies*, eds. Mark Robert Rank and Edward Kain (Englewood Cliffs, NJ: Prentice Hall, 1981); Scott Coltrane, "Changing Patterns of Family Work: Chicano Men and Housework," in *Shifting the Center*, ed. Susan Ferguson (Mountain View, CA: Mayfield Publishing, 1998); and Lillian Rubin, *Families on the Fault Line: America's Working Class Speaks About the Family, the Economy, Race, and Ethnicity* (New York: Harper Collins, 1994).
3. Kathleen Gerson, "Dilemmas of Involved Fatherhood," in *Reconstructing Gender*, ed. Estelle Disch (Mountain View, CA: Mayfield Publishing, 1997); and Teresa L. Jump and Linda Haas, "Fathers in Transition," in *Changing Men: New Directions in Research on Men and Masculinity*, ed. Michael Kimmel (Newbury Park, CA: Sage Publications, 1987).
4. Kjersti Ericsson, "Gender, Delinquency and Child Welfare," *Theoretical Criminology* 2, no. 4 (1998), 455.
5. R. W. Connell, *Masculinities* (Berkeley: University of California Press, 1995).
6. See Philippe Bourgois, *In Search of Respect: Selling Crack in El Barrio* (Cambridge: Cambridge University Press, 1995); Johnnie David Spraggins, Jr., "African American Masculinity: Power and Expression," *Journal of African American Men* 4, no. 3 (1999); and Sally Holland and Jonathan Scourfield, "Managing Marginalised Masculinities: Men and Probation," *Journal of Gender Studies* 9, no. 2 (2000). For examples of how low-income men and men of color demonstrate masculinity in alternative ways, Elijah Anderson describes inner-city black men's need to use the "code of the street" to survive in their communities. Anderson, *Code of the Street: Decency, Violence and the Moral Life of the Inner City* (New York: W.W. Norton & Co., 2000).
7. These men epitomize what R. W. Connell calls "marginalized masculinities." Connell, *Masculinities*; and Holland and Scourfield, "Managing Marginalised Masculinities." According to Connell, such masculinities represent "configurations of practice generated in particular situations in a changing structure of relationships." Connell, *Masculinities*, 81.
8. Arguably a father's lack of support, failure to intervene on his child's behalf, or even lack of knowledge of the child's birth can be construed as indirect responsibility in some cases.
9. California Welfare and Institutions Code (WIC) 316.2 specifies how fathers should receive notice.
10. In the case of *DeShaney v. Winnebago County Department of Social Services* (1989), the U.S. Supreme Court denied the civil suit brought by a mother whose husband severely beat her son. In this ruling, the Court explained that the state is not required to "affirmatively protect citizens from the private actions of a third party" (489 US 189). Other rulings have established that "once the state assumes custody of a person, it owes him a rudimentary duty of safekeeping no matter how perilous his circumstances when he was free" (*K. H. ex. Rel. Murphy v. Morgan*, 914 F.2d 846 (7th Cir. 1990)). See also *Meador v. Cabinet for Health Resources*, 902 F.2d 474 (6th Cir. 1990).
11. Although Leonard was not certain of the specific cause of death of Traci's child, an event that happened before he met her, accidental ingestion of iron is the leading cause of poisoning deaths in children less than six years old, with the U.S. Food

and Drug Administration (FDA) identifying at least 110,000 reported deaths from children ingesting iron between 1986 and 1994. FDA, P94-18, "Childhood Iron Poisoning," press release (Rockville, MD: FDA, 1994).

12.   Chantelle's case and the county's move to deny her services are discussed in greater detail in chapter 5.

13.   Chris's housing and child care struggles are discussed in chapter 5.

14.   Sue Boney-McCoy and David Finkelhor, "Psychosocial Sequelae of Violent Victimization in a National Youth Sample," *Journal of Consulting and Clinical Psychology* 63, no. 5 (1995); Karen M. Fondacaro and John C. Holt, "Psychological Impact of Childhood Sexual Abuse of Male Inmates: The Importance of Perception," *Child Abuse & Neglect* 23, no. 4 (1999); Juliette D. G. Goldman and Usha K. Padayachi, "Some Methodological Problems in Estimating Incidence and Prevalence in Child Sexual Abuse Research," *Journal of Sex Research* 37, no. 4 (2000).

15.   Robin Weeks and Cathy Spatz Widom, "Self-Reports of Early Childhood Victimization Among Incarcerated Adult Male Felons," *Journal of Interpersonal Violence* 13, no. 3 (1998).

16.   Esther Madriz, *Nothing Bad Happens to Good Girls: Fear of Crime in Women's Lives* (Berkeley: University of California Press, 1997). See also Boney-McCoy and Finkelhor, "Psychosocial Sequelae of Violent Victimization."

17.   WIC 316.2 details how alleged fathers should be identified, noticed, and treated by the court. Putative means commonly believed, supposed, or claimed. Thus a putative father is one believed to be the father unless proved otherwise.

18.   About twenty-five states keep a "putative father registry" that records paternity for unmarried fathers. Other states maintain biological parent registries. See the Evan B. Donaldson Adoption Institute website (www.adoptioninstitute.org) for more information.

19.   A declaration of paternity is signed by both the unmarried mother and father and is legally binding. Men can disclaim their paternity by signing a rescission of paternity within sixty days of signing the declaration, so long as no court proceedings or child support orders relating to the child in question have occurred. Beyond sixty days, there is a lengthier process to renounce paternity, which must be completed by the time the child is two years old. For teen parents, the rules are slightly different.

20.   Effective January 1, 1997, as part of the implementation of federal welfare reform legislation, in cases where the parents of a child are not legally married, the father's name will not be added to the birth certificate unless they sign a Declaration of Paternity in the hospital, or sign the form later or legally establish paternity through the courts and pay a fee to amend the birth certificate.

21.   See California Family Code 7611 for more information on how California law defines paternity. Family Code 7631 grants men not presumed to be the father the right to initiate a proceeding to establish paternity in cases where the mother is relinquishing the child for adoption. Recent legal cases also solidify linkages between paternal rights and marital status. For example, the U.S. Supreme Court determined that foreign-born children whose American fathers are not married to their mothers are not entitled to derivative citizenship in the cases of *Miller v. Albright* (523 U.S. 420 (1998)) and *Nguyen v. INS* (533 US 53 (2001)).

22.   De facto parent status is a legal term derived from the Latin for "as a matter of fact," or something which, while not necessarily lawful or legally sanctified, exists in fact. A common law spouse may be referred to a de facto wife or de facto husband: although not legally married, they live their lives as if they are married.

23.   *Elizabeth Miscovich v. Gerald Allan Miscovich*, 455 Pa. Super. 437, 688 A. 2d 726 (1997). For denial of cert, see also 526 U.S. 1113; 119 S. Ct. 1757; 143 L. Ed. 2d 789 (1999).

24. *Michael H. v. Gerald D.*, 491 U.S. 110; 109 S. Ct. 2333 (1989).

25. *Dawn D., Petitioner, v. The Superior Court of Riverside County, Respondent; JERRY K., Real Party in Interest*, 17 Cal. 4th 932; 952 P.2d 1139 (1998).

26. Julie Gannon Shoop, "Marriage Trumps Biology in California Paternity Fight," *Trial* 34, no. 7 (1998), 18.

27. California Civil Code, Section 7005 specifies that the donor of semen provided to a *licensed physician* for use in artificial insemination in a woman other than the donor's wife is not considered the legal father.

28. *Jhordan C. v. Mary K.*, 179 Cal. App. 3d 386.

29. Ralph Lindgren and Nadine Taub, *The Law of Sex Discrimination* (Eagen, MN: West Publishing, 1993), 449.

30. Laura Curran and Laura S. Abrams, "Making Men into Dads: Fatherhood, the State, and Welfare Reform," *Gender & Society* 14, no. 5 (2000).

31. The choice to bill parents for the cost of foster care resides with the county, often with the district attorney's office. The study county did bill parents for the costs, although many counties do not.

32. Capitalization is in the original of this distributed form letter from the juvenile court.

33. Both mothers and fathers can voluntarily relinquish their children. In surrendering their parental rights, they allow their children to be adopted or made permanent wards of the state, but are not saddled with a record of having failed to reunify. For example, Maya and Joe, described in chapter 6, chose this route.

34. David Blankenhorn, *Fatherless America: Confronting Our Most Urgent Social Problem* (New York: Harper Collins, 1996); George Gilder, *Wealth and Poverty* (New York: Basic Books, 1981); Charles Murray, "The Coming White Underclass," *Wall Street Journal*, October 29, 1993; David Popenoe, "A World Without Fathers (Consequences of Children Living Without Fathers)," *Wilson Quarterly* 20, no. 2 (1996); Barbara Dafoe Whitehead, "Dan Quayle Was Right," *The Atlantic*, April (1993). On criminal activity specifically, see William S. Comanor and Llad Phillips, *The Impact of Income and Family Structure on Delinquency: Working Paper* (University of California–Santa Barbara, 1998), http://www.econ.ucsb.edu/.

35. Sanford Bates, "Should a Father Have a Mother's Pension? (Originally Published in July 1952 in this journal)," *Public Welfare* 51, no. 1 (1993), 12.

36. See Tommy Thompson, "HHS Announces Decline in TANF Caseloads," *HHS News*, December 2 (2003). Further pointing to the incompatibility of paid employment and reunification, one longitudinal study using administrative data found that children whose mothers lost income from welfare but gained income from paid employment reunified with their children more slowly than mothers who maintained aid or had never received aid. Kathleen Wells and Shenyang Guo, "Mothers' Welfare and Work Income and Reunification with Children in Foster Care," *Children and Youth Services Review* 25, no. 3 (2003). Although the exact mechanism is unclear, it does suggest that paid employment among low-income workers may itself inhibit parents' ability to focus on reunification. For a discussion of the inability of families to survive solely on low-paid work, see Sharon Hays, *Flat Broke with Children* (New York: Oxford University Press, 2003).

37. "Father Makes Two: Unmarried Men Who Raise Their Children Are One of the Fastest-Growing Groups in America," *Time*, November 19 (2001).

38. Mary Ann Mason, *The Custody Wars: Why Children Are Losing the Legal Battle and What We Can Do About It* (New York: Basic Books, 2000), 4.

39. Alliance for Non-Custodial Parents, *Joint Custody Laws in the U.S.* (Alliance for Non-Custodial Parents, 2003), http://www.ancpr.org/joint_custody_laws_in_the_united.htm.

40. *Stanley v. Illinois*, 405 U.S. 645; 92 S. Ct. 1208 (1972).

41. *Quilloin v. Walcott*, 434 U.S. 246; 98 S. Ct. 549 (1978).
42. *Caban v. Mohammed*, 441 U.S. 380; 99 S. Ct. 1760 (1979).
43. Katherine T. Bartlett, *Gender and the Law: Theory, Doctrine, Commentary* (Boston: Little, Brown & Co., 1993); Lindgren and Taub, *The Law of Sex Discrimination*; and Theodore J. Stein, *Child Welfare and the Law*, rev. ed. (Washington, DC: CWLA Press, 1998). Shortly after *Caban*, a subsequent challenge to the same New York law (*Lehr v. Robertson* 463 US 248 (1983)) by a man without a relationship to his child was unsuccessful. Bartlett, *Gender and the Law: Theory, Doctrine, Commentary*; Lindgren and Taub, *The Law of Sex Discrimination*; and Stein, *Child Welfare and the Law*, further clarify the centrality of an ongoing relationship to nonmarital paternal rights.
44. See DHHS, "Nurturing Fatherhood: Improving Data and Research on Male Fertility, Family Formation, and Fatherhood" (Washington, DC: Federal Interagency Forum on Child and Family Statistics, 1998); Kathryn Edin and Laura Lein, *Making Ends Meet: How Single Mothers Survive Welfare and Low-Wage Work* (New York: Russell Sage Foundation, 1997); Michael E. Lamb, "The History of Research on Father Involvement: An Overview," *Marriage & Family Review* 29, no. 2–3 (2000); Robert Lerman and Elaine Sorenson, "Father Involvement with Their Nonmarital Children: Patterns, Determinants, and Effects on Their Earnings," *Marriage & Family Review* 29, no. 2–3 (2000); William Marsiglio et al., "Scholarship on Fatherhood in the 1990s and Beyond," *Journal of Marriage and the Family* 62, no. 4 (2000); William Marsiglio, Randal Day, and Michael E. Lamb, "Exploring Fatherhood Diversity: Implications for Conceptualizing Father Involvement," *Marriage & Family Review* 29, no. 4 (2000); Anne Nurse, *Fatherhood Arrested* (Nashville, TN: Vanderbilt University, 2002); and Ellen K. Scott et al., "Unstable Work, Unstable Income: Implications for Family Well-Being in the Era of Time-Limited Welfare," *Journal of Poverty* 8, no. 1 (2004).
45. Some research suggests that unwed fathers are more likely to have substance abuse, mental, and physical health problems (Melvin Wilson and Jeanne Brooks-Gunn, "Health Status and Behaviors of Unwed Fathers," *Children and Youth Services Review* 23, no. 4/5 (2001)) and have criminal records than married fathers (Christopher Mumola, "Incarcerated Parents and Their Children" (Washington, DC: Bureau of Justice Statistics, 2000)). They also visit with their children less than married fathers and provide far less in child support than fathers who were married to their children's mother (see DHHS, "Nurturing Fatherhood.") Arguing for the differential treatment of married and never-married fathers, social welfare historian Mary Ann Mason argues that "we assume that unwed fathers are like married fathers except for ceremony. In fact, few unwed fathers live with their children or seriously participate in their upbringing, and as a group unwed fathers exhibit far more socially undesirable characteristics such as criminal records and drug and alcohol addiction than do married fathers." Mason, *The Custody Wars*, 116. However, understanding causality is difficult. This body of research also shows that unwed men who are employed visit their children more often than unemployed unwed fathers. At the same time, other research shows how underemployed men are less desirable spouses and thus are less likely to marry (e.g., Kathryn Edin, "Few Good Men," *American Prospect*, January 3 (2000). This points to the indelible role of class in determining which men marry in the first place.
46. As mentioned, parents are responsible for financially supporting their children, even while they don't have custody, and may be billed for some portion of foster care costs as assessed by a judge (usually on the recommendation of the district attorney) when the case ends.
47. Andrea G. Hunter and James Earl Davis, "Hidden Voices of Black Men: the Meaning, Structure, and Complexity of Manhood," *Journal of Black Studies* 25, no. 1 (1994).

48. Vivian L. Gadsen and Ralph R. Smith, "African American Males and Fatherhood: Issues in Research and Practice," *Journal of Negro Education* 63, no. 4 (1994), 634.

49. Joan Acker, "Symposium: From Sex Roles to Gendered Institutions," *Contemporary Sociology* 21, no. 5 (1992), 567.

50. Technically fathers should receive automatic placement of their children if they are not part of the allegation that led to the child being placed in protective custody. However, the study county's efforts to assess future risk led to the practice where a man's criminal history was interpreted as creating significant risk, which eliminates the possibility of automatic placement.

51. Bureau of Justice Statistics, "Criminal Offender Statistics" (Washington, DC: Department of Justice, 2001).

52. Tina Dorsey, Marianne Zawitz, and Priscilla Middleton, "Drugs and Crime Facts" (Washington, DC: Department of Justice, 2001); and Bureau of Justice Statistics, "Sourcebook 2000" (Washington, DC: Department of Justice, 2000).

53. DHHS, "The AFCARS Report" (Washington, DC: Department of Health and Human Services, Administration for Children and Families, 2001); and National Clearinghouse on Child Abuse and Neglect, "Foster Care National Statistics: April 2001" (Fairfax, VA: National Clearinghouse on Child Abuse and Neglect, 2001).

54. One only need note O. J. Simpson's easy bid for his own children after he was found civilly responsible for killing their mother to understand the veracity of this claim.

55. I could not verify Richie's account of his legal custody arrangement with Laquanda since she was not involved with CPS, and thus was not the subject of social work investigation or scrutiny.

56. It is important to note that Richie does not share this perception. He contends that his more confrontational approach of calling his social worker's supervisor and complaining led to the change in her attitude. I have applied more credibility to his attorney's version of the social worker's transformation, based on my experience with social workers, the frequency with which they are threatened, and the attorney's position as Richie's advocate and insider to the system.

Chapter 8

1. Given the intentional vagueness of the best interests standard and use, it is difficult to find a coherent discussion of the term's actual meaning. See the American Bar Association "Law Day" discussion of best interests for some elucidation of these issues, http://www.abanet.org/publiced/lawday/talking/children.html.

2. This priority was articulated in the Adoption Assistance and Child Welfare Act of 1908 (P.L. 96-272) and reiterated with the passage of the Adoption and Safe Families Act of 1997 (P.L. 105-89), which clearly delineated a preference for adoption above all other placements when reunification fails (§ 101(B)(i) and (ii)). See Richard P. Barth, "After Safety, What Is the Goal of Child Welfare Services: Permanency, Family Continuity or Social Benefit?" *International Journal of Social Welfare* 8, no. 4 (1999); Ada Schmidt-Tieszen and Thomas McDonald, "Children Who Wait: Long Term Foster Care or Adoption?" *Children and Youth Services Review* 20, no. 1/2 (1998); and Barbara Bennett Woodhouse, "Making Poor Mothers Fungible: The Privitization of Foster Care," in *Child Care and Inequality: Re-Thinking Carework for Children and Youth*, ed. Francesca M. Cancian et al. (New York: Routledge, 2002).

3. Federal law allows for the termination of services if a child has been in state care for 15 of the prior 22 months, even if the time in state care was not continuous. AB 1524, which granted shorter time limits, was passed in California in 1996. AB 740 created shorter time limits for siblings of children less than three years of age in out-of-home care. This means that an entire sibling group could adhere to the six-month time limit so long as one child is less than three years-old. A judge may decide that

there is a strong likelihood a child will be safely returned to a parent in the near future or that it would be in a child's best interest for a parent to receive additional services. In this unusual instance, a case might be allowed to continue for a few more months, but cases are not supposed to continue beyond the eighteenth consecutive month.

4. Demonstrating this preference, then-President Bill Clinton's declaration of November 1997 as National Adoption Month stated, "While foster care offers these children a safe and nurturing temporary haven in their time of greatest need, as many as 100,000 foster care kids will need permanent homes in the next few years...Adoption allows these and other children to have the permanent home they deserve." Bill Clinton, "Proclamation 7048—National Adoption Month, 1997" (Weekly Compilation of Presidential Documents, 1997). Thus biological parents are limited in the time they have to prove their rehabilitation to regain custody of their children.

5. See chapter 5 for a discussion of the relative right to services.

6. Jennifer Ayres Hand, "Preventing Undue Terminations: A Critical Evaluation of the Length-of-Time-Out-of-Custody Ground for Termination of Parental Rights," *New York University Law Review* 71, no. 5 (1996), 1263. Parental success in services does not, on its own, necessarily determine whether a child will be reunified with their parents. Other research suggests that outside of services, placement decisions are influenced by "formal and informal administrative policies, the presence or absence of resources and the discretion of juvenile court judges to name a few." Anthony Maluccio and James K. Whittaker, "Learning from the 'Family Preservation' Initiative," *Children and Youth Services Review* 19, no. 1/2 (1997), 8.

7. It is important to maintain perspective on children's experience of time in out-of-home care.

8. Jill Duerr Berrick et al., *The Tender Years: Toward Developmentally-Sensitive Child Welfare Services for Very Young Children* (Oxford: Oxford University Press, 1998).

9. Toni Terling found that 37 percent of children reunited with their families reenter the system within three-and-a-half years. Terling, "The Efficacy of Family Reunification Practices: Reentry Rates and Correlates of Reentry for Abused and Neglected Children Reunited with Their Families," *Child Abuse & Neglect* 23, no. 12 (1999). Federal estimates from data reported from thirty states indicate that about 17 percent of children entering foster care had previously been in foster care. National Clearinghouse on Child Abuse and Neglect, "Foster Care National Statistics: April 2001" (Fairfax, VA: National Clearinghouse on Child Abuse and Neglect, 2001). In California that figure is about 20 percent. Barbara Needell et al., "Performance Indicators for Child Welfare Services in California: 1997" (Berkeley: University of California at Berkeley, Center for Social Services Research, 1998).

10. This prioritization of adoption tends to ignore that adoptions from foster care have high rates of disruption; that is, placements slated for adoption that end following the placement but prior to legalization of the adoption, or that terminate after the adoption is finalized. Although rates vary by year, state, and study population, the proportion of adoptions that disrupt is approximately 10 to 15 percent. Richard P. Barth and M. Berry, *Adoption and Disruption: Rates, Risks and Resources* (New York: Aldine de Gruyter, 1988). Based on a review of the numerous studies of adoption disruption, J. A. Rosenthal indicates some of the most important factors that predict disruption: older age of the child at placement, inadequate parental preparation and information, unrealistic expectations of the child, low social support, a history of physical or sexual abuse prior to adoption, significant acting out behaviors, and adoptive placement with a nonfoster parent or known relative. Other factors do not appear to be significantly associated with disruption, such as the gender of the child, level of developmental disability, ethnicity of the parents or child, or income level of

the adoptive parents. See Rosenthal, "Outcomes of Adoption of Children with Special Needs," *Adoption* 3, no. 1 (1993).

11. Leslie Atkinson and Stephen Butler, "Court-Ordered Assessment: Impact of Maternal Non-Compliance in Child Maltreatment Cases," Child Abuse & Neglect 20, no. 3 (1996); and Michael S. Jellinek, et al, Murphy "Serious Child Mistreatment in Massachusetts: The Course of 206 Children Through the Courts," Child Abuse & Neglect 16 (1992).

12. Soren Holm, "What Is Wrong with Compliance?," *Journal of Medical Ethics* 1993, no. 19 (1993), 109. See also Rose Weitz, *The Sociology of Health, Illness, and Health Care* (Belmont, CA: Wadsworth Publishing, 1996), 427.

13. For a discussion of medicalization of deviance, see Peter Conrad, "The Meaning of Medications: Another Look at Compliance," *Social Science in Medicine* 20, no. 1 (1985).

14. See Linda Blum, *At the Breast: Ideologies of Breastfeeding and Motherhood in the Contemporary United States* (Boston: Beacon Press, 1999); Cindy A. Stearns, "Breastfeeding and the Good Maternal Body," *Gender and Society* 13, no. 3 (1999); and Patricia Stuart-Macadam and Katherine A. Dettwyler, *Breastfeeding: Biocultural Perspectives on Breastfeeding* (New York: Aldine de Gruyter, 1995) for a discussion of this issue.

15. Holm, "What Is Wrong with Compliance?," 108.

16. As discussed in chapter 1, family court uses a preponderance of the evidence standard to establish culpability in this civil proceeding.

17. *Alcoholics Anonymous: The Story of How Many Thousands of Men and Women Have Recovered from Alcoholism*, 2nd ed. (New York: Alcoholics Anonymous World Services, 1955), 59.

18. James L. Nolan, *The Therapeutic State: Justifying Government at Century's End* (New York: New York University Press, 1998).

19. *In re Jessica B.*, 207 Cal. App. 3d 504 (1989).

20. For cohort data, see Center for Social Services Research, "California Children's Services Archives: Foster Care Placement Stability from CWS/CMS" (Berkeley: University of California at Berkeley, 2003).

21. Center for Social Services Research, "California Children's Services Archive: Child Welfare Foster Care Exits Over Time from CWS/CMS" (Berkeley: University of California at Berkeley, 2003).

22. Administration for Children and Families, "Child Welfare Outcomes 2001: Annual Report to Congress. Safety, Permanency, Well-Being" (Washington, DC: Department of Health and Human Services, 2004).

23. Theodore J. Stein, *Child Welfare and the Law*, rev. ed. (Washington, DC: CWLA Press, 1998), 154.

24. The state must find "clear and convincing evidence" that termination is in the child's best interest. This is a higher legal standard than the preponderance of the evidence standard used in earlier dependency court proceedings to evaluate the reasonableness of child removal, but not as rigorous as the beyond a reasonable doubt standard used in criminal proceedings.

25. WIC 366.3(c)(1)(A)–(E). As of January 1, 2002, the fifth condition regarding siblings was added. Its impact is not discussed in detail because it was not in place at the time I conducted my research. California law requires that if none of the exceptions apply and "it is likely the child will be adopted, the court shall terminate parental rights and order the child placed for adoption. A child is not unadoptable simply because she or he is not yet placed in a preadoptive home or with a relative or foster family who is prepared to adopt the child" (California Welfare and Institutions Code [WIC] 366.26(c)(1)). In instances where a potentially adoptive home has not been identified for a child in question, counties are allowed 180 days to "home-find." A parent's

case is usually continued during the search; the social worker then embarks on a search for a potentially adoptive home to justify terminating parental rights. After the 180-day period of home-finding, another hearing is scheduled to assess adoptability and determine parental rights. Should the county fail to find an adoptive home, a judge must determine whether an adoptive home will likely be identified in the near future.

26. See Jill Duerr Berrick, Barbara Needell, and Meredith Minkler, "The Policy Implications of Welfare Reform for Older Caregivers, Kinship Care, and Family Configuration," *Children and Youth Services Review* 21, no. 9/10 (1999). Rates of kinship care increased following the 1979 case of *Miller v. Youakim* (440 U.S. 125; 99 S. Ct. 957; 59 L. Ed. 2d 194). In this decision, the U.S. Supreme Court ruled that states had to pay kinship care providers the same rate as licensed foster parents if the relatives could meet the requirements for foster care licensing. Not all relatives can meet foster care licensing regulations, which typically require "adequate space" in the home, fire and safety inspections, a criminal background or CPS history check, cardiopulmonary resuscitation (CPR) certification, an adequate income to meet the needs of present family members without reliance on foster care payments, and physical exams, including tuberculosis (TB) tests. States have different requirements for foster care licensing for relatives, with California having among the most lenient requirements. Shelley Waters Boots and Rob Geen, "Family Care or Foster Care? How State Policies Affect Kinship Caregivers" (Washington, DC: Urban Institute, 2001). Relatives are not entitled to the same rates of reimbursement for the children in their care unless they also have a foster care license, although they are eligible for public assistance grants under TANF. Of the 44,000 children in kinship care in California in January 1996, approximately 20,000 received AFDC payments and 24,000 received foster care payments. League of Women Voters of California, "Juvenile Justice in California, Part II: Dependency System. Facts & Issues" (Sacramento: League of Women Voters of California, 1998). These differing levels of eligibility have monetary consequences. In 1996, foster care payments ranged from $345 to $484 a month per child depending on age, with additional funds made available depending on the level of disability. AFDC payments for that same year were $293 per month. Jill Duerr Berrick, "When Children Cannot Remain Home: Foster Family Care and Kinship Care," *Protecting Children from Abuse and Neglect* 8, no. 1 (1998). Fully licensed kinship foster care providers are also entitled to state-sponsored respite care and other support services, whereas unlicensed providers are not. Boots and Geen, "Family Care or Foster Care?" In these cases, this exception to termination of parental rights to facilitate adoption is least controversial when the child is over the age of three years and is therefore seen as less likely to be adopted by strangers and less able to establish an equally strong bond with adoptive parents. It is worth noting that African American children are up to eight times as likely as all other children to be in formal kinship care. House Ways and Means Committee, "2000 Green Book. Section 11: Child Protection, Foster Care, and Adoption Assistance" (Washington, DC: U.S. Government Printing Office, 2000), 712.

27. According to California law, "when the child is living with a relative or a foster parent who is willing and capable of providing a stable and permanent environment, but not willing to become a legal guardian, the child shall not be removed from the home if the court finds the removal would be seriously detrimental to the emotional well-being of the child because the child has substantial psychological ties to the relative caretaker or foster parents."

28. WIC 366.26.

29. Goldstein, Freud, and Solnit, *Beyond the Best Interests of the Child* (New York: Free Press, 1973); Goldstein, Freud, and Solnit, *Before the Best Interests of the Child* (New

York: Free Press, 1979); Goldstein, Freud, and Solnit, *In the Best Interests of the Child: Professional Boundaries* (New York: Free Press, 1986).

30. Hand, "Preventing Undue Terminations," 1257.

31. David E. Arredondo and Leonard P. Edwards, "Attachment, Bonding, and Reciprocal Connectedness: Limitations of Attachment Theory in the Juvenile and Family Court," *Journal of the Center for Families, Children and the Courts* 2, no. 1 (2000); and Hand, "Preventing Undue Terminations."

32. Arredondo and Edwards, "Attachment, Bonding, and Reciprocal Connectedness," 112.

33. Ibid., 113. For a critique of their use, including the ways that the dominant use of bond may be insensitive to the life experiences and cultural norms of many children, see also Tiffany Field, "Attachment and Separation in Young Children," *Annual Review of Psychology* 47, no. 1 (1996).

34. *In re Autumn H.*, 27 Cal. App. 4th 567 (1994).

35. *In re Casey D.*, 70 Cal. App. 4th 38 (1999).

36. *In re Casey D.*, 70 Cal. App. 4th 38 (1999). Other cases that also uphold *Autumn H.* include *In re Amanda D.*, 55 Cal. App. 4th 813 [64 Cal. Rptr. 2d 108] (1997); *In re Lorenzo C.*, 54 Cal. App. 4th 1330, 1338–1339 (1997); *In re Taneka W.*, 37 Cal. App. 4th 721, 728–729 (1995); and *In re Beatrice M.*, 29 Cal. App. 4th 1411, 1416 (1994).

37. WIC 366.26.

38. Mark Courtney and Yin-Ling Wong, "Comparing the Timing of Exits from Substitute Care," *Children and Youth Services Review* 18, no. 4–5 (1996); Charles Glisson, James W. Bailey, and James A. Post, "Predicting the Time Children Spend in State Custody," *Social Service Review* 74, no. 2 (2000); Stephen A. Kapp, Thomas P. McDonald, and Kandi L. Diamond, "The Path to Adoption for Children of Color," *Child Abuse & Neglect* 25, no. 2 (2001); and Schmidt-Tieszen and McDonald, "Children Who Wait." Other research suggests that children with more than one sibling in foster care, sexually abused children, and children who are physically or emotionally disabled are also less likely to be tracked toward adoption. Glisson, Bailey, and Post, "Predicting the Time Children Spend in State Custody;" and Schmidt-Tieszen and McDonald, "Children Who Wait."

39. Children's Bureau, "Adoption Data" (Washington, DC: Administration for Children and Families, 2003). See also Administration for Children and Families, "AFCARS Report: Preliminary FY 2001 Estimates as of March 2003" (Washington, DC: Department of Health and Human Services, 2003).

40. Bill Clinton, "The President's Radio Address" (Weekly Compilation of Presidential Documents, 1996), 2512.

41. Charmaine Crouse Yoest, "No Child Is Unadoptable," *Policy Review*, January–February, no. 18 (1997), 13.

42. This case is discussed in chapter 5.

43. See http://www.CAKidsConnection.com for an example of such sites.

44. John McCormick, "Chicago Hope: How a Judge Bucked the System by Putting Children First," *Newsweek*, March 24 (1997).

45. Toni Terling-Watt, "Permanency in Kinship Care: An Exploration of Disruption Rates and Factors Associated with Placement Disruption," *Children and Youth Services Review* 23, no. 2 (2001), 118.

46. Ibid.

47. For a discussion of the postmodern family condition, see Judith Stacey, *Brave New Families: Stories of Domestic Upheaval in Late Twentieth Century America* (New York: Basic Books, 1991).

48. Openness and contact in public adoptions are increasing in popularity and use. See Annette R. Appell, "Increasing Options to Improve Permanency: Considerations in

Drafting an Adoption with Contact Statute," *Children's Legal Rights Journal* 18, no. 4 (1998); Karie M. Frasch, Devon Brooks, and Richard P. Barth, "Openness and Contact in Foster Care Adoptions: An Eight-Year Follow-up Family Relations," *Family Relations* 49, no. 4 (2000); and Joan Heifetz Hollinger, "Response to CWLA 'Analysis' of Uniform Adoption Act" (Kevin McCarty, 1997; accessed on-line February 20, 2004, www.webcom.com/kmc/adoption/law/uaa/hollinger.html. See also Karie Frasch et al., "Enhancing Positive Outcomes in Transracial Adoptive Families" (Berkeley: University of California at Berkeley, Social Work Education Center, 2004).

49.   The right to procreate was established through a series of legal decisions. In *Skinner v. Oklahoma* (316 U.S. 535 (1942)), the Supreme Court struck down a law authorizing the sterilization of persons with two or more felonies "involving moral turpitude." Further articulating the fundamental right to reproduce, and to control ones own reproduction, *Griswold v. Connecticut* (318 U.S. 479 (1965)) struck down a ban on the use of contraceptives by married couples, and *Eisenstadt v. Baird* (405 U.S. 438, 453 (1972)) extended that right to unmarried persons. *Roe v. Wade* (410 U.S. 113 (1973)) also identified a constitutional right to abortion.

Chapter 9

1.   For example, see Jacques Donzelot, *The Policing of Families* (New York: Pantheon, 1979); Michel Foucault, *Discipline and Punish: The Birth of the Prison* (New York: Vintage Books, 1995); Linda Gordon, "Family Violence, Feminism, and Social Control," in *Women, the State, and Welfare*, ed. Linda Gordon (Madison: University of Wisconsin Press, 1990); Linda Gordon, *Heroes of Their Own Lives* (New York: Penguin Books, 1988); Linda Gordon, *Pitied, but Not Entitled* (Cambridge, MA: Harvard University Press, 1994); Christopher Lasch, *Haven in a Heartless World: The Family Besieged* (New York: W.W. Norton & Co., 1995); Andrew J. Polsky, *The Rise of the Therapeutic State* (Princeton, NJ: Princeton University Press, 1991).

2.   Bureau of Labor Statistics, *Occupational Outlook Handbook* (Washington, DC: U.S. Department of Labor, 2002).

3.   The total percentage of all forms of maltreatment equals more than 100 percent, as children are sometimes subjected to more than one form of abuse. Administration for Children and Families, "Child Maltreatment 2002" (Washington, DC: Department of Health and Human Services, 2004). California data provided by Center for Social Services Research, "California Children's Services Archive: Child Abuse Referral Highlights from CWS/CMS," (Berkeley: University of California at Berkeley, 2003).

4.   National Clearinghouse on Child Abuse and Neglect, "Child Abuse and Neglect Fatalities: Statistics and Interventions" (Washington, DC: Administration for Children and Families, 2004). See also Nancy Peddle et al., "Current Trends in Child Abuse Prevention and Fatalities: The 2000 Fifty State Survey." Working paper 808 (Chicago: Prevent Child Abuse America, 2002). Most researchers believe that the estimated numbers of fatalities caused by abuse or neglect are undercounted. For example, see T. Crume et al., "Underascertainment of Child Maltreatment Fatalities by Death Certificates, 1990–1998," *Pediatrics* 102, no. 2 (2002). Crume et al. found that "only half of the children who died as a result of maltreatment had death certificates that were coded consistently with maltreatment. Black race and female gender were associated with higher ascertainment, whereas death in a rural county was associated with lower ascertainment." As such, official estimates are likely not reliable, but provide some guidance in understanding at least the minimum number of deaths.

5.   Estimates of prior CPS involvement are also hard to calculate, as such deaths may be more likely to be classified as caused by abuse or neglect than in cases where CPS has

not been involved. See Peddle et al., "Current Trends in Child Abuse Prevention and Fatalities."

6. Law dramas like *Law and Order, The Guardian, Judging Amy, ER*, and movies like *Losing Isaiah* and *I am Sam* grapple with these very issues.

7. Gordon, "Family Violence, Feminism, and Social Control," 183.

8. Roberts, *Shattered Bonds: The Color of Child Welfare* (New York: Basic Civitas Books, 2002), 80.

9. A more detailed account of Cindy's case is provided in Jennifer A. Reich, "Investigating Child Abuse Investigations," in *Sourcebook of Family Theory and Research*, eds. Vern L. Bengtson et al. (Thousand Oaks, CA: Sage Publications, 2004).

10. For California data, see B. Needell et al., *Child Welfare Services Reports for California* (University of California at Berkeley, 2004), http://cssr.berkeley.edu/CWSCMS reports. The national average is harder to identify, given the significant variation by state. Of children who exited care in 2001, about 59 percent exited to be reunified with their parents. However, this does not reveal how long children had been in foster care before exiting. For the 47 states, the District of Columbia, and Puerto Rico, the percentages of exits to reunifications that occurred within 12 months of entry into foster care in 1999 ranged from 33.8 in Illinois to 87.3 in New Mexico, with a median of 67.3. In 44 states, more than 50 percent of the exits to reunification were achieved within 12 months, and in 45 states less than 10 percent of the exits to reunification involved children who had been in foster care for 48 months or more. Administration for Children and Families, "Child Welfare Outcomes 1999: Annual Report" (Washington, DC: Department of Health and Human Services, 2001). Time in care is an important predictor of reunification: about 81 percent of children that are reunified with their parents will be reunified in less than 24 months, with 54 percent of those children reunifying in less than 12 months. (Administration for Children and Families, "Child Welfare Outcomes 1999"). See also Administration for Children and Families, "The AFCARS Report" (Washington, DC: Department of Health and Human Services, 2001).

11. Barbara Needell et al., "Performance Indicators for Child Welfare Services in California: 1997" (Berkeley: University of California at Berkeley, 1998); and Toni Terling, "The Efficacy of Family Reunification Practices: Reentry Rates and Correlates of Reentry for Abused and Neglected Children Reunited with Their Families," *Child Abuse & Neglect* 23, no. 12 (1999). For information on reentry within 12 months, see also Administration for Children and Families, "Child Welfare Outcomes 2001: Annual Report to Congress. Safety, Permanency, Well-Being," (Washington DC: Department of Health and Human Services, 2004).

12. This exception from services was created under the Adoption and Safe Families Act (ASFA) and is discussed in greater detail in chapter 5.

13. Administration for Children and Families, "Child Welfare Outcomes 2001."

14. Polsky, *The Rise of the Therapeutic State*, 16.

15. Annette R. Appell, "On Fixing 'Bad' Mothers and Saving Their Children," in *"Bad" Mothers*, eds. Molly Ladd-Taylor and Lauri Umansky (New York: New York University Press, 1998), 376.

16. Ibid., 377.

17. See Children's Defense Fund for information on the status of American children. Sentencing Project provides information on how the war on drugs affects families. See also Laura E. Gomez, *Misconceiving Mothers: Legislators, Prosecutors, and the Politics of Prenatal Drug Exposure* (Philadelphia: Temple University Press, 1997); and Amanda Noble et al., "Gender Issues in California's Perinatal Substance Abuse Policy," *Contemporary Drug Problems* 27, no. 1 (2000).

18. Roberts, *Shattered Bonds*, 113.

19. Examples of recent ethnographic works include Daniel Dohan, *The Price of Poverty: Money, Work, and Culture in the Mexican American Barrio* (Berkeley: University of California Press, 2003); Barbara Ehrenreich, *Nickel and Dimed: On (Not) Getting by in America* (New York: Henry Holt & Co., 2002); John Gilliom, *Overseers of the Poor: Surveillance, Resistance, and the Limits of Privacy* (Chicago: University of Chicago Press, 2001); Lynnell Hancock, *Hands to Work: The Stories of Three Families Racing the Welfare Clock* (New York: William Morrow-Harper Collins, 2002); Sharon Hays, *Flat Broke with Children* (New York: Oxford University Press, 2003); Jennifer Johnson, *Getting by on the Minimum: The Lives of Working-Class Women* (New York: Routledge, 2002); Mark Rank, *Living on the Edge: The Realities of Welfare in America* (New York: Columbia University Press, 1994); Ellen Scott, Andrew London, and Nancy Myers, "Dangerous Dependencies—The Intersection of Welfare Reform and Domestic Violence," *Gender and Society* 16, no. 6 (2002); and Ellen K. Scott et al., "Unstable Work, Unstable Income: Implications for Family Well-Being in the Era of Time-Limited Welfare," *Journal of Poverty* 8, no. 1 (2004).

20. For examples, see Sarah Begus and Pamela Armstrong, "Daddy's Right: Incestuous Assault," in *Families, Politics, and Public Policy*, ed. Irene Diamond (New York: Longman, 1983); Catherine McKinnon, "Sex and Violence," in *Gender Inequality: Feminist Theories and Politics*, ed. Judith Lorber (Los Angeles: Roxbury Press, 1998); and Kate Millett, "Beyond Politics: Children and Sexuality," in *Pleasure and Danger: Exploring Female Sexuality*, ed. Carole S. Vance (London: Pandora, 1984).

21. Appell, "On Fixing 'Bad' Mothers and Saving Their Children," 358; Roberts, *Shattered Bonds*; Roberts, "Welfare's Ban on Poor Motherhood," in *Whose Welfare?*, ed. Gwendolyn Mink (Ithaca, NY: Cornell University Press, 1999).

22. M. V. Lee Badgett and Nancy Folbre, "Assigning Care: Gender Norms and Economic Outcomes," *International Labour Review* 138, no. 3 (1999); Gordon, *Pitied, but Not Entitled*; Gwendolyn Mink, "The Lady and the Tramp: Gender, Race, and the Origins of the American Welfare State," in *Women, the State, and Welfare*, ed. Linda Gordon (Madison: University of Wisconsin Press, 1990); and Francis Fox Piven and Richard A. Cloward, *Regulating the Poor: The Functions of Public Welfare* (New York: Vintage Books, 1993).

23. Kathryn Edin and Laura Lein, *Making Ends Meet: How Single Mothers Survive Welfare and Low-Wage Work* (New York: Russell Sage Foundation, 1997); Gwendolyn Mink, "Welfare Cant," *Crossroads*, March (1995); Gwendolyn Mink and Rickie Solinger, eds., *Welfare: A Documentary History of U.S. Policy and Politics* (New York: New York University Press, 2003); Roberts, "Welfare's Ban on Poor Motherhood."

24. Zillah Eistenstein, *The Female Body and the Law* (Berkeley: University of California Press, 1988); John Hagan, "The Everyday and the Not So Exceptional in the Social Organization of Criminal Justice Practices," in *Everyday Practices and Trouble Cases*, eds. Austin Sarat et al. (Chicago: Northwestern University Press, 1998); and Lynne Haney, "Feminist State Theory: Applications to Jurisprudence, Criminology, and the Welfare State," *Annual Review of Sociology* 26 (2000).

25. Demie Kurz, *For Richer, for Poorer: Mothers Confront Divorce* (New York: Routledge, 1995); MaryAnn Mason, *The Custody Wars: Why Children Are Losing the Legal Battle and What We Can Do About It* (New York: Basic Books, 2000); and Nancy D. Polikoff, "Gender and Child-Custody Determinations: Exploding the Myths," in *Families, Politics, and Public Policy*, ed. Irene Diamond (New York: Longman, 1983).

26. Mark E. Courtney et al., "Foster Youth Transitions to Adulthood: A Longitudinal View of Youth Leaving Care," *Child Welfare* 80, no. 6 (2001).

27. Administration for Children and Families, "Child Welfare Outcomes 2001."

28. Carole Joffe, "Why the United States Has No Child-Care Policy," in *Families, Politics, and Public Policy*, ed. Irene Diamond (New York: Longman, 1983), 177.

29. Judith Stacey, *In the Name of the Family: Rethinking Family Values in a Postmodern Age* (Boston: Beacon Press, 1996), 7.

30. Karie M. Frasch, Devon Brooks, and Richard P. Barth, "Openness and Contact in Foster Care Adoptions: An Eight-Year Follow-up Family Relations," *Family Relations* 49, no. 4 (2000), 443.

31. Devon Brooks and Sheryl Goldberg, "Gay and Lesbian Adoptive and Foster Care Placements: Can They Meet the Needs of Waiting Children?," *Social Work* 46, no. 2 (2001).

32. For examples, see Andrew J. Cherlin and Frank F. Furstenberg, Jr., "Stepfamilies in the United States: A Reconsideration," *Annual Review of Sociology* 20 (1991); Patricia Hill Collins, *Black Feminist Thought: Knowledge, Consciousness, and the Politics of Empowerment* (New York: Routledge, 1991); Susan Dalton, "Nonbiological Mothers and the Legal Boundaries of Motherhood," in *Ideologies and Technologies of Motherhood: Race, Class, Sexuality, Nationality*, eds. Helena Ragone and France Winddance Twine (New York: Routledge, 2000); Barbara Katz Rothman, *Recreating Motherhood: Ideology and Technology in a Patriarchal Society* (New York: W.W. Norton & Co., 1989); and Mary L. Shanley, "Fathers' Rights, Mothers' Wrongs? Reflections on Unwed Fathers' Rights and Sex Equality," *Hypatia* 10, no. 1 (1995).

Appendix

1. This differs from my ability to discuss cases with social workers while accompanying social workers, because in those cases, I only observed what the workers were observing.

2. One mother was interviewed for several hours, but was referred to me through a friend of hers from their shared drug treatment program. Her case was in the process of closing, which provided a different perspective on the process. She is the only parent included who was not identified through the court process or through a parents' attorney.

3. Jennifer A. Reich, "Pregnant with Possibility: Reflections on Embodiment, Access, and Inclusion in Field Research," *Qualitative Sociology* 26, no. 3 (2003).

4. Deborah Tannen, "Marked Women, Unmarked Men," in *The World Is a Text: Writing, Reading, and Thinking About Culture and its Contexts*, eds. Jonathan Silverman and Dean Rader (Englewood Cliffs, NJ: Prentice Hall, 2002).

5. Carol A. B. Warren and Jennifer Kay Hackney, *Gender Issues in Ethnography*, 2nd ed. (Thousand Oaks, CA: Sage Publications, 2000), 21.

6. See Susan Bordo, *Unbearable Weight* (Berkeley: University of California Press, 1993); Adrienne Rich, *Of Woman Born: Motherhood as Experience and Institution* (New York: W.W. Norton and Co., 1976); and Rosemary Tong, *Feminist Thought: A Comprehensive Introduction* (Boulder, CO: Westview Press, 1989).

7. Dorothy Roberts, *Killing the Black Body: Race, Reproduction, and the Meaning of Liberty* (New York: Vintage Books, 1997), 202.

8. Monica Casper, "Feminist Politics and Fetal Surgery: Adventures of a Research Cowgirl on the Reproductive Frontier," *Feminist Studies* 23, no. 2 (1997), 246–47.

9. Kath Weston, *Families We Choose: Lesbians, Gays, Kinship* (New York: Columbia University Press, 1991); Kath Weston, "The Virtual Anthropologist," in *Is Academic Feminism Dead? Theory in Practice*, ed. The Social Justice Group (New York: New York University Press, 2000), 150.

INDEX